MICROSOFT® PROFESSIONAL EDITIONS

# Building Applications
Microsoft®
## with Outlook™ 97

PUBLISHED BY
Microsoft Press
A Division of Microsoft Corporation
One Microsoft Way
Redmond, Washington 98052-6399

Library of Congress Cataloging-in-Publication Data
Building Microsoft Outlook 97 applications / Microsoft Corporation.
     p.   cm.
  ISBN 1-57231-536-9
  1. Microsoft Outlook. 2. Time management--Computer programs.
  3. Personal information management--Computer programs.
  I. Microsoft Corporation.
  HD69.T54B85 1997
  005.369--dc21                                97-2408
                                                 CIP

Printed and bound in the United States of America.

1 2 3 4 5 6 7 8 9   MLML   2 1 0 9 8 7

Distributed to the book trade in Canada by Macmillan of Canada, a division of Canada Publishing Corporation.

A CIP catalogue record for this book is available from the British Library.

Microsoft Press books are available through booksellers and distributors worldwide. For further information about international editions, contact your local Microsoft Corporation office. Or contact Microsoft Press International directly at fax (206) 936-7329.

Microsoft, Microsoft Press, PowerPoint, Visual Basic, and Visual C++ are registered trademarks and ActiveX, Developer Studio, IntelliSense, and Outlook are trademarks of Microsoft Corporation. Other product and company names mentioned herein may be the trademarks of their respective owners.

**Acquisitions Editor:** Casey D. Doyle
**Project Editor:** Maureen Williams Zimmerman

# Acknowledgments

Because the process of producing a book is a group effort, I'd like to thank all those people who helped make this possible. Thanks go to Casey Doyle, Gwen Lowery, Laura Brenner, Donalee Edwards, Lori Fields, Kristin Lynn Bergsma, Stephanie McKinney, Darlene Rudd, Cheryl Channing, Peter Ashmore, Jeff Gilbert, Robin Lyle, Bart McKeirnan, Frank Lee, David Goodhand, Darrique Barton, Bill Metters, Warren Halcott, and Jay Abbott.

And special thanks to my wife Gloria for her constant kindness, love, and support.

Peter J. Krebs

# Contents

**Introduction   vii**

**Part 1   Introducing Microsoft Outlook 97   1**

Chapter 1   Applications You Can Create with Outlook   3

Chapter 2   Outlook Design Tools   15

**Part 2   Quick Guide to Building Applications   27**

Chapter 3   Customize Built-In Modules   29

Chapter 4   Design a Custom Application   61

**Part 3   Building Blocks of Applications   95**

Chapter 5   Forms   97

Chapter 6   Controls, Fields, and Properties   139

Chapter 7   Actions   185

Chapter 8   Folders   223

**Part 4   Beyond the Basics   271**

Chapter 9   Use Visual Basic Scripting Edition with Outlook   273

Chapter 10   The Business Card Request Application   331

Chapter 11   The Help Desk Application   385

Chapter 12   The Document Tracking Application   427

Chapter 13   Distribute and Maintain Applications   475

**Index   493**

# Introduction

**In This Chapter**

Who Should Use This Book   viii

How This Book Is Organized   ix

Use the Companion CD-ROM   x

In the six months that I've worked with Microsoft Outlook 97, I've been continually impressed with its quality, flexibility, vast array of features, and, perhaps most important, its overall usefulness. The process of researching and writing about Microsoft Outlook has been an adventure of constant discovery. In fact, the further I got into writing this book, the more I realized that I was only scratching the surface of the wide variety of tasks you can accomplish with this powerful new technology. It's not often that I rave about a software product. But I will about this one. Microsoft Outlook 97 is a great piece of software. Here are five reasons why I think you'll come to the same conclusion.

**Instant workgroup solutions**   With Outlook, creating groupware applications has never been faster or easier. That's because Outlook ships with full-featured Calendar, Tasks, and Contacts modules that can be created and customized in Public Folders. This offers instant groupware capabilities, so users can share calendars, schedules, task lists, and customer contact information among their workgroup or across the organization.

**Fast application development**   With Outlook application design tools such as the Forms Designer, you can get information-sharing applications up and running quickly—often without programming. And you can easily modify solutions on the fly because Outlook Forms are interpreted, not compiled. When building an application, you always start with either a built-in module, a sample application, or a standard form, so most of the functionality is already there. In fact, you can often build high-quality applications in a matter of days.

**Scalable application development**  Many groupware applications grow in popularity and require additional functionality as their use becomes more widespread. Outlook provides for this by supporting a scalable set of development tools. For example, you can create procedures to control forms and folders using Microsoft Visual Basic Scripting Edition (VBScript) supplied with Outlook. If your application requires additional functionality, you can use the full power of Automation and Visual Basic or Visual Basic for Applications to create and program Outlook objects and meet your organization's communication needs.

**Office integration**  Outlook is tightly integrated with the other Office 97 applications, so you can create solutions applications that bring the best features of each application under one umbrella. For example, you can create an Outlook Form that serves as a mail-enabled front-end to a Microsoft Access 97 database. Or you can use Microsoft Visual Basic for Applications to create a macro in Microsoft Excel that automatically mails a sales report to a distribution list when a command button is clicked in a Microsoft Excel worksheet.

**Centralized management and security**  Because Outlook runs on Microsoft Exchange Server, Outlook applications can take full advantage of the central administration, replication, and security features of Microsoft Exchange Server. For example, you can develop an application on your computer, and then turn it over to an administrator who installs it on Microsoft Exchange Server. Once on the server, the administrator can set access permissions and replication properties for the folder, so the folder is both secure and replicated across the organization.

# Who Should Use This Book

Both programmers and non-programmers can pick up this book and find the information they need to develop groupware applications. In Part 2, "Quick Guide to Building Applications," I show how just about anyone can quickly create a completely usable groupware application without programming. You don't need to be a hard-core developer to build Outlook applications, although programming experience is certainly a plus. Regardless of your experience level, this book gives you an inside view of the components that make up a groupware application. It also offers helpful hints from the Microsoft Outlook development team to get you around some rough spots in the product. In Part 4, "Beyond the Basics," I provide plenty of Visual Basic Scripting Edition examples, along with several sample applications that show how you can streamline processes in your office with Microsoft Outlook applications.

# How This Book Is Organized

This book consists of the following four parts.

## Part 1   Introducing Outlook

Chapter 1, "Applications You Can Create with Outlook," discusses the processes and problems best suited for Outlook solutions and shows you the kind of Request, Discussion, Tracking, and Reference applications you can build to streamline communications in your organization. Chapter 2, "Outlook Design Tools," showcases the tools available for creating Outlook applications.

## Part 2   Quick Guide to Building Applications

Chapter 3, "Customize Built-In Modules," shows you how to create instant groupware applications by modifying the built-in Contacts application, customizing it for tracking customer correspondence related to a beta program, and then copying it to Public Folders on Microsoft Exchange Server. Chapter 4, "Design a Custom Application," shows you how to build a Discussion application called Products Ideas that makes it possible for users to submit, read, and respond to new products ideas.

## Part 3   Building Blocks of Applications

Chapter 5, "Forms," introduces the form design process, and covers fundamental form design tasks such as adding controls and fields, creating new actions, setting form properties, and publishing forms. Chapter 6, "Controls, Fields, and Properties," covers the fundamental skills and information you need to effectively use controls, fields, and properties on a form. It also explains the unique features of each commonly used control, and then offers some strategies for implementing these controls and fields in an application. Chapter 7, "Actions," discusses the easiest way to create responses for Message forms, explains how to create custom Reply actions for Message forms, and then shows how to create custom Reply to Folder actions for Post forms. Chapter 8, "Folders," takes an in-depth look at the folder design process, discusses how to manage forms, and explains how to create custom views. It also covers setting folder permissions and building rules.

## Part 4   Beyond the Basics

Chapter 9, "Use Visual Basic Scripting Edition with Outlook," introduces Visual Basic Scripting Edition and provides a wide variety of code examples for the most commonly performed tasks using Visual Basic Scripting Edition in Outlook. Chapter 10, "The Business Card Request Application," takes you step-by-step through the process of building an application that automates a request process. Chapter 11, "The Help Desk Application," showcases a variety of design techniques, including how multiple folder and form types can be used in an application. Chapter 12, "The Document Tracking Application," is a good example of an application that provides a user-friendly and mail-enabled front-end to a Microsoft Access 97 database. Chapter 13, "Distribute and Maintain Applications," shows you how to distribute forms in folders and provides some techniques for maintaining applications.

# Use the Companion CD-ROM

The companion CD-ROM contains most of the applications covered in this book. Add the Building Microsoft Outlook 97 Applications.pst file to your Microsoft Exchange system, and then use the applications provided in the Building Microsoft Outlook 97 Applications folder as reference as you work your way through this book. You might want to make a copy of the applications and dissect the ones you're most interested in to see how they're developed. You can also customize these applications and put them to work in your organization.

▶ **To install the companion CD-ROM**

1  Insert the CD-ROM into your CD-ROM drive.

2  Run the Setup.exe program.

# Add the Personal Folder (.pst) File to Outlook

The Setup program installs a Building Microsoft Outlook 97 Applications file in the destination folder you specified during installation. The Building Microsoft Outlook 97 Applications file is actually a personal folder (.pst) file that contains sample forms and files, Help files, shortcuts to Web sites, a database, and a custom utility that rebuilds the forms cache.

While it's not required that you add the Building Microsoft Outlook 97 Applications file to your Microsoft Exchange system, it serves as a valuable reference tool, and the sample applications can be used as a starting point for building applications that are customized for your environment.

▶ **To add the Building Microsoft Outlook 97 Applications (.pst) file**

1   On the **File** menu, point to **Open Special Folder**, and then click **Personal Folder**.

2   Locate the Building Microsoft Outlook 97 Applications file you installed from the companion CD-ROM, and then double-click the file.

3   The file is now added as the Building Microsoft Outlook 97 Applications Personal Information folder on your Microsoft Exchange system and appears in the Folder List in Outlook.

# Technical Support for the Companion CD-ROM

Every effort has been made to ensure the accuracy of this book and the contents of the companion CD-ROM. Microsoft Press provides corrections for books through the World Wide Web at the following address:

http://www.microsoft.com/mspress/support/

If you have comments, questions, or ideas regarding this book or the companion CD-ROM, please mail or e-mail them to Microsoft Press at the following addresses:

## Postal Mail

Microsoft Press

Attn: Building Microsoft Outlook 97 Editor

One Microsoft Way

Redmond, WA 98052-6399

## E-mail

mspinput@microsoft.com

Please note that product support is not offered through the above mail addresses. For support information on Microsoft Outlook, see the documentation for the appropriate product support phone number.

# What's on the Companion CD-ROM

The companion CD-ROM, which is arranged much like the book, is divided into five parts.

# Help and References Folder

The Help and References folder provides supplemental information to help you design Outlook applications. As such, it provides three folders.

**Outlook Forms Help**   This Help file contains information about creating Outlook applications and up-to-date information about the objects, methods, and properties supported in the Forms 2.0 object model.

**Outlook Visual Basic Help**   This Help file provides information about the objects, methods, properties, and constants in the Microsoft Outlook object library.

**Web Sites**   As shown in Figure I-1, the Web Sites folder contains shortcut items that you can double-click to open the Microsoft Outlook Web site or the Microsoft Visual Basic Scripting Edition Web site.

**Figure I-1   The Web Sites folder**

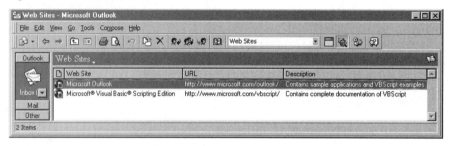

# Quick Guide to Building Applications Folder

The Quick Guide to Building Applications Folder contains two folders that showcase how you can quickly build Microsoft Outlook applications.

**Beta Contacts**   As shown in Figure I-2, the Beta Contacts folder demonstrates how you can easily customize built-in Outlook modules, such as Contacts, to build instant groupware.

**Figure I-2   The Beta Contacts folder**

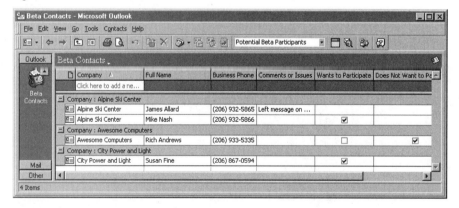

**Products Ideas**   Provides a Discussion application that makes it possible for users to submit, read, and respond to new products ideas.

# Building Blocks of Applications Folder

The Building Blocks of Applications folder contains several folders and forms that serve as good examples for implementing controls, fields, properties, and actions. In addition, the Classified Ads and Training Management folders provide excellent examples of how custom views can be designed.

**Classified Ads**  Enables users to post, view, and make purchase offers on items in the Classified Ads folder, as shown in Figure I-3. This application provides a good example of building views in a folder.

**Figure I-3  The Classified Ads folder**

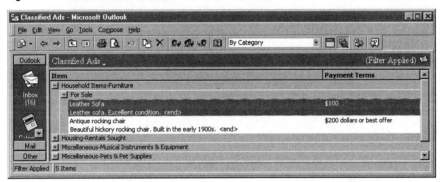

**Training Management**  Enables course administrators to create an online catalog and potential students to register for and evaluate classes. Provides a good example of building views and creating response actions.

**Vacation Request**  Automates the vacation request and approval process with several forms and custom actions that enable the supervisor to automatically approve or deny a vacation. In this book, this application is used to demonstrate how actions work and how controls, properties, and fields can be implemented on a form.

**While You Were Out**  Contains a While You Were Out form that provides a good example of how Message forms can be customized to standardize communication in your organization.

# Beyond the Basics Folder

Contains applications that demonstrate how Microsoft Visual Basic Scripting Edition can be used to program Outlook applications.

**Business Card Request**  Shows how a Message form and a public folder can be used to automate a Request process in your organization. Also provides a good example of how properties and controls are implemented on a form.

**Document Tracking**  This application shows how forms, folders, documents, and a database can be integrated to streamline request and tracking processes. As shown in Figure I-4, the Document Tracking folder shows the status of a document as well as the tasks that have been performed on the document. When a document is saved in this folder, a record is created for the item in a Microsoft Access 97 database.

**Figure I-4  The Document Tracking folder**

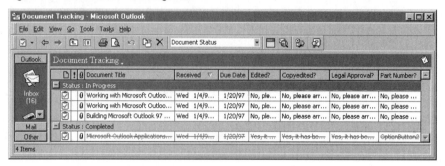

**Help Desk**  Automates the process of submitting, assigning, and tracking Help Desk Requests. Provides a good example of a multiple-folder application and how to use Entry IDs to identify and locate items in a folder.

**VBScript**  Contains the Library Orders folder and the VBScript Samples folder. The Library Orders folder provides a sample application that shows how you can use Visual Basic Scripting Edition to automate the process of ordering library materials. The VBScript Samples folder provides a variety of items that contain command buttons that trigger sample VBScript procedures.

# Miscellaneous Folder

This folder contains an application that demonstrates how OLE calls can be used to access information in the Address Book. It also provides a utility for restoring the default forms in your forms cache.

**Get User Info**  Contains a form that demonstrates how OLE Messaging can be used to return user information from the Address Book.

**Switch Forms**  Provides a utility that restores the default forms in your forms cache. You use this utility when you want to clean the forms cache.

**See Also**  For more information about how to use the Switch Forms utility, see "The Switch Forms Utility" in Chapter 13, "Distribute and Maintain Applications."

# Introducing Microsoft Outlook 97

## Contents

Chapter 1   Applications You Can Create with Outlook   3
Chapter 2   Outlook Design Tools   15

# Applications You Can Create with Outlook

## In This Chapter

Types of Applications You Can Create   5

Folder Applications   10

For More Form and Folder Ideas   13

As I was nearing the end of this project, a production manager at Microsoft came to my office and asked me how long it would take to build a form that would enable her to track the progress of marketing documents from the time they are submitted to the time they are printed or posted on the network. Before I answered, I asked her to describe the process she wanted to use the form for. She said writers in Marketing or User Assistance submit documents to a production manager who is responsible for arranging a variety of tasks, including editing, copyediting, legal approval, part number assignment, virus checking, and printing or posting the document on the network. Like most processes, producing marketing materials is a group effort, requiring a variety of people from different departments to perform a disparate set of tasks to complete a job.

When I asked her how the processes are currently handled, she told me that after writers hand off a document, they are required to enter the document information into a database. Task assignment and tracking, she said, is handled on an informal basis. She also explained that the writers don't like using the database because they find it hard to use. After listening to her describe the process, I agreed to develop the application, with the understanding that she would provide me with a flowchart of the process and a document describing the fields she wanted on the form. In the end, it took three days to build the application, which you'll find in Chapter 12, "The Document Tracking Application." Perhaps most important, it proved to me how valuable Outlook can be in an organization.

The Document Tracking application brings out the best in Outlook for several reasons. First, it automates and streamlines a real-world process. Now writers can submit documents and document information using a form in electronic mail. The submitted items are stored in a public folder so production managers can track the status of the document's progress. In addition, task assignment is automated, so production managers can click a button to send a part number or legal approval request via electronic mail. Perhaps equally important, each participant in the process collaborates on the same item in the Document Tracking folder, so the production process is never held up because a piece of paper is sitting on someone's desk. In addition, after a person completes a task such as copyediting, he can update the Document Tracking form and save it in the Document Tracking folder. When this happens, the item is not only updated in the Document Tracking folder, but is also written to a Microsoft Access database, so production managers can run queries and end-of-the-month performance reports.

As demonstrated in this example, you can create Outlook applications to accomplish a wide variety of tasks. Here are just a few of the things you can accomplish with Outlook applications.

**Share information**   You can build applications that make it possible for users to share all types of information, including schedules, tasks, contacts, documents, product ideas, and customer feedback.

**Structure information**   You can build forms and folders to structure information so it's not only easy to read but easy to find. For example, you can create a Preferred Vendors public folder so managers can quickly find qualified vendors that have been referred by other managers in the organization. Or you can use the Product Ideas application supplied with this book to make it possible for users to submit, organize, and view new product ideas in a public folder.

**Distribute information**   You can create forms that make it possible for users to send announcements, sales reports, documents, and request-for-services items. For example, you can create a Bulk Mailer form so you can automatically notify all users in a particular contact list when a product update is available.

**Collect information**   You can create forms and folders for collecting information. For example, you can create a User Feedback form and public folder for collecting information about a product under development. Or you can use the Classified Ads application supplied with this book to make it possible for users to submit and respond to classified ads.

**Collaborate on information**   One of the benefits of Outlook is that it makes it possible for each user to collaborate on the same item. For example, with the Product Ideas application, a variety of users from different locations can all participate in an online discussion about a particular product feature. With the Document Tracking application, users can collaborate on a task in the Document Tracking public folder.

**Streamline processes**   You can create applications that are modeled on paper-based processes in your organization. For example, you can create forms and folders that make it possible for users to electronically submit vacation requests, travel plans, copier requests, purchase orders, status reports, classified ads, and training class registration.

# Types of Applications You Can Create

The two main building blocks of Outlook applications are forms and folders. With the Outlook design tools described in Chapter 2, you can create the following types of applications:

- **Applications that consist entirely of forms**   These are forms that are not associated with a specific folder, such as the While You Were Out form.

- **Applications that consist of a custom folder and standard forms**   Often when you create a folder, you create custom views for the folder but use the standard Outlook forms. For example, you might create a Contacts folder in a public folder and create custom views for the folder, but not change the standard forms supplied with the folder.

- **Applications that consist of a custom folder and custom forms**   In many cases, you customize both the folder and the form to build an application. For example, the Training Management, Classified Ads, and Document Tracking applications all consist of customized forms and folders.

## Forms You Can Create

With the Outlook Form Designer, you can create a wide spectrum of forms to perform a variety of tasks. When you create forms with Outlook, you never start from scratch. Instead, you base the forms you create on a standard form of a specific type supplied with Outlook. Standard form types include the Message, Post, Office Document, and built-in module form (such as those supplied in Contacts or Calendar). Because most of the functionality is already available in these forms, you can often create custom forms by adding or removing fields and controls from the form.

In this section, we look at the different types of forms you can create using the Outlook Form Designer.

### Message Forms

Message forms are forms that are based on the Outlook Mail Message form. As such, Message forms make it possible for users to send information to other users or to a public folder. Message forms are often used to streamline a request process or approval process. Here are some examples of Message forms.

**Vacation Request**  The Vacation Request application, covered in Part 3, "Building Blocks of Applications," consists of a Vacation Request form, as shown in Figure 1.1. The Vacation Request form makes it possible for a user to send a vacation request to a manager. The Vacation Request application also consists of a Vacation Approved form and a Vacation Denied form so a manager can respond to a request.

**Figure 1.1   The Vacation Request form**

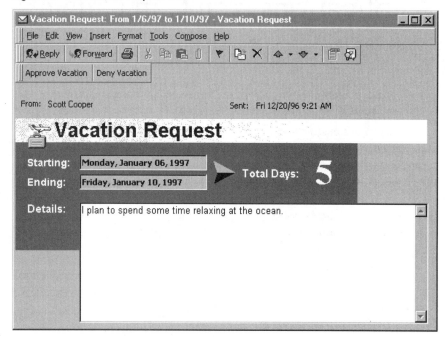

**Business Card Request**  This form makes it possible for users to automatically fill in and send a Business Card Request to the Business Card Requests public folder. Form more information, see Chapter 10, "The Business Card Request Application."

**Status Report**  This form makes it possible for users to send weekly or monthly status reports to their manager. Submitted status reports can be stored in a personal folder or public folder and used for reference at review time.

**Mileage Report**  This form makes it possible for users to submit their monthly mileage reports to their manager for approval. When approved, the information in the Mileage Report item can be written to a database.

# Post Forms for Posting Items in a Folder

Post forms are used to post items in a folder and to post responses to items in a folder. Post forms are used in applications that enable users to conduct online discussions, such as the Product Ideas folder covered in Chapter 4, "Design a Custom Application." As such, Post forms serve as the foundation for creating threaded conversations in views. Post forms are also used for applications that require users to respond to a particular item, such as the Training Management application, in which the Evaluation form is used to post a response to a Course Offering item.

Here are a few ideas for Post forms using the Outlook Forms Designer.

**Job Posting**   As shown in Figure 1.2, the Job Posting form structures information and makes it possible for Human Resources to post a job opening in the Job Postings folder.

**Figure 1.2   The Job Posting form with the Job Postings folder in the background**

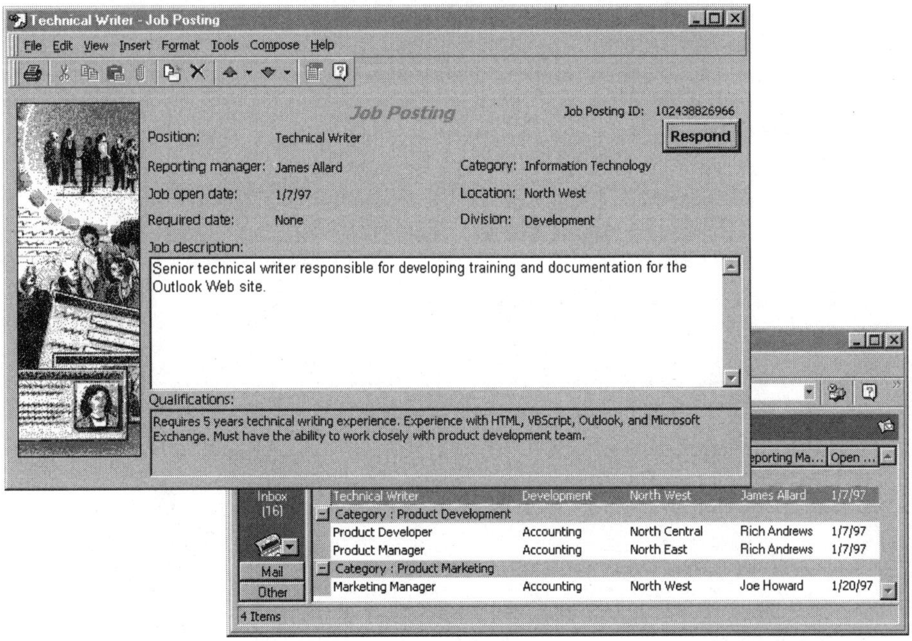

**Job Candidate**   The Job Candidate application consists of a Job Candidate form and a Response form. A manager or human resource administrator can submit a Job Candidate item to the Job Candidates public folder. After each user interviews the candidate, they use the Response form to submit their hiring recommendations to the Job Candidates folder, where the summary of opinions can be reviewed by the manager.

**Product Ideas**   The Product Ideas application consists of a Product Idea form for posting product ideas in the Product Ideas folder and a Product Idea Response form for posting responses to product ideas in the folder. For more information, see Chapter 4, "Design a Custom Application."

# Office Document Forms

With Office Document forms, you can create forms using Microsoft Excel, Microsoft Word, or Microsoft PowerPoint. For example, you might want to streamline a scheduling process by creating a Weekly Schedule form for managers, so they can fill out a Microsoft Excel Weekly Schedule worksheet that's embedded in the form. In this way, managers can distribute a schedule to their workgroup.

Here are a few more examples of the kinds of Office Document forms you can create.

**Purchase Request**   As shown in Figure 1.3, the Purchase Request form is based on a Microsoft Excel worksheet. To submit a Purchase Request, the user opens the Purchase Request form in the Purchase Requests folder, fills in the worksheet, and then clicks the **Post** button on the form. An administrator can open the Purchase Request item in the Purchase Requests folder to process the request.

**Figure 1.3   The Purchase Request form**

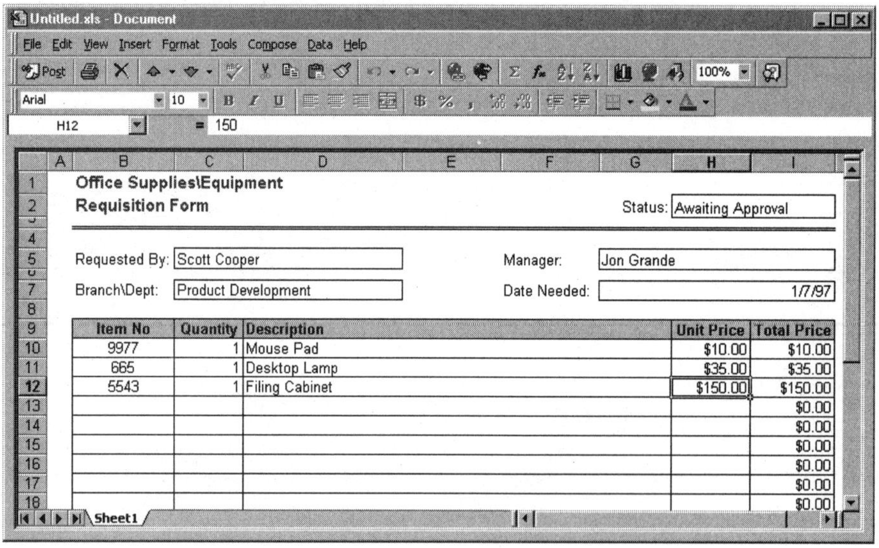

**Sales Report**   You can create a Sales Report form based on a Microsoft Excel chart for mailing weekly sales reports to a distribution list.

**Invoice**   You can create an Invoices form based on a Microsoft Excel worksheet for mailing invoices or for posting them in a folder.

**Service Contract**   You can create forms based on a Microsoft Word document for beta contract agreements, exit interview forms, or for a variety of other purposes that require semi-structured information in a form.

## Built-In Modules Forms

You can customize forms based on the forms in the built-in modules—Calendar, Task, Contacts, and Journal—to take advantage of the specific functionality of the module.

Here are a few ideas for the types of forms you can create based on the forms in the Outlook built-in modules.

**Assigned Help Task form**   You can create forms such as the Assigned Help Task form, as shown in Figure 1.4, that make it possible to update and track the progress of a task. As shown below, the standard **Task** page is hidden, and a custom page is added to the form. The standard Status and % Complete fields are added to the custom page.

**Figure 1.4   The Assigned Help Task form with the Assigned Help Tasks folder in the background**

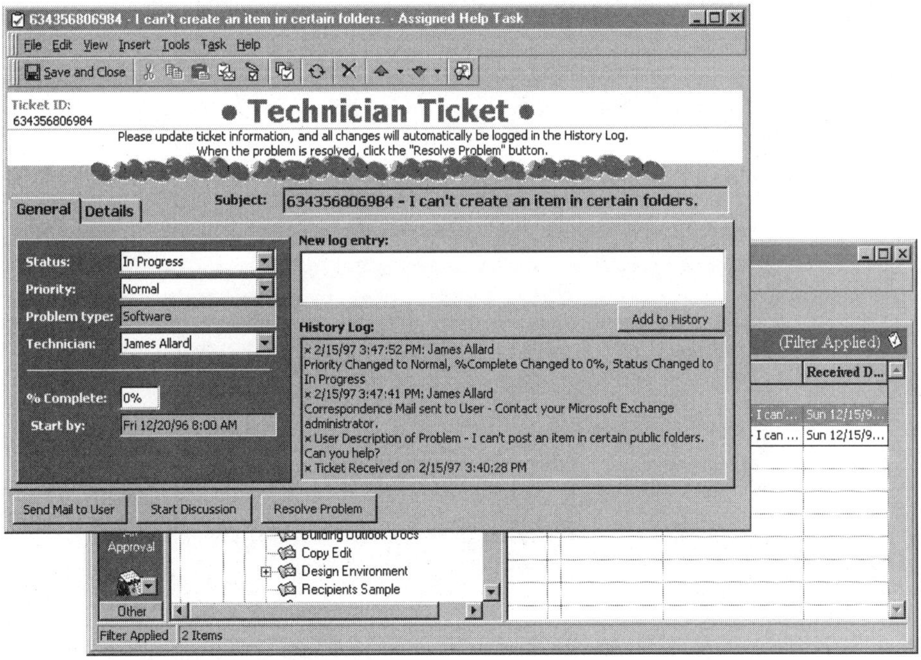

**Document Tracking form**   The Document Tracking application, covered in Chapter 12, contains a Document Tracking form based on the standard Task form. For this application, the Document Tracking form is used by different people involved in the document production process to update the Document Tracking item after a task is completed.

# Folder Applications

Folders in Outlook are generally used for the following purposes:

- To facilitate online discussions about a particular topic, as demonstrated with the Product Ideas folder.

- To store, organize, and share information, as demonstrated with the Job Postings, Classified Ads, Training Management, and Web Sites folders.

- To record and track information that is constantly updated, as demonstrated with the Assigned Help Tasks folder and the Document Tracking folder.

# Folders Based on Built-in Modules

With the built-in modules such as Calendar, Tasks, and Contacts, you can create an instant workgroup solution by creating a folder in Public Folders. You can then modify the folder for the specific purpose of your workgroup or organization. Here are a few ideas for the types of applications you can build based on built-in module folders.

**Preferred Vendors folder**   With the Preferred Vendors folder, managers can post references for vendors they recommend. The Preferred Vendors folder, as shown in Figure 1.5, is based on the built-in Contacts module.

**Figure 1.5   The Preferred Vendors folder based on the built-in Contacts folder**

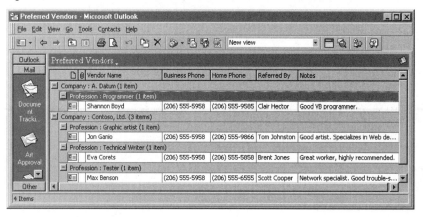

**Shared Calendar application**   You can create a Calendar folder in Public Folders, so events relating to a particular group can be easily recorded and shared. For example, you might want to create a shared Calendar that contains events related to the product development cycle, so that product announcements, press releases, trade shows, and shipping dates are accessible to the entire workgroup.

# Discussion Folders

Most often, Discussion folders serve as a central location for users to submit, share, and respond to ideas and information. Discussion folders feature views with *threaded conversations*, so users can view the history of responses to a particular item.

**New Product Ideas folder**  The New Products Ideas folder makes it possible for users to post product ideas and to respond to new product ideas in the Product Ideas folder. In addition, users can post responses to product idea responses. Responses to a particular item are located underneath and indented from the original item, creating the threaded conversation view.

**Job Candidates folder**  With the Job Candidates folder, managers or human resource personnel can post a job candidate item in a public folder. Those people who interview the candidate can then post their opinions of the candidate and hiring recommendations as a response item to the Job Candidate item. A manager can then view the history of interview responses to get the group's overall impression of the candidate.

**Training Management folder**  With the Training Management folder, training personnel can post Course Catalog items in the folder, as shown in Figure 1.6. After a Course Catalog item is posted, personnel can post a Course Offering item as a response to the Course Catalog item. After a user completes a course, she can post an Evaluation item as a response to the Course Offering item.

**Figure 1.6   The Training Management folder**

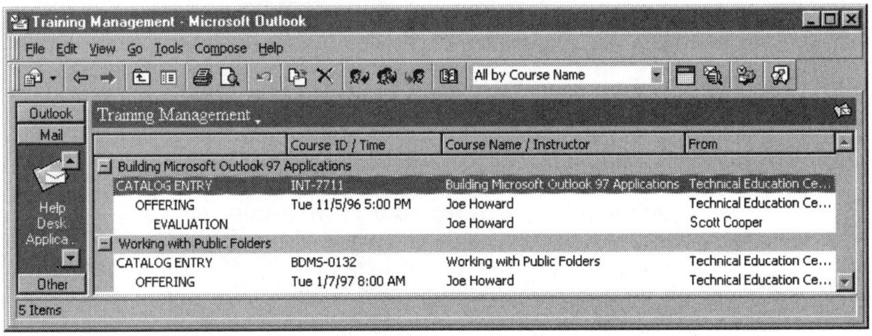

# Tracking Folders

Tracking folders makes it possible for users to record and review information that is constantly updated.

**Document Tracking folder**  The Document Tracking folder, as discussed earlier, contains Document Tracking items that are constantly updated by participants in the production process, such as those people who edit, copyedit, and post the document on the server.

**Assigned Help Tasks folder**   This folder, as shown in Figure 1.7, makes it possible for a Help Desk technician or manager to view the status of a Help Desk Request. When a technician changes the status of a task or completes a task, the status is updated in the By Status view in the Assigned Help Tasks folder.

**Figure 1.7   The Assigned Help Tasks folder**

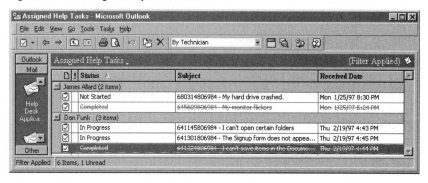

# Reference Applications

You can store just about any kind of information in a folder, including product specifications, feature proposals, sales reports, software prototypes, employee status reports, Web site addresses, and training materials.

**Specification Library**   As a development team works on a project, they can store product specifications in a public folder so other members of the development team, as well as sales and marketing personnel, have access to the documents.

**Status Reports**   Managers as well as employees may want to store weekly status reports in a public folder for reference at review time.

**Web Sites**   These folders are great for storing Web addresses. Web Site folders can be personal folders for private use or public folders that the entire workgroup can contribute to.

**Training Materials**   These folders provide a good medium for delivering training materials. As shown in Figure 1.8, the Microsoft Visual Basic Scripting Edition (VBScript) Samples folder contains sample procedures for a variety of commonly performed tasks that can be accomplished using Visual Basic Scripting Edition.

**Figure 1.8  The VBScript Samples folder**

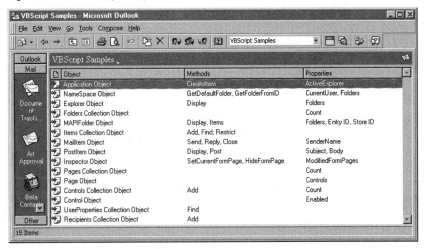

# For More Form and Folder Ideas

For additional information about the types of applications you can create, visit the Microsoft Outlook Web site at:

http://www.microsoft.com/outlook

# CHAPTER 2

# Outlook Design Tools

### In This Chapter
Help and Web Sites   15
Outlook Form Designer   17

Microsoft Outlook offers great design tools for creating custom forms and folders. For example, the Outlook Form Designer provides an AutoLayout feature that automatically positions controls as you add them to a form. In addition, the Form Designer provides a Script Editor window, so you can use Microsoft Visual Basic Scripting Edition in your forms to control folders, forms, fields, and controls. And when working with Outlook folders, you can create custom views directly in the folder by dragging fields to or from the Column Heading row. In many cases, you don't even need to open a dialog box to create a view.

In this chapter, you'll get a quick introduction to the tools that you use to design Outlook applications. Along the way, you'll see some of the features that you can use to make designing applications quicker and easier.

# Help and Web Sites

In the Building Microsoft Outlook 97 Applications folder supplied with this book, you'll find a Help and Web Sites folder, as shown in Figure 2.1. From this folder, you can install the Outlook Forms Help and Outlook Visual Basic Help. If you have the Microsoft Internet Explorer 3.0 installed, you can also click an item in the Web Sites folder to go directly to the Microsoft Visual Basic Scripting Edition Web site or the Microsoft Outlook Web site.

**Important**  If you have not added the Building Microsoft Outlook 97 Applications folder, see the Introduction of this book for instructions.

▶ **To open the Help and Web Sites folder**

- In the Folder List, open the Building Microsoft Outlook 97 Applications folder, and then open the Help and Web Sites folder, as shown in Figure 2.1.

**Figure 2.1   The contents of the Help and Web Sites folder in the Building Microsoft Outlook 97 Applications folder**

Double-click the item to open it. You can then double-click the icon in the item to install Help. ⌐

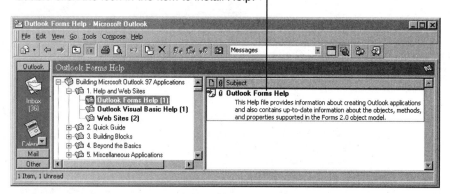

Here is a quick summary of the contents of the Help and Web Sites folder.

**Outlook Forms Help Folder**   This folder contains an item from which you can install Outlook Forms Help. The Outlook Forms Help file provides comprehensive information about supported properties and methods for Outlook controls. It also provides valuable tips and techniques supplied by the Outlook development team.

▶ **To install Outlook Forms Help**

1   In the Folder List, open the Outlook Forms Help folder.

2   Double-click the **Outlook Forms Help** item in the folder, and then double-click the icon in the message box of the item.

**Outlook Visual Basic Help Folder**   This folder contains an item from which you can install Outlook Visual Basic Help. The Outlook Visual Basic Help file includes the Outlook object model and descriptions of supported Outlook objects, methods, properties, and events.

▶ **To install Outlook Visual Basic Help**

1   In the Folder List, open the Outlook Visual Basic Help folder.

2   Double-click the Outlook Visual Basic Help item in the folder, and then double-click the icon in the message box of the item.

**Web Sites Folder**   This folder contains shortcuts you can click (if you have the Microsoft Internet Explorer 3.0) to go to the following sites:

- **http://www.microsoft.com/vbscript/**   The Visual Basic Scripting Edition Web site contains comprehensive Visual Basic Scripting Edition, code samples, and a tutorial.

- **http://www.microsoft.com/outlook/**   The Outlook Web site contains Visual Basic Scripting Edition samples, form samples, and valuable tips and techniques for creating Outlook applications.

▶ **To visit a Web site**

1   In the Folder List, open the Web Sites folder.

2   Double-click an item in the folder to go to the Web site you want.

# Outlook Form Designer

The Outlook Form Designer is built directly into Outlook, so opening the Form Designer is as easy as opening a form in Outlook, and then clicking **Design Outlook Form** on the **Tools** menu. When the form is in Design mode, the **Form Design** toolbar and the Field Chooser appear. As shown in Figure 2.2, you can add fields and controls to the form by dragging the fields from the Field Chooser to the form. When you add a field to a form using the Field Chooser, Outlook automatically creates a control and a label for the field and binds the control to the field. With the Outlook AutoLayout feature, the controls are automatically aligned with existing controls on the form. To exit Design mode, you click **Design Outlook Form** on the **Tools** menu again. In this way, you can easily switch back and forth between Design and Run mode to check the layout of a form at run time.

▶ **To view the Form Designer**

1   On the Outlook **Compose** menu, click **New Mail Message**.

2   On the form's **Tools** menu, click **Design Outlook Form**.

**Figure 2.2   The Outlook Form Designer**

With the AutoLayout feature, the controls are automatically aligned on the form.

When the form is in Design mode, the Outlook **Form Design** toolbar appears.

You can drag fields from the Field Chooser to the form.

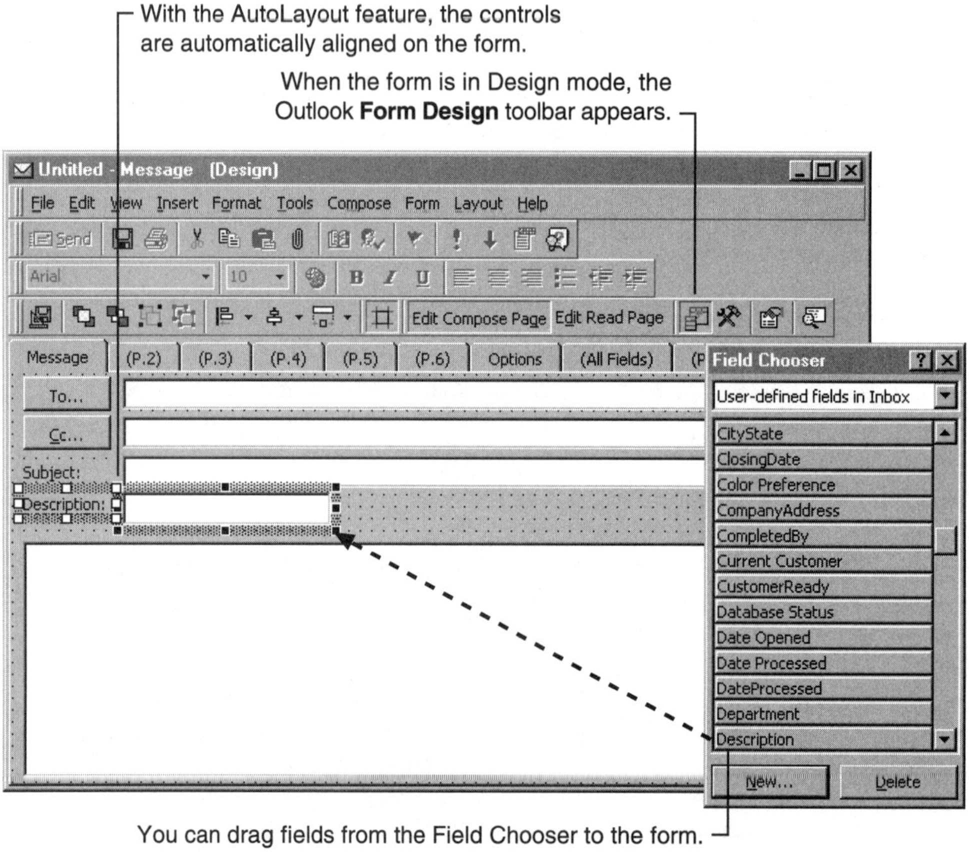

Here are just a few advantages of developing forms with the Outlook Forms Designer.

**Outlook forms are fully 32-bit forms**   so they're fast, and perhaps equally important, they're small, averaging about 10K.

**Outlook forms are interpreted**   so they're easy for designers to keep track of and update. With Outlook forms, designers don't need to worry about searching through folders or directories to find uncompiled source files to make changes to a form.

**The Outlook Form Designer provides a grid and a variety of alignment tools**   including AutoLayout, to make sure your forms have a professional appearance.

# Properties Dialog Box

To set properties for controls and fields that you add to forms, you use the **Properties** dialog box in the Form Designer, as shown in Figure 2.3.

▶ **To view the Properties dialog box**

- With the form in Design mode, right-click an existing control on the form. For this example, you can right-click the Subject control, and then click **Properties** on the shortcut menu.

**Figure 2.3   The Properties dialog box in the Form Designer**

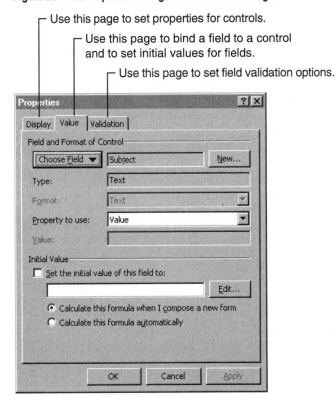

Use this page to set properties for controls.

Use this page to bind a field to a control and to set initial values for fields.

Use this page to set field validation options.

# Advanced Properties Dialog Box

With the advanced **Properties** dialog box, you can set properties for controls. As shown in Figure 2.4, the advanced **Properties** dialog box is used to set the **ControlTipText** property for a control.

▶ **To view the advanced Properties dialog box**

• With the form in Design mode, right-click an existing control (the Subject control in this example), and then click **Advanced Properties** on the shortcut menu.

**Figure 2.4   The advanced Properties dialog box in the Form Designer**

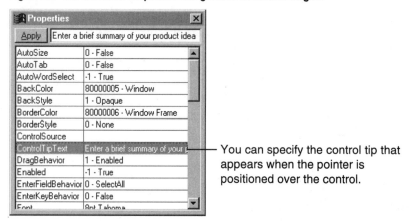

You can specify the control tip that appears when the pointer is positioned over the control.

**See Also**   For more information about using the **Properties** dialog box or the advanced **Properties** dialog box, see Chapter 6, "Controls, Fields, and Properties."

# The Visual Basic Expression Service

Using the Visual Basic Expression Service provided in Outlook, you can create validation criteria for fields, you can create formulas to calculate field values, and you can create formulas that combines text strings in a field.

▶ **To open the Visual Basic Expression Service**

1   With the form in Design mode, right-click an existing control (the **CardAddress** control in this example), and then click **Properties** on the shortcut menu.

2   Click the **Value** tab, and then click **Edit**.

As shown in Figure 2.5, the Visual Basic Expression Service is used to create a formula for a field in the Business Card Request form.

**Figure 2.5.   With the Visual Basic Expression Service, you can create formulas for fields.**

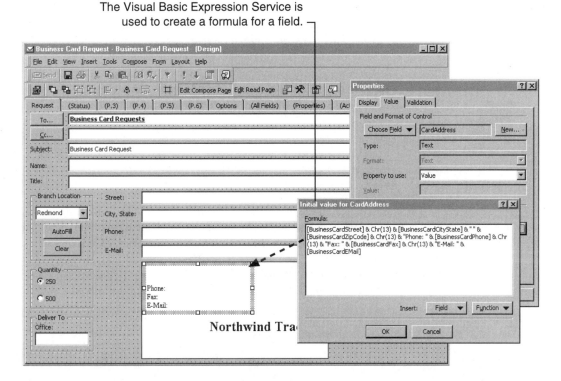

The Visual Basic Expression Service is
used to create a formula for a field.

With the Visual Basic Expression Service, you can:

- **Validate fields**   You can create validation formulas to ensure that a specific value or a value range is entered in a field, or to ensure that a field value is not exceeded.

- **Create formulas for calculating values in fields**   For example, you can create a formula for a Total field that multiplies hours by hourly rate.

- **Create Combination fields**   You can create formulas that combine field values and text fragments together or you can create Combination fields that show the value of the first non-empty field in the item.

**See Also**   For more information about the Visual Basic Expression Service, see Chapter 6, "Controls, Fields, and Properties."

# Script Editor and Visual Basic Scripting Edition

With the Forms Designer Script Editor, you can program Outlook forms using Visual Basic Scripting Edition. Visual Basic Scripting Edition is a subset of the Visual Basic language and is designed to be a small, lightweight interpreted language. Using Visual Basic Scripting Edition, the Outlook Object Library, and the Forms 2.0 Object Library, you can accomplish a wide variety of programming tasks. For example, you can set the current form page when the form opens in Compose mode. Or you can create a procedure that automatically sends a notification message to a distribution list when a new item in posted in a folder.

▶ **To view the Script Editor**

- With the form in Design mode, click the **View Code** button on the **Form Design** toolbar.

The Script Editor has templates for all the item events. To add an event template to your script in the Script Editor, click **Event** on the **Script** menu, click an event name in the list, and then click **Add**. The appropriate **Sub...End Sub** or **Function...End Function** statement is inserted. As shown in Figure 2.6, the **Item_Open** function is added to the Script Editor window for the Business Card Request form, and code is added to the event to hide the **Status** page of the form when the form is in Compose mode.

**Figure 2.6   The Script Editor window shows the Item_Open function.**

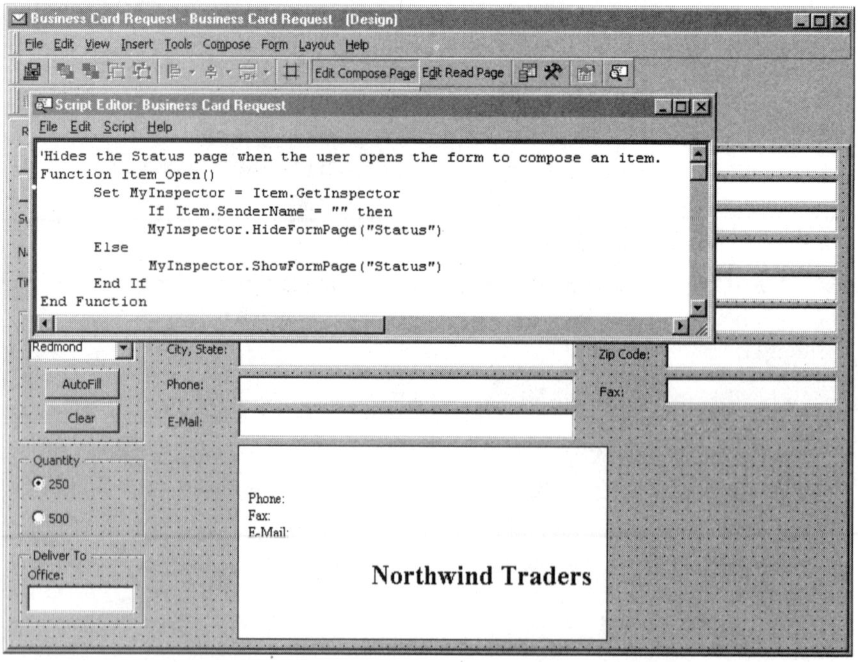

**See Also**   For more information about using Visual Basic Scripting Edition, see Chapter 9, "Use Visual Basic Scripting Edition with Outlook."

# Visual Basic and Automation

You can use Visual Basic and Automation to control an Outlook session. For example, you can copy data from a Microsoft Excel worksheet into a new mail message and send it to a list of recipients, all from within Microsoft Excel. To automate Outlook from another Microsoft Office application, you reference the Outlook Object Library; and then use the **CreateObject** function to start a new session of Outlook, or use the **GetObject** function to automate a session that's already running. After returning the Outlook **Application** object by using one of these two functions, you can write code in your controlling module that uses the objects, properties, methods, and constants defined in the Outlook Object Library.

# Folder View Design Tools

With Outlook, you can create custom views by adding, removing, and rearranging fields in the Column Heading row. For example, you can create a column by dragging a field from the Field Chooser to the Column Heading row.

▶ **To add or remove column using the Field Chooser**

1   On the **View** menu click **Field Chooser**.

2   Drag the field you want to add as the new column to the Column Heading row, as shown in Figure 2.7. Use the double-arrow marker to position the new column heading in the Column Heading row.

3   To remove the column heading, drag the column heading you added away from the Column Heading row until an X appears, and then release the mouse button.

As shown in Figure 2.7, the **Comments or Issues** column is created by dragging the **Comments or Issues** field from the Field Chooser to the Column Heading row.

**Figure 2.7   The Beta Contacts folder and the Field Chooser**

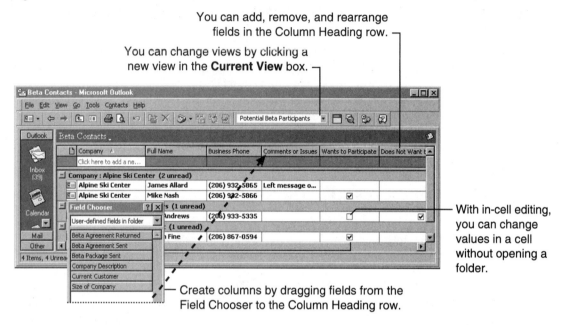

You can add, remove, and rearrange fields in the Column Heading row.

You can change views by clicking a new view in the **Current View** box.

With in-cell editing, you can change values in a cell without opening a folder.

Create columns by dragging fields from the Field Chooser to the Column Heading row.

**Drag and Drop Grouping**   You can group items in a folder by a particular field simply by dragging the field you want to group by above the Column Heading row.

**Format Columns**   The ability to format columns gives you great flexibility in designing views. For example, in many cases, you want the column label to be different than the name of the field the column is based on. To format a column, right-click the column heading, and then click **Format Columns** on the shortcut menu. You can then choose the options you want.

**In-cell Editing**   When the in-cell editing option is turned on for a folder, users can edit and enter information in cells within the folder without opening a form. For example, in the Beta Contacts folder, as shown earlier in Figure 2.7, users can click in a **Wants to Participate** cell to add or remove a check box icon in the cell. To select in-cell editing, click **Format View** on the **View** menu, and then select the **Allow in-cell editing** check box.

**Best Fit Feature**   This feature automatically arranges the column size to fit the text in the column heading label. To choose the **Best Fit** option for a column, right-click the column heading, and then click **Best Fit** on the shortcut menu.

**Show Only Custom Views**   Quite often, users are confused by the large number of views available in a folder. To alleviate this problem, Outlook makes it possible to show only the custom views created for the folder. To select this option, click the **View** menu, and then click **Define Views**. Then select the **Show only those views created for only this folder** check box.

# Folder Properties Dialog Box

With the folder **Properties** dialog box, as shown in Figure 2.8, you define folder attributes and behavior. For example, you can define who can access the folder and the functions they can perform, and you can create rules that automatically process items as they arrive in a folder.

▶ **To view the folder Properties dialog box**

- In the Folder List, right-click the folder, and then click **Properties** on the shortcut menu.

**Note**  To view all available **Properties** dialog box pages for a folder, the folder must be located in the Mailbox folder or Public Folders. Also note the **Outlook Address Book** page is only available for Contact type folders.

**Figure 2.8  The folder Properties dialog box**

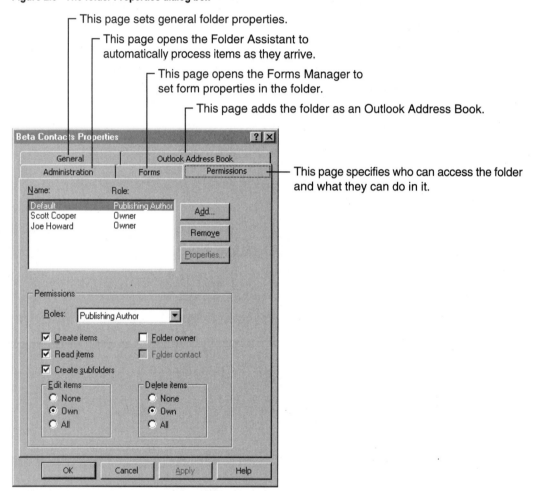

This page sets general folder properties.

This page opens the Folder Assistant to automatically process items as they arrive.

This page opens the Forms Manager to set form properties in the folder.

This page adds the folder as an Outlook Address Book.

This page specifies who can access the folder and what they can do in it.

**See Also**  For more information about designing folders or designing folder views, see Chapter 8, "Folders."

# Quick Guide to Building Applications

## Contents

Chapter 3   Customize Built-In Modules   29

Chapter 4   Design a Custom Application   61

# Customize Built-In Modules

## In This Chapter

Overview of the Folder You Create   31

Create New Folders   34

Create Custom Views   36

Create Items for the Beta Contacts Folder   43

Enter Dates in the Beta Participants View   45

Customize the Contacts Form   46

Test the Form at Design Time   55

Publish the Form   55

Specify the Default Form for the Folder   56

Test the Application   56

Delete the Items You Created   57

Copy the Folder to Public Folders   57

Set Permissions   57

Release the Application   59

What's Next   59

As a desktop information manager, Outlook provides built-in personal management tools such as Calendar, Tasks, Contacts, and Journal that can significantly increase user productivity. While these modules work great for individual use, their value is dramatically increased when they're located in a public folder because they allow users to share calendars, schedules, task lists, and customer information among workgroups or across the organization. In fact, with the built-in modules in Outlook, creating groupware is as simple as creating a module in Public Folders.

This chapter is designed to show how you can easily customize built-in Outlook modules to suit the needs of your workgroup or organization. In this chapter, you transform the Contacts module into a groupware application that enables users to record, share, and track the history of customer correspondence. When you're finished with this chapter, you should have a better understanding of both the limits and possibilities of customizing built-in modules. Perhaps equally important, you should have a whole new set of ideas about the kinds of applications you can create using these modules as a starting point. Here are a few ideas.

 **Calendar**   can be created in Public Folders and used to post, share, and update schedules for activities such as training classes, sporting events, and company functions. For a product launch, you might want to post milestone events such as trade shows, press tours, and product ship date in the Calendar folder.

 **Tasks**   can be created in Public Folders and used to post and track the tasks completed by each member of a project team. In addition, the Tasks folder can be used to delegate responsibilities to a staff of temporary workers or to track workgroup member's hours, billing information, and mileage.

 **Contacts**   can be created in Public Folders and used to post contact names, phone numbers, addresses, and company information, so it can be shared by a workgroup. With Contacts, users can post and track correspondence with sales contacts, potential customers, vendors, contractors, and co-workers.

 **Journal**   Can be created in Public Folders and used to log and track information such as the amount of time an individual or workgroup spends on a particular task, on a project, or with a specific customer.

**Note**   For the Notes module, you can add custom views to the folder but you cannot modify the built-in form.

# Overview of the Folder You Create

The Contacts module is designed primarily for individuals to keep track of their personal contacts. As such, it offers a built-in Contact form and a variety of views, including an Address Cards view, a Phone List view, and a By Company view, as shown in the Figure 3.1. In this chapter, you will transform the Contacts module into the Beta Contacts application, as shown in Figure 3.1.

**Figure 3.1  The Beta Contacts folder you create**

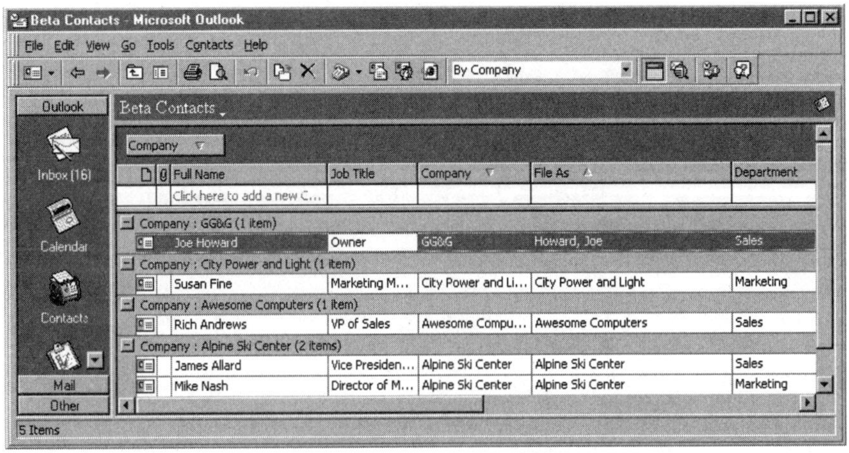

In this chapter, you transform the Contacts module into a groupware application that is used to track correspondence with participants in a beta software program. For those of you not involved in the software industry, most software companies send early copies of their software to their preferred customers for early testing and feedback. This process, also known as beta testing, usually involves close communication between the people running the beta program and the beta participants.

To build the Beta Contacts application based on the Contacts module, you first create a new Contacts folder in Public Folders. You then rename the folder and add custom views to it. Next, you modify the built-in Contacts form. Finally, you set permissions on the folder so only those individuals involved in the beta program can access it.

**The Beta Contacts folder**  that you build is based on the built-in Contacts module. The Beta Contacts folder is created in Public Folders so the information in the folder can be shared among members of a workgroup. In this chapter, you first create the Design Environment folder so you have a place for creating and testing applications, as shown in Figure 3.2.

**Figure 3.2   The Beta Contacts folder is first created in the Design Environment personal folder.**

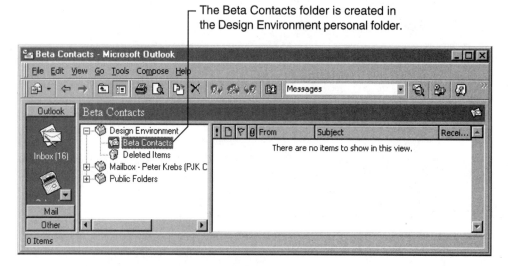

**The Potential Beta Participants view**  As part of the customization process, you create a Potential Beta Participants view. This view groups contacts by company and enables users of the Beta Contacts application to select a check box in a column to specify that the contact wants to participate in the beta program. The Potential Beta Participants view is shown in Figure 3.3.

**Figure 3.3   The Beta Contacts folder with the Potential Beta Participants view selected**

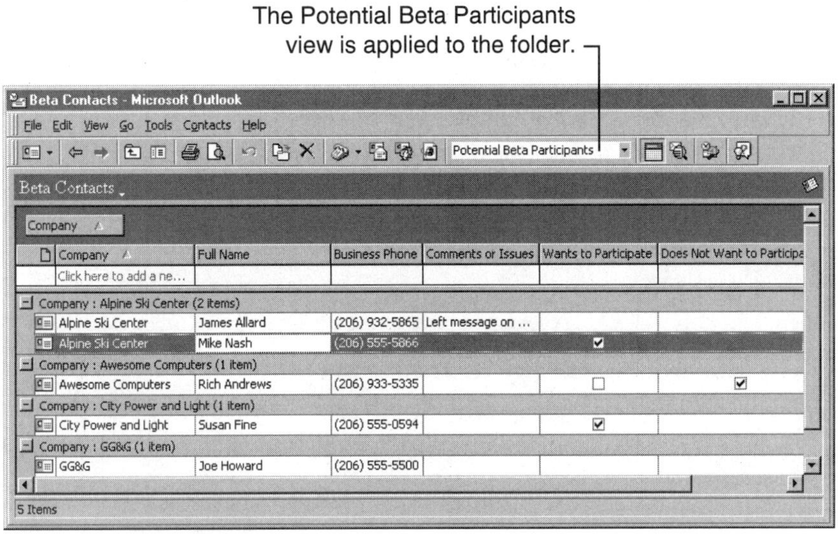

The Potential Beta Participants
view is applied to the folder.

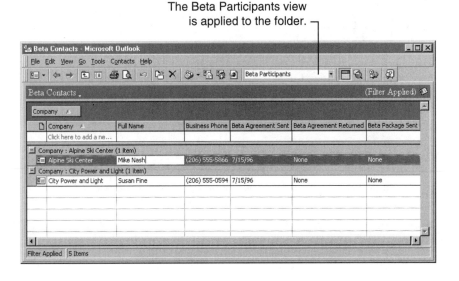

**The Beta Participants view**   You also add a view to the Beta Contacts folder that uses a filter to show only the contacts that have agreed to participate in the beta program. In addition, you add fields to the Beta Participants view that enable users of the Beta Contacts folder to update and track the status of correspondence either sent or returned by customers, as shown in Figure 3.4.

**Figure 3.4   The Beta Contacts folder with the Beta Participants view selected**

The Beta Participants view
is applied to the folder.

**The Beta Contacts form**   Finally, you customize the form that comes with the Contacts module by adding an additional page to the form. You then add controls to the page, and bind the controls to custom fields that you add to the Beta Contacts folder. Figure 3.5 shows the additional page you design for the Beta Contacts form.

**Figure 3.5   The Beta Contacts form with the Company Profile page selected**

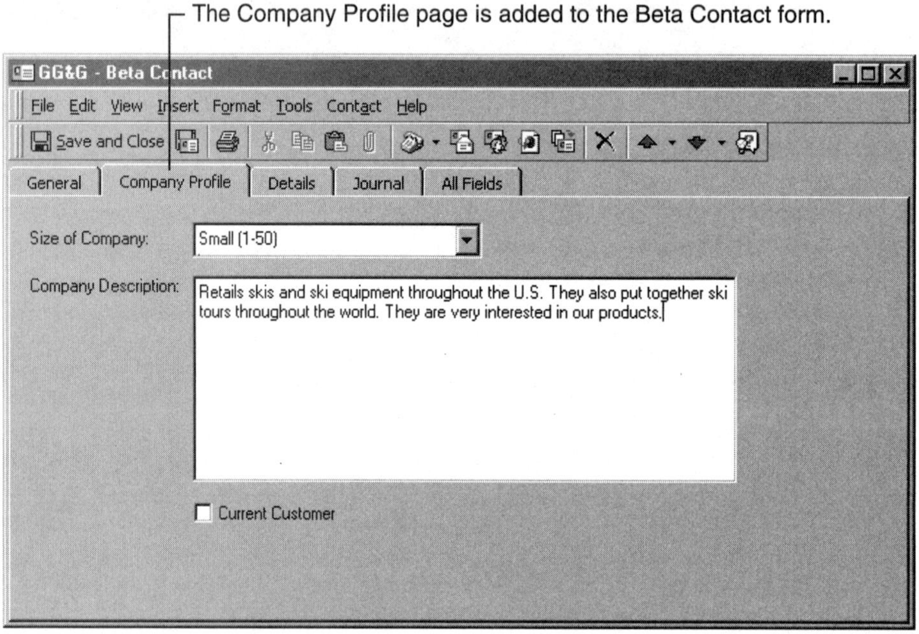

— The Company Profile page is added to the Beta Contact form.

# Create New Folders

To start, you create a new personal folder (.pst) called Design Environment. This is the folder you use throughout this book for creating and testing folders. We recommend you start building your Outlook applications by creating forms and views in a personal folder. After you've tested the forms and views, you can then copy the folder to a public folder, if necessary.

## Create the Design Environment Personal Folder

The Design Environment personal folder you create is a private folder, meaning that only you can view its contents. This secure environment is ideal for building applications.

▶ **To create the Design Environment folder**

1  On the **Tools** menu, click **Services**.

2  Click **Add**.

3  In the **Available information services** box, click **Personal Folders**, and then click **OK**.

4  In the Folder List, select a folder location. This is the location of the .pst file in which the contents of the folder are stored.

5  In the **File Name** box, type **Design Environment**, and then click **Open**.

6  In the **Name** box, type **Design Environment**, and then click **OK** twice.

# Create the Beta Contacts Folder

Now you create the Beta Contacts folder as a subfolder of the Design Environment folder. When you create the Beta Contacts folder, you specify that the folder contains Contact items, so the folder automatically inherits the properties and functionality of the built-in Contacts module.

▶ **To create the Beta Contacts folder**

1  In the Folder List, right-click the **Design Environment** folder.

2  Click **Create Subfolder**.

3  In the **Name** box, type **Beta Contacts**.

4  In the **Folder contains** box, select **Contact Items**.

   When you click **Contact Items**, the folder automatically takes on the characteristics of the Contacts module.

5  In the **Description** box, type the following:

   **This folder contains beta program contacts. It also contains beta program status that shows whether the company is a beta customer, and whether they have returned their beta material**.

6  Clear the **Create a shortcut to the folder in the Outlook Bar** check box, and then click **OK**.

# Create Custom Views

With Outlook, you can create custom views to organize and show information in the folder so the information users want is easy to find. For the Beta Contacts folder, you create two views:

**The Potential Beta Participants view**  lets users keep track of those people who agree over the telephone to participate in the beta program.

**The Beta Participants view**  lets users view only those contacts who have agreed to participate in the beta program.

# Create the Potential Beta Participants View

Let's assume you and a few others in your workgroup are responsible for contacting a list of companies to see if they want to participate in the beta program. To keep track of who agrees to participate, you can create the Potential Beta Participants view. To create this view, you adding user-defined fields to the Beta Contacts folder. Once you create these fields, you build a view with columns based on these fields.

▸ **To create the Potential Beta Participants view**

1   In the Folder List, click the **Beta Contacts** folder.

2   On the **View** menu, click **Define Views**.

3   In the **Views for Folder "Beta Contacts"** box, click **By Company**, and then click **Copy**.

   In this case, you save time by basing the new view on the existing By Company view.

4   In the **Name of new view** box, type **Potential Beta Participants**.

5   Click **This folder, visible to everyone**, and then click **OK** twice, and then **Apply View**.

## Remove Fields

Many of the fields in the By Company view aren't necessary for the Potential Beta Participants view, so you can remove them by dragging them from the Column Heading row.

▸ **To remove fields**

- Drag the following column headings away from the column heading row until an **X** appears through the column heading, and then release the mouse button.
  - Attachment (shown as a paper clip in the column heading)
  - Job Title
  - File As
  - Department
  - Business Fax
  - Home Phone
  - Mobile Phone
  - Categories

## Add New Fields

Next you add the Comments or Issues, Wants to Participate, Does Not Want to Participate, and Primary Contact fields to the view.

▸ **To add new fields**

1  In the **View** menu, click **Field Chooser**, and then click **New**.

2  In the **Name** box, type **Comments or Issues**, and then click **OK**.

3  Click **New**.

4  In the **Name** box, type **Wants to Participate**.

5  In the **Type** box, click **Yes/No**, and then click **OK**.

6  Repeat steps 3, 4, and 5, but in step 4, type **Does Not Want to Participate** in the **Name** box. Make sure you choose a Yes/No type field.

7  Repeat steps 3, 4, and 5, but in step 4, type **Primary Contact** in the **Name** box. Make sure you choose a Yes/No type field.

## Change the Order of the Company and Full Name Columns

With Outlook, you can change the order of column headings by dragging them to new locations.

▶ **To drag the Company column heading**

- Drag the Company column heading until a double-arrow marker appears over the border where you want to place the column, as shown in Figure 3.6.

**Figure 3.6   The Company column is placed in front of the Full Name column.**

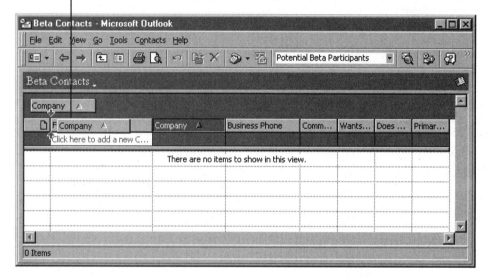

## Add the Column Headings to the Column Heading Row

To add column headings, you drag the fields you created earlier from the Field Chooser to the Column Heading row.

▶ **To drag the fields to the Column Heading row**

1   Drag the Comments or Issues field from the Field Chooser to the Column Heading row and position it to the right of the Business Phone column heading. The double-arrow marker shows you where the new column heading will be inserted in the column heading row.

2   Drag the Wants to Participate field from the Field Chooser to the Column Heading row and position it to the right of the Comments or Issues column heading.

3   Drag the Does Not Want to Participate field from the Field Chooser to the Column Heading row and position it to the right of the Wants to Participate column heading.

4   Drag the Primary Contact field from the Field Chooser to the Column Heading row and position it to the right of the Does Not Want to Participate field.

# Adjust the Column Widths to Best Fit

To resize columns, you can right-click the column heading, and then click **Best Fit**.

▶ **To adjust the column widths**

1 Right-click the Comments or Issues column heading, and then click **Best Fit**.

2 Repeat for the Wants to Participate, Does Not Want to Participate, and Primary Contact column headings.

The view should now look similar to the view as shown in Figure 3.7.

**Figure 3.7   The column widths are adjusted for Best Fit in the Potential Beta Participants view.**

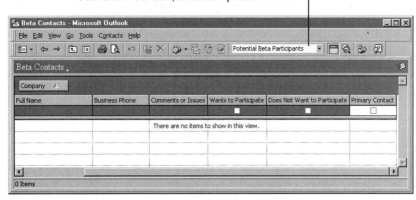

After making changes to the view, click the
**Current View** box, and then press ENTER. ⌐

# Save the Potential Beta Participants View

Since you have made changes to the view since you clicked the **Apply View** button, you must save the view to retain the changes.

▶ **To save the view**

1 Click the **Current View** box, and then click the ENTER key.

2 Click **Update the view "Potential Beta Participants" with the current settings**, and then click **OK**.

# Create the Beta Participants View

Next you create a view that shows only the people who are primary contacts and who have agreed to participate in the beta program. This view enables folder users to track what has been sent by beta coordinators and returned by the beta participants. For example, once a contact agrees to participate in the beta program, you send them a Beta Agreement to read and sign. Then, once the Beta Agreement has been returned, you send out the Beta Package, complete with the product and the necessary feedback forms.

▶ **To create the Beta Participants view**

1   In the Folder List, click the **Beta Contacts** folder.

2   On the **View** menu, click **Define Views**.

3   In the **Views for Folder "Beta Contacts"** box, click **Potential Beta Participants**, and then click **Copy**.

4   In the **Name of new view** box, type **Beta Participants**.

5   Click **This Folder, Visible to Everyone**, and then click **OK twice**, and then click **Apply View**.

## Remove Fields

Many of the fields in the Potential Beta Participants view aren't necessary for the Beta Participants view, so you can remove them.

▶ **To remove fields from the view**

- Drag the following column headings away from the Column Heading row until an **X** appears through the column heading, and then release the mouse button.

  - Comments or Issues
  - Wants to Participate
  - Does Not Want to Participate
  - Primary Contact

## Add New Fields

Next you add the Beta Agreement Sent, Beta Agreement Returned, and Beta Package Sent fields to the view. The user can directly enter information in these fields without opening the form.

▶ **To add new fields**

1  On the **View** menu, click **Field Chooser**.

2  Click **New**.

3  In the **Name** box, type **Beta Agreement Sent**.

4  In the **Type** box, click **Date/Time**.

5  In the **Format** field, click the XX/XX/XX format, and then click **OK**.

6  Repeat steps 2–5 for both the Beta Agreement Returned and Beta Package Sent fields.

7  Click **OK**.

## Add the Column Headings to the Column Heading Row

Now you add the new fields to the Column Heading row.

▶ **To drag the fields to the Column Heading row**

1  Drag the Beta Agreement Sent field from the Field Chooser to the Column Heading row and position it to the right of the Business Phone column heading. The double-arrow marker shows you where the new column heading will be inserted in the column heading row.

2  Drag the Beta Agreement Returned field from the Field Chooser to the Column Heading row and position it to the right of the Beta Agreement Sent field.

3  Drag the Beta Package Sent field from the Field Chooser to the Column Heading row and position it to the right of the Beta Agreement Sent field.

## Adjust the Column Widths to Best Fit

Next, you adjust the column widths for the Beta Agreement Sent, Beta Agreement Returned, and Beta Package Sent column headings.

▶ **To adjust the column widths**

1  Right-click the **Beta Agreement Sent** column heading, and then click **Best Fit**.

2  Repeat for the **Beta Agreement Returned** and **Beta Package Sent** column headings.

Your Beta Participants view should now look similar to the view shown in Figure 3.8.

**Figure 3.8   The Beta Participants view**

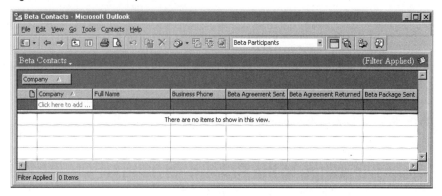

# Create a Filter for the Beta Contacts View

With a filter, you can create a set of criteria that determines the items that are shown in a view. For the Beta Participants view, you create a filter that displays only items that have a check in the Wants to Participate and Primary Contact fields.

▶ **To create a filter**

1   On the **View** menu, click **Filter**.

2   Click **Filter**, and then click the **Advanced** tab.

3   Click **Field**, point to **User-defined fields in Inbox**, and then click **Wants to Participate**.

4   In the **Value** box, click **Yes**, and then click **Add to List**.

5   Click **Field**, point to **User-defined fields in Inbox**, and then click **Primary Contact**.

6   In the **Value** box, click **Yes**, and then click **Add to List**.

7   Click **OK**.

# Save the Beta Participants View

Now you must save the view to retain your most recent changes.

▶ **To save the view**

1   Click the **Current View** box, and then click the ENTER key.

2   Click **Update the view "Beta Participants" with the current settings**, and then click **OK**.

# Create Items for the Beta Contacts Folder

Now let's assume you're ready to call potential beta participants and you want to keep track of those customers who either agree or do not agree to participate. You might also want to type the results of your calls, such as "Left message on answering machine," in the Comments or Issues field.

Before you create items, you switch to the Potential Beta Participants view. This is the view in which you enter new contacts.

▶ **To switch to the Potential Beta Participants view**

- On the Outlook toolbar, click **Potential Beta Participants** in the **Current View** box.

▶ **To create a Beta Contacts item**

- In the folder view, click the **Click here to add...** cell in the Company column, and then fill in the cells, as shown in Figure 3.9. After you finish typing in an item, click outside the cell. The item is then added to the folder. The values for the cells are shown in the following table.

**Figure 3.9   The top row in the view lets you create a new item for the view.**

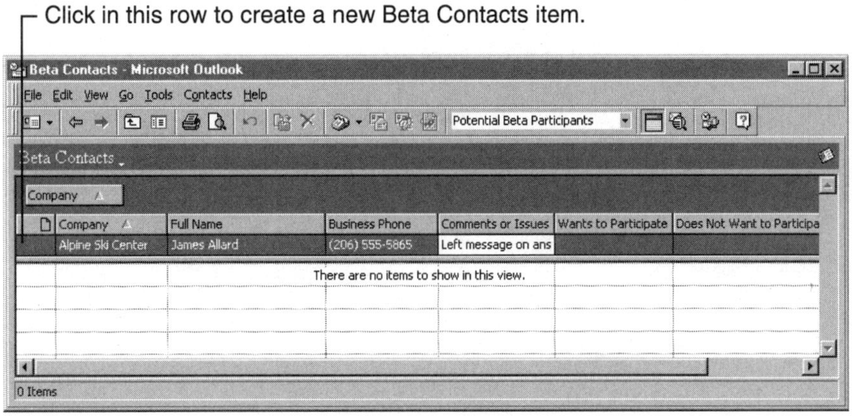

Click in this row to create a new Beta Contacts item.

| Cell column | Value |
| --- | --- |
| Company | Alpine Ski Center |
| Full Name | James Allard |
| Business Phone | (206) 555-5865 |
| Comments or Issues | Left message on answering machine 7-10 |
| Wants to Participate | |
| Does Not Want to Participate | |
| Primary Contact | |

Now let's assume you talked to Mike Nash and he agreed to participate in the program and to be the primary contact for the beta program for Alpine Ski Center.

▶ **To create a second Beta Contacts item**

- In the folder view, click the **Click here to add...** cell in the Company column, and then fill in the cells with the options shown in the following table.

| Cell column | Value |
| --- | --- |
| Company | Alpine Ski Center |
| Full Name | Mike Nash |
| Business Phone | (206) 555-5866 |
| Comments or Issues | |
| Wants to Participate | X |
| Does Not Want to Participate | |
| Primary Contact | X |

To keep things interesting, let's create another item.

▶ **To create a third Beta Contacts item**

- In the folder view, click the **Click here to add...** cell in the Company column, and then fill in the cells with the options shown in the following table.

| Cell column | Value |
| --- | --- |
| Company | Awesome Computers |
| Full Name | Rich Andrews |
| Business Phone | (206) 555-5335 |
| Comments or Issues | |
| Wants to Participate | |
| Does Not Want to Participate | X |
| Primary Contact | |

Here's one more to create.

| Cell column | Value |
|---|---|
| Company | City Power and Light |
| Full Name | Suzan Fine |
| Business Phone | (206) 555-5596 |
| Comments or Issues | |
| Wants to Participate | X |
| Does Not Want to Participate | |
| Primary Contact | X |

Your view should now look like the view shown in Figure 3.10.

**Figure 3.10   The Potential Beta Participants view with the Beta Contact items**

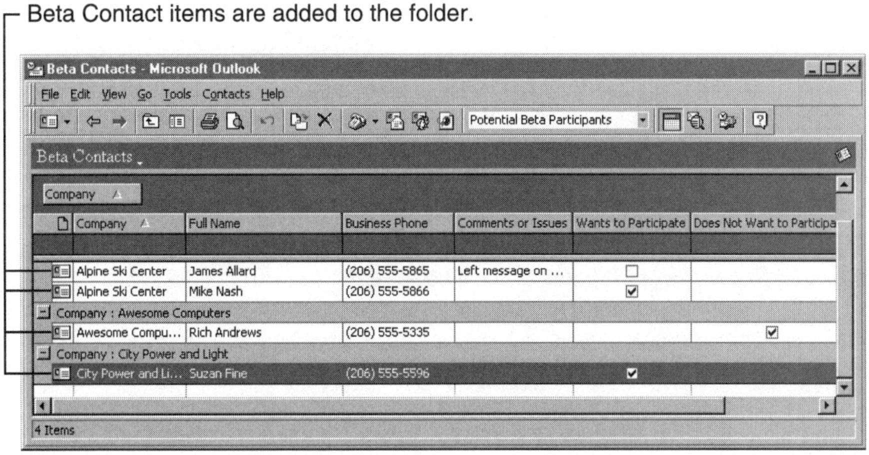

Beta Contact items are added to the folder.

# Enter Dates in the Beta Participants View

Now let's assume you send Beta Agreement contracts to those people who agree to participate in the program. To do this, you use the Beta Participants view to enter the date that the Beta Agreement contracts are sent.

▶ **To switch to the Beta Participants view**

- On the Outlook toolbar, click **Beta Participants** in the **Current View** box.

▶ **To enter the Beta Agreement Sent date in the fields**

- Click the Beta Agreement Sent field for Mike Nash, and then type the date, as shown in Figure 3.11.

**Figure 3.11   The Beta Participants view with dates entered directly in the Beta Agreement Sent fields**

Dates can be entered directly into the cells. ┐

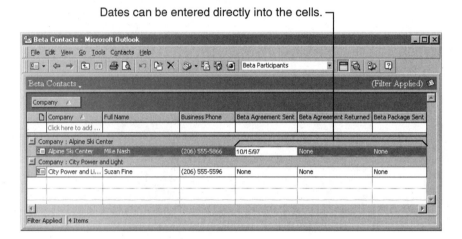

# Customize the Contacts Form

Up to this point, we've focused on modifying the Beta Contacts application by adding custom views. Now we'll further customize the Beta Contacts application by modifying the built-in Contacts form. While you cannot customize the General page of the Contacts form, you can specify that additional pages are shown on the form, and you can add controls to these pages.

In this example, you add a Company Profile page to the Contacts form, as shown in Figure 3.12.

Figure 3.12   The Company Profile page you add to the Contacts form

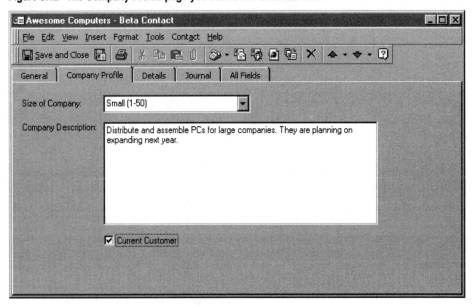

# Open the Contacts Form

To customize a built-in form, you first open it as you would to create an item. After the form is open, you switch between Design mode and Run mode.

▶ **To open the Contacts form in Design mode**

1   On the Outlook toolbar, click **New Contact**.

2   On the **Tools** menu of the **Untitled - Contact** window, click **Design Outlook Form**.

3   Click the **(P.2)** tab.

# Rename the New Page

The Contacts form provides several additional pages that you can add controls to. Notice that the additional pages are in parentheses. This indicates that the pages are hidden at run time. When you add controls to a page, the parentheses are automatically removed, so the page is visible at run time. For this example, you rename (P.2) to Company Profile.

▶ **To rename and show the page**

1  On the **Form** menu, click **Rename Page**.

2  In the **Page name** box, type **Company Profile**, and then click **OK**.

3  On the **Form** menu, click **Display This Page**.

# Add Controls to the Form

Now you use the Control Toolbox to add controls to the Company Profile page. After you add a control, you create a new field, and then bind the control to the field. In Outlook, a control is the physical component on the form in which the user enters, views, or clicks values. The field is the storage area in which the values from the controls are saved or loaded.

▶ **To show the Control Toolbox**

• On the **Form Design** toolbar, click **Control Toolbox**.

## Add a ComboBox Control

The ComboBox control you add to the Company Profile page enables users to select and view the size of a company, such as Small (1–50), Medium (51–500), and Large (501–1000+).

▶ **To add the ComboBox control**

• From the Control Toolbox, drag a ComboBox control to the form. Then drag the sizing handle on the right border of the control until the field is approximately the size of the field shown in Figure 3.13.

**Figure 3.13  The ComboBox control is added to the Company Profile page.**

┌─ The ComboBox control is dragged to the form.

The Control Toolbox from which you drag controls ─┐

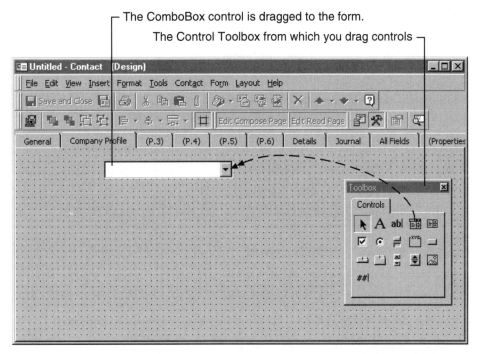

## Set Properties for the ComboBox Control

When you set properties for the ComboBox control, you create a Size of Company field. When you create a new field for a control from the Properties dialog box, the field is automatically bound to the control. When a control is bound to a field, the values in the control are saved to the field when an item is composed. When an item is opened in a folder, the values from the fields are loaded into the controls.

▶ **To set properties for the ComboBox control**

1   Right-click the ComboBox control, click **Properties**, and then click the **Value** tab.

2   Click **New**.

3   In the **Name** box, type **Size of Company**, and then click **OK**.

4   In the **List Type** box, click **Droplist**.

With a Droplist ComboBox control, the user must select a value from the list as opposed to typing in an arbitrary value. If you intend to group fields in a view based on values in a combo box, it's usually best to specify that the combo box is a drop list, so you can control the values upon which you group items in the folder.

5   In the **Possible Values** box, type the following:

**Small (1–50); Medium (51–500); Large (501–1000+)**

6   Select the **Set the initial value of this field to** check box, type **"Small (1–50)"** in the box below it, and then click **OK**.

**Figure 3.14   Properties for the ComboBox control**

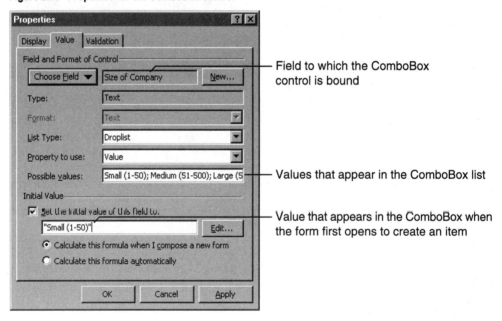

— Field to which the ComboBox control is bound

— Values that appear in the ComboBox list

— Value that appears in the ComboBox when the form first opens to create an item

## Add a Label for the ComboBox Control

Now you add a label for the ComboBox control to identify the control and to help the user understand the purpose of the control.

▶ **To add a label**

1  From the Control Toolbox, drag a Label control to the form.

2  In the label, select the word **Label1** and then type **Size of Company**, as shown in Figure 3.15.

**Figure 3.15   A label is added for the ComboBox control to identify its purpose.**

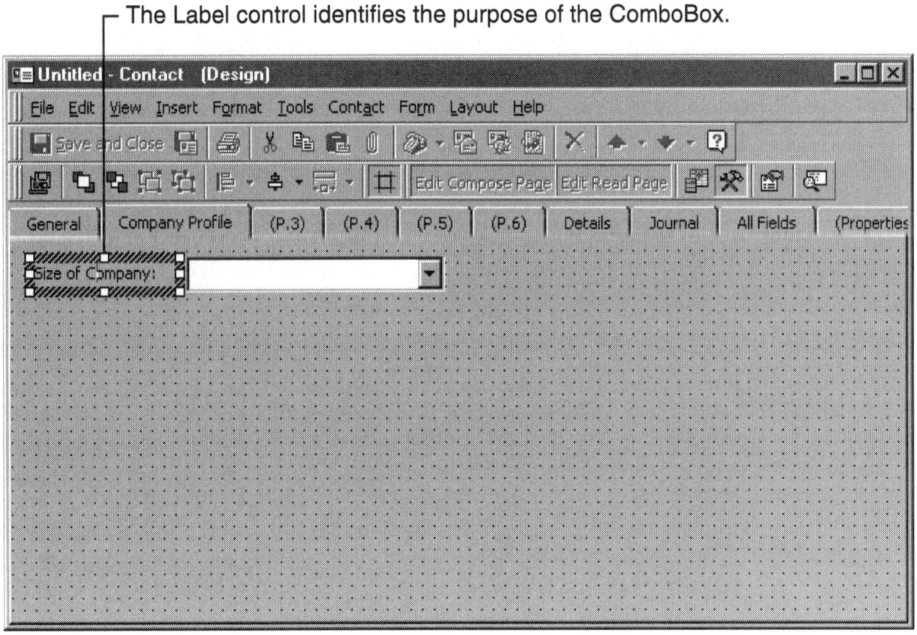

┌─ The Label control identifies the purpose of the ComboBox.

# Add a TextBox Control

Now you add a TextBox control to the Company Profile page. This control enables users to enter and view a company description on the Company Profile page.

▶ **To add a TextBox control**

- From the Control Toolbox, drag a TextBox control to the form. Then drag the sizing handle on the right border of the control until the field is approximately the size of the field shown in Figure 3.16.

**Figure 3.16   A TextBox control is added to the Company Profile page.**

A TextBox control is added to the form. ⌐

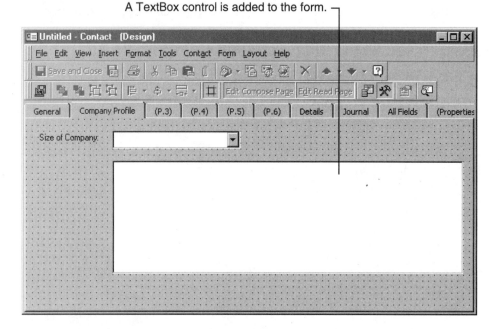

## Set Properties for the TextBox Control

Now you create a Company Description field that is automatically bound to the TextBox control. In addition, you select the MultiLine option for the control so the user can enter multiple lines of text in it. You also select the Resize with form option so the control size is adjusted to the size of the form.

▶ **To set properties for the TextBox control**

1  Right-click the TextBox control, click **Properties**, and then click the **Value** tab.

2  Click **New**.

3  In the **Name** box, type **Company Description**, and then click **OK**.

4  Click the **Display** tab.

5  Select the **Resize with form** check box.

6  Select the **Multi-line** check box.

7  Click **OK**.

## Add a Label for the TextBox Control

Now you add a label for the TextBox control so users know the purpose of the control.

▶ **To add a label**

1  From the Control Toolbox, drag a Label control to the form, and position it to the left of the TextBox control.

2  In the label, select the word **Label2** and then type: **Company Description:**

3  To resize the label, drag the sizing handle on the right border of the label until all text in the label is visible.

# Add a CheckBox Control

Finally, you add a CheckBox control to the form. This control enables users to specify if a company is a current customer.

▶ **To add a CheckBox control**

1  From the Control Toolbox, drag a CheckBox control to the form.

2  Click the CheckBox control, and then type **Current Customer**, as shown in Figure 3.17.

**Figure 3.17   A CheckBox control is added to the Company Profile page.**

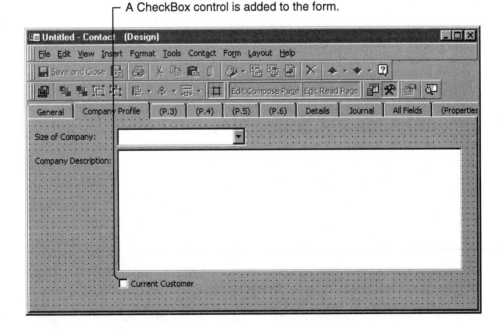

Building Microsoft Outlook 97 Applications  **53**

### Set Properties for the CheckBox Control

Next, you create a Current Customer field to which the CheckBox control is bound.

**1** Right-click the CheckBox control, and then click **Properties**.

**2** Click **New**.

**3** In the **Name** box, type **Current Customer**

**4** In the **Type** box, click **Yes/No**.

**5** In the **Format** box, click **Icon**, and then click **OK** twice.

# Set Form Properties

The Properties page of the form lets you name the form and specify a contact in case someone has suggestions for improvements or problems with the form.

▶ **To set form properties**

**1** Click the **Properties** tab.

**2** In the **Version** box, type **1.0**

**3** In the **Form Number** box, type **1.1**

**4** In the **Contact** box, type your name, and in the **Description** box type the following:

**Use this form to post, view, and update Beta Contact items in the Beta Contacts folder**.

**Figure 3.18  The Properties page of the Beta Contact form**

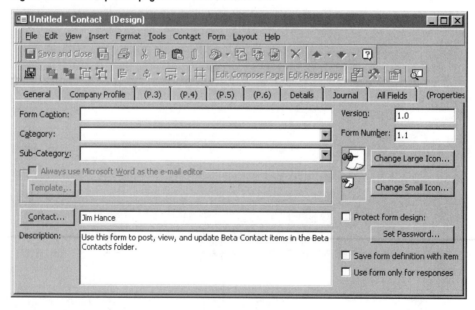

**Important**   Notice in this example that the **Form Caption** box is left blank. In most cases, you should leave this field blank and name the form when you publish it. Publishing the form is covered later in this chapter. This is done for the following reason. If you specify a form caption, and later republish the form with a different form name, the old form caption name still appears on the Outlook **Compose** menu.

**See Also**   For more information about setting form properties, see Chapter 5, "Forms."

# Test the Form at Design Time

Before you save a form or publish a form to a folder, it's a good idea to run the form to see how the form layout appears at run time. With Outlook, you can easily switch between Design mode and Run mode for the form.

▸ **To switch between Design mode and Run mode**

- On the **Tools** menu, click **Design Outlook Form**.

# Publish the Form

After you run the form and you're satisfied with its layout, you can publish the form in the Beta Contacts folder. When you publish the form, the form is saved and registered in the Beta Contacts folder form library and a menu item appears for the form on the **Contacts** menu of the folder.

▸ **To publish the form to the Beta Contacts folder form library**

1   On the **File** menu, click **Publish Form As**.

2   In the **Form Name** box, type **Beta Contact**

   If for some reason the Beta Contacts folder is not selected (next to the **Publish In** button), click **Publish In** to select it.

3   Click **Publish**.

4   Close the form.

**Figure 3.19   The Publish Form As dialog box is automatically filled in for you.**

# Specify the Default Form for the Folder

Now that you've created a custom form, you no doubt want to run it to see if it works as expected. However, at this point, there are two possible forms that you can open. One form is the built-in Contacts form that's provided with Outlook. The other is the Beta Contact form you created. At this point, if you click the New Contact button on the Outlook toolbar, the built-in Contacts form appears. To open the Beta Contact form you created, you must click New Beta Contact on the Outlook Compose menu. This is not exactly intuitive.

To avoid this step, you make the Beta Contact form the default form for the folder. Then, when the user clicks the New Contact button, the Beta Contact form appears.

▶ **To make the Beta Contact form the default form**

1   In the Folder List, right-click the **Beta Contacts** folder, and then click **Properties**.

2   Click the **General** tab.

3   In the **When posting to this folder, use** box, click **Beta Contact**, and then click **OK**.

# Test the Application

Let's test the Beta Contacts application and make sure the Beta Contact form opens when you click the **New Contact** button. First, however, let's switch to the Potential Beta Participants view.

▶ **To select the Potential Beta Participants view**

•   In the Current View box, click Potential Beta Participants.

▶ **To test the Beta Contact form**

1   Click the **New** button.

You should see the Beta Contact form with the Company Profile tab.

2   Fill in the form, and then click **Save and Close**.

The new item is posted in the Beta Contacts folder.

**See Also**   For more information about how forms and views work together, see Chapter 8, "Folders."

# Delete the Items You Created

Before you make the form available to other users, you delete the items you created earlier in this chapter. You do this because the items you created earlier in the chapter without the Beta Contact form will show in the Contacts form when opened.

▸ **To delete the items in the Beta Contacts folder**

1   Hold down the SHIFT key, and then click the items in the Beta Contacts folder.

2   Press the DEL key.

# Copy the Folder to Public Folders

Now that you've created forms and views for the Beta Contacts folder, and you've tested the folder to make sure it works as planned, you copy the folder from the Design Environment personal folder to Public Folders so the folder can be shared by a workgroup or across the entire organization. Before you copy the folder, you might want to see your administrator to find out the best location for the folder. In addition, you might need to see your administrator to get the appropriate permissions to copy the folder to its destination in Public Folders.

▸ **To copy the Beta Contacts folder**

1   In the Folder List, click the **Beta Contacts** folder.

2   On the **File** menu, point to **Folder**, and then click **Copy "Beta Contacts"**.

3   In the **Copy the selected folder to the folder** box, click the location you want the folder copied to, and then click **OK**.

**See Also**   For more information about distributing folders, see Chapter 13, "Distribute and Maintain Applications."

# Set Permissions

With Permissions, you define who can open the folder and the functions they can perform in the folder. When you create a folder in Outlook, you are automatically given an Owner role for the folder. This means you have full permissions to create, edit, and delete items in the folder, and you have full permissions to change any folder properties. Also when you create a folder, a Publishing Author role is assigned to Default. This means that all users in the Microsoft Exchange system are automatically given permissions to create and open items in the folder, to delete and edit their own items, and to create subfolders.

For the Beta Contacts folder, you will limit access to the folder to only a few users by first setting the Default role to None. You then give a few of your co-workers a Publishing Author role so they can create, edit and delete items in the folder.

### ▶ To set permissions for the Beta Contacts folder

1  In the Folder List, right-click the **Beta Contacts** folder, and then click **Properties**.

2  Click the **Permissions** tab.

3  In the **Name** box, click **Default**, and then in the **Roles** box, click **None**.

   This prevents all users on the Microsoft Exchange System from opening the folder.

4  Click **Add**, select several of your co-workers names from the list, click **Add**, and then **OK**.

5  In the **Name** box, click one of the names you added, and then in the **Role** box, click **Publishing Author**.

6  Repeat Step 5 for each name you added to the **Name** box.

The Permissions page should now look similar to the illustration shown in Figure 3.20.

**Figure 3.20   The Permissions page for the Beta Contacts folder.**

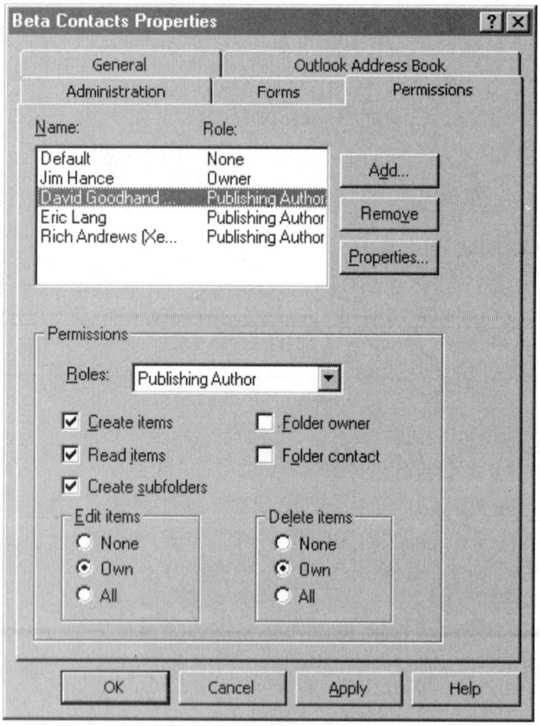

# Release the Application

Before you release the application, you set the **Initial View on Folder** property to
**Potential Beta Participants**. This will be the view users first see when they open the
Beta Contacts folder.

▶ **To set administration properties**

1  In the Folder List, right-click the **Beta Contacts** folder, and then click **Properties**.

2  Click the **Administration** tab.

3  In the **Initial view on folder** box, click **Potential Beta Participants**, and then
   click **OK**.

Now that the folder is ready for use, send a message to your co-workers to notify them
that the application is available.

# What's Next

In this chapter, we covered how to build a groupware application based on a built-in
module. With built-in modules, most of the functionality is already defined, so
generally all you need to do is make a few modifications to create an application with
a specific purpose.

In the next chapter we'll take a look at building a custom discussion application based
on the Post to Folder form supplied with Outlook. Unlike the forms in built-in
modules, the Post to Folder form can be completely customized, so you can use it for
building a wide range of applications. To begin working with the Post to Folder form,
you'll design a Product Ideas application that lets users post, read, and respond to new
product ideas in a public folder.

# CHAPTER 4

# Design a Custom Application

## In This Chapter

Overview of the Product Ideas Application   62

Create the Product Ideas Folder   65

Create the Product Idea Form   66

Create the Product Idea Response Form   78

Set the Actions   81

Create the By Product Category View   87

Specify the Default Form for the Folder   90

Set the Hidden Property for the Product Idea Response Form   90

Test the Application   91

Copy the Folder to Public Folders   92

About Folder Permissions   92

Release the Application   92

What's Next   93

The Microsoft Outlook Post form can be used in conjunction with a public folder to build custom discussion applications that let users submit, share, and collaborate on ideas and information. Discussion applications provide a great way to facilitate communication in your organization because they enable users across the enterprise to conduct online conversations. Perhaps equally important, the history of correspondence is saved and organized in a public folder, so important ideas or critical conversations are always available for viewing at a later date. Discussion applications are especially useful for virtual corporations or flexible workgroups where members work together on a project, but work different hours or in different locations.

In this chapter, you'll build a Product Ideas application that lets users submit, read, and respond to new product ideas in a public folder. This application provides a good example of how a discussion application can be used in your organization to not only collect, store, and organize ideas, but also foster enterprise-wide dialog about subjects that are vital to your company's interest.

By the end of this chapter, you'll have the basic skills and concepts you need for building one of the most common types of groupware applications—the discussion application. As a result, you'll be able to build a wide variety of new applications to foster communication in your company. In addition, you'll also have a working discussion application that you can use as a basis for building other information-sharing applications.

Here are just a few suggestions for the types of discussion applications you can build:

**Product Feedback**   Lets users post feedback about existing products and features in a public folder. Other users, such as product developers, marketing, or sales personnel, can then respond to existing feedback items, thus creating an online discussion. Product Planners can review the folder on a periodic basis to get an overall idea of what users like and dislike about a particular product.

**Technical Users Group**   Serves as a forum for posting issues and problems, as well as solutions to problems. For example, if a person is having difficulty with a particular task, he can post his problem to the Technical Users Group public folder. In turn, another user can post a solution to the problem item, perhaps suggesting a workaround he discovered working on a similar task.

**Vendor Services Application**   Enables members of your organization to post, respond to, and read reviews of professional services provided by your company's vendors. For example, if a supervisor is looking for temporary word processing help, she can search the folder for a highly recommended vendor that's already been used in the company.

**Restaurants and Accommodations Application**   Lets users post, read, and respond to restaurant and hotel/motel reviews in a public folder. With this application, your company can quickly develop an online travel guide to help business travelers plan where to eat and stay when they're working away from the office.

# Overview of the Product Ideas Application

The Product Ideas application consists of a Product Ideas folder and two forms: the Products Idea form and the Product Idea Response form. Here's how the Products Idea application might by a used by a Sporting Equipment Manufacturer to help generate new ideas for products.

Let's assume Rich Andrews in Chicago opens the Product Ideas public folder, and then uses the Product Idea form to post an idea for a wooden kayak construction kit. Later in the day Joe Howard in Boston reads the idea, and then uses the Product Idea Response form to post a response asking what kind of wood is best to use. A few minutes later, Suzan Fine reads the items posted by Rich Andrews and Joe Howard and uses the Product Idea Response form to post a response to Joe Howard's item. As shown in Figure 4.1, the resulting conversation is stored and organized in the folder.

**Figure 4.1   The Product Ideas folder**

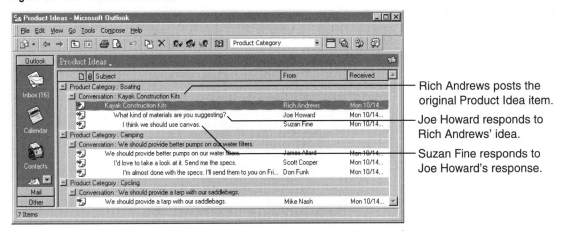

Rich Andrews posts the original Product Idea item.

Joe Howard responds to Rich Andrews' idea.

Suzan Fine responds to Joe Howard's response.

**The Product Category View**   As part of the application design process, you add a custom view to the Product Ideas folder that groups items first by Product Category field, then by the Conversation field, as shown in Figure 4.2.

**Figure 4.2   The Product Category view in the Product Ideas folder**

Items are grouped by Product Category.

The custom Product Category view is selected in the **Current View** box.

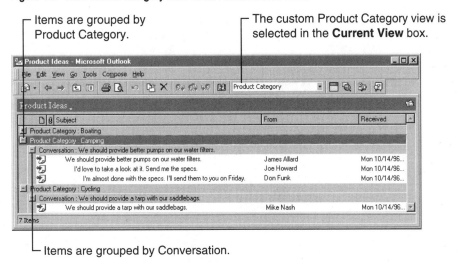

Items are grouped by Conversation.

**The Product Idea Form**   The Product Idea form is a modified Post to Folder form. The New Product Idea form has both a **Compose** page and a **Read** page. With the **Compose** page, as shown in Figure 4.3, the user posts a new item in the New Product Idea folder. With the **Read** page, the user opens and views a posted item.

**Figure 4.3   The Compose page of the Product Idea form**

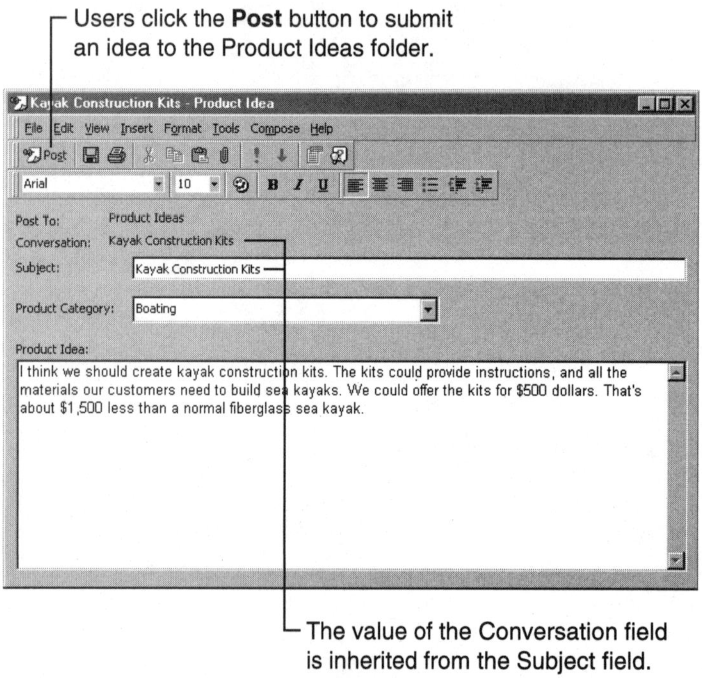

Users click the **Post** button to submit an idea to the Product Ideas folder.

The value of the Conversation field is inherited from the Subject field.

**The Product Idea Response Form**   The Product Idea Response form, as shown in Figure 4.4, serves two purposes. It lets users post a response to a product idea. In addition, it lets users post a response to the response. We'll take a look at how this is done later in this chapter.

**Figure 4.4   The Compose page of the Product Idea Response form**

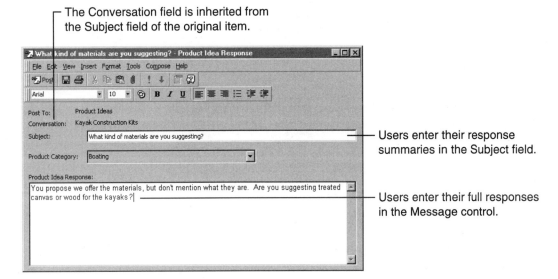

The Conversation field is inherited from the Subject field of the original item.

Users enter their response summaries in the Subject field.

Users enter their full responses in the Message control.

# Create the Product Ideas Folder

To get started, you create the Product Ideas folder in the Design Environment personal folder, as shown in Figure 4.5.

If you haven't yet created the Design Environment folder, refer to "Create the Design Environment Personal Folder" in Chapter 3.

▶ **To create the Product Ideas folder**

1   In the Folder List, right-click the Design Environment folder, and then click **Create Subfolder** on the shortcut menu.

2   In the **Name** box, type **Product Ideas**.

3   In the **Folder contains** box, click **Mail Items**.

4   In the **Description** box, type **Use this folder to post, view, and respond to product ideas**.

5   Clear the **Create a shortcut to the folder in the Outlook Bar** check box.

**Figure 4.5   The Product Ideas folder is created in the Design Environment personal folder.**

# Create the Product Idea Form

The Product Idea form that you create will enable users to post new ideas to the Product Ideas folder. The Product Idea form is based on the standard Outlook Post form. The Outlook Post form supplies most of the functionality you need, so all you need to do to build the Product Idea form is add and remove a couple controls, and then set a few properties for the controls and the form. To design the Product Idea form, you'll modify the **Message** tab of the Post form, as shown in Figure 4.6.

**Figure 4.6   The finished version of the Compose page you create. The form is shown in Design mode.**

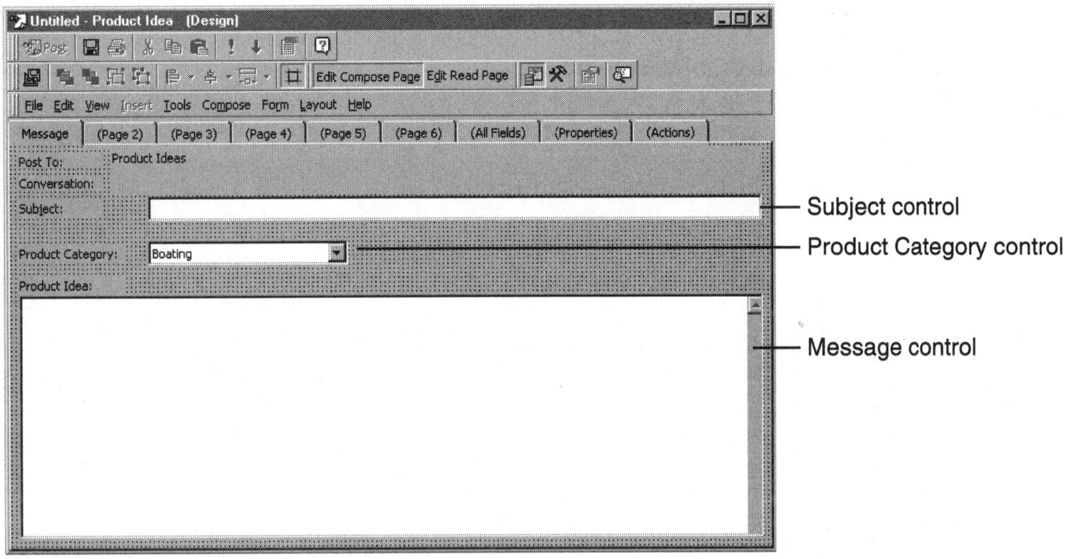

— Subject control
— Product Category control
— Message control

# Open the Post to Folder Form

To build the Product Idea form, you open the Post form in the Product Ideas folder, and then switch to Design mode to modify the form.

▶ **To open the Post form in Design mode**

1   In the Folder List, click the Product Ideas folder.

2   On the **Compose** menu, click **New Post in This Folder**.

3   On the **Tools** menu of the form, click **Design Outlook Form**.

# Edit the Compose Page

Most forms consist of two pages—a **Compose** page for submitting items and a **Read** page for opening and viewing items. In most cases, the **Compose** page is slightly different from the **Read** page. For example, the **Compose** page has a Post To control that shows where the item is posted, while the **Read** page has a From control to show who posted the item.

To edit the **Compose** page, you remove the Categories control, you resize the Message control, and you add a Product Category control. You also add or remove the associated labels for the controls.

## Remove the Categories Control

For the form you're creating, the Categories control serves no purpose, so you delete it from the **Compose** page.

▶ **To remove the Categories control and its label**

1   Click the **Categories** control, and then press DELETE.

2   Click the **CategoriesLabel** control, and then press DELETE.

## Adjust the Message Control

Now you move the Message control and resize it to make room for the Product Category control that you add to the form.

▶ **To adjust the Message control**

1   Drag the Message control bottom until it is near the bottom of the **Compose** page as shown in Figure 4.7.

2   Drag the Message control top border until it's approximately the size and location of the control in Figure 4.7.

▶ **To horizontally center the Message control**

•   On the **Layout** menu, point to **Center in Form**, and then click **Horizontally**.

**Figure 4.7   The Message control is adjusted to make room for the Product Category control.**

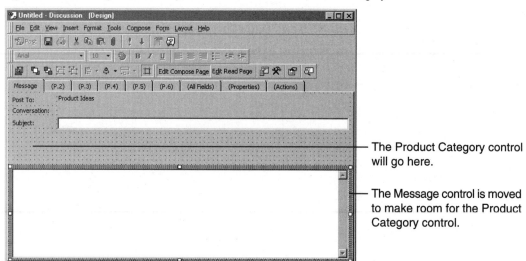

The Product Category control will go here.

The Message control is moved to make room for the Product Category control.

# Add the Product Category Control

The Product Category control is a ComboBox control that lets users select a product category, such as Boating or Fishing, or enter a new product category. Later in this chapter, you will build a view that groups items in the Product Ideas folder by product category. When product ideas are grouped in the folder by Product Category, it becomes much easier for the user to find ideas about a particular product.

▶ **To add the Product Category control**

1 On the **Form Design** toolbar, click the **Control Toolbox** button.

2 From the **Control Toolbox**, drag a ComboBox control to the form. Then place the pointer over a sizing handle on the right border of the control and drag the border until the field is approximately the size and position of the control shown in Figure 4.8.

**Figure 4.8   The Product Category control is added to the Compose page.**

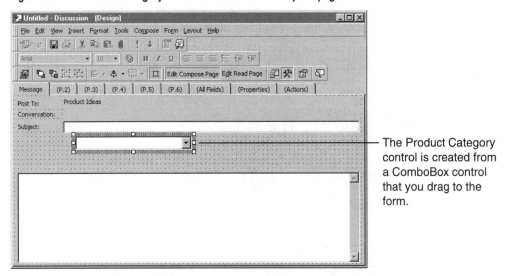

The Product Category control is created from a ComboBox control that you drag to the form.

## Set the Properties for the Product Category Control

When you set properties for the Product Category control using the **Properties** dialog box, as shown in Figure 4.9, you name the control, and then you create a Product Category field for the control. When you create the field from the **Properties** dialog box, you automatically bind the field to the control. When a field is bound to the control, the value in the control at run time is saved to the field when the item is posted. The value is loaded into the control from the field when a posted item in a folder is opened.

### ▶ To set the properties for the Product Category control

1   Right-click the ComboBox control you added to the form, and then click **Properties** on the shortcut menu.

2   Click the **Display** tab.

3   In the **Name** box, type **Product Category**.

4   Click the **Value** tab.

5   Click **New**.

6   In the **Name** box, type **Product Category**, and then click **OK**.

   The Product Category control is now bound to the Product Category field.

7   In the **Possible Values** box, type **Boating;Camping;Cycling;Fishing;Hiking; Running**.

8   Select the **Set the initial value of this field to** check box, and then type **Boating** in the box.

   The initial value is the value that first appears in the control when the form first opens at run time.

9   Click **OK**.

**Figure 4.9   The Properties dialog box for the Product Category control**

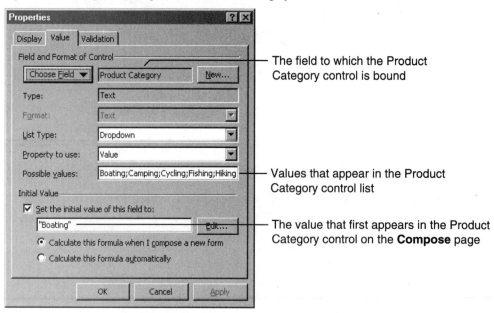

## Add a Label for the Product Category Control

Now you add a label for the Product Category control so users know the purpose of the control.

▶ **To add a Label control**

1  From the **Control Toolbox**, drag a Label control to the **Compose** page, as shown in Figure 4.10.

2  Click the Label control, and then change its text to **Product Category:**.

**Figure 4.10   The Product Category label is added to the form.**

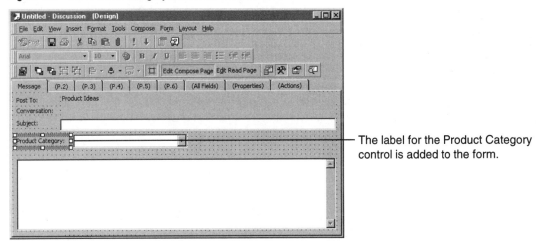

The label for the Product Category control is added to the form.

## Align the Subject and Product Category Control

One way to make sure your forms have a professional look is to align the controls on the form. Outlook offers a variety of layout options, but in most cases you can align items simply by dragging the borders of controls until they are aligned they way you want. For example, on the **Compose** page, you can align the Subject and Product Category controls by dragging the left edge of the Subject control until it is aligned with the left edge of the Product Category control. Because the **Snap to Grid** option is on, the Subject control is automatically adjusted for you.

▶ **To align the Subject and Product Category controls**

• Click the Subject control, and then drag the left border of the Subject control until it is aligned with the left border of the Product Category control, as shown in Figure 4.11.

**Figure 4.11   The Subject control is aligned with the Product Category control.**

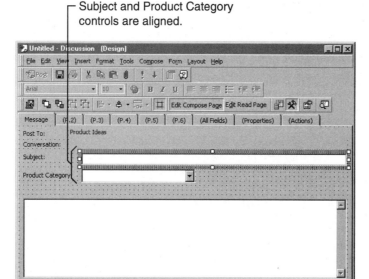

## Add a Label for the Message Control

Now you add a label for the Message control to indicate to users the type of information they're supposed to type into the control. To make room for the label, you may need to make the Message control slightly smaller.

▶ **To add a Label control**

1   Drag a Label control from the **Control Toolbox** to the **Compose** page, as shown in Figure 4.12.

2   Click the Label control, and then type **Product Idea:**.

**Figure 4.12   The Product Idea label is added to the Compose page.**

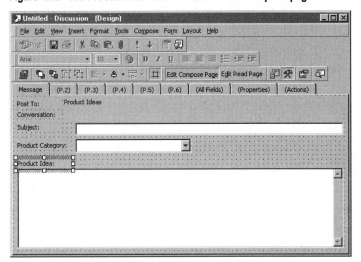

## Set the Tab Order

The tab order defines the sequence in which the controls become active on the form when the user presses TAB. When you add controls to the form, the control name is added to the bottom of a list of controls in the **Tab Order** box. For the **Compose** page, you must move the Product Category control up the list so it follows directly after the Subject control.

▶ **To set the Tab Order for the Compose page**

1   On the **Layout** menu, click **Tab Order**.

2   In the **Tab Order** box, click **Product Category**, then click **Move Up** until **Product Category** is above **Message**.

**Note**   Label controls, such as ConversationLabel and SubjectLabel, are listed in the **Tab Order** box but are not included in the tab order.

# Edit the Read Page

To edit the **Read** page, you copy the controls you added to the **Compose** page. Before you do this, however, you must switch to the **Read** page, adjust grid settings, delete the Categories control, and adjust the Message control to make room for new controls.

▶ **To switch to the Read page**

• On the **Form Design** toolbar, click **Edit Read Page**, as shown in Figure 4.13.

▶ **To delete the Categories control and its label**

1  Hold down the CTRL key, and then click the **Categories** control and its associated label.

2  Press DELETE.

▶ **To adjust the Message control**

1  Drag the Message control bottom border until is near the bottom of the **Compose** page as shown in Figure 4.13.

2  Drag the Message control top border until it's approximately the size and position of the control shown in Figure 4.13.

**Tip**  If necessary, you can automatically center the Message control on the form. To do this, click the Message control, point to **Center in Form** on the **Layout** menu, and then click **Horizontally**.

**Figure 4.13   The Read page of the Product Idea form**

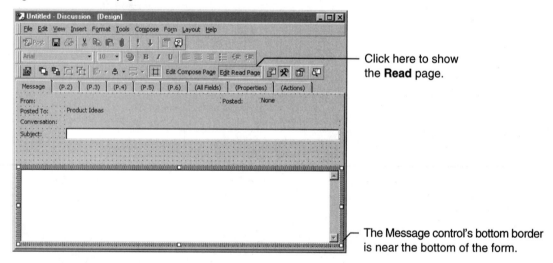

Click here to show the **Read** page.

The Message control's bottom border is near the bottom of the form.

## Copy Controls from the Compose Page

Now you switch to the **Compose** page and copy the Product Category control, its label, and the Product Idea label. Then you switch back to the **Read** page where you paste the controls.

▶ **To copy the controls from the Compose page**

1 On the **Form Design** toolbar, click **Edit Compose Page**.

2 Hold down the CTRL key and click the Product Category control, the Product Category label, and the Product Idea label.

3 On the **Standard** toolbar, click **Copy**.

4 On the **Form Design** toolbar, click **Edit Read Page**.

5 When the **Read** page appears, click **Paste**, and then position the pasted controls on the page as shown in Figure 4.14.

6 Click the Subject control, and then drag the left border of the Subject control until it is approximately aligned with the left border of the Product Category control.

7 Hold down SHIFT and click the Product Category control.

8 In the **Layout** menu, point to **Align**, and then click **Left**.

**Figure 4.14   The Read page of the Product Idea form**

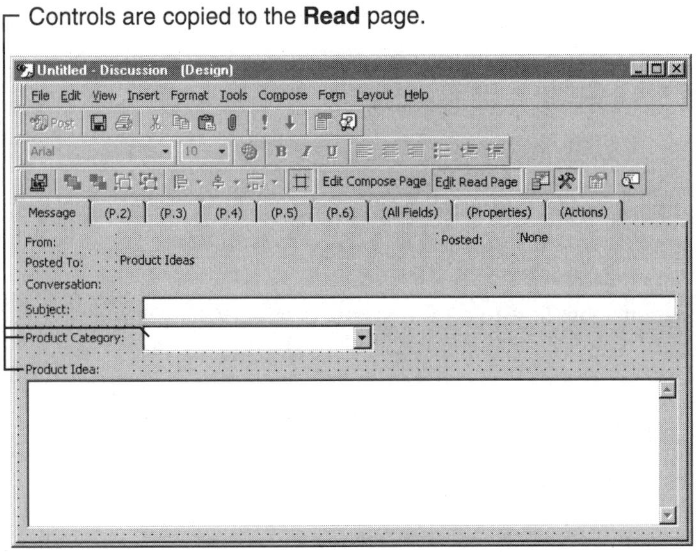

Controls are copied to the **Read** page.

## Set the Tab Order for the Read Page

When designing forms, it's important to remember that when you change a design element on the **Compose** page, you most often need to make the same change on the **Read** page.

▶ **To set the tab order**

1   On the **Layout** menu, click **Tab Order**.

2   In the **Tab Order** box, click **Product Category**, and then click **Move Up**.

# Set Product Idea Form Properties

The Outlook **Properties** tab lets you define the overall attributes for the form, including the Caption property that appears in the title bar of the form window and the Contact property for specifying who to contact for upgrades or maintenance of the form. There are a variety of other properties you can set for the form, but for now, only set the properties listed in Table 4.1.

▶ **To set Product Idea form properties**

• Click the **Properties** tab, and then fill in the values as shown in Table 4.1. Remember, there is no need to specify a form caption.

**Table 4.1   Product Idea Item Form Properties**

| Property | Value |
| --- | --- |
| Form caption | |
| Contact | *Your name* |
| Description | Use this form to post and view product ideas in the Product Ideas folder. |
| Version | 1.0 |
| Form Number | 1-1 |

**See Also**   For more information about how to set form properties, see Chapter 5, "Forms."

# Test the Form at Design Time

Before you save a form or publish it to a folder, it's a good idea to run the form to see how the form layout appears at run time.

▶ **To switch between Design mode and Run mode**

• On the **Tools** menu, click **Design Outlook Form**.

# Make a Backup Copy of the Product Idea Form

While it's not absolutely necessary, it's usually a good idea to make a backup copy of the form before you publish it to a form library.

▶ **To save the Product Idea form**

1   On the **Tools** menu, click **Design Outlook Form** to switch to Design mode.

2   On the **File** menu, click **Save As**.

3   In the **Save in** box, click a folder in which to save the form.

4   In the **File Name** box, type **Product Idea**, and then click **Save**.

# Publish the Product Idea Form

When you publish the Product Idea form to the Product Ideas folder, you register the form definition in the folder. As a result, a menu command appears on the **Compose** menu of Outlook when the user opens the Product Ideas folder. This is the menu command that enables users to open the Product Idea form and create a new Product Idea item.

▶ **To publish the form to the Product Ideas folder**

1   On the **Form Design** toolbar, click **Publish Form As**.

2   In the **Form Name** box, type **Product Idea**.

3   If the text to the right of the **Publish In** button is not Product Ideas, click **Publish In**, then select the Product Ideas folder in the Folder Forms Library list, and then click **OK**.

4   Click **Publish**.

**Tip**   Click the Outlook **Compose** menu. You'll notice the **New Product Idea** command is added to the menu. Outlook automatically constructs the menu command by combining the word "New" with the Form Caption property—"Product Idea."

# Create the Product Idea Response Form

The Product Idea Response form, as shown in Figure 4.15, is very similar to the Product Idea form. Therefore, to create the Product Idea Response form, all you need to do is modify a few properties of the Product Idea form, change the form name, and then publish the form in the Product Ideas folder.

**Figure 4.15   The Compose page of the Product Idea Response form**

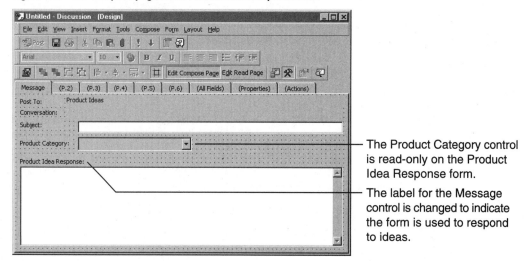

The Product Category control is read-only on the Product Idea Response form.

The label for the Message control is changed to indicate the form is used to respond to ideas.

# Edit the Compose Page

To edit the **Compose** page, you change several properties for the Product Category control, and you change the label associated with the Message control. First, however, you must switch from the **Read** page to the **Compose** page.

▶ **To switch to the Compose page**

• On the **Form Design** toolbar, click **Edit Compose Page**.

## Make the Product Category Control Read-Only

On the Product Idea Response form, you make the Product Category control a "read-only" control so the Product Category selected by the person who posted the New Idea cannot be changed by the person responding to the idea.

▶ **To make the Product Category control read-only**

**1**   On the **Compose** page, right-click the Product Category control, and then click **Properties**.

**2**   Click the **Display** tab, and then select the **Read only** check box.

## Clear the Initial Value Property for the Product Category Field

Now you specify that the **Initial Value** property for the Product Category field is cleared. This ensures that the value from Product Category field in the Product Idea item is copied to the Product Category field in the Product Idea Response item.

▶ **To clear the Initial Value property**

**1**   Right-click the Product Category control, and then click **Properties**.

**2**   Click the **Value** tab, and then clear the **Set the initial value of this field to** check box.

## Change the Product Idea Label

Now you change the label above the Message control from "Product Idea:" to "Product Idea Response:". This helps to clarify the purpose of the Message control on the Product Idea Response form.

▶ **To change the label**

**1**   Click the Product Idea label (located above the Message control), and then click it again.

**2**   Change the text in the label to **Product Idea Response:**.

# Edit the Read Page

Now you switch to the **Read** page, set the Product Category control to read-only, and then change the Product Idea label to Product Idea Response.

▶ **To switch to the Read page**

•   On the **Form Design** toolbar, click **Edit Read Page**.

▶ **To make the Product Category control read-only**

**1**   Right-click the Product Category control, and then click **Properties**.

**2**   Click the **Display** tab, and then select the **Read only** check box.

▶ **To change the Product Idea label**

1 Click the Product Idea label (above the Message control), and then click it again.

2 Change the label to **Product Idea Response:**.

# Set the Form Properties

Now you set the form properties for the Product Idea Response form.

▶ **To set the form properties**

1 Click the **Properties** tab, and then fill in the values as shown in the following table.

Table 4.2   Product Idea Response Form Properties

| Property | Value |
|---|---|
| Form caption | |
| Contact | *Your name* |
| Description | Use this form to post or view a response to a product idea or to post or view a response to a product idea response. |
| Version | 1.0 |
| Form Number | 1-1 |

# Make a Backup Copy of the Product Idea Response Form

Now you save the Product Idea Response form in the folder where you saved the Product Idea form.

▶ **To make a backup copy of the Product Idea Response form**

1 On the **File** menu, click **Save As**.

2 In the **Save In** box, make sure the folder is the same folder where the Product Idea form is saved.

3 In the **Name** box, type **Product Idea Response**, and then click **Save**.

# Publish the Form

Before you publish the Product Idea Response form, you change the **Form Name** option in the **Publish Form As** dialog box to Product Idea Response. You then publish the Product Idea Response form to the Product Ideas Form Library.

▶ **To publish the Product Idea Response form**

1   On the **Form Design** toolbar, click the **Publish Form As** button.

2   In the **Form Name** box, change the name to **Product Idea Response**.

The **Message class** property automatically updates when you change the name.

3   Click **Publish**.

4   Close the Product Idea Response form.

# Set the Actions

Actions determine how a form handles responses. For example, the action that you create for the Product Idea form will enable users to respond to a Product Idea item with the Product Idea Response form. In addition, the action that you create for Product Idea Response form will enable users to respond to a Product Idea Response item with the Product Idea Response form. In essence, the form will call itself for a response.

# Set the Actions for the Product Idea Form

First you open the Product Idea form in the Product Ideas folder. Then you switch to Design mode for the form and set its actions.

▶ **To open the Product Idea form in Design mode**

1   On the Outlook **Compose** menu, click hold down the SHIFT key and click **New Product Idea**.

Holding down the SHIFT key when you open a form for design purposes is a good practice because it prevents any code in the form from executing when the form is opened. Note that the Product Ideas folder must be open for the **New Product Idea** command to appear on the **Compose** menu.

2   On the **Tools** menu of the Product Idea form, click **Design Outlook Form**.

# Make the Reply to Folder Action Unavailable

When you create a new action for a Post form, you usually make the standard Post to Folder action unavailable. You do this for two reasons: First, you don't want standard Post items in the Product Ideas folder because they won't group correctly in custom views. Second, you want to avoid the confusion of presenting the user with two commands—**New Post in This Folder** and **New Product Idea**—that enable them to post an item in the folder.

▶ **To make the Reply to Folder action unavailable**

1  On the Product Idea form, click the **Actions** tab.

2  Double-click the **Reply to Folder** action.

3  Clear the **Enabled** check box, and then click **OK**.

The **Actions** page should now look like the **Actions** page shown in Figure 4.16.

**Figure 4.16  The Reply to Folder action is made unavailable for the Product Idea form.**

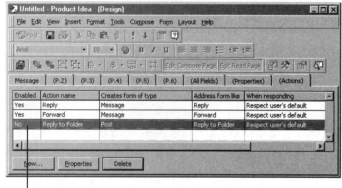

└ The Reply to Folder action is not
enabled for the Product Idea form.

# Create a New Action

Now you create a new action that specifies a Product Idea Response button appears on the Product Idea form when the user opens a posted Product Idea. When the user clicks the Product Idea Response button, as shown in Figure 4.17, the Product Idea Response form appears. The user can then use this form to post a response in the folder.

**Figure 4.17   The Product Idea Response button is added to the Product Idea form when a Product Idea item is opened in the folder.**

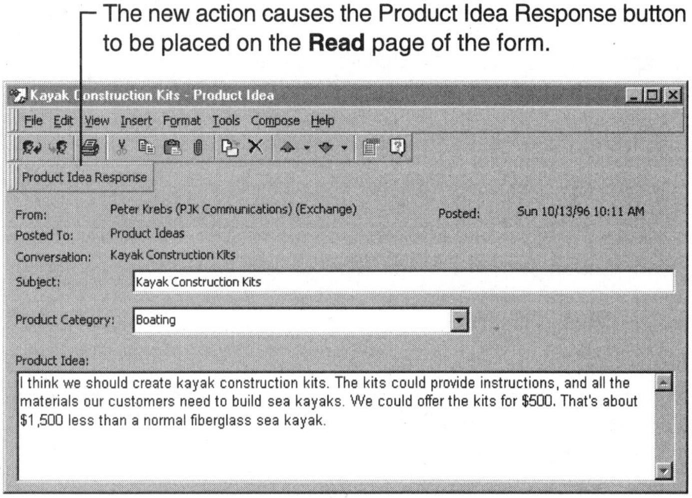

The new action causes the Product Idea Response button to be placed on the **Read** page of the form.

▶ **To create a new action**

1  On the **Actions** tab, click **New**.

2  In the **Action name** box, as shown in Figure 4.18, type **Product Idea Response**.

"Product Idea Response" is the name of the command that appears on the Product Idea Response button on the Product Idea form when a posted item is opened. The **Product Idea Response** command also appears on the **Compose** menu of the folder when a Product Idea item is selected in the Product Ideas folder.

3  In the **Form name** box, click **Product Idea Response**.

4  In the **Address form like a** box, click **Reply to Folder**.

**Figure 4.18  The Form Action Properties dialog box for the Product Idea form specifies the Product Idea Response form opens when the user clicks the Product Idea Response button.**

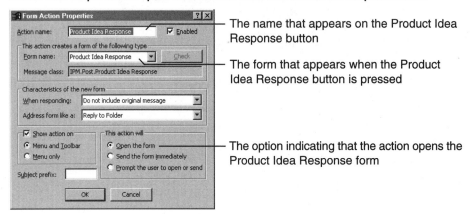

The name that appears on the Product Idea Response button

The form that appears when the Product Idea Response button is pressed

The option indicating that the action opens the Product Idea Response form

# Make a Backup Copy of the Product Idea Form

Before you publish the form, it's a good idea to make a backup copy.

▶ **To make a backup copy of the form**

1  On the **File** menu, click **Save As**.

2  In the **Save In** box, make sure the folder is the same folder where the Product Idea form is saved.

3  Click **Save**.

# Publish the Product Idea Form

▶ **To publish the form**

1 On the **Form Design** toolbar, click **Publish Form As**.

2 Click **Publish**.

3 Close the Product Idea form.

# Set the Actions for the Product Idea Response Form

Now you open the Product Idea Response form and create a new Product Idea Response action so users can respond to a Product Idea Response item. In effect, users can create a "response to a response" by opening another instance of the Product Idea Response form. When you create the new action, the Product Idea Response button is added to the form when a posted Product Idea Response item is opened in the Product Idea folder, as shown in Figure 4.19.

**Figure 4.19   The Product Idea Response button appears on the form when the user opens a Product Idea Response item in the folder.**

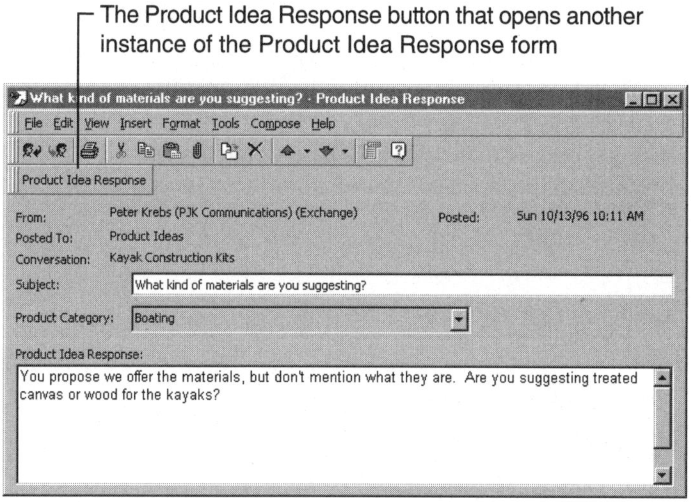

The Product Idea Response button that opens another instance of the Product Idea Response form

## Open the Product Idea Response Form

To create a new action for the Product Idea Response form, you first open the form in Run mode, and then switch to Design mode so you can add the new actions to the form. Note that the Product Ideas folder must be open for the **New Product Idea Response** command to appear on the **Compose** menu.

▶ **To open the Product Idea Response form in Design mode**

1   On the Outlook **Compose** menu, hold down the SHIFT key and click **New Product Idea Response**.

2   On the **Tools** menu of the Product Idea form, click **Design Outlook Form**.

## Make the Reply to Folder Action Unavailable

Just as you made the Reply to Folder action unavailable for the Product Ideas form, you make it unavailable for the Product Ideas Response form.

▶ **To make the Reply to Folder action unavailable**

1   On the Product Idea Response form, click the **Actions** tab.

2   Double click the **Reply to Folder** action.

3   Clear the **Enabled** check box, and then click **OK**.

## Create a New Action

Now you create a new action that causes the Product Idea Response button to appear on the Product Idea Response form when the user opens a posted Product Idea Response item.

▶ **To create a new action**

1   On the Product Idea Response form, click the **Actions** tab.

2   Click **New**.

3   In the **Action name** box, type **Product Idea Response**.

4   In the **Form name** box, click **Product Idea Response**.

5   In the **Address form like a** box, click **Reply to Folder**.

# Make a Backup Copy of the Product Idea Response Form

It's always a good idea to have a backup copy of the form.

▶ **To make a backup copy of the form**

1   On the **File** menu, click **Save As**.

2   In the **Save In** box, make sure the folder is the same folder where the Product Idea form is saved.

3   In the **Name** box, type **Product Idea Response**, and then click **Save**.

# Publish the Product Idea Response Form

▶ **To publish the form**

1   On the **File** menu, click **Publish Form As**.

2   Click **Publish**.

3   Close the Product Idea Response form.

# Create the By Product Category View

Custom views organize information in folders so the information is meaningful and can be analyzed more quickly. For example, take a look at the Messages view in Figure 4.20. In this view, items are listed chronologically according the order they were posted in the folder. With this flat presentation of information, you'd never know that discussions are taking place within the folder.

**Figure 4.20   The Product Ideas folder with the Messages view selected**

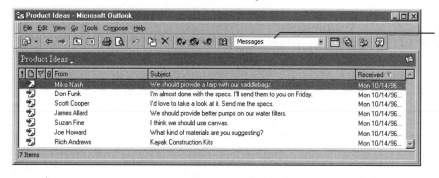

The Messages view shows items in the order they were received.

Now take a look at the same information in Figure 4.21. With the custom Product Category view applied to the folder, items are grouped first by the Product Category field, and then by the Conversation field. In addition, each item in a conversation group is sorted by the Conversation Index field, so you can see the history of responses to each item.

**Figure 4.21   The Product Ideas folder with the Product Category view selected**

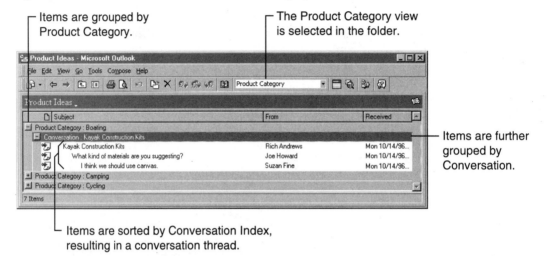

Items are grouped by Product Category.

The Product Category view is selected in the folder.

Items are further grouped by Conversation.

Items are sorted by Conversation Index, resulting in a conversation thread.

▶ **To create the Product Category view**

1   Click the **Product Ideas** folder in the Folder List.

2   On the **View** menu, click **Define Views**.

3   Click **New**.

4   In the **Name of new view** box, type **Product Category**, then click **OK** twice, and click **Apply View**.

# Remove Fields

Now you remove the fields that aren't necessary for the Product Category view.

▶ **To remove fields**

- Drag the following column headings away from the column heading row until an **X** appears through the column heading, and then release the mouse button.

   - Importance (the ! column heading).

   - Flag Status (the column heading with the flag symbol).

# Group Items

For the Product Category view, you group items first by the Product Category field, and then by the Conversation Topic field.

When you group items in a view by Product Category, all items in the Product Ideas folder that have the value Camping selected in the Product Category box are grouped together. Similarly, all items that have the value Fishing selected in the Product Category box are grouped together.

When a user first submits an Product Idea item, the Subject of the item becomes the Conversation Topic property. Any response items to the item, whether a direct response, or a response to a response, inherit this Conversation Topic property. As a result, all items about a particular Conversation Topic are grouped together.

▶ **To group items by Product Category, then by Conversation**

1  In the **View** menu, click **Group By**.

2  In the **Select available fields from** box, click **User-defined fields in folder**.

3  In the **Group items by** box, click **Product Category**.

4  In the **Select available fields from** box, click **Frequently-used fields**.

5  In the **Then by** box, click **Conversation**.

6  Click **OK**.

# Sort Items

The Conversation Index field is the field that makes conversation threading come to life. When you group items by Conversation Topic, and then sort them by Conversation Index, you can suddenly see the relationship between items in a discussion application because a response to an item immediately follows the item. Plus the response is indented from the associated item, so it's easy for a user who hasn't been part of the online conversation to quickly come up to speed on an issue by simply following the thread of conversation up to the last posted item.

▶ **To sort items by the Conversation Index field**

1  In the **View** menu, click **Sort**.

2  In the **Select available fields from** box, click **Frequently-used fields**.

3  In the **Sort items by** box, click **Conversation Index**, and then click **OK**.

# Arrange the Column Heading Order

Usually for discussion applications the Subject column heading precedes the From column heading. In Outlook, you can make adjustments to the view directly in the folder, so changing the column heading order is a simple matter of drag and drop editing.

▶ **To arrange the column heading order**

• Drag the Subject column heading to the left until the red double arrow appears, then drop the column heading.

# Save the Potential Beta Participants View

Now you save the view so the changes you made are retained.

▶ **To save the view**

1 Click the **Current View** box, and then click the ENTER key.

2 Click **Update the view "Product Category" with the current settings**, and then click **OK**.

# Specify the Default Form for the Folder

Now you make the Product Idea form the default form for the Product Idea folder so that when the user clicks the New button on the Outlook **Standard** toolbar, the Product Idea form appears.

▶ **To specify that the Product Ideas form is the default form**

1 In the Folder List, right-click the Product Ideas folder.

2 Click **Properties**.

3 Click the **General** tab.

4 In the **When Posting to this folder, use** box, click **Product Idea**.

# Set the Hidden Property for the Product Idea Response Form

Before you test the Product Idea application to make sure it's working as expected, you set the **Hidden** property for the Product Idea Response form. This ensures that users can only open the Product Idea Response form by first selecting or opening a posted item. Therefore, the Product Idea Response form can be used only for posting responses, not for creating new items to start a conversation topic.

When you set the **Hidden** property of the Product Idea Response form, you remove the **Product Idea Response** command from the Outlook **Compose** menu. With the **Hidden** property set, the Product Idea Response form can only be opened by clicking one of action commands you specified for the Product Idea and Product Idea Response forms.

▶ **To set the Hidden property for the Product Idea Response form**

1   In the Folder List, right-click the Product Ideas folder.

2   Click **Properties**.

3   Click the **Forms** tab, and then click **Manage**.

4   In the right forms box, click **Product Idea Response**, and then click **Properties**.

5   Select the **Hidden** check box.

# Test the Application

Before you copy the Product Ideas application to Public Folders and make it available to other users, it's a good idea to test the application to make sure everything is working as expected.

▶ **To test the Product Ideas application**

1   With the Product Ideas folder open, click **New Product Idea** on the Outlook **Compose** menu.

2   Fill in the form, and then click **Post**.

    The new item is posted in the Product Ideas folder.

3   Double-click the Product Idea item you posted.

4   When the Product Idea form appears, click the Product Idea Response button on the form.

5   Fill in the Product Idea Response form, and then click **Post**.

6   In the Product Idea folder, double-click the Product Idea Response item you just posted.

7   When the Product Idea Response form appears, click the Product Idea Response button.

8   Fill in the Product Idea Response form, and then click **Post**.

9   Repeat Steps 1–7 several times. Each time you perform step 2, click a different value in the **Product Category** box and enter different text in the **Subject** box.

# Copy the Folder to Public Folders

Now that you've created forms and a custom view for the Product Ideas folder, and you've tested the folder to make sure it works as planned, you copy the folder from the Design Environment personal folder to Public Folders so the folder can be shared by a workgroup or across the entire organization. Before you copy the folder, you might want to contact your administrator to find out the best location for the folder. In addition, you might need to contact your administrator to get the appropriate permissions to copy the folder to its destination in Public Folders.

▶ **To copy the Product Ideas folder**

1   In the Folder List, click the **Product Ideas folder**.

2   On the **File** menu, point to **Folder**, and then click **Copy "Product Ideas"**.

3   In the **Copy the selected folder to the folder** box, click the location you want the folder copied to.

# About Folder Permissions

When you create the Product Ideas folder, you are automatically given owner permissions for the folder. In addition, all users are given Publishing Author permissions so they can post and open items in the folder, and modify and delete items they create. At this time, you can leave the folder permissions alone.

**See Also**   For more information about how to set permissions, see Chapter 8, "Folders."

# Release the Application

Before you make the application available to co-workers, you set the **Initial View on Folder** property to Product Category. This is the view users first see when they open the folder.

▶ **To set administration properties**

1   In the Folder List, right-click the Product Ideas folder, and then click **Properties**.

2   Click the **Administration** tab.

3   In the **Initial view on folder** box, click **Potential Beta Participants**.

Now that the folder is ready for use, you can send a message to your co-workers to notify them that the application is available.

**See Also**  For more information about releasing applications, see Chapter 13, "Distribute and Maintain Applications."

# What's Next

In this chapter, we've taken a quick look at how to build an information-sharing groupware application based on the Post form. In the next chapter, "Forms," we'll take an in-depth look at the forms design environment, the different types of forms you can create, how forms work, and how to set form properties.

# Building Blocks of Applications

## Contents

Chapter 5 Forms 97
Chapter 6 Controls, Fields, and Properties 139
Chapter 7 Actions 185
Chapter 8 Folders 223

# Forms

## In This Chapter

Become Familiar with the Form Designer and Form
  Components  98

Learn How Forms Work  112

Create a Folder  116

Open the Form and Switch to Design Mode  116

Edit Form Pages  118

Add Controls  123

Create and Bind Fields  124

Polish the Layout  129

Create Help (Optional)  130

Edit the Read Page  131

Set Action Properties  132

Set Form Properties  132

Publish the Form  135

Test and Release the Form  138

With the Outlook Form Designer, you can build custom forms to streamline request processes, collect and distribute information, and save and show information that is structured so it's not only easy to find, but easy to read. For example, you can create Travel Request forms to automate the approval of business travel plans. You can create Product Feedback forms to collect valuable feedback from your customers. Or you can create Job Candidate forms to post information about a potential employee, so that other members of your organization can view the candidate's background before interviewing the candidate. After the interview, interviewers can post their impressions of the candidate in a public folder, so a manager can quickly get an overall impression of the candidate.

This chapter discusses form design concepts, introduces the form design process, and then covers fundamental form design tasks such as adding controls and fields, creating new actions, setting form properties, and publishing forms. When you're done with this chapter, you should have the basic knowledge and skills you need to create and publish forms in your organization.

Throughout this chapter, there are numbered graphic blocks, such as Step 1 below, that represent major steps in the form design process. Within each step, you can find detailed information that can help you complete the subtasks involved in the step.

# Become Familiar with the Form Designer and Form Components

This section covers the components of the Form Designer and discusses the parts of an Outlook form.

## Outlook Form Designer

The Outlook Form Designer consists of the following elements.

**Figure 5.1   Outlook Form Designer environment**

With the **Display** page, you set properties for a control.

With the **Value** page, you create fields and bind them to controls.

Click the **Field Set** box to select a category of fields.

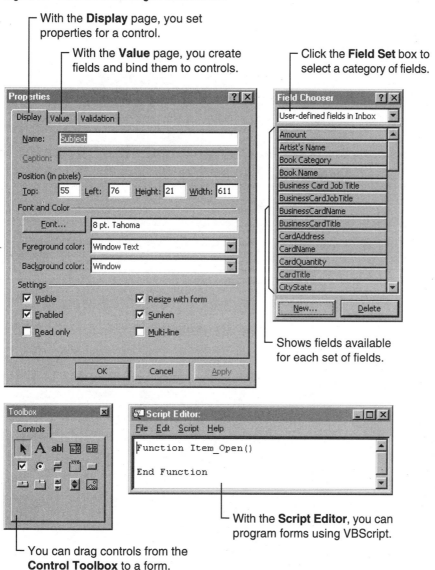

Shows fields available for each set of fields.

With the **Script Editor**, you can program forms using VBScript.

You can drag controls from the **Control Toolbox** to a form.

Click here to publish a form in a
forms library.

You can hide or show the **Message**
page and add controls to it.

Click here to switch to the
Read page of a form.

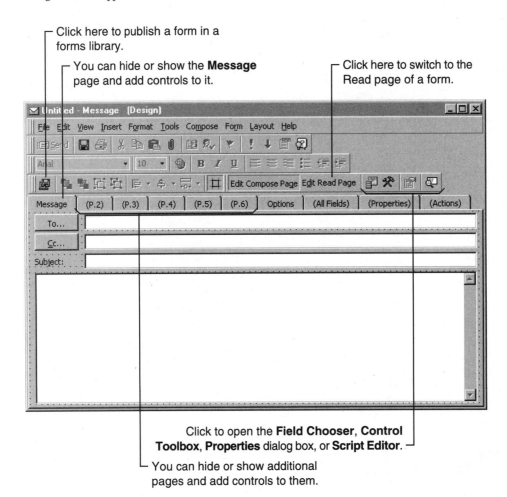

Click to open the **Field Chooser**, **Control
Toolbox**, **Properties** dialog box, or **Script Editor**.

You can hide or show additional
pages and add controls to them.

# Types of Forms

Outlook provides four basic types of forms you use as starting points for all forms that
you build. To effectively design forms, you need to know the basic characteristics of
these four forms: Message, Post, Office Document, and built-in forms.

# Message Form

You use the Message form as a starting point for building forms that let users send information to another user, distribution list, or folder. The Message form is fully customizable. When Message forms are sent, they travel through the Exchange Server's messaging transport agent and are routed to the specified address. Examples of Message forms are the Vacation Request form, the While You Were Out form, and the Business Card Request form.

**Figure 5.2   The Mail Message form is the starting point for Message forms.**

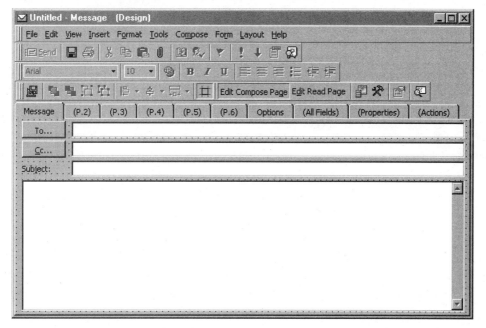

## Post Form

You use the Post form as a starting point for building forms that enable users to post, open, and respond to information in a personal or public folder. The Post form is fully customizable. Post forms submit items directly to the active folder. As such, Post forms are tightly integrated with folders. Examples of Post forms are the Product Idea and Product Idea Response forms found in the Product Ideas application, which is discussed in Chapter 4, "Design a Custom Application."

**Figure 5.3  The Post form is the starting point for forms that are integrated with a personal or public folder.**

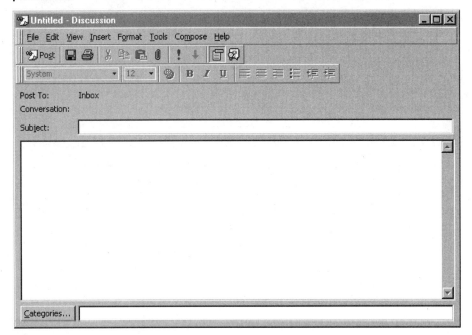

# Office Document Form

You use the Office Document form as a starting point for building forms that have a Word, PowerPoint, or Microsoft Excel document embedded in them. Office Document forms are essentially an Office document wrapped in either a Message or Post form. You can create Office Document forms to send documents to other users and to post documents in a folder. Examples of Office Document forms are an Expense Report form or a Purchase Request form supplied with the Outlook sample applications. These forms include a Microsoft Excel worksheet embedded in an Outlook form.

**Figure 5.4   The Document form is the starting point for Office Document forms.**

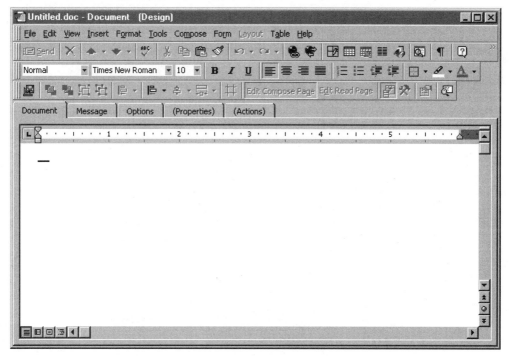

**Important**   Office Document forms do not contain pages you can customize. However, you can customize the document embedded in the Document page of the form. To create a form in a Microsoft Office 97 document, see Help for the specific application you want to create a form for.

## Built-In Forms

You can modify built-in forms in Calendar, Contacts, Journal, and Tasks modules by showing additional pages on the form. You can then add controls and fields to the form to suit the needs of your application. The characteristics of each built-in form vary, depending on the application. For example, with the Task Request form, users send a Task Request to another user. With the Task form, however, users save the task in the current folder.

**Figure 5.5   The built-in Appointment form can be customized to meet your personal needs or those of your workgroup or organization.**

You can show additional pages and add controls to them.

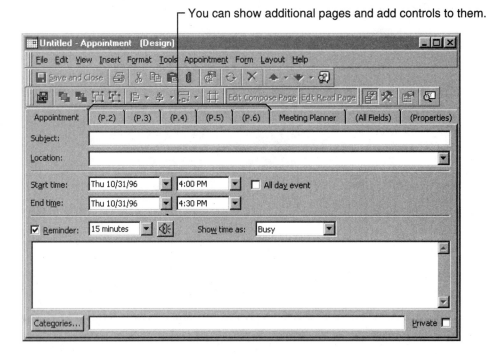

# Parts of a Form

Before you get started designing forms, you need to know about the different components of a form and what each component is used for. This section dissects a form and discusses the purpose of each of its components.

# The Compose and Read Pages

An Outlook form can consist of one page. But in most cases it consists of two pages: a Compose page and a Read page. Although the Compose and Read pages are often similar in appearance, they serve very different purposes. The Compose page enables users to create items and to send or post items. The Read page enables users to open and read submitted items in a folder, and to respond to items.

**Figure 5.6   The Message form consists of a Compose page and a Read page.**

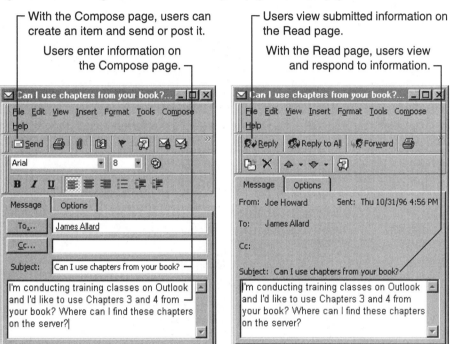

# Pages

Forms also have a series of pages that you view by clicking their respective tabs. In addition to the default **Message** or **General** page, forms have five custom pages that you can add controls to. Forms also have pages such as the **Properties** and **Actions** pages that enable you to set properties for the form to define how it functions, as shown in Figure 5.7.

**Figure 5.7   Pages of the Message form**

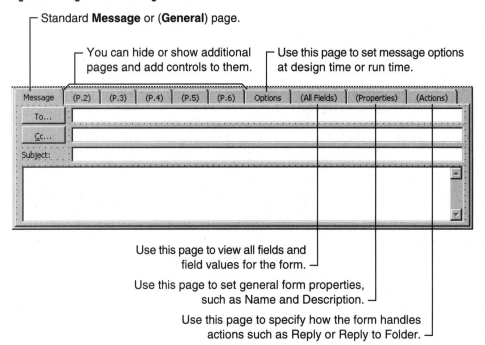

┌ Standard **Message** or (**General**) page.

┌ You can hide or show additional
  pages and add controls to them.

┌ Use this page to set message options
  at design time or run time.

Use this page to view all fields and
field values for the form. ┘

Use this page to set general form properties,
such as Name and Description. ┘

Use this page to specify how the form handles
actions such as Reply or Reply to Folder. ┘

# Controls

Controls are the components of a form that enable users to enter information and view information. Controls are the means through which users interact with the form. You add controls to the form by dragging them from the Control Toolbox.

**Figure 5.8   Controls and the Control Toolbox**

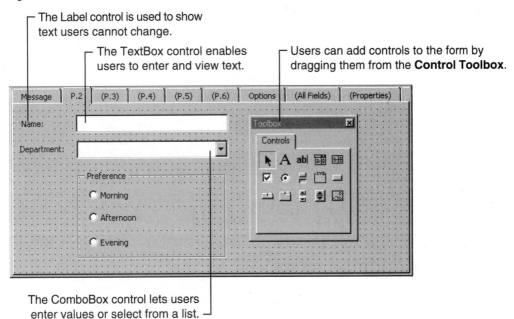

The Label control is used to show text users cannot change.

The TextBox control enables users to enter and view text.

Users can add controls to the form by dragging them from the **Control Toolbox**.

The ComboBox control lets users enter values or select from a list.

# Fields

A form field is MAPI field that defines how information in a control or in a folder is saved and displayed. In addition, the field is a physical storage location in the item where the specified data is saved. To specify that the information in a control is to be saved, you bind the control to a field. For example, as shown in Figure 5.9, the TextBox control is bound to the Name field, so the information in the control is saved to the field when an item is sent. When the item is opened, the information is loaded from the field into the control.

**Figure 5.9   The TextBox control is bound to the Name field.**

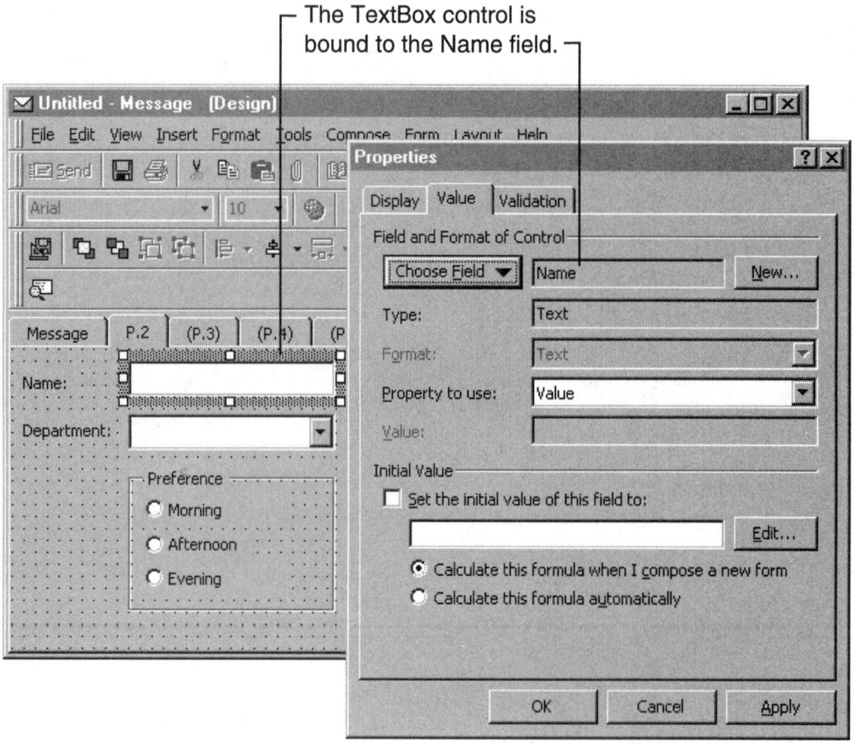

# Properties

Properties define the characteristics of form components. With Outlook, you can define properties for forms, controls, and fields. Figure 5.10 shows display properties that are set for the Name control.

**Figure 5.10   Properties of the Name control**

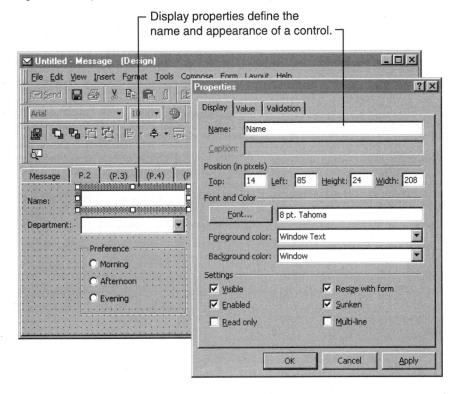

# Actions

Actions define how a form handles responses. You can create new actions or you can modify existing actions. For example, you can create a new action that specifies that a custom form is opened when the user clicks the **Reply** button on a form. Or you can create a new action that adds a custom response button to the form. As shown in Figure 5.11, new actions have been created for the Vacation Request form that enable users to respond to a Vacation Request item by clicking an Approve Vacation or Deny Vacation button on the Vacation Request form.

**Figure 5.11   The Actions page for the Vacation Request form**

This action sends a Vacation Approved reply to the requester.

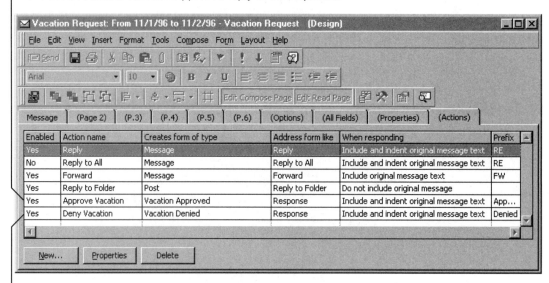

This action sends a Vacation Denied reply to the requester.

# Form Scripts

With the Script Editor, you can use Microsoft Visual Basic Scripting Edition to add functionality to a form. You can add code for a command button that creates and sends a response item, you can launch other applications from a form, and you can create procedures that automatically fill in or clear values on the form, as shown in Figure 5.12.

**Figure 5.12   The Script Editor shows code that automates a Business Card Request form.**

The AutoFill_Click procedure automatically fills in Address field values.

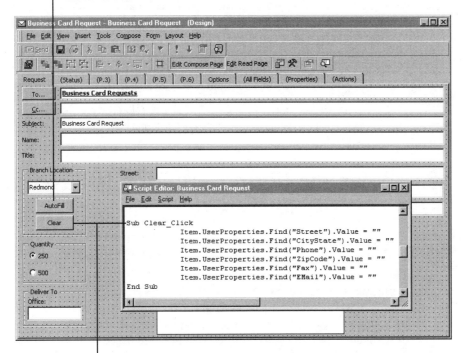

The Clear_Click procedure automatically clears values from the fields.

# Learn How Forms Work

 This section briefly covers some fundamental form concepts, such as the meaning of the term *item*, how saving the form definition with an item affects the form, and how shared fields work.

## What Is an Item?

Throughout the book, the term *item* is often used. In the past, an item was simply called a message. So why change the terminology? Because the term message can no longer encompass the vast array of information that can be included in an item. In Outlook, an item is a container for information. In addition to text and number values entered by users, this container known as an item can hold just about anything, including Uniform Resource Locators (URLs), voice mail, office documents, video clips, PowerPoint presentations, and so on. An item also contains properties that define the item, such as message class, that associates the item with a specific form.

**Note**   You may be wondering where items are stored. Public folder items are stored in the Microsoft Exchange Store on a Microsoft Exchange Server. Personal folder and mailbox items are stored in the location specified by the user.

## What Happens When the Form Definition Is Saved with the Item?

The Outlook Form Designer provides an option on the form **Properties** page called **Save form definition with item**. The **Save form definition with item** option serves two purposes:

- **It enables users to send Message forms to other users**   When the **Save form definition with item** option is selected for a Message form, the form definition is included in the item. This enables users who receive the item to view the item in the custom form, even though they do not have the custom form published in a forms library on their Exchange system. As such, it provides a useful way to send items created with custom forms to locations outside your immediate Exchange System. For example, you may want to send a customer feedback item over the Internet to a customer site. If the **Save form definition with item** option is selected, the customer sees the item in the custom form when they open it, even though they do not have the form published on their Exchange System.

- **It provides a security measure**   If a user opens a Message form that has the **Save form definition with item** option selected, and the form is not available on the Exchange Server or on the user's Outlook system, and the form has VBScript included with it, then the user sees the **Warning** message box, as shown in Figure 5.13. In this case, the **Save form definition with item** provides a security measure to prevent a user from opening a potentially harmful form. For example, with Visual Basic Scripting Edition, you can create a procedure that returns to your Inbox an item that contains the contents of another user's Inbox. When you finish designing a Message form, you can:

  - Clear the **Save form definition with item** option and publish the form in the Personal Forms Library or a Folder Forms Library.

  - Submit the form to an administrator who checks it for harmful macros. If none exist, the administrator clears the **Save form definition with item** check box and then publishes the form to the Organization Forms Library.

**Figure 5.13   Users see this message box when they try to open an item that contains the form definition and VBScript.1**

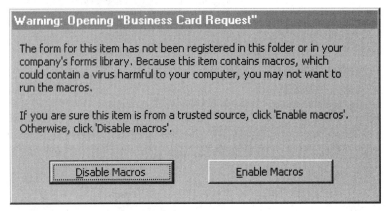

**Important**   By default, the **Save form definition with item** option is only turned on for Message forms.

**See Also**   For more information about the **Save form definition with item** option, see Step 12, "Set Form Properties" later in this chapter.

# How Is a Form Opened?

In theory, before an administrator publishes a form to the Organization or Folder Forms Library, he clears the **Save form definition with item** check box. The question then arises: If the form definition doesn't travel with the item, how is the form opened? The answer is that the form is launched from a Personal, Organization, or Folder Forms Library when the user attempts to create or view an item associated with the form. The form is associated with the item by its message class. Each form has a message class that identifies it internally to Microsoft Exchange. For example, the standard Post form has the message class IPM.Post, while the standard Contact form has the message class IPM.Contact. When an item is created, the message class of the form used to create the item is saved as one of the attributes of the item. When the user double-clicks an existing item to open it, the message class of the item is passed to Microsoft Exchange and is used to locate and launch the form associated with the item.

As shown in Figure 5.14, when a user opens the form to create a Volunteer Registration item, the form is launched from the Organization Forms Library. The item, and not the form, is then sent to a recipient. When the recipient opens the item in his or her Inbox, the Volunteer Registration form is launched and the information from the item is shown in the form.

**Figure 5.14  The Compose page creates and sends the item. The Read page shows the item. The form is loaded from the Organization Forms Library.**

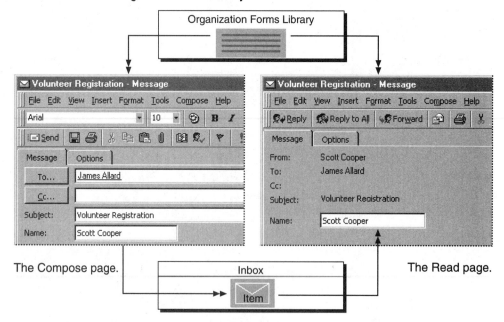

| For more information about | See |
|---|---|
| Saving the form definition with an item property | Step 12, "Set Form Properties," later in this chapter. |
| Submitting a form to an administrator | Chapter 13, "Distribute and Maintain Applications." |
| How forms are cached | Chapter 13, "Distribute and Maintain Applications." |

# How Do Shared Fields Work?

If you're new to designing forms, it helps to understand how the form saves information in the item and how it loads information from the item to the form. One of the central concepts behind the storing and loading of information is shared fields. A shared field is a field that is bound to controls on both the Compose and Read pages of a form. As shown in Figure 5.15, the Name control is bound to the Name field on the Volunteer Registration form.

**Figure 5.15  When the item is created and sent, the information is saved from the control to the field. When the item is opened, the information is loaded from the field into the control.**

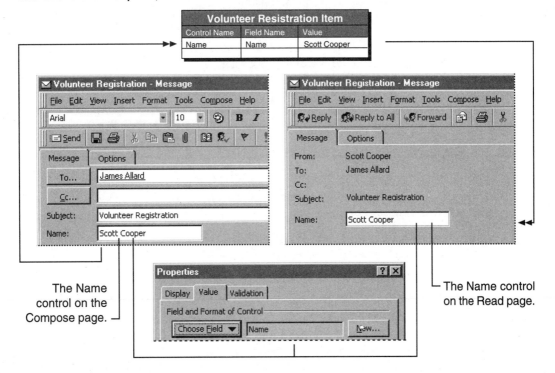

The Name control on the Compose page.

The Name control on the Read page.

Shared fields can also be used between forms. For example, when a user creates a response to an item, the information in fields that are common between both forms is copied from the first-opened form to the response form.

**See Also**   For more information about creating shared fields, see Chapter 6, "Controls, Fields, and Properties."

# Create a Folder

Generally, it is a good idea to create a form in a personal folder. This method offers a couple of advantages. First, it lets you store forms in a central and private location while you're designing them. Second, it enables you to easily test the form because you can open the form by clicking the menu command that Outlook adds to the *<Compose>* menu of the folder when you publish the form in the folder's Forms Library. Note that the name of the *<Compose>* menu will differ, depending on the type of folder that you're working with.

▸ **To create a personal folder**

1   In the Folder List, right-click a personal folder under which you want to create a folder, and then click **Create Subfolder**.

2   In the **Name** box, enter a name for the folder.

3   In the **Folder contains** box, do one of the following:

   • Click **Mail Items** to create a folder that will contain items created with Message, Post, or Office Document forms.

   • Click **Appointment Items**, **Contact Items**, **Journal Items**, **Note Items**, or **Task Items** to create a folder for items of that type. For example, if you click **Appointment Items**, Outlook creates a Calendar folder.

4   In the **Description** box, type a description for the folder.

5   If you want a shortcut to the folder, select the **Create a shortcut to this folder in the Outlook Bar** check box.

**See Also**   For more information about creating folders, see Chapter 8, "Folders."

# Open the Form and Switch to Design Mode

When you design an Outlook form, you always start with an existing form. Outlook gives you a variety of standard and custom forms to choose from. In addition to forms supplied in Outlook, you can design a form based on custom templates created by someone in your organization.

- To open a form and switch to Design mode, first click the folder in which you want to create the form.

**Important**   If you select the Calendar, Contacts, Tasks, Journal, or Notes folder, the **Compose** menu changes to reflect the nature of the folder. For example, the **Compose** menu in the Calendar folder is changed to **Calendar**. In this book, this menu is referred to as the *<Compose>* menu.

▶ **To create a Message form**

1   On the Outlook **Compose** menu, click **New Mail Message**.

   To create a Message form, you must be in the Inbox folder or a folder that contains Mail items.

2   On the **Tools** menu of the form, click **Design Outlook Form**.

▶ **To create a Post form**

1   On the Outlook **Compose** menu, click **New Post in This Folder**.

   To create a Post form, you must be in the Inbox folder or a folder that contains Mail items.

2   On the **Tools** menu of the form, click **Design Outlook Form**.

▶ **To create an Office Document form**

1   Click the folder in which you want to create the form.

2   On the **File** menu, point to **New**, and then click **Office Document**.

3   Double-click the template you want.

4   Do one of the following:

   - To create an Office Document form for posting items, click **Post the document in this folder**.

   - To create an Office Document form for sending items, click **Send the document to someone**.

▶ **To create a Calendar, Contacts, Tasks, Journal, or Notes form**

1   On the *<Compose>* menu, click the menu command associated with the form you want to modify. The name of the *<Compose>* menu will differ for each type of module.

   For example, to modify the Appointment form in a Calendar folder, click **New Appointment** on the **Calendar** menu.

2   On the form **Tools** menu, click **Design Outlook Form**.

▶ **To create a form based on a custom Outlook template**

1  On the *<Compose>* menu, click **Choose Template**.

2  Click the **Outlook** tab.

3  Double-click the template you want.

4  If the template is a Post template, select the folder the form will be associated with.

5  On the form **Tools** menu, click **Design Outlook Form**.

| For more information about | See |
|---|---|
| Creating a Message form | Chapter 10, "The Business Card Request Application." |
| Creating a Post form | Chapter 4, "Design a Custom Application" and Chapter 11, "The Help Desk Application." |
| Modifying a built-in form | Chapter 3, "Customize Built-In Modules." |

# Edit Form Pages

Usually forms consist of two pages: a Compose page and a Read page. There are other pages contained within the Compose or Read pages, such as (P.2)—(P.6) that you can customize or use to set properties on the form. These pages are covered later in the chapter.

The Compose page appears when the user opens the form to create an item. The Read page appears when the user double-clicks an existing item and opens it. When you create forms, you usually edit both the Compose and Read pages. In fact, when you first start designing forms, it's a common mistake to make adjustments to the Compose page, but forget to make the same adjustments to the Read page.

When working with forms, you can switch back and forth between the Read and Compose pages by clicking the **Edit Compose Page** or **Edit Read Page** buttons on the **Form Design** toolbar, as shown in Figure 5.16. While the Compose and Read pages look very similar, they both have unique characteristics that you need to be aware of.

**Figure 5.16  The Edit Compose Page and Edit Read Page buttons**

Click here to show the Compose page. ⌐        ⌐ Click here to show the Read page.

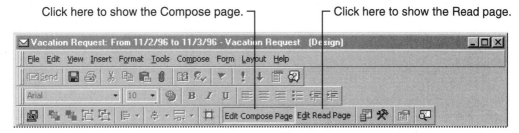

## The Compose Page

The Compose page of a form contains controls in which the user enters information. For example, in Figure 5.17 the user can enter information in the Starting and Ending boxes. When the item is sent or posted, the information in these controls is saved in the item. In addition, the Compose page of Message forms provides controls such as the **To** button and **To** box that enable users to specify an address for an item.

**Figure 5.17  The user enters information in the controls on the Compose page.**

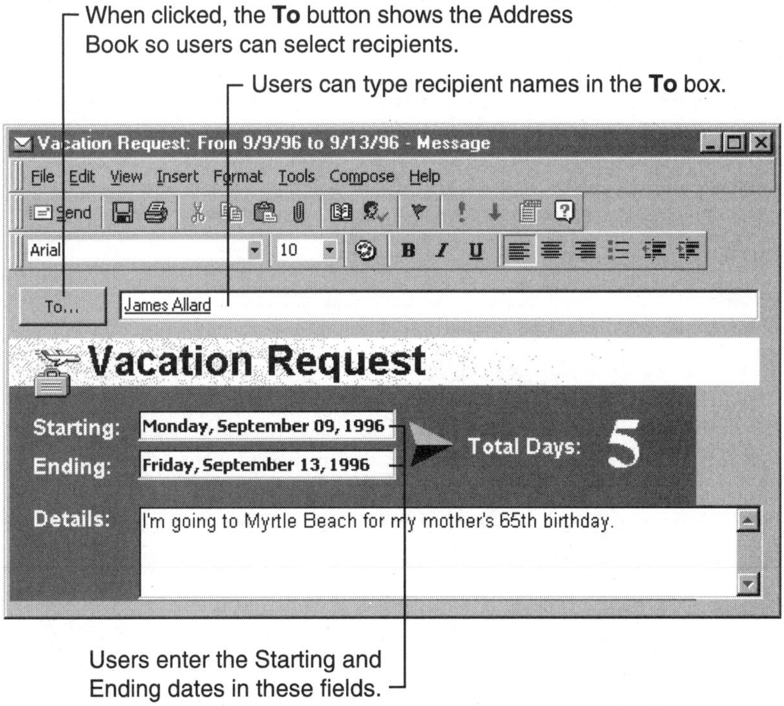

⌐ When clicked, the **To** button shows the Address
Book so users can select recipients.

⌐ Users can type recipient names in the **To** box.

Users enter the Starting and
Ending dates in these fields. ⌐

## The Read Page

The Read page of a form lets the user open and read an item. Quite often, many controls on the Read page are read-only, especially when the form involves money or sensitive information. As shown in Figure 5.18, the Starting and Ending boxes on the Read page of the Vacation Request form are read-only, so the reader cannot change them.

**Figure 5.18   The Read page of the Vacation Request form. Many of the controls on the Read page are read-only, so they cannot be changed by the reader.**

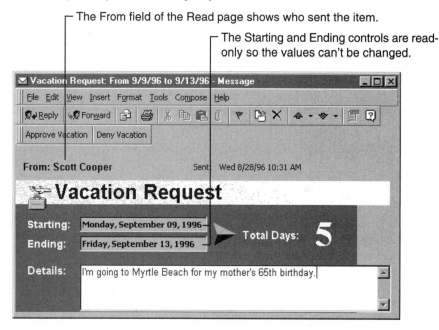

## About Separate Read Layout

The Outlook Form Designer provides a **Separate Read Layout** option that lets you specify if an individual form page has a Read page layout that is different than the Compose page layout. By default, the **Separate Read Layout** option, located on the **Form** menu, is selected for the **Message** page of Message and Post forms. However, for a custom page, this option is not automatically selected.

Most often when designing forms, you edit the Compose page first, and then edit the Read page. When you open a Message or Post form, the **Message** page is visible. For many of the forms you create, the **Message** page may be the only page you edit. However, you can also edit pages **P. 2** through **P. 6**, as shown in Figure 5.19.

**Important**   If you decide to add controls to a custom form page, you must select the **Separate Read Layout** option (**Form** menu) if you want the Compose layout of this page to differ from the Read layout, as shown in Figure 5.19.

**Figure 5.19   For the Message form, the Separate Read Layout option is selected for the custom page.**

When a control is added to a page, the page is automatically visible in Run mode.

Pages in parentheses are visible in Design mode but not in Run mode.

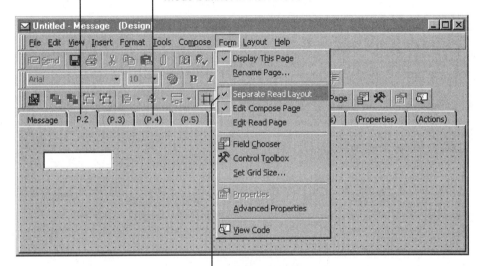

When you add controls to an additional page, click **Separate Read Layout** if you want the Read page layout to differ from the Compose page layout.

**Note**   If the **Separate Read Layout** option is not selected for a page, then you cannot switch between the Compose and Read pages when the individual page is active.

▶ **To view either the Read or Compose page**

• Click the **Edit Compose Page** or **Edit Read Page** button on the **Form Design** toolbar.

▶ **To specify the Separate Read Layout option for a page**

1  Click the page for which you want to specify the **Separate Read Layout** option.

2  On the **Form** menu, click **Separate Read Layout**.

**Note**   The **Edit Compose Page** and **Edit Read Page** buttons are enabled only when the **Separate Read Layout** option is selected for the active page.

# Hide or Show a Page

Outlook uses parentheses to designate the pages that are hidden at run time. For example, in the preceding Figure 5.19, notice the text is in parentheses for pages 3 through 6 to specify that these pages are hidden.

The capability to hide and show pages gives you great flexibility when designing forms. For example, quite often there isn't enough room on the **Message** page for all the controls you need to add. In this case, you can add additional controls to a custom form page. When you add controls to a page, the parentheses are removed from text in the page's tab, indicating that the page is visible at run time.

For some forms, you may want to hide the **Message** page. This can be especially useful for preaddressing forms. For example, you can specify an address in the To field of a form at design time, and then hide the page. This prevents the user from changing the address and also lets users submit items without ever seeing the destination address on the form. In addition, you may also want to hide the **Options** page of the form. Keep in mind, however, that at least one page must be visible on the form.

▶ **To hide or show a page at run time**

1  Click the page.

2  On the **Form** menu, click **Display This Page**.

**Note**  If you drag a field or a control to a hidden page, the page will display at run time.

| For more information about | See |
| --- | --- |
| Preaddressing forms | "To Field" in Chapter 6, "Controls, Fields, and Properties." |
| Hiding and showing pages | "Hide a Form Page" in Chapter 9, "Use Visual Basic Scripting Edition with Outlook," and Chapter 11, "The Help Desk Application." |

# Rename a Page

When you make a page visible, you should rename it to convey the purpose of the page.

▶ **To rename a page**

1  Click the page.

2  On the **Form** menu, click **Rename Page**.

3  Type the new name for the page.

# Add Controls

Controls are the means through which users enter and view information on the form. When creating forms with Outlook, you usually add controls to the Compose page of the form first. Then, if you want the information in the controls to be saved to the item, you create a field for the control and bind the field to the control. Binding fields is covered in Step 7.

To add controls to the form, you use the Control Toolbox.

▶ **To show the Control Toolbox**

• On the **Form Design** toolbar, click **Control Toolbox**.

With Outlook, you can add .ocx controls and ActiveX controls to the toolbox to provide added flexibility on your forms.

▶ **To add additional controls to the Control Toolbox**

1  Right-click the **Controls** page on the **Control Toolbox**, and then click **Custom Controls** on the shortcut menu.

2  In the **Available Controls** box, click the controls you want.

▶ **To add a control to a form**

• Drag the control from the **Control Toolbox** to the form.

▶ **To set Display properties for a control**

1  Right-click the control, and then click **Properties**.

2  On the **Display** page, set the properties you want.

▶ **To set Advanced properties for a control**

1  Right-click the control, and then click **Advanced Properties**.

2  In the Properties window, set the properties you want and then close the window.

# Create and Bind Fields

Fields are the means through which information in a control gets saved and shown in an item. Therefore, you only need to create fields for those controls that contain information that you want to save in the item. For example, you generally don't need to create an associated field for a Label control, as shown in Figure 5.20, because there's no reason to save the values in such controls to the item. However, for controls in which users enter information, such as the TextBox and ComboBox controls, you usually create a new field or bind an existing field to the control so that the value in the control is saved to the item.

**Figure 5.20   Fields in which the user enters or selects information are generally bound to fields. Label and Image controls are usually not bound to fields.**

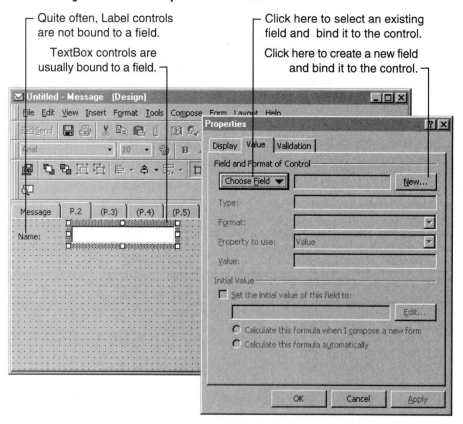

# Create a New Field and Bind It to a Control

When you create a new field by using the **Properties** dialog box, the field you create is automatically bound to the currently selected control. In addition, the field you create is automatically added to the User-defined fields in <Folder> set of fields.

▶ **To create a new user-defined field**

1   Right-click the control, and then click **Properties**.

2   Click the **Value** page.

3   Click **New**.

4   In the **Name** box, type the field name.

5   If necessary, change the **Type** and **Format** of the field.

**See Also**   For more information about specifying the type and format for a field, see Chapter 6, "Fields, Controls, and Properties."

# Bind a Control to an Existing Field

In addition to the user-defined fields that you create, Outlook supplies several different sets of fields that you can use. These sets include Frequently-used fields, Address fields, Date/Time fields, and All Mail fields. These are built-in MAPI fields that in most cases perform advanced functions not easily attained with user-defined fields. To select an existing field to bind to a control, you use the **Properties** dialog box, as shown in the preceding illustration in Figure 5.20.

▶ **To bind a control to an existing field**

1   Right-click the control, and then click **Properties**.

2   Click the **Value** page.

3   Click **Choose Field**, point to the set of fields you want, and then click the field.

# Select Fields from Other Forms

Outlook conveniently categorizes fields by the forms with which they're associated. This is often very useful if you want to create a form that has many of the same fields as another form. Rather than looking through the User-defined fields in <Folder> set of fields, you can view a shortened list of fields for a form.

▶ **To add a set of fields from a form to the Field List**

**1** Right-click the control, and then click **Properties**.

**2** Click the **Value** tab.

**3** Click **Choose Field**, and the click **Forms**.

**4** In the upper left-hand library box, click the forms library that contains the forms you want, as shown in Figure 5.21.

**5** In the left-hand forms box, double-click the form to add it to the **Selected Forms** box.

**6** Click **Close**.

**Figure 5.21  You can add a field set from another form to the Field List.**

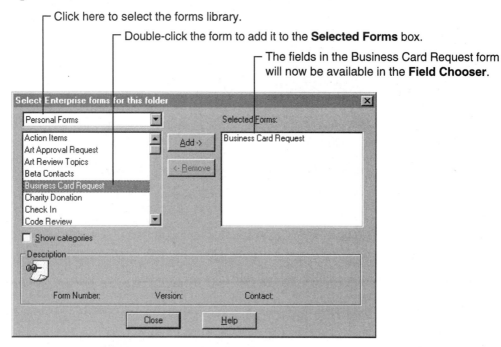

Click here to select the forms library.

Double-click the form to add it to the **Selected Forms** box.

The fields in the Business Card Request form will now be available in the **Field Chooser**.

# When to Use the Field Chooser

The Field Chooser enables you to view fields, add fields, and delete fields. You add a field from the Field Chooser by dragging it from the Field Chooser to the form. When you drag a field from the Field Chooser, Outlook adds a control and a control label to the form and automatically binds the control to the associated field. In addition, it automatically positions the controls on the form if the **AutoLayout** option is selected on the **Layout** menu. The control added to the form depends on the field you add. For example, if you add a Yes/No type field to a form from the Field Chooser, a CheckBox control is added to the form. If you add a Text type field, a TextBox control is added to the form.

In addition to providing a shortcut for adding TextBox and CheckBox controls to a form, the Field Chooser provides several other purposes:

- If you accidentally delete a standard control such as a Message, To, or From control on a form, you can add it back to the form by dragging it from the Field Chooser.

- The Field Chooser enables you to delete fields.

- The Field Chooser enables you to view fields available in the active folder and in other forms, as shown in Figure 5.22.

▶ **To add a field from the Field Chooser**

1 On the **Field Chooser**, click the set of fields you want.

2 Drag the field from the **Field Chooser** to the form, as shown in Figure 5.22.

**Figure 5.22   You can drag fields directly from the Field Chooser to the form.**

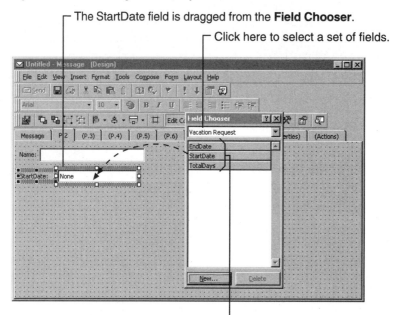

The StartDate field is dragged from the **Field Chooser**.

Click here to select a set of fields.

Shows the fields available from
the Vacation Request form.

# Delete a Field

To delete a field, you use the Field Chooser.

▶ **To delete a field**

1 On the **Field Chooser**, click the set of fields you want.

2 Click the field you want to delete, and then click **Delete**.

3 In the message box, click **Yes**.

# Polish the Layout

After you add controls to the form, you can use Outlook's layout options to add professional polish to your forms. Outlook provides a great set of layout options that will save you countless hours of finish work. This section covers how to select, edit, align, and space controls. However, you are encouraged to experiment with the remainder of the layout options.

## Select and Edit Controls

To select a control on a form, you click the control. To edit the control, you click it again. For example, to select a Label control, you click it once. To type text into the label, you click it again, and then type the text. To exit Edit mode, you click outside the Label control.

## Align Controls

With Outlook alignment options, you can align the borders of a control. When you align controls, the alignment is always based on the last control selected. The sizing handles of the last control selected are white, as opposed to black sizing handles on the other controls, to indicate the control upon which the alignment is based.

▶ **To align controls**

1   Hold down CTRL and then click the controls you want to align.

2   On the **Layout** menu, point to **Align**, and then click one of the alignment menu commands.

## Space Controls

After you align the controls, you can space them so they are evenly separated.

▶ **To space controls:**

1   Hold down CTRL and then click the controls you want to space.

2   On the **Layout** menu, point to **Horizontal Spacing** or **Vertical Spacing**, and then click one of the spacing options.

# Set Tab Order

The tab order defines the sequence in which the controls become active on the form when a user presses the TAB key. When you add controls to the form, the control name is added to the bottom of a list of controls in the **Tab Order** box.

Label controls, such as ConversationLabel and SubjectLabel, are listed in the **Tab Order** box but are not included in the tab order at run time. Also, when the Message control is active, pressing the TAB key will cause the Insert bar to advance to the next tab stop in the control. Therefore, it's usually best, if possible, to put the Message control as the last control in the tab order.

▸ **To set the tab order for the Compose page**

1   On the **Layout** menu, click **Tab Order**.

2   In the **Tab Order** box, click **Move Up** or **Move Down** to put the controls in the proper tab sequence.

**Tip**   You can select more than one control at a time in the **Tab Order** box. To do this, hold down the CTRL key, and then click the controls you want in the **Tab Order** box.

# View the Form in Run Mode

When you've finished with the layout of a page, it's a good idea to switch from Design mode to Run mode to see how the form will look at run time.

▸ **To switch between Design mode and Run mode**

• On the **Tools** menu, click **Design Outlook Form**.

# Create Help (Optional)

Not all forms require Help. In fact, most forms should be simple enough that Help is not required. However, in some cases, you may want to specify Control TipText for a control. With Control TipText, the TipText appears when the user positions the pointer over the control.

▸ **To create Control TipText**

1   Right-click the control you want to specify Control TipText for, and then click **Advanced Properties** on the shortcut menu.

2   Double-click the **ControlTipText** cell, and then type the text you want.

3   Close the **Advanced Properties** box.

# Edit the Read Page

Quite often, the Compose and Read pages of a form are very similar. As a result, you can design most of the Read page by copying controls from the Compose page. As a rule, you must edit the pages of the Read page if the page has a separate Read layout.

**Important**  Each individual page on a Read or Compose page can have different settings for the **Separate Read Layout** option.

▶ **To copy controls to the Read page**

1  On the **Form Design** toolbar, click **Edit Read Page**.

2  Click the individual page you want to edit.

3  Adjust or remove any unnecessary controls on the page to make room for the controls you want to copy from the **Compose** page.

4  On the **Form Design** toolbar, click **Edit Compose Page**.

5  Click the individual page that contains the controls you want to copy.

6  Hold down CTRL and click the fields that you want to copy.

7  Click the **Copy** button.

8  Click **Edit Read Page**.

9  Click the **Paste** button.

10  Repeat steps 2–9 for each Read page you want to edit.

## Set Properties for Controls on the Read Page

Quite often, you make many of the controls on the Read page read-only. This prevents readers from changing the contents of an item after it has been sent or posted.

▶ **To make a control read-only**

1  Right-click the control, and then click **Properties**.

2  On the **Display** page, select the **Read only** check box.

## Set the Tab Order for the Read Page

With Outlook forms, you must set the tab order for the Compose and Read pages separately. In addition, you must the set the tab order for each individual page separately. For instructions on setting the tab order for a page, see Step 8, "Polish the Layout," earlier in this chapter.

# About Viewing the Read Page in Run Mode

To view the Read page in Run mode, you must first send or post an item with the form, or for some built-in forms, you must save an item. For this reason, you should test the Read page after you publish the form. Publishing and testing the Read page of the form is covered later in this chapter.

▶ **To switch between Design mode and Run mode**

- On the **Tools** menu, click **Design Outlook Form**.

# Set Action Properties

With form action properties, you specify how a form handles responses. Form actions are one of the most important aspects of Outlook because they enable users to respond to existing items in an Outlook folder.

**Important**   Throughout this book, the term *response* is used to encompass Reply, Forward, Reply to All, Reply to Folder, and all user-defined response actions.

With Outlook actions, you can specify:

- Whether a **Reply**, **Reply to All**, **Forward**, **Post to Folder**, or custom menu command appears on the Outlook **Compose** menu and the form *<Compose>* menu.
- Whether an action button appears on the form toolbar.
- The form to activate to enable the user to send or post a response.
- Whether the action opens the response form, sends the response immediately, or whether the user is prompted to open the response form.

▶ **To set actions**

- See Chapter 7, "Actions." It provides a detailed look at how to create actions for Message and Post forms, and provides several detailed examples to help you understand how actions can be applied in applications.

# Set Form Properties

With the form **Properties** page, you give the form a name and a description and you specify who to contact for questions about the form.

▶ **To set form properties**

- With the form open in Design mode, click the **Properties** page, as shown in Figure 5.23.

**Figure 5.23   The form Properties page**

Input here appears in the Title Bar of the form at run time.

Shows who is responsible for maintaining the form.

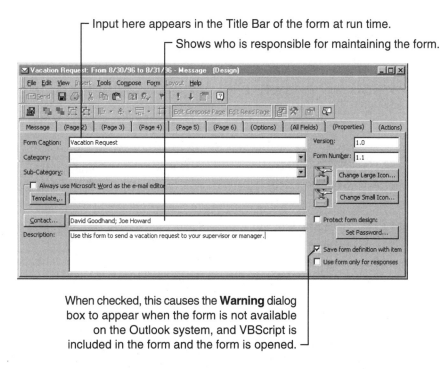

When checked, this causes the **Warning** dialog box to appear when the form is not available on the Outlook system, and VBScript is included in the form and the form is opened.

**Form Caption**   Is the text that appears in the title bar of the form. Outlook also uses the form caption to automatically construct the form name. The form caption only appears in the title bar of the form when the **Save form definition with item** check box is cleared. It is not recommended that you specify a form caption. Instead, you can leave the **Form Caption** box empty, and then specify the form name when you publish the form. For more information, see "Publish the Form" later in this chapter.

**Category**   Lets you create or specify a category for forms to help organize the forms in the **New Form** dialog box.

**Sub-Category**   Lets you create or specify a sub-category for the form.

**Always Use Microsoft Word as the E-mail Editor**   Lets you specify that Microsoft Word runs in the Message control of the form, so users have spell checking, thesaurus, and full formatting options available with Microsoft Word. The Word editing features are only available to recipients who use Word as their e-mail editor.

**Template**   Enables you to specify the Microsoft Word template that is used to format the text in the Message control of the form.

**Contact**   Click the **Contact** button to select the names of those people who are responsible for maintaining and upgrading the form. Contact information shows in the **Forms Manager** dialog box and the form **Properties** page.

**Description**   Type a description for the form. The form description shows in the form **About** dialog box on the **Help** menu and also in the **Properties** dialog box for the form.

**Change Large Icon**   Click to change the icons for the form. Large icons appear in the form **Properties** dialog box.

**Change Small Icon**   Click to change the icons that appear in the Outlook folder to represent an item of the type created with the form.

**Protect Form Design**   Select this check box to have password protection for your form. This prevents other users from changing the form after you've published it.

**Save Form Definition with Item**   Specifies the form definition is included with the item. This check box is selected by default for Message forms and cleared for Post forms. This option provides convenience and security for forms. It provides convenience because it enables you to send items to other users. Those users can then open the item in the form on their computer, even though the form is not installed on their Outlook system.

It provides a security measure for this reason: If a form contains VBScript and is not available on the user's Outlook system, and the **Save form definition with item** option is checked, the user sees a **Warning** dialog box, as shown earlier in this chapter in Figure 5.13. It prevents users from opening an unauthorized form that contains macros that can delete or copy their mail, or send mail from their mailbox to another user.

After you create a Message form that is intended for general use, you submit it to an administrator for approval. The administrator checks the form for viruses and potentially harmful code. If the administrator approves the form, he clears the **Save form definition with item** check box, and then publishes the form in the Organization Form Library.

**See Also**   For more information about form security and managing forms in your organization, see Chapter 13, "Distribute and Maintain Applications."

**Use Form Only for Responses**   Certain forms, such as the Approve Vacation and Deny Vacation forms, are used solely for responding to existing items. As a result, these forms are opened only if a related item is first selected or opened.

**See Also**   For more information about this option and creating response forms, see Chapter 7, "Actions."

# Publish the Form

When you finish designing a form, you publish it to a forms library. Optionally, you can make a backup copy of the form, although it is not required.

- When you publish a form, you register the form in a forms library and expose the form to the Outlook user interface. For example, after the form is published, the form menu commands and form name are visible in the Outlook user interface.

- When you make a backup copy of the form, you save the form definition as an .oft file.

Outlook forms are interpreted, not compiled. Therefore, there's no source code to worry about. And because only the form definition is saved, rather than the form and all of its associated controls, the file size is only about 10K on average.

# Make a Backup Copy of the Form

Before you publish the form, you may want to make a backup copy of the form on your hard disk or on your organization's server. When you make a copy of the form, you save it as an .oft file in much the same manner as you save a Microsoft Word document.

▶ **To save the form as a file**

1   On the **File** menu, click **Save As**.

2   In the **Save In** box, select the folder where you want to save the form file.

3   In the **File name** box, type a name for the form.

4   Click **Save**.

# Publish the Form

When you publish a form, you accomplish three things:

- You make the form available to be run in Outlook.

- You register the form in the designated form library.

- You expose the form's properties, such as form name, description, and menu commands in Outlook.

## About the Form Name and Message Class

It is not recommended that you type a name for the form in the **Form Caption** box on the **Properties** page. Instead, you leave the **Form Caption** box empty and specify the form name in the **Form Name** box in the **Publish Form** As dialog box.

When you click the **Publish Form As** button on the **Form Design** toolbar, and type a name in the **Form Name** box, Outlook automatically sets the message class for the form by appending the form name to IPM.<*xxx*>. For example, if the form is a Message form, and you type **Business Card Request** in the **Form Name** box, Outlook constructs the message class for the form by appending the form name to IPM.Note, so the message class is IPM.Note.Business Card Request. The message class is the internal identifier of the form, and is used to locate and activate a form when an item associated with the form is created or opened.

▶ **To specify the form name**

1   On the **Form Design** toolbar, click **Publish Form As**.

2   Type a name in the **Form name** box.

▶ **To change the message class**

•   In the **Form Name** box, change the name of the form.

   The **Message class** box is automatically updated.

When you publish a form, you publish it to a forms library. After the form is published in a library, you can then open the form to compose, submit, and read items in a folder. Where you publish the form determines how the form will be available to other users. The following table provides a description of the forms libraries where you can publish forms.

**Important**   When publishing and naming forms, the form name should be unique. Also, if the form is published in more than one forms library and you make changes to the form, the form must be updated in all the forms libraries in which it is published. For more information about distributing forms, see Chapter 13, "Distribute and Maintain Applications."

| Location | Description | Advantage |
|---|---|---|
| Organization Forms Library | A public container of forms that is located on a Microsoft Exchange Server. | Allows forms to be used by anyone who has access to the Microsoft Exchange Server. |
| Personal Forms Library | A private container of forms. | Allows forms to be available for personal use. Also handy for designing and testing forms. |
| Public Folders Forms Library | A public container of forms. Each folder has its own Folder Forms Library. The container exists in the folder on the Microsoft Exchange Server. | Allows forms to be used by anyone who has access to the server and has permissions to use the folder. |
| Personal Folders Forms Library | A private container of forms. Each folder has its own Folder Forms Library. | Allows forms to be organized in a personal folder. Also enables designers to distribute a large number of forms and folders by using a .pst personal folder file. |

▶ **To publish a form**

1  On the **Form Design** toolbar, click the **Publish Form As** button.

2  In the **Form name** box, type the name for the form.

3  To change the location (library) where the form is stored, click **Publish In**, and then do one of the following:

- To select a form in the Organization Forms Library, click **Organization Forms** in the **Forms Library** box, and then click **OK**.

- To select a form in the Personal Forms Library, click **Personal Forms** in the **Forms Library** box, and then click **OK**.

- To select a form in a Folder Forms Library, select the folder in the **Folder Forms Library** box, and then click **OK**.

4  Click **Publish**.

**See Also**   For more information about how to make forms available to users, see Chapter 13, "Distribute and Maintain Applications."

# Test and Release the Form

After you publish the form, you need to test it to make sure it works as expected.

### ▸ To test a Message form in the Personal or Organization Forms Library

1  On the Outlook bar, click **Inbox**.

2  On the Outlook **Compose** menu, click **Choose Form**.

3  Click **Organization Forms** or **Personal Forms**.

4  Double-click the form.

5  Fill out the form options, and then send the form to yourself.

6  When the item arrives in your Inbox, double-click it to make sure the Read page of the form works as expected.

### ▸ To test a Post form in a Folder Forms Library

1  In the Folder List, click the folder that contains the form you want to test.

2  On the Outlook **Compose** menu, click the form's associated menu command to open the form.

3  Fill out the form options, and then click **Post**.

4  After the item is posted in the folder, double-click it to open it and make sure the Read page of the form works as expected.

# Release the Form

**See Also**  For more information about releasing forms, see Chapter 13, "Distribute and Maintain Applications."

# CHAPTER 6

# Controls, Fields, and Properties

## In This Chapter

Set Control Display Properties   140

Layer Controls   143

Set Advanced Control Properties   143

Bind a Control to an Existing Field   144

Create User-Defined Fields   146

Set Initial Field Values   155

Validate and Restrict Data   156

Set Field-Specific Properties   160

Set Control-Specific Properties   168

In this chapter, you'll cover the fundamental skills and information you need to effectively use controls, fields, and properties on a form. In addition, you'll take a look at the unique features of each commonly used control and then get some strategies for implementing these controls and fields in an application.

Specifically, we'll cover how to:

**Set display properties for controls**   including foreground and background colors.

**Set advanced properties**   such as the **BackStyle**, **BorderStyle**, **ControlTipText**, and **WordWrap** properties for a control.

**Create combination fields**   that show the results of combined text strings.

**Create formula fields**   that automatically perform calculations and show the results in the field. For example, for a Grand Total field, you can create a formula to show the result of adding the value of the Total field to the value of the SubTotal field.

**Set initial values**   in a field to determine the value that appears in the field when the form first appears at run time.

**Validate and restrict information in a field.**   For example, you will learn how to create validation formulas that Microsoft Outlook checks before it closes the form. For example, you can create a validation formula that shows a message box if a value in a field exceeds a certain number.

**Use the To, Subject, and Message field.**   Specifically, you'll see how to preaddress a form by setting the initial value of a To field. You will also take a look at how the Subject field works, and how to insert files, items, and hyperlinks to World Wide Web pages in the Message field.

**Set control-specific properties.**   For example, you'll learn about creating check boxes, how to bind option buttons to a field, and how to create list boxes so users can select multiple values.

# Set Control Display Properties

Each control, regardless of whether it is bound to a field or not, has a unique set of display properties that you can change. With display properties, you can change the name of the control, specify its exact position on the form, set its foreground or background color, and specify settings such as read-only or multi-line, as shown in Figure 6.1.

▶ **To view the display properties for a control**

1   Right-click the control, and then click **Properties** on the shortcut menu.

2   Click the **Display** tab.

**Figure 6.1   Display properties for the StartDate TextBox control**

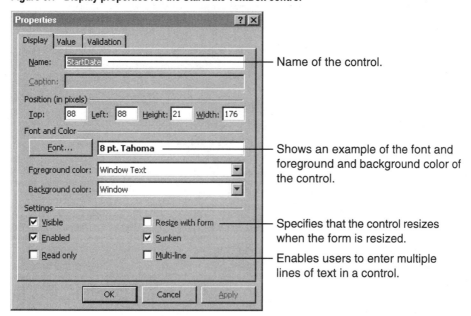

— Name of the control.

— Shows an example of the font and foreground and background color of the control.

— Specifies that the control resizes when the form is resized.

— Enables users to enter multiple lines of text in a control.

**Tip**   When you add a control to a form, the control is given a default name such as TextBox1, Label1, and so on. If you'll be referencing the control in Microsoft Visual Basic Scripting Edition procedures for the form, it's a good idea to give the control a unique name, as shown earlier in Figure 6.1.

# Change Foreground and Background Colors

The background or foreground color for a control corresponds to the color specified for the component on the **Appearance** tab of the Display icon in Windows Control Panel. As shown earlier in Figure 6.1, the foreground color of the StartDate control is set to Window Text, so the color of the foreground text in the StartDate control matches the color of Window text in the **Display Properties** dialog box in Windows. Similarly, the background color of the StartDate control matches the color defined for Window. If you have Window defined as green on your system, the background of the control is green.

▶ **To set foreground and background colors for a control**

1 Right-click the control, and then click **Properties**.

2 Click the **Display** tab.

3 In the **Foreground** or **Background color** box, click the component that you wish to map the control to.

The Vacation Request form, as shown in Figure 6.2, provides a good example of how color effects can be achieved on a form. The background color for the Label8 control is set to Button Shadow, so it will have a dark gray color for almost all users. Also, many of the controls on the form have a white background. In this case, the background color is set to Window, which maps to white in Windows Control Panel. Notice that most of the controls actually sit on top of the Label8 control. This is done using the Form Designer **Bring to Front** and **Send to Back** options. For this form, the Label8 control is sent to the back layer of the page.

**Figure 6.2   The Vacation Request form**

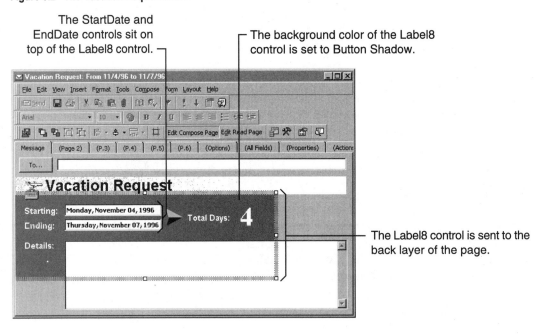

**Tip**   Generally, you can make a dark gray background for a control by setting the background color to Button Shadow. You can make the background color white by setting the background color to Window.

# Layer Controls

The Label8 control on the Vacation Request form provides a good example of how you can layer controls on a form. As shown earlier in Figure 6.2, several controls, such as StartDate and EndDate, are located on top of the Label8 control. This is done by using the **Send to Back** and **Bring to Front** buttons on the **Form Design** toolbar. With these buttons, you can layer controls by bringing them to the front layer or sending them to the back layer.

▶ **To send a control to a back layer**

• Click the control, and then click the **Send to Back** button on the **Form Design** toolbar.

▶ **To bring a control to a front layer**

• Click the control, and then click the **Bring to Front** button on the **Form Design** toolbar.

**See Also**   For more information about setting control Display Properties, see "Set Control-Specific Properties" later in this chapter.

# Set Advanced Control Properties

The advanced **Properties** window provides even more capabilities for customizing a control. For example, with the advanced **Properties** window, you can:

• Define a transparent background for a control.

• Specify the **ControlTipText** property—the text that appears when the user moves the pointer over the control.

• Specify if the control has the **WordWrap** property turned on.

• Specify the **BorderStyle** property for the control.

▶ **To open the advanced Properties window**

• Right-click the control, and then click **Advanced Properties** on the shortcut menu.

In the example shown in Figure 6.3, the Label2 control sits on top of the textured Image1 control. However, the Label2 text appears to be part of the image because the Label2 **BackStyle** property is set to Transparent. The **BackStyle** property for a control can only be set in the advanced **Properties** window.

**Figure 6.3   The BackStyle property of the Label2 control is set to Transparent so the control appears to be part of the Image1 control behind it.**

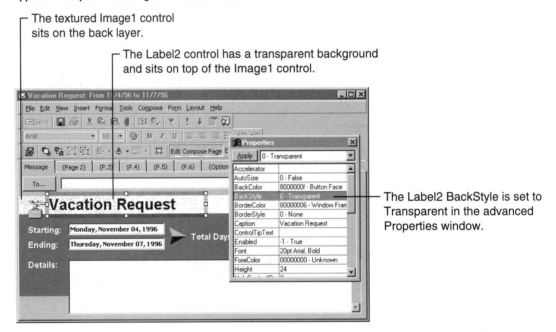

# Bind a Control to an Existing Field

In many cases, you can bind a control to an existing field, rather than creating a new field. For example, you can bind a control to a field supplied by Outlook, or you can bind a control to an existing user-defined field. You can view a list of available fields in the field list in the **Properties** dialog box, as shown in Figure 6.4.

**Figure 6.4   The Field Set and field list in the Properties dialog box**

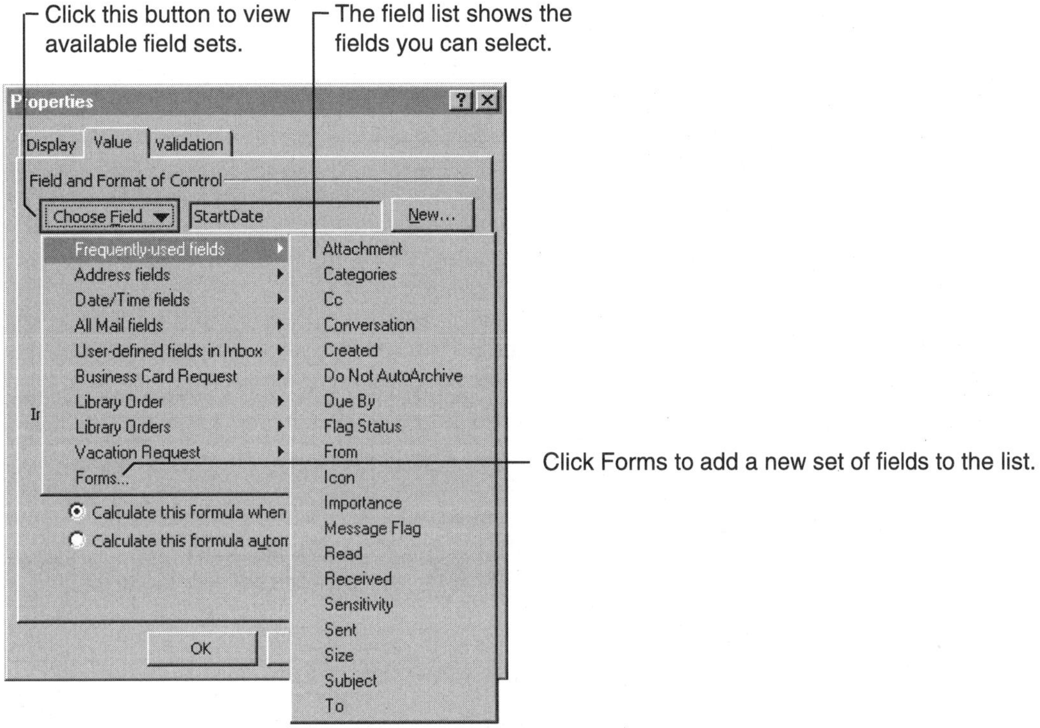

Click this button to view available field sets.

The field list shows the fields you can select.

Click Forms to add a new set of fields to the list.

▶ **To bind a control to an existing field**

1   Right-click the control you want to define a field for, and then click **Properties** on the shortcut menu.

2   Click the **Value** tab.

3   Click **Choose Field**, point to the set of fields you want, and then click the field.

The sets of fields available in the field list in the **Properties** dialog box differ for each type of form. For example, if you create a Message form, the field list does not show the field categories for built-in forms, such as All Contact fields, All Appointment fields, and All Task fields. In addition, when creating a Message form, all user-defined fields are created in the Inbox, regardless of the active folder.

The following table shows the field sets that are available for each type of form, shows where the user-defined fields are created for the form. It also shows if the Field Chooser is available for the form type.

| Form type | Available field categories | User-defined fields are created in | Field Chooser available |
|-----------|---------------------------|-----------------------------------|------------------------|
| Message | Field sets from built-in forms, such as Appointment, are not available | Inbox | Yes |
| Post | All | Active folder | Yes |
| Office Document | N/A | N/A | N/A |
| Built-in | All | Active folder | Yes |

**Important**   For Office Document forms, you must create fields in the document itself using the application (Microsoft Word, Microsoft Excel, or Microsoft PowerPoint) **Forms** toolbar. For example, for a Word document, you use the Word **Forms** toolbar to add fields directly to the document.

**See Also**   For more information about creating controls in a Office 97 document, see the Help for the specific application.

# Create User-Defined Fields

With Outlook, there are two ways to create fields. You can use the Field Chooser, which offers the advantage of automatically creating and positioning controls for you when you drag the field on the form. Or you can use the **Properties** dialog box, which enables you to edit field properties. In this section, we cover using the **Properties** dialog box to create new user-defined fields. Before you can create a field using the **Properties** dialog box, however, you must first select a control on the form that you want to bind the field to.

▶ **To create a user-defined field**

**1**  Right-click the control you want to define a field for, and then click **Properties** on the shortcut menu.

**2**  Click the **Value** tab.

**3**  Click **New**.

**4**  In the **Name** box, type a name for the field.

**5**  In the **Type** box, click a field type.

**6**  In the **Format** box, click a format, as shown in Figure 6.5.

**Figure 6.5   You can create user-defined fields from the Properties dialog box.**

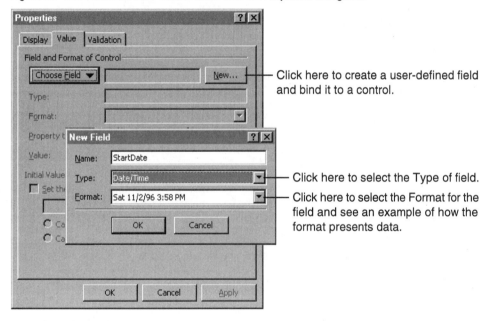

Click here to create a user-defined field and bind it to a control.

Click here to select the Type of field.

Click here to select the Format for the field and see an example of how the format presents data.

**Note**  After you create a field, you cannot change its type. Rather, you must create a new field with a different name with the desired properties. You can then delete the old field. To delete a field, use the Field Chooser.

# Specify Field Type

When you create a new field, you use the **Type** property to specify the type of data stored in a field in the item. The following table describes the uses for the various field types.

| Field types | Description |
| --- | --- |
| Text | Text or numbers that don't require calculations, such as phone numbers. |
| Number | Numeric data used in mathematical calculations, with the exception of currency. |
| Percent | Numeric data as a percentage. |
| Currency | Numeric data as currency or mathematical calculations that involve money. |
| Yes/No | Fields that are bound to a CheckBox control. |
| Date/Time | Date and time data. |
| Duration | Use to show time expired. This control has no inherent intelligence built-in. |
| Keywords | Fields that are bound to a ListBox control from which the user can select multiple values. |
| Combination | Fields that show the result of combined text strings. Combination fields are read-only. |
| Formula | Fields that show the result of a formula. For example, a Totals field might contain a formula that multiplies the value of the Hours field by the Hourly Rate field. Formula fields are read-only |
| Integer | Nondecimal numeric data. |

# Specify Field Formats

Field formats determine how information is saved and shown in a control. Each field type has a different set of formats that you can choose from. Each format in the **Field Format** box, as shown earlier in Figure 6.5, includes an example of how the format presents information in the control.

# Create Combination Fields

With Combination fields, you can create a formula for a field that combines string values from other fields and shows the results in the control bound to the field. This section describes the general procedure for creating Combination fields, and then provides several examples of the types of Combination fields you can create.

▶ **To create a Combination field**

1   Right-click the control that you want to bind to a Combination field, and the click **Properties** on the shortcut menu.

2   Click the **Value** tab.

3   Click **New**.

4   In the **Name** box, type a name for the field.

5   In the **Type** box, click **Combination**.

6   Click **Edit**.

7   Do one of the following:

   • Click **Joining fields and any text fragments to each other** to show combined string values in the field.

   • Click **Showing only the first non-empty field, ignoring subsequent ones** if you want only the first value entered in the specified fields to show in the Combination field.

8   Type text in the **Formula** box or click **Field** to specify the fields you want inserted in the expression.

**Note**   The **Showing only the first non-empty field, ignoring subsequent other ones** option is generally used in the context of folder fields. For example, when you have a folder that contains different types of items, one type of item may have the user name in the Author field, while another type of item might have the user name in the From field. To combine these two field values into one field in the folder, you can use the **Showing only the first non-empty string field, ignoring subsequent ones** option.

## Combine Field Strings

With the Visual Basic Expression Service provided with Outlook, you can easily build expressions for Combination fields without worrying about concatenating values. As shown in Figure 6.6, the FullName control shows the combined values from the FirstName and LastName fields.

**Figure 6.6   The formula for the FullName field combines the values from the FirstName and LastName fields and shows the results in the FullName control. Notice the field is read-only.**

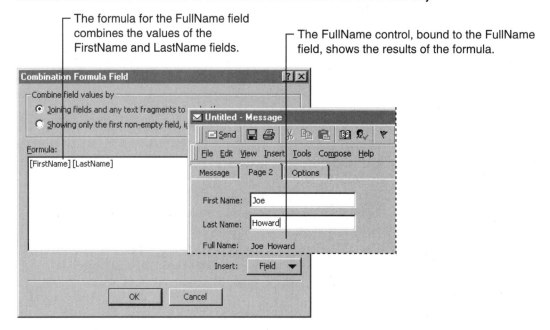

The formula for the FullName field combines the values of the FirstName and LastName fields.

The FullName control, bound to the FullName field, shows the results of the formula.

## Combine Field Value Strings with Text Fragments

Quite often, you combine text fragments that you type into the **Formula** box with string values from other fields. In the following example, the Combination field named UserName is located on the **Read** page of a form. At run time, when the user opens a submitted item, the value of the From field is combined with the User Name: fragment to create the result shown in Figure 6.7.

**Figure 6.7   The User Name: [From] formula automatically combines the text fragment with the value in the From field.**

Shows the User Name: text fragment in the User Name field.

Shows the value of the From field in the User Name field.

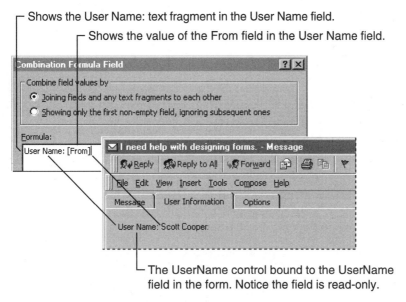

The UserName control bound to the UserName field in the form. Notice the field is read-only.

# Combine Field Values by Showing Only the First Non-Empty Field

In general, this option makes more sense when applied to a folder than applied to a form. In fact, it is described in detail in Chapter 8, "Folders." However, it can have some use when applied to a form. For example, let's assume a folder contains items created with a form that has a variety of phone number fields, such as home phone, car phone, business phone, and fax number. Also assume that you want to create a new form that consolidates the numbers so that only the primary phone number shows on the form. To do this, you can create a Combination field named Primary Phone that combines the phone numbers, but only displays the value in the first non-empty phone field in the item.

**See Also**   For more information about using Combination fields in folders, see Chapter 8, "Folders."

# Create Formula Fields

With Formula fields, you can create formulas that automatically calculate values and show the result in a control. Here are a few examples:

- For a Time Card form, you can create a formula for a field that totals the hours for the day, and then totals the hours for the week and shows the results in the Totals field.

- For the sample While You Were Out form supplied in Outlook, the Subject field contains a formula that combines the values from several fields into a message that shows in the Subject field.

- For the Vacation Request form supplied in Outlook, the TotalDays field contains a formula that automatically calculates the number of vacation days by finding the difference between the Starting date and the Ending date.

- For an Invoice form, you can create a Totals field that contains a formula to show the result of the number of hours multiplied by the hourly rate.

Although you can create a Formula field, it's really just as easy to create a formula for a Text, Number, or Currency field. As a result, there is really no compelling reason to create a Formula field. Instead, it's preferable to create the type of field you want, and then create the formula for the field. As you'll see in the examples in this section, the fields include formulas, but are not defined as Formula fields.

### ▶ To create a Formula field when you create the field

1  Right-click the control you want to bind to the Formula field, and then click **Properties** on the shortcut menu.

2  Click the **Value** tab.

3  Click **New**.

4  In the **Name** box, type a name for the field.

5  In the **Type** box, click the type of field you want. You do not have to select **Formula**. You can select any type of field—Currency, Number, Date/Time—and then click **OK**.

6  On the **Value** page, click **Edit**.

7  In the **Formula** box, type in the formula or use the **Field** or **Function** buttons to insert the field or function you want.

## Specify the Field Automatically Calculates the Results

After you create the formula for the field, you must set the **Calculate this formula automatically** option so the field is updated when field values referenced in the formula are changed. For example, for the Invoice form shown in Figure 6.8, the TOTAL field automatically updates when the values in the Hours or Hourly Rate controls change.

▶ **To specify that the field automatically calculates the result**

1   Right-click the control that you want to create a formula for, and then click **Properties** on the shortcut menu.

2   On the **Value** page, select the **Set the initial value of this field to** check box.

3   Click **Calculate this formula automatically**.

4   To make the control read-only, click the **Display** tab, and then select the **Read only** check box.

## Calculate Totals

In Figure 6.8, the TOTAL field is a formula field that shows the result of the expression:

```
[Hours] * [Hourly Rate]
```

This expression multiplies the number of hours in the Hours field by the value in the Hourly Rate field and shows the result in the TOTAL field.

**Figure 6.8   The TOTAL field automatically multiplies the hours by the hourly rate and shows the results.**

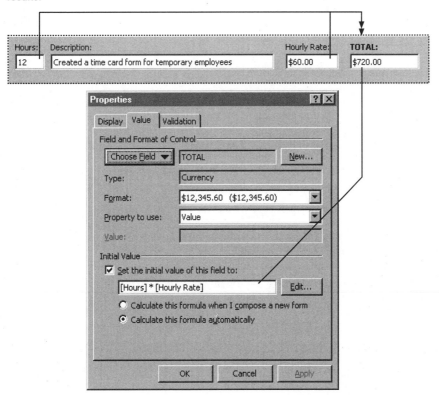

# Build Text Strings

The While You Were Out form, as shown in Figure 6.9, provides an example of a Formula field that shows the results of combined values in the Subject field, which is not visible on the form at run time. When the While You Were Out item is created, the values from the You Received and Please Contact fields are combined with the You Received text fragment to create the value in the Subject field. This is the value that appears in the user's Inbox when they receive the message.

**Figure 6.9  The While You Were Out form. The Subject field is hidden on the form at run time.**

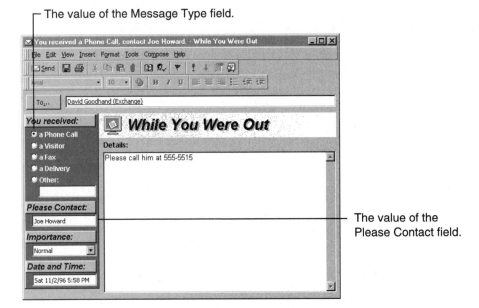

The value of the Message Type field.

The value of the Please Contact field.

When the item arrives in the user's Inbox, the Subject field shows the following result:

You received a Phone Call, contact Joe Howard.

In the formula, as shown earlier in Figure 6.9, the **IIf** function evaluates the expression and returns one of two parts, based on whether the expression evaluates as True or False. For example, if the Message Type field value is not Other, then the Subject field shows the value of the Message Type field (a Phone Call). In the next line, if the Please Contact field is not empty, then the value of the Please Contact field is added to the Subject field.

# Calculate Date Differences

On the Vacation Request Form, as shown in Figure 6.10, the Total Days field contains a formula that automatically calculates the difference between the Starting and Ending fields and shows the result.

**Figure 6.10   The Total Days field calculates the difference between the StartDate and EndDate fields and adds 1.**

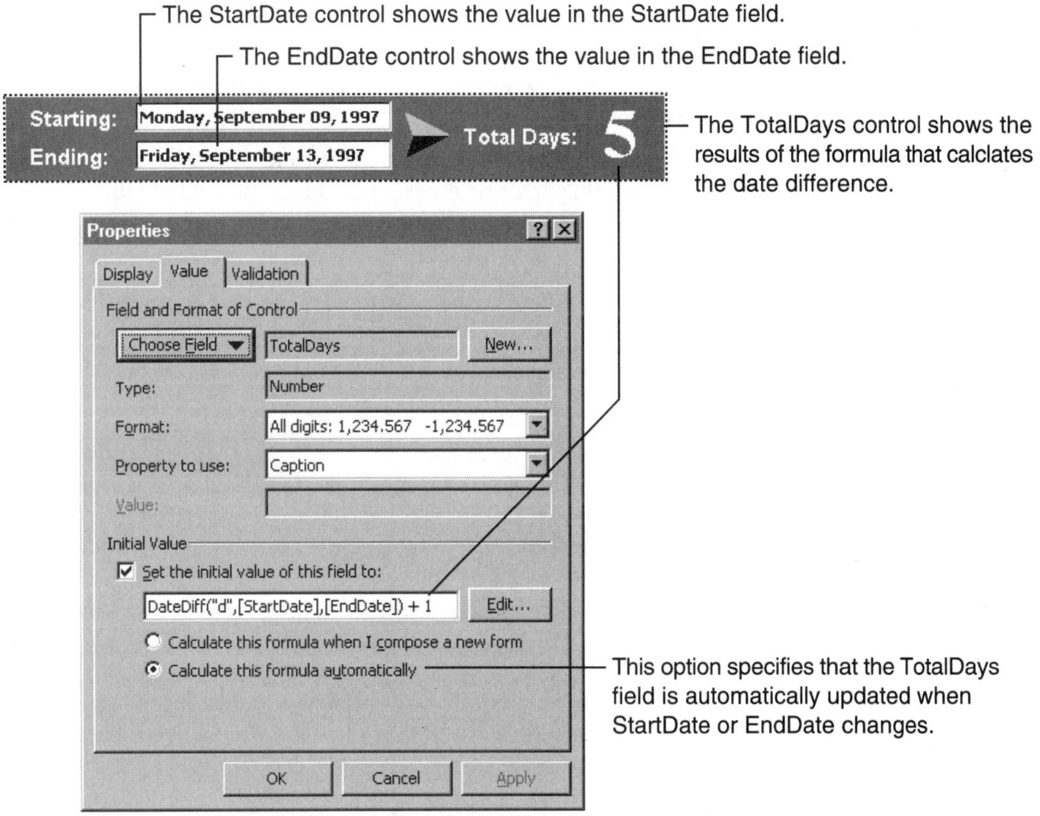

The StartDate control shows the value in the StartDate field.

The EndDate control shows the value in the EndDate field.

Starting: Monday, September 09, 1997
Ending: Friday, September 13, 1997    Total Days: 5

The TotalDays control shows the results of the formula that calclates the date difference.

Properties — Display | Value | Validation

Field and Format of Control
Choose Field ▼   TotalDays   New...
Type: Number
Format: All digits: 1,234.567  -1,234.567 ▼
Property to use: Caption ▼
Value:

Initial Value
☑ Set the initial value of this field to:
DateDiff("d",[StartDate],[EndDate]) + 1   Edit...
○ Calculate this formula when I compose a new form
◉ Calculate this formula automatically

OK   Cancel   Apply

This option specifies that the TotalDays field is automatically updated when StartDate or EndDate changes.

**Tip**  The StartDate and EndDate fields in the Vacation Request form offer IntelliSense. For example, if you enter "Next Tuesday" into the EndDate field, Outlook translates "Next Tuesday" into the correct date.

# Set Initial Field Values

When you create an initial value for a field, you specify the values that are available in the field when the user opens the form to create a new item. With Outlook, the way the initial value is set is handled somewhat differently based on the control to which the field is bound. As a result, we'll cover the general concept of initial values in this section, and then cover how to set the initial value for each control separately.

Here are a few examples of why you set initial values for fields:

- To set the default values in Label, TextBox, ComboBox, ListBox, CheckBox, and OptionButton controls.

- To set the initial value of the Subject field of a form to summarize the content of the form. For example, for an Art Approval form, you can set the initial value of the Subject field to "Art Approval".

- To set the initial value of the To field on a Message form to preaddress the form. For example, for an Employee Feedback form, you can preaddress the To field to an Employee Feedback public folder so all responses are automatically routed to that folder.

The following table lists the sections in this chapter that explain how to set initial values for the control to which the field is bound. Therefore, each control contains a separate section on how to set the initial value.

| To set the initial value for a | See later in this chapter |
| --- | --- |
| To field | "To Field" |
| Subject field | "Subject Field" |
| Message field | "Message Field" |
| Field bound to a Label control | "Label Controls" |
| Field bound to a TextBox control | "TextBox Controls" |
| Field bound to an OptionButton control | "OptionButton Controls" |
| Field bound to a CheckBox control | "CheckBox Controls" |
| Field bound to a ListBox control | "ListBox Controls" |

# Validate and Restrict Data

Outlook provides a couple ways to validate and control how information is entered into a form.

- At the simplest level, you can specify that a value is required for a field. As a result, if the user tries to submit or save the item and no value is in the field, the user sees a message saying a value is required in the field.

- You can create a validation formula for a field. If the field validation fails, the users sees a message box showing the types of values allowed in the field.

# Specify a Field Value Is Required for a Field

Many forms contain Text fields in which the user is required to enter information. For example, on the Business Card Request form, as shown in Figure 6.11, the Name field requires a value. If a value is not entered in the Name field when the user attempts to send the form, Outlook shows a message box that tells the user that a field on the form requires a value.

**Figure 6.11   On the Business Card Request form, a value is required in the Name field. If no value is entered, users see a message when they attempt to send the item.**

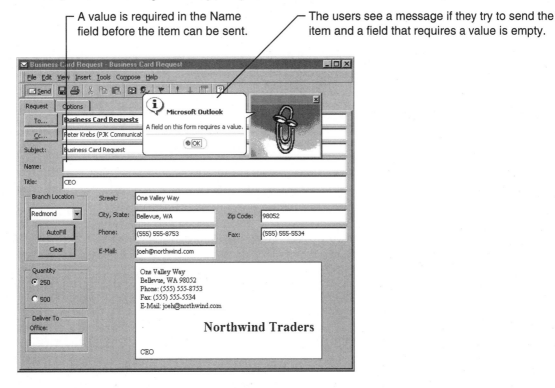

A value is required in the Name field before the item can be sent.

The users see a message if they try to send the item and a field that requires a value is empty.

▶ **To specify that a value is required for a Text field**

1   Right-click the control that is bound to the field, and then click **Properties** on the shortcut menu.

2   Click the **Validation** tab.

3   Select the **A value is required for the field** check box.

> **Important**  Many of the Outlook field types automatically supply a value in the field by default. For example, the Date field automatically has the value "None" by default. For field types such as Date, Currency, and Number that automatically supply a value, you must create a formula or use a script to validate that the field contains the specified information.

# Create Validation Formulas

Outlook performs field validation when the user attempts to save, send, or post an item. In addition, Outlook performs field validation when the user attempts to close a form. With validation formulas, you can limit the type of information that can be saved to the item. For example, you can define:

```
>=10 And <=100
```

as the validation formula for a Number field that accepts only values from 10 to 100. When users attempt to submit or save the item, they see a message only if the number entered in the field does not fall within the range of 10 to 100.

> **Tip**  If you want to validate the field immediately after the user enters information in the field, you can do so using the ChangeProperty event in Visual Basic Scripting Edition. For more information, see Chapter 9, "Use Visual Basic Scripting Edition with Outlook."

### ▶ To create a validation formula

1  Right-click the control you want to create a validation expression for, and then click **Properties** on the shortcut menu.

2  Click the **Validation** tab, and then under **Validation Formula**, click the **Edit** button.

3  Type the validation formula or use the **Field** or **Function** button to build the formula.

4  In the **Display this message if the validation fails** box, type the message you want to appear in the message box the user sees if the validation fails.

# Formulas That Validate Amounts

For many forms, you can create validation formulas for fields to check if a value in the field is more or less than a specified value. For example, in Figure 6.12, the validation formula for the Amount field in the Charity Donation form specifies that the value in the field must be at least one dollar. If the user enters a value less than one dollar in the Amount field, a message appears.

**Figure 6.12   The Amount field contains a value that is less than one dollar. When the user attempts to send the form, a message box appears indicating what is acceptable in the field.**

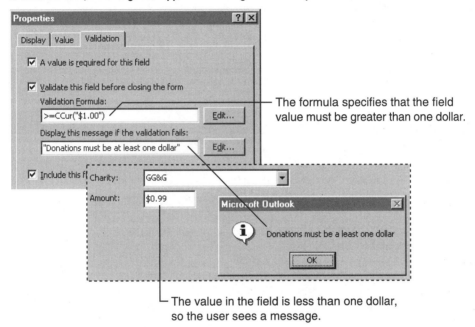

The formula specifies that the field value must be greater than one dollar.

The value in the field is less than one dollar, so the user sees a message.

**See Also**   Note that the **CCur** function (Currency Conversion) is used in the validation formula. For more information on the **CCur** function, see the Outlook Forms Help.

## Validation Formulas That Compare One Field Value with Another

In some cases, you might want to create a validation formula that compares one field value against another field value. For example, for the Vacation Request form as shown in Figure 6.13, the value of the StartDate field is compared to the value of the EndDate field to make sure the EndDate value falls after the StartDate value.

**Figure 6.13   The validation formula for the Amount field specifies that the validation passes if the value is equal to or greater than one day.**

The validation formula for the EndDate field compares the value of the EndDate and StartDate field values.

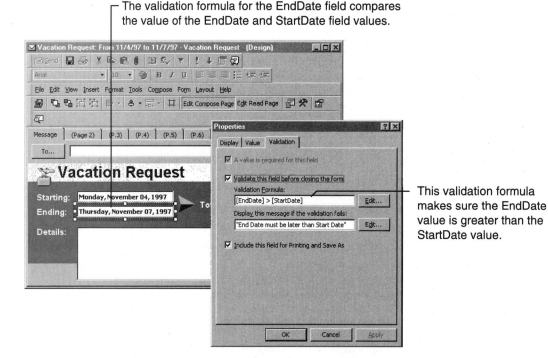

This validation formula makes sure the EndDate value is greater than the StartDate value.

# Set Field-Specific Properties

The **Message** page of standard Message and Post forms contains three Outlook-supplied fields that provide fundamental functionality on the form. These fields are:

**To field**   Used to address the form.

**Subject field**   Used to summarize the message. The text in the Subject field appears in the title bar of the form window. The value in the Subject field also sets the value of the Conversation field in the item.

**Message field**   Used to enter text or insert files, items, or objects or insert shortcuts to them.

This section describes how the To, Subject, and Message fields work, and then describes strategies for effectively using these fields in a form.

# To Field

With Outlook, you can preaddress forms by setting the initial value of the To field. Preaddressing a form is much like providing a self-addressed envelope. Because the address is already provided on the form, the user just fills in the form and clicks the **Send** button.

## Preaddress a Form to a Distribution List or Person

In some cases, you want to preaddress a Message form to a distribution list or to a user. For example, you want to preaddress a form such as a Weekly Schedule form to a distribution list. In addition, you may want to preaddress a Reply form so the item created with the form is sent to your Inbox.

▶ **To set the initial value of the To field**

1   On the Outlook **Compose** menu, click **New Mail Message**.

2   On the form, click the **To** button.

3   Double-click the names or distribution list name you want, and then click **OK**.

   If the distribution list you want to specify does not exist, you must ask your administrator to create it. If you create a Personal Distribution List or use an existing Personal Distribution List, the form will work correctly only on your computer.

4   Click **To**, and then click **OK**.

5   On the **Tools** menu, click **Design Outlook Form** to switch to Design mode.

# Preaddress a Form to a Folder

In some cases, you might want to preaddress a form to a folder. For example, the Business Card Request form, as shown in Figure 6.14, can be opened from the Organization Forms Library. However, the form is preaddressed to the Business Card Request folder, so the user can automatically submit the item simply by clicking the **Send** button.

**Figure 6.14  The Business Card Request form is preaddressed to the Business Card Request folder.**

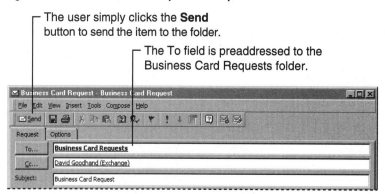

┌ The user simply clicks the **Send**
button to send the item to the folder.

┌ The To field is preaddressed to the
Business Card Requests folder.

Before you can preaddress a form to a folder, the folder address must exist in the Global Address Book or your Personal Address Book. If the folder address does not exist in the Global Address Book, you ask your administrator to make the folder address available in the Global Address book or you can publish the folder address to your Personal Address Book.

**Important**  To publish a folder address in your Personal Address Book, the folder must be located in Public Folders.

▶ **To add a folder address to your Personal Address Book**

1  In the Folder List, right-click the folder, and then click **Properties** on the shortcut menu.

2  Click the **Administration** tab, and then click **Personal Address Book**.

3  Click **Personal Address Book**.

▶ **To preaddress the To field to a folder**

1  On the Outlook **Compose** menu, click **New Mail Message**.

2  On the Message form, click the **To** button.

3  In the **Show Names from the** box, click **Personal Address Book**.

4  Double-click the folder name in the list, and then click **OK**.

5  On the **Tools** menu, click **Design Outlook Form** to switch to Design mode.

# Subject Field

The Subject field provides several important functions on a form:

- It summarizes the information in the item.
- It sets the value of the Conversation field. The Conversation field is the field used to create threaded conversations in views.
- The value in the Subject field appears in the title bar of the window.

**Figure 6.15   Shows how the Subject field functions in the New Product Idea form**

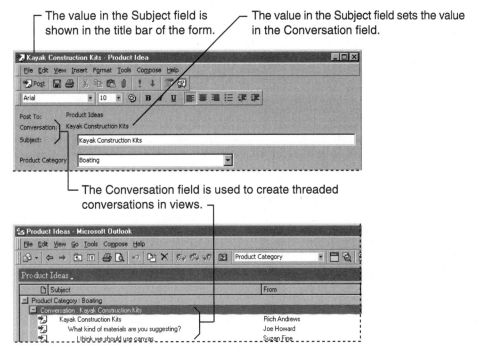

## Set the Initial Value of the Subject Field

In some cases, you may want to set the initial value of the Subject field. For example, for single-purpose forms such as the Business Card Request form, you can set the initial value of the Subject field to "Business Card Request".

▶ **To specify the initial value of the Subject field**

1  Right-click the Subject control, and then click **Properties** on the shortcut menu.

2  In the **Initial Value** box, type a value or click **Edit** to build an initial value formula for the Subject field.

# Message Field

With the Message field, you can:

- Insert file attachments and shortcuts. For example, for a Copier Request form, the user can insert attached files into the Message field. If the files are too large to send through the Microsoft Exchange system, the user can insert shortcuts to the attached files instead. In addition, you, the designer, can insert files or shortcuts, and hyperlinks. For example, you may want to insert attachments for ReadMe files that explain how to use the form or application. Or you may want to insert a hyperlink to a file or folder address.

- Insert item attachments and shortcuts. For example, this enables users to insert messages from other users into the Message field.

- Insert a shortcut to a World Wide Web page. Recipients must have an Web browser installed on their computer to use the shortcuts.

- Insert linked or embedded objects. These objects can be Word documents, Microsoft Excel workbooks, and PowerPoint presentations.

**Figure 6.16   At design time or run time, you can insert files, items, and objects in the Message field. You can also insert shortcuts.**

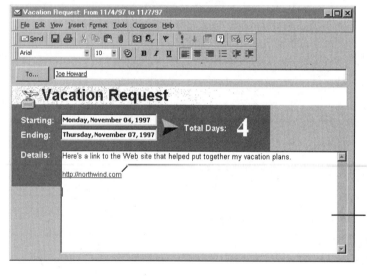

A hyperlink is automatically created when the user types **http://** in the Message control.

The Message control is linked to the Message field—the only field in which you can insert files, items, objects, and hyperlinks.

Each of these scenarios is covered in more detail in the following sections.

# Restrictions and Rules for the Message Control Usage

The Message field is automatically bound to the Message control in Outlook. When working with the Message field and control, there are a few guidelines you should be aware of:

- Each form can contain one Message control per page. For example, the **Compose** page of a form can contain a Message control and the **Read** page can contain a Message control.

- You cannot have a Message control on the **Message** page and another control on a separate page of the **Compose** or **Read** page.

- If the form does not have the **Separate Read Layout** option selected on the **Form** menu for the page that contains the Message control, the form can only contain one Message control.

- The Message control is automatically bound to the Message field.

- The Message control is the only control on a form in which you or the user can insert files, items, or objects.

▶ **To insert a file attachment or shortcut in the Message control**

1 Click in the Message control where you want to insert the file attachment or shortcut.

2 On the **Insert** menu, click **File**.

3 Locate and click the file you want to insert.

4 Under **Insert as**, click an option.

▶ **To insert an item in the Message control**

1 Click in the Message control where you want to insert the item.

2 On the **Insert** menu, click **Item**.

3 In the **Look in** box, click the folder that contains the items you want to insert.

4 Under **Insert as**, click an option.

▶ **To insert a folder shortcut in the Message control**

1   On the form **Tools** menu, click **Design Outlook Form** to switch to Run mode.

2   With the right mouse button, drag the folder from the Folder List to the Message control.

▶ **To insert a URL shortcut in the Message control**

1   First create the Universal Resource Locator (URL) shortcut using your Web browser.

2   On the form **Tools** menu, click **Design Outlook Form** to switch to Run mode.

3   Drag the URL shortcut icon from desktop to the Message control.

▶ **To insert a hyperlink in the Message control**

1   On the form **Tools** menu, click **Design Outlook Form** to switch to Run mode.

2   Type the hyperlink in the Message control. When you type **http://** or one of the supported protocols, the text is automatically underlined and the color is changed to blue. For example, to create a hyperlink to the Building Microsoft Outlook 97 Applications folder using the Outlook protocol, you specify the following hyperlink in the Message control:

<Outlook://Building Microsoft Outlook 97 Applications>

If the hyperlink includes spaces, you must enclose the entire address in angle brackets (< >).

Here are the supported protocols:

| Protocol | Description |
|---|---|
| file:// | A protocol used to open files on an intranet. |
| ftp:// | File Transfer Protocol (FTP), the most common method used to transfer files over the Internet. |
| gopher:// | Gopher protocol, by which hyperlinks and text are stored separately. |
| http:// | Hypertext Transfer Protocol (HTTP). |
| https:// | Hypertext Transfer Protocol Secure. A protocol designed to provide secure communications using HTTP over the Internet. |
| mailto: | A protocol used to send mail to an e-mail address. When the recipient clicks this hyperlink, a new message opens with the mailto e-mail address filled in. |
| news: | A protocol used to open an Internet newsgroup for recipients who are connected to an NNTP server. |
| nntp;// | Network News Transfer Protocol. A protocol used to distribute, inquire, retrieve, and post Usenet articles over the Internet. |
| Outlook:// or Outlook;// | A protocol used to open an Outlook folder or an item or file in Outlook. This protocol is supported only in Outlook. |
| prospero:// | A protocol used to organize Internet resources in your personal set of hyperlinks that go to information on remote file servers, for your personal virtual file system. |
| telnet:// | The Internet standard protocol for logging on from remote locations. |
| wais | Wide Area Information Servers Protocol. A distributed information system used to retrieve documents based on keywords you supply. |

▶ **To insert an object in the Message control**

**1** On the form **Tools** menu, click **Design Outlook Form** to switch to Run mode.

**2** Click in the Message control where you want to insert the object.

**3** On the **Insert** menu, click **Object**.

**4** In the **File name** box, type the name of the fi'e that you want to link or embed in the Message control, or click **Browse** to select from a list.

  - To create a linked object, select the **Link to file** check box.

  - To show the object as an icon, select the **Display as icon** check box.

# Set Control-Specific Properties

Each of the controls in the Outlook **Control Toolbox** serves a unique purpose. As a result, the properties for each control are set in a slightly different way. This section covers setting the properties for the most commonly used controls.

# Label Controls

Label controls can be used to show text on the page. As such, they are useful for company logos, address information, or a heading on a form page, as shown in Figure 6.17.

### When to Bind a Label Control

Generally, you bind Label controls to fields when you want to save the value to the item. For example, in the Vacation Request form, as shown in Figure 6.17, the Total Days label is bound to the TotalDays field. In this way, the value in the field is saved to the item when the item is saved or sent. However, also notice that Label2 and Label5 are not bound. As a result, the value in the Vacation Request field is not saved to the item. Rather, it exists in the form definition and is recreated each time an instance of the form is activated.

**Figure 6.17   Label controls on the Vacation Request form**

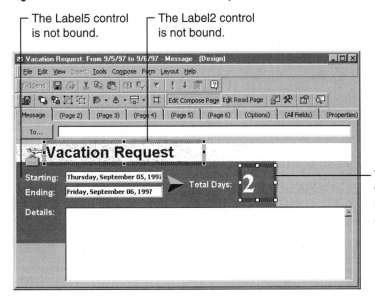

┌ The Label5 control   ┌ The Label2 control
  is not bound.          is not bound.

The TotalDays control is bound to the TotalDays field and shows the result of the values in the StartDate and EndDate fields.

# Set the Initial Value of a Label Control

In some cases, you may want to set the initial value of a Label control. For example, in the Vacation Request form, the TotalDays Label control on the **Compose** page contains a formula that automatically shows the result in the field.

▸ **To set the initial value of a Label control**

1   Right-click the control, and then click **Properties** on the shortcut menu.

2   On the **Value** tab, type the initial value in the **Initial Value** box or click **Edit** to create an initial value formula.

 • To automatically calculate a formula, click **Calculate this formula automatically**.

 • To show the initial value in the Label control when the form is opened to create an item, click **Calculate this formula when I compose a new form**.

**Note**   Before you can set the initial value of a Label control, the control must be bound to a field.

# TextBox Controls

Use TextBox controls on a form to let the user enter, edit, and view information, as shown in Figure 6.18. For example, you can place a TextBox control on a **Compose** page to let the user enter information and on the **Read** page to let the user view information.

**Note**   In some cases, you may want to insert attachments, shortcuts, or hyperlinks. To do this, you must use the Message control. For more information about the Message control, see "Message Field" earlier in this chapter.

**Figure 6.18   TextBox controls on the Business Card Request form**

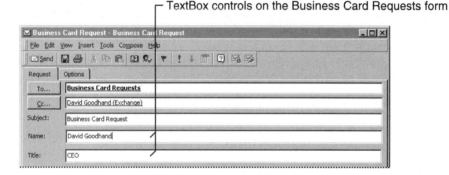

┌─ TextBox controls on the Business Card Requests form

The TextBox control has a variety of display properties that give you great flexibility in determining how the TextBox control looks and functions. For example, you can specify the **Multi-line** property so the user can enter more than one line of text in the control. Before you can specify the initial value for a control, it must be bound to a field.

▶ **To specify the Multi-line option for a TextBox control**

1   Right-click the control, and then click **Properties** on the shortcut menu.

2   Click the **Display** tab, and then select the **Multi-line** check box.

▶ **To specify the initial value for a TextBox field**

• On the **Value** page, type a value in the box under **Initial Value** or click **Edit** to build an initial value formula for the field.

# OptionButton Controls

Use OptionButton controls on a form when you want to present a limited number of choices to the user. For example, on the Business Card Request form, OptionButton controls are used to enable the user to select the quantity of cards they want, as shown in Figure 6.19.

**Figure 6.19 OptionButton controls on the Business Card Request form**

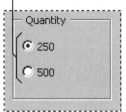

OptionButton controls offer a choice
of mutually exclusive options.

Quantity

○ 250
○ 500

▶ **To specify a caption for an OptionButton control**

**1** Drag the OptionButton control from the **Control Toolbox** to the form.

**2** Click the OptionButton control. When the insertion pointer appears, type the caption for the control.

# Set Value Properties for an OptionButton Control

For OptionButton controls that you want to group together, you bind the controls to the same field. For example, the OptionButton controls in the earlier Figure 6.19 are bound to the Quantity field. When you bind one OptionButton control to a field, all other option buttons in the group are automatically bound to the same field. Option buttons on a page that are not included in a container, such as a Frame or MultiPage control, are automatically grouped together. Options buttons in a container control are grouped with the option buttons in that container.

▶ **To bind an OptionButton control to a field**

**1** Right-click the control, and then click **Properties** on the shortcut menu.

**2** Click the **Value** tab.

**3** Do one of the following:

- Click **New** to create a new field. You can create a Currency, Text, or Number field. Choose the type of field to match the data in the control. In this example, the Quantity field is a Number field.

- Click **Choose Field**, point to **User-defined fields in folder**, and then click the field that you want to bind the OptionButton control to. In this example, the OptionButton control is bound to the Quantity field.

When you bind one option button in the group to a field, all option buttons in the group are automatically bound to the same field.

### Set the Value Property of Each Option Button Separately

After you bind the option buttons in a group to an existing field, you must set the **Value** property of each option button separately. The **Value** property is the value that is written to the field when the option button is selected at run time. As such, this value appears in folder views to represent the option button if it is selected in an item.

▶ **To set the Value property of an option button**

1  Right-click the OptionButton control that you want set the **Value** property for, and then click **Properties** on the shortcut menu.

2  Click the **Value** tab.

3  In the **Value** box, type a value for the option button.

4  Click **OK**.

▶ **To set the initial value of an OptionButton control**

1  Right-click the OptionButton control that you want selected when the form first appears at run time, and then click **Advanced Properties** on the shortcut menu.

2  Click the **Value** cell, and then type **True**.

3  Click **Apply**, and then close the advanced **Properties** window.

# CheckBox Controls

Use CheckBox controls to give the user an On/Off or Yes/No choice, as shown in Figure 6.20. Because check boxes work independently of each other, the user can select any number of check boxes at one time.

**Figure 6.20   A CheckBox control**

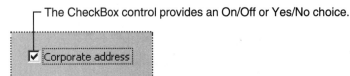

The CheckBox control provides an On/Off or Yes/No choice.

☑ Corporate address

▶ **To bind a CheckBox control to a field**

1 Right-click the field, and then click **Properties** on the shortcut menu.

2 On the **Value** page, do one of the following:

   • Click **New** to create a new field. You can create a Yes/No, On/Off, True/False, or Icon field. When you select a Yes/No field, the selected value appears in the cell in the folder. If you select Icon, the CheckBox icon appears in the folder as selected or cleared.

   • Click **Choose Field**, point to **User-defined fields in folder**, and then choose the field that you want to bind the CheckBox control to. In this example, the CheckBox control in Figure 6.20 is bound to the Corporate field.

**Note**   The CheckBox control must be bound to a Yes/No field type for the check box to operate properly.

▶ **To set the initial value of a CheckBox control**

1 Right-click the CheckBox control, and then click **Advanced Properties** on the shortcut menu.

2 Click the **Value** cell, and then type **True**.

3 Click **Apply**, and then close the advanced **Properties** window.

# ComboBox Controls

Use ComboBox controls so users can either choose a value from the list portion of the control or enter text in the edit box portion of the control, as shown in Figure 6.21. When working with the ComboBox control, you create the control, bind it to a field, and then specify the values for the items in the combo box list.

**Figure 6.21   A Dropdown ComboBox control**

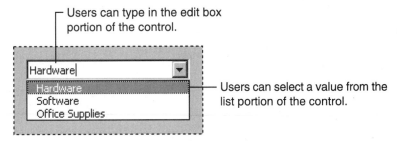

▶ **To bind the CheckBox control to a field**

1  Right-click the control, and then click **Properties** on the shortcut menu.

2  On the **Value** page, do one of the following:

- To create a new field, click **New**.

- To bind the ComboBox control to an existing field, click **Choose Field**, point to **User-defined fields in folder**, and then click the field you want to bind the ComboBox control to.

▶ **To select a list type**

- In the **List Type** box on the **Value** page, click either **Dropdown** or **Droplist**.

   Outlook provides two types of combo boxes that you can use.

| List type | Description |
| --- | --- |
| Dropdown | Users can either select a value from the list or type a value in the edit box. |
| Droplist | Users must select a value from the list. |

▶ **To add values to the combo box list**

- In the **Possible values** box on the **Value** page, type the values you want to appear in the list. Separate each value with a semicolon (;), as shown in Figure 6.22.

▶ **To set the initial value of a ComboBox control**

- In the **Initial Value** box on the **Value** page, type in the value that you want to appear in the edit box portion of the control when the form first appears, as shown in Figure 6.22.

**Figure 6.22   A ComboBox control**

The ComboBox control is bound to this field.

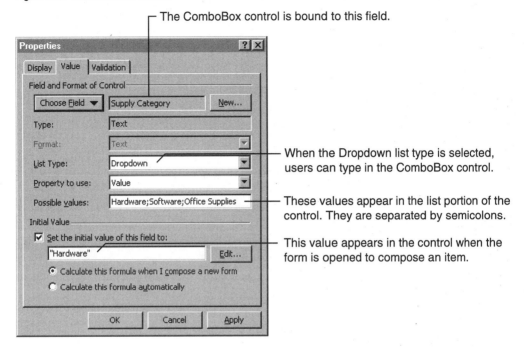

When the Dropdown list type is selected, users can type in the ComboBox control.

These values appear in the list portion of the control. They are separated by semicolons.

This value appears in the control when the form is opened to compose an item.

# ListBox Controls

Use ListBox controls to show a list of values from which the user can select one or many values. To create a list box that enables users to select more than one value, you must bind the ListBox control to a Keywords field. List boxes that are bound to Keywords fields have check boxes that enable users to select multiple values, as shown in Figure 6.23. When the user selects multiple values in the ListBox control, the values appear in the view in an Outlook folder as comma-separated values.

**Figure 6.23   Values selected in a list box bound to a Keywords field are shown as comma-separated values in an Outlook view.**

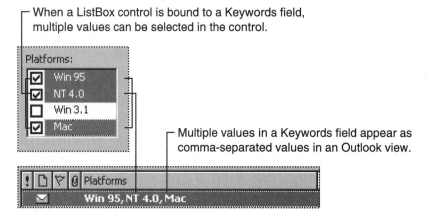

When a ListBox control is bound to a Keywords field, multiple values can be selected in the control.

Multiple values in a Keywords field appear as comma-separated values in an Outlook view.

▶ **To bind the ListBox control to a field**

1   Right-click the control, and then click **Properties** on the shortcut menu.

2   On the **Value** page, do one of the following:

- To create a Keywords field, click **New**, and then click **Keywords** in the **Type** box.

- To create a ListBox control without a Keywords field, click **Text**, **Number**, **Currency**, or **Date/Time** in the **Type** box, and then in the **Format** box, click a format.

- To bind the ListBox control to an existing field, click **Choose Field**, point to **User-defined fields in folder**, and then click the field that you want to bind the ListBox control to.

**Note**   Do not bind the ListBox control to a Yes/No, Combination, or Formula field.

▶ **To add values to the ListBox control**

- In the **Possible values** box on the **Value** page, type the values you want to appear in the list. Separate each value with a semicolon, as shown in Figure 6.24.

▶ **To set the initial value of a ListBox control**

- In the **Initial Value** box on the **Value** page, do one of the following:

  - To set the initial value to a single value, type the value that you want to appear as checked in the ListBox control when the user opens the form to compose an item, as shown in Figure 6.24.

  - To set the initial value to multiple values, type the values that you want to appear as checked in the ListBox control when the user opens the form to compose an item. Separate each value in the **Initial Value** box with a semicolon.

**Figure 6.24   The values that you want to appear in the list are typed in the Possible Values box.**

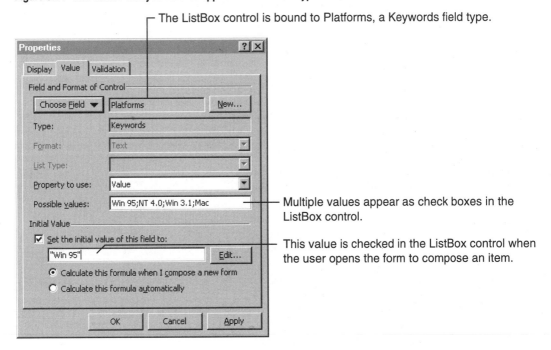

# Frame Controls

Use the Frame control to contain controls that are logically related, as shown in Figure 6.25. Frame controls are often used to contain OptionButton controls, but they can also contain other controls such as CheckBox, ComboBox, Label, and TextBox controls.

**Figure 6.25 The Frame control**

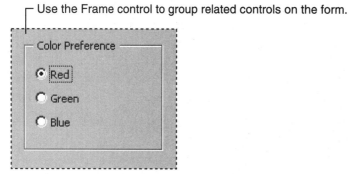

Use the Frame control to group related controls on the form.

▶ **To add a Frame control**

• Drag the control from the **Control Toolbox** to the form.

▶ **To add or remove controls from a Frame control**

• To add a control, drag the control into to the frame. To remove a control, drag it outside the borders of the frame.

▶ **To change the caption of the Frame control**

• Right-click the border of the Frame control, and then click **Properties** on the shortcut menu.

• In the **Caption** box on the **Display** page, type a new caption for the Frame control.

# CommandButton Controls

The CommandButton control, when clicked, triggers the Click event. As such, you can write Visual Basic Scripting Edition Click event procedures in the Script Editor for each CommandButton control, as shown in Figure 6.26.

**Important** Outlook only supports the Click event for controls.

**Figure 6.26   CommandButton controls on the Business Card Request form**

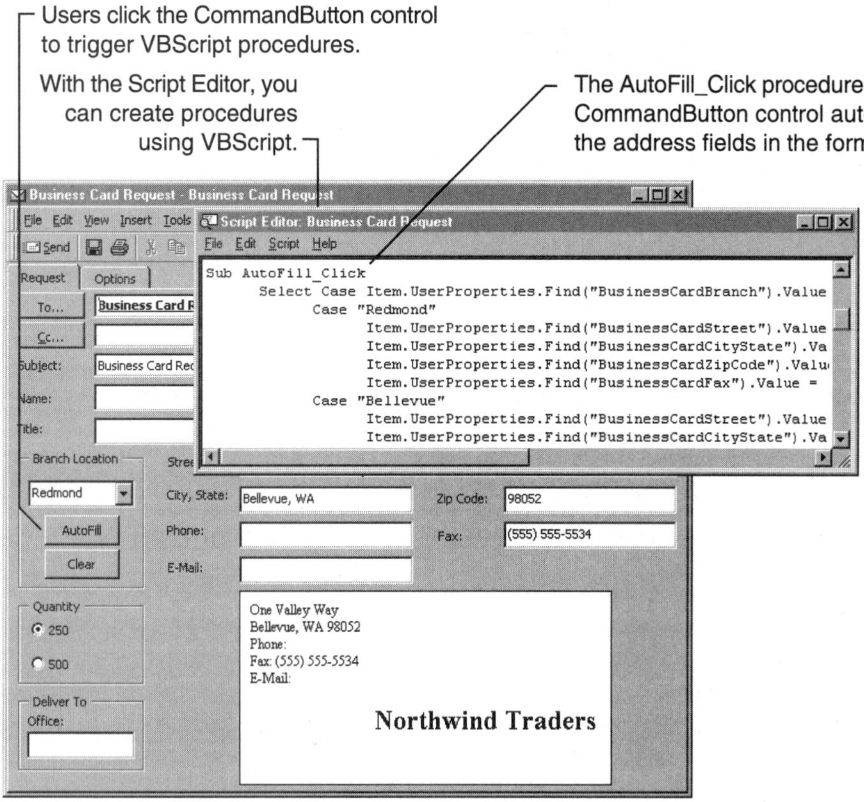

Users click the CommandButton control
to trigger VBScript procedures.

With the Script Editor, you
can create procedures
using VBScript.

The AutoFill_Click procedure for the AutoFill
CommandButton control automatically fills
the address fields in the form.

▶ **To add a CommandButton control**

1   Drag the control from the **Control Toolbox** to the form.

2   To set the caption for a CommandButton control, click the control. When the edit
    pointer appears, type the name in the control.

3   To specify a name for the CommandButton control, right-click the control, and
    then click **Properties** on the shortcut menu.

4   In the **Name** box, type a name, and then click **OK**.

▶ **To create a procedure for a CommandButton control**

1   Click the **View Code** button on the **Form Design** toolbar.

2   In the Script Editor window, type **Sub** followed by a space, followed by **CommandButton1_Click**, where CommandButton1 is the name of the control. Add the necessary code to the procedure. End the procedure with an **End Sub** statement, as shown in the following example:

```
Sub CommandButton1_Click
    MsgBox "This is a procedure for a CommandButton control."
End Sub
```

▶ **To test a CommandButton control Click procedure**

1   On the **Tools** menu, click **Design Outlook Form** to switch the form into Run mode.

2   Click the command button.

3   To switch back to Design mode, click **Design Outlook Form** again on the **Tools** menu.

**See Also**   For more information about creating procedures for forms using Visual Basic Scripting Edition, see Chapter 9, "Use Visual Basic Scripting Edition with Outlook."

# MultiPage Controls

Use MultiPage controls to provide multiple pages of information on a form, as shown in Figure 6.27.

**Figure 6.27   The MultiPage control on the Read page of the Help Request form.**

Users click this tab to show the **Ticket** page.

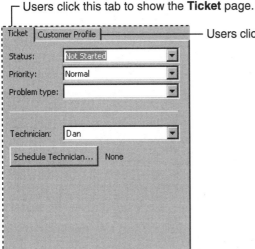

Users click this tab to see the **Customer Profile** page.

▶ **To add a MultiPage control**

• Drag the MultiPage control from the **Control Toolbox** to the form.

▶ **To add controls to the MultiPage control**

• Switch to the page you want to add controls to, and then drag the controls you want from the **Control Toolbox** to the MultiPage control.

▶ **To insert, rename, delete, or move a page**

• Right-click a tab on the MultiPage control, and then click the shortcut menu command to insert, rename, delete, or move a page, as shown in Figure 6.28.

**Figure 6.28   The shortcut menu of the MultiPage control**

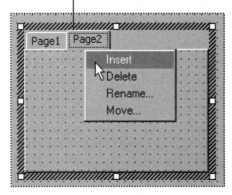

Right-click on a tab on the MultiPage control to show the shortcut menu.

## How the TabStrip Control Differs from the MultiPage Control

With a MultiPage control, each page on the control usually contains a different set of controls. However, with the TabStrip control, each page contains the same controls. For example, you might use a TabStrip control to present the addresses of various companies. You set the title of each tab to the name of the company, and then you write code that, when you click a tab, updates the controls to show the address of that company.

**See Also**   For more information about the TabStrip control, see the Outlook Forms Help.

# Image Controls

Use Image controls to contain graphic images, as shown in Figure 6.29.

**Figure 6.29   Image controls on the Vacation Request form**

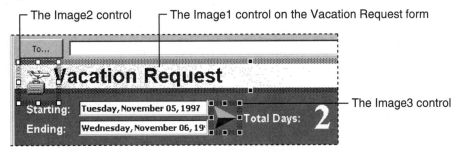

┌ The Image2 control          ┌ The Image1 control on the Vacation Request form

The Image3 control

▶ **To add a picture to an Image control**

1  Right-click the Image control, and then click **Advanced Properties** on the shortcut menu.

2  Double-click the **Picture** cell, and then select the image.

▶ **To delete the picture in the Image control**

•  You must delete the Image control, so click the Image control, and then press the DELETE key.

▶ **To size an image in the Image control**

1  Right-click the Image control, and then click **Advanced Properties**.

2  Do one of the following:

| To | Do this |
| --- | --- |
| Automatically size the control to the picture: | In the **AutoSize** cell, click **True**. |
| Maintain the size of the picture, regardless of the size of the Image control: | In the **PictureSizeMode** cell, click **Clip**. |
| Stretch the picture to fill the Image control: | In the **PictureSizeMode** cell, click **Stretch**. |
| Enlarge the picture, but still maintain the **PictureAlignment** property setting: | In the **PictureSizeMode** cell, click **Zoom**. |

# SpinButton Control

Use the SpinButton control to enable the user to increment or decrements numbers in a control. Although you can write script for the SpinButton control, it is not required to create a SpinButton control. To create a spin button for a control, you can bind the spin button to the same field that a TextBox control is bound to. Here is an example of how you can create a SpinButton control.

▶ **To add the TextBox control and bind it to a field**

1  From the **Control Toolbox**, drag a TextBox control to the form.

2  Right-click the TextBox control, and then click **Properties** on the shortcut menu.

3  Click the **Value** tab, and then click **New**.

4  In the **Name** box, type a name for the field.

5  In the **Type** box, click **Number**.

6  Click **OK**, and then click **OK** again.

▶ **To add the SpinButton control and bind it to a field**

1  From the **Control Toolbox**, drag a SpinButton control to the form and position it to the right of the TextBox control you just added.

2  Right-click the SpinButton control, and then click **Properties** on the shortcut menu.

3  Click the **Value** tab.

4  Click **Choose Field**, point to **User defined fields in folder**, and then click the field you just added.

5  Click **OK**.

6  Hold down the CTRL key, and then right-click the SpinButton and TextBox controls.

7  On the shortcut menu, point to **Make Same Size**, and then click **Height**.

8  To test the SpinButton control, click **Design Outlook Form** on the **Tools** menu to exit Design mode, and then click the SpinButton control to increment or decrement the number in the TextBox control.

**See Also**  For more information about the SpinButton control, see the Outlook Forms Help.

# Controls that Require VBScript

In addition to the CommandButton control, the **Control Toolbox** provides several other controls that require VBScript to operate. These are the ToggleButton, TabStrip, and ScrollBar controls.

**See Also**  For more information about these controls, see the Outlook forms Help.

# CHAPTER 7

# Actions

## In This Chapter

Voting Buttons for Message Forms   185
Reply Actions   196
Reply to Folder Actions for Post Forms   210

Action properties make it possible for you to define custom responses for forms, instead of using the standard Reply and Reply to Folder actions. For example, with the Vacation Request form, supervisors can reply to a vacation request item by choosing an Approve Vacation or Deny Vacation action, rather than using the standard Reply action.

In this chapter, we take a close look at the different ways of creating responses for forms. Specifically, we look at:

**The easiest way to create responses for Message forms**  by using Voting buttons. As an example, we cover how Voting buttons are created for an Art Approval form.

**How to create custom Reply actions for Message forms**  As an example, we cover how Reply actions are implemented for the Vacation Request form.

**How to create custom Reply to Folder actions for Post forms**  As an example, we take a look at how custom responses are designed for the Course Catalog Entry in the Training Management folder.

# Voting Buttons for Message Forms

Voting buttons, which are only available with Message forms, provide an easy way for users to collect quick feedback from other users. When you specify Voting button options for a form, you cause two important things to happen.

You specify that Voting buttons are added to the **Read** page of the form, as shown in Figure 7.1.

**Figure 7.1   The Read page of the Art Approval form. This page is used by members of the Art Approval Committee to approve or reject the art submitted by the artist.**

Voting buttons are added to the **Read** page of the Art Approval form.
Reviewers click **Approve** or **Reject** to send their response to the artist.

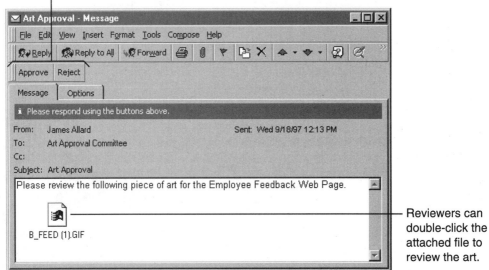

Reviewers can double-click the attached file to review the art.

You also specify where the Tracking item is located. The Tracking item contains the results of the voting responses and shows the results on the Tracking page, as shown in Figure 7.2.

**Figure 7.2   The Tracking page of the Art Approval form tallies the results of the responses from the Art Approval Committee members.**

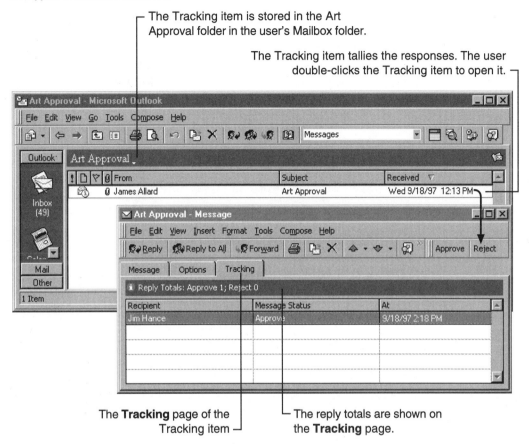

— The Tracking item is stored in the Art Approval folder in the user's Mailbox folder.

The Tracking item tallies the responses. The user double-clicks the Tracking item to open it. ⌐

The **Tracking** page of the Tracking item ⌐

└ The reply totals are shown on the **Tracking** page.

In this section, we create an Art Approval form that has Voting buttons and a Tracking item. When you're done, you will understand how Voting buttons work and how they can be used to collect feedback from other users. You'll also know how to create simple Art Approval application.

# Overview of the Art Approval Form

The Art Approval form is a very simple form based on the standard Message form. The Art Approval form, as shown in Figure 7.3, is for use by an artist to send an attached file of electronic art to users on the Art Approval Committee distribution list for review. The recipients review the attached file, and then vote to approve or reject. To see the voting results, the artist opens the Art Approval Tracking item in the Art Approval folder.

**Figure 7.3   The Compose page of the Art Approval form**

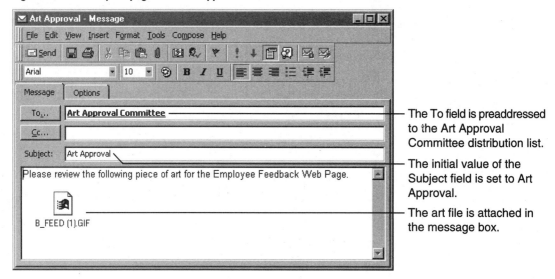

The To field is preaddressed to the Art Approval Committee distribution list.

The initial value of the Subject field is set to Art Approval.

The art file is attached in the message box.

# Create the Art Approval Folder

Before you create the Art Approval form, create an Art Approval folder in your Mailbox folder. That's where you'll store the Tracking item that tallies responses.

▶ **To create the Art Approval folder**

1   In the Folder List, right-click the Mailbox folder, and then click **Create Subfolder**.

2   In the **Name** box, type **Art Approval**.

3   Clear the **Create a shortcut to this folder in the Outlook Bar** check box.

# Create the Art Approval Form

For this example, you create the Art Approval form. First you open the standard Message form and then set the initial value of the To and Subject fields. Then you switch to Design mode, specify Voting button options for the form, and then publish the form in your Personal Forms Library.

▶ **To open the standard Message form**

1 In the Outlook bar, click the **Inbox** icon, and then on the **Compose** menu, click **New Mail Message**.

2 On the form **Tools** menu, click **Design Outlook Form**.

## Preaddress the To Field

Quite often, you'll want to preaddress a form to the people you send the form to on a regular basis. To preaddress a form, you set the initial value of the To field. In the example in this chapter, the initial value of the To field is set to the Art Approval Committee distribution list. For the form that you create, however, you preaddress the form to your own address. You must set the initial value of the To field at run time because you cannot open the Address Book from the To field at design time.

**See Also**   To create a distribution list, see Microsoft Outlook Help.

▶ **To preaddress the form**

1 On the **Tools** menu, click **Design Outlook Form** to switch to Run mode.

2 On the form, click the **To** button.

3 Double-click the address you want to set as the initial value in the To field. (For this example, you can select your own address.)

4 Click **OK**.

5 On the **Tools** menu, click **Design Outlook Form** to switch back to Design mode.

## Set the Initial Value of the Subject Field

For forms that serve a specific purpose, such as the Art Approval form, it makes sense to set the initial value of the Subject field. This saves the user the time of filling in the Subject field and ensures that a recipient sees a consistent Subject field each time he receives an Art Approval item in his Inbox.

▶ **To set the initial value of the Subject field**

1  Right-click the Subject field, and then click **Properties** on the shortcut menu.

2  Click the **Value** tab.

3  In the **Initial Value** box, select the **Set the initial value of this field to** check box, and then in the box below it type **Art Approval** or whatever value you want for this form.

4  Click **Calculate this formula when I compose a new form**.

5  Click **OK**.

You don't see the initial value in the Subject field immediately. It only appears when the form is opened to compose an item at run time.

## Set Options for the Art Approval Form

In the form window, click the **Options** page. Remember, the **Options** page is only available for Message forms. With the **Options** page, you specify Voting button options and you indicate where you want to store the Tracking item.

### Set Voting Button Options

Voting buttons appear on the **Read** page of the form and enable the user to respond to the Art Approval item by clicking the **Approve** or **Reject** button. The **Read** page of the form appears when the user double-clicks an Art Approval item in the Inbox.

▶ **To specify Voting buttons**

1  Select the **Use voting buttons** check box.

2  In the **Use voting buttons** box, type the text you want to appear on the Voting buttons or select the values from the list. If you type values, you must separate the values with a semicolon.

### Specify Who the Replies Are Sent To

When you select the **Have replies sent to** check box, your address is automatically added to the box. You can add additional addresses to the box or you can replace your address with another.

▶ **To specify the reply address**

1  Select the **Have replies sent to** check box.

2  To specify additional names, click **Select Names**, and then double-click the names you want.

## Specify Where the Tracking Item is Stored

With forms that have Voting buttons, Outlook provides an automatic tally of the Voting button responses in a saved item in a folder. This folder must be located in your Mailbox folder. The default folder is the Sent Items folder. However, you can change it.

▶ **To specify where the Tracking item is stored**

1  On the **Options** page, click **Browse**.

2  In the **Folder** box, click the Art Approval folder, and then click **OK**.

As shown in Figure 7.4, the **Save sent messages to** option is set to the Art Approval folder. So when an Art Approval item is sent, an Art Approval item is also saved in the Art Approval folder in your Mailbox folder. After you receive and open voting responses in your Inbox, the responses are written to the Tracking item in the Art Approval folder. If this seems a little confusing right now, don't worry. We'll go through the process step by step.

**Figure 7.4  Voting button options for the Art Approval form**

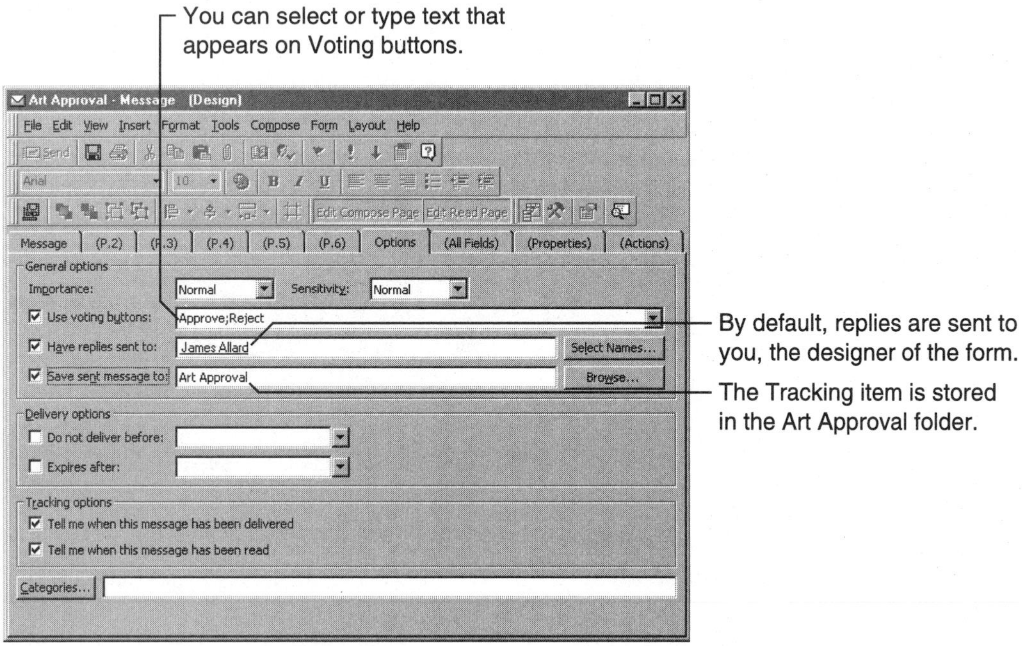

You can select or type text that appears on Voting buttons.

By default, replies are sent to you, the designer of the form.

The Tracking item is stored in the Art Approval folder.

# How Actions are Automatically Set for Voting Buttons

When you specify Voting buttons for a form, Outlook automatically adds custom actions to the **Actions** page. There are two important points to remember about these actions. First, when you specify Voting buttons, the **Creates form of type** property is set to the standard Message form (IPM.Note). Second, the **Address form like** property is set to **Response**, as shown in Figure 7.5.

**Figure 7.5  The Actions page of the Art Approval form. Approve and Reject actions are automatically added when you specify the Voting buttons on the Options page.**

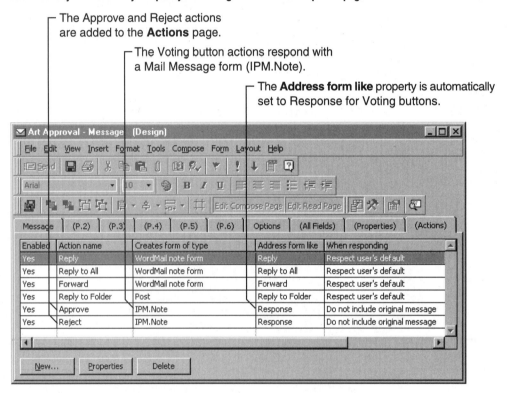

The Approve and Reject actions
are added to the **Actions** page.

The Voting button actions respond with
a Mail Message form (IPM.Note).

The **Address form like** property is automatically
set to Response for Voting buttons.

# Publish the Form to the Personal Forms Library

Now you publish the form to your Personal Forms Library so you can open and test the form.

▶ **To publish the form**

1   Click the **Publish Form As** button on the **Forms Designer** toolbar.

2   If the **Personal Forms** text does not appear next to the **Publish In** button, click **Publish In**, click **Personal Forms** in the **Forms Library** box, and then click **OK**.

3   In the **Form name** box, type **Art Approval** or whatever you want to name the form, and then click **Publish**.

4   Close the form.

**See Also**   For more information about where to publish forms, see Chapter 13, "Distribute and Maintain Applications."

# Test the Art Approval Form

Now you open the Art Approval form and then send an Art Approval item to your Inbox.

## Send an Art Approval Item

First, you open the Art Approval form from your Personal Forms Library. When you open the form, you see the **Compose** page of the form. Using the **Compose** page, you send an Art Approval item to your Inbox.

▶ **To send the Art Approval form**

1   On the Outlook **Compose** menu, click **Choose Form**.

2   Click **Personal Forms**, and then double-click **Art Approval**.

3   On the **Insert** menu, click **File**, and then double-click a file to insert in the message box on the Art Approval form.

4   Click the **Send** button.

## Use the Voting Buttons to Respond

Now you open the Art Approval item in your Inbox. Then you click one of the Voting buttons.

▶ **To vote in the item:**

1   Double-click the Art Approval item in your Inbox.

2   Normally, you open the attached item to review it. However, in this case there is no need to.

3   Click **Approve**.

4   Click **Send the response now**, and then click **OK**.

# Review Replies

Now you open the Art Approval reply in your Inbox. Then you open the Tracking item in the Art Approval folder.

**Important**   The Voting button responses are tallied in the Tracking item only after the response items are opened in your Inbox. If the items are not opened, the results are not tallied in the Tracking item. If no response items are opened, the Tracking page is not available on the Tracking form.

▶ **To open the response item in your Inbox**

• In your Inbox, double-click the Art Approval item.

▶ **To open the Tracking item**

1   In the Folder List, open the Art Approval folder.

2   Double-click the Tracking item, as shown in Figure 7.2 earlier in this chapter.

   The Tracking item is identified by an information icon, as shown in Figure 7.2, earlier in this chapter.

3   Click the **Tracking** tab.

**Figure 7.6   The Tracking item is opened in the Art Approval folder.**

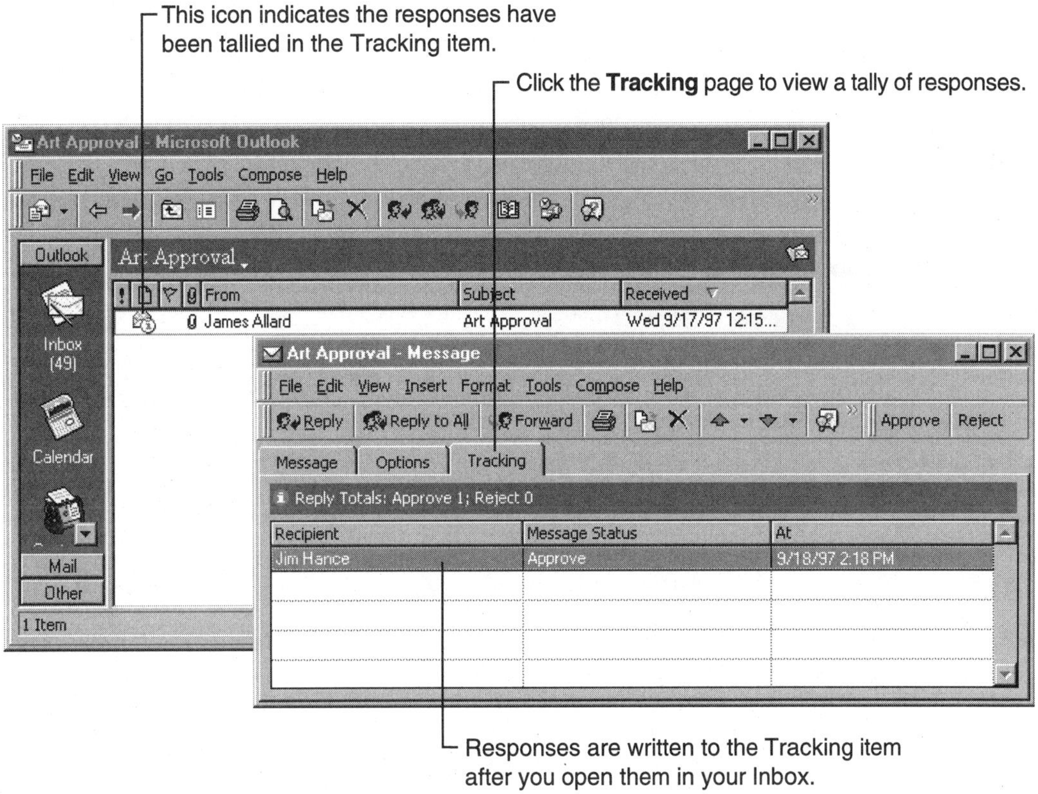

This icon indicates the responses have
been tallied in the Tracking item.

Click the **Tracking** page to view a tally of responses.

Responses are written to the Tracking item
after you open them in your Inbox.

# Reply Actions

When creating applications with Message forms, you often create Reply actions that open custom forms, instead of the standard Message form. For example, the Vacation Request form has two custom actions: The Approve Vacation action activates the Request item using either a Vacation Approved form or a Vacation Denied form.

In this section, we create custom Reply actions for Message forms. Throughout this section, we use the Vacation Request application for examples of how to implement Reply actions with Message forms.

▶ **To open the Vacation Request folder**

- In the Folder List, expand the **Building Microsoft Outlook 97 Applications** folder, and then expand the **3. Building Blocks** folder. Then click the **Vacation Request** folder.

**Note**   If you haven't installed the Building Microsoft Outlook 97 Applications folder, see the Introduction of this book for instructions.

# Overview of the Vacation Request Application

The Vacation Request application consists of four forms. All forms are intentionally left unhidden in this folder so you can view them.

▶ **To view a Vacation Request form**

- On the **Compose** menu, click **New Vacation** *formname*.

**Vacation Request form**   The **Compose** page enables the user to compose a Vacation Request item and send it to his supervisor. The **Read** page, the page seen by the supervisor when she opens the vacation request, contains the **Approve Vacation** and **Deny Vacation** buttons, as shown in Figure 7.7.

**Figure 7.7   The Read page of the Vacation Request form**

This action button opens the
Vacation Approved form.

This action button opens the
Vacation Denied form.

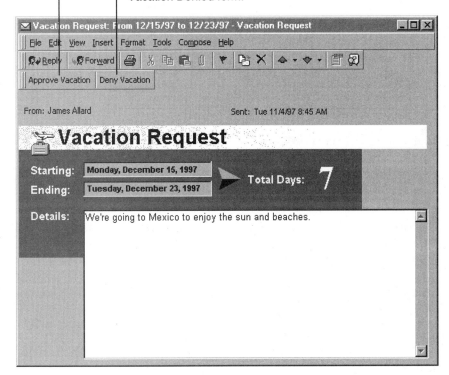

**Vacation Approved form**   The supervisor sees the **Compose** page of the Vacation Approved form when she clicks the **Approve Vacation** button on the Vacation Request form. She then clicks **Send** to route the approved vacation request to the user.

**Vacation Denied form**   The supervisor sees the **Compose** page of this form when she clicks the **Deny Vacation** button on the Vacation Request form. She can then click **Send** to route the denied vacation request to the user.

**Vacation Report form**   Lets the user send the supervisor a report of the vacation days taken. The supervisor can then track the days available for each employee.

Because we're discussing actions, we focus primarily on the Vacation Request form and its associated actions in this part of the chapter. Along the way, we take a look at a custom Reply action.

# Actions for the Vacation Request Form

To get familiar with actions, let's take a look at the **Actions** page for the Vacation Request form, as shown in Figure 7.8.

▶ **To view the Actions page for the Vacation Request form**

1   In the Folder List, expand the **Building Microsoft Outlook 97 Applications** folder, and then expand the **Building Blocks** folder. Then click the **Vacation Request** folder.

2   On the **Compose** menu, click **New Vacation Request**.

3   On the Vacation Request form **Tools** menu, click **Design Outlook Form**.

4   Click the **Actions** page.

**Note**   If you haven't installed the Building Outlook 97 Applications folder, see the instructions in the Introduction to this book.

**Figure 7.8   The Actions page for the Vacation Request form**

┌ This action places an **Approve Vacation** button on the **Read** page.
When the button is clicked, it opens the Vacation Approved form.

┌ This action places a **Deny Vacation** button on the **Read** page.
When the button is clicked, it opens the Vacation Denied form.

Click here to show the **Actions** page. ┐

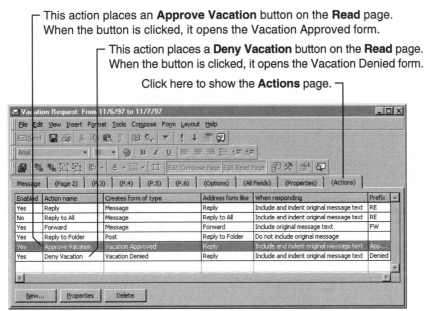

## New Reply Actions

When you create new Reply actions, you specify that custom command buttons and menu commands are added to the form. The menu commands and buttons, when clicked, activate a custom form that lets the user reply to an item. For example, the Vacation Request form has a custom Approve Vacation action. When a supervisor opens a vacation request in his Inbox, he can click the **Approve Vacation** button to open the Vacation Approved form, as shown in Figure 7.9.

The supervisor can then click the **Send** button to send the Vacation Approved item to the person who requested it. When the Vacation Approved form is opened, the original message is copied from the Vacation Request form to the message box of the Vacation Approved form. Likewise, the From field is copied to the To field, and the values in the StartDate, EndDate, and TotalDays fields are copied from the Vacation Request form to the Vacation Approved form.

**Figure 7.9   The Read page (partial) of the Vacation Request form and the Compose page of the Vacation Approved form**

On the **Read** page of the Vacation Request form, the **Approve Vacation** button opens the Vacation Approved form.

The supervisor clicks the **Send** button to send the response to the requester.

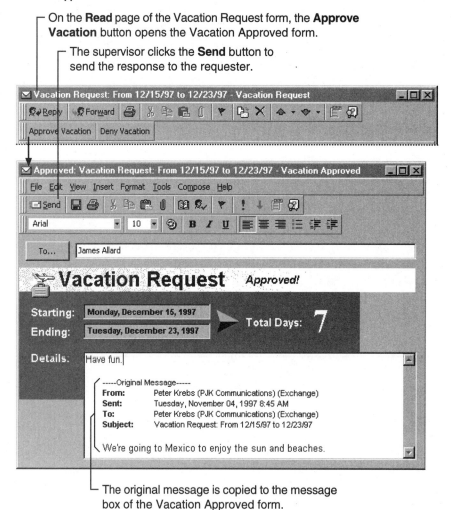

The original message is copied to the message box of the Vacation Approved form.

## Approve Vacation Action

Now let's take a look at the properties associated with the Approve Vacation action.

▶ **To view the Approve Vacation action**

• On the **Actions** page, double-click the **Approve Vacation** action.

The **Form Action Properties** dialog box, as shown in Figure 7.10, enables you to create new actions and to modify existing actions. With this dialog box, you specify the text that appears on the **Action** button, the form that appears when the button is clicked, and whether the original message is copied to the Reply item.

**Figure 7.10   The Form Action Properties dialog box .**

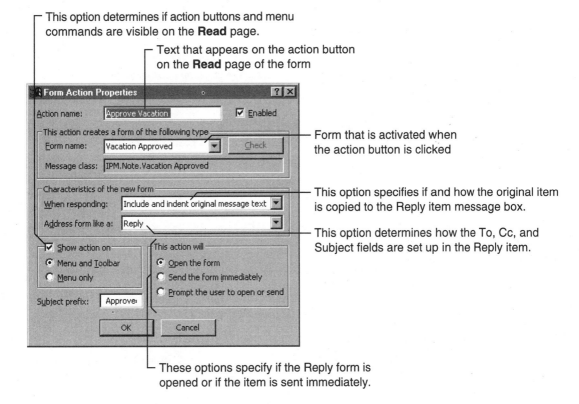

This option determines if action buttons and menu commands are visible on the **Read** page.

Text that appears on the action button on the **Read** page of the form

Form that is activated when the action button is clicked

This option specifies if and how the original item is copied to the Reply item message box.

This option determines how the To, Cc, and Subject fields are set up in the Reply item.

These options specify if the Reply form is opened or if the item is sent immediately.

## Action Name

The **Action name** box, as shown in the preceding Figure 7.10, defines the name of the menu command and command button that open the associated custom Reply form. The custom action button, as discussed earlier in this chapter, appears on the **Read** page of the form.

The custom menu command appears in two places:

- On the Outlook **Compose** menu when an item created with the associated form is selected in a folder. For example, with the Vacation Request form, the **Approve Vacation** command appears on the **Compose** menu when a Vacation Request item is selected in the Inbox.

- On the **Compose** menu of the **Read** page of the form.

## Form Name and Message Class

The **Form name** box contains the name of the form that is opened when the menu command or command button is selected. The **Message class** box contains the internal identifier for the form. When you select a form in the **Form name** box, the message class automatically appears in the **Message class** box.

The **Form name** list contains the names of the forms published in the active folder. In addition, it contains a **Forms** value that you can use to select from forms in the Organization, Personal, or Application Forms Library.

▶ **To specify a form name**

- Do one of the following:

  - In the **Form name** box, type a form name, and then click **Check** to search for the form.

    If Outlook cannot find the form, you see a message box. If this happens, I highly recommended you create the form before you specify the form name. After you create the form and publish it in a forms library, you can return to the original form and click the name of the form in the **Form name** box.

  - In the **Form name** box, click a form name from the drop-down list.

  - In the **Form name** box, click **Forms** on the drop-down list. In the **New Form** box, double-click the form you want.

## Characteristics of the New form

Under **Characteristics of the new form**, you can specify how the original message is copied to the message box of the Reply form. In addition, you can use the Form Action Properties dialog box to specify how the values in the From, Cc, and Subject fields are copied from the original form to the Reply form.

### When Responding

For Reply actions, you can specify if the contents of the original item are copied to the message box of the Reply item. You can also specify how the contents of the message box are copied. The default setting for this property is **Respect user's default**. In Outlook, the user can set the **When replying to a message** option on the **Reading** page of the **Options** dialog box (**Tools** menu). By default, this property is set for the user to **Include and indent original message text**. Therefore, if you have **Respect user's default** selected in the **When Responding** box, you can assume that for most users the message box on the reply form includes and indents the original message. If you want to override the user's **When replying to a message** preference, click another option in the When Responding box to explicitly define how you want the contents of the message box to appear on the Reply form.

Here are a few general guidelines for setting the **When responding** option for Message forms.

- If the amount of information in the original message is small, click **Include and indent the original message text**. As shown in the preceding Figure 7.10, this is the option that is selected for the Approve Vacation action in the Vacation Request form.

- If you want to include a shortcut to the message in the response item, click **Attach link to original message**.

### Address Form Like A

For Message forms, you almost always choose **Reply** for this option. When you choose **Reply**, The To field of the Reply form contains the contents of the From field of the original item, and the Cc field is empty. The Subject field, unless otherwise specified, contains RE:, followed by the contents of the Subject field of the original item.

The following table describes how the **Address form like a** options set up the Reply form.

| Option | Description |
| --- | --- |
| Reply | Sets up the Reply form so the To field contains the contents of the From field of the original item. The Cc field is empty. The Subject field contains RE:, followed by the contents of the Subject field of the original item. |
| Reply to All | Sets up the Reply form so the To field contains the contents of the From and Cc fields of the original item. The Subject field contains **RE:**, followed by the contents of the Subject field of the original item. |
| Forward | Sets up the form so the To and Cc fields are empty and the Subject field contains **FW:** followed by the contents of the Subject field of the original item. |
| Reply to Folder | Sets up the Reply form so the Post To field contains the active folder address, the Conversation field contains the subject of the original item, and the Subject field is empty. In most cases, the Conversation field is not visible on a form. The Conversation field contains the value of the Subject of the original item. |
| Response | Used exclusively for Voting button actions. |

## Show Action On

Most of the time, you can leave the default **Menu and Toolbar** option for a form. However, there might be times when you want to control the placement of the custom action buttons on the form. For example, you might want to add a command button to the bottom of the form and then write a macro for the command button to activate the Reply form when the button is clicked. If this is the case, you can click the **Menu only** option.

### This Action Will

For the Vacation Request form, the Approve action, when initiated, opens the Vacation Approved form. For most actions, you specify **Open the form** in the **This action will** box. However, there might be cases when you choose the **Send the form immediately** option. For example, you might send a form to a user requesting their updated phone number and address. Rather than opening a Reply form, the user can fill in the fields on the original form, and then click the custom action button. The Reply form is then activated, but isn't visible to the user. Values from the originating form are then copied to the Reply form. If you specify the **Send the form immediately** option, you must still create the Reply form. And you must ensure that the fields you want filled in on the invisible Reply form are included on the original form.

### Subject Prefix

Shows the prefix that appears in the **Subject** box of the Reply form. The prefix is **RE** by default. For example, for the Approve Vacation action, the **Approve** prefix appears in the **Subject** box of the Vacation Approved form. When the person who requested the vacation receives the Approved Vacation item in his Inbox, the text in the Subject column in the folder tells him his vacation is approved.

# How Field Values Are Copied to the Reply Form

Outlook does not provide a way to explicitly define the field values that are copied from custom fields on the original form to custom fields on the Reply form. Rather, you accomplish this by using the same fields for both forms, as shown in Figure 7.11. When the field is shared between the original and Reply form, the values are automatically copied from the original form to the Reply form at run time.

For example, the following fields are located on both the Vacation Request form and the Vacation Approved form. When an Approve Vacation action is initiated, the values in these fields are copied from the Vacation Request form to the Vacation Approved form.

- Subject
- TotalDays
- StartDate
- EndDate

**Figure 7.11   Values between fields common to both the original and Reply form are copied to the Reply form.**

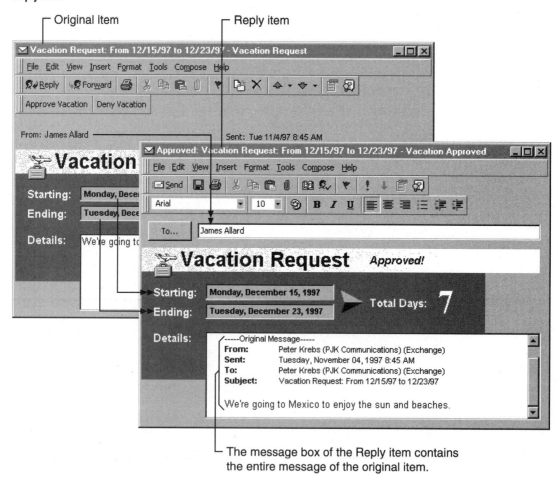

**Important**   To ensure that field values are copied between the original form and the Reply form, use the same fields for both forms. For example, for the Vacation Request applications, the TotalDays, StartDate, and EndDate fields are used for the Vacation Request form, the StartDate form, and the EndDate form.

**Note**   In Figure 7.11 the Subject field is not visible. Instead it is located on Page 2, a hidden page. The Subject text, however, is copied from the original item to the Reply item and does appear in the **Subject** box on the **Read** page of the Reply item.

# Vacation Request Reply Forms

In most cases, the custom Reply form is very similar to the original form. Quite often, you can use the original form as a template for the Reply form. For example, the Vacation Approved form is a Reply form based on the Vacation Request form. Only a few modifications have been made:

- The custom Reply actions are removed.

- The form **Description** is changed, as shown in Figure 7.12.

**Figure 7.12   The form description is changed for the Reply form.**

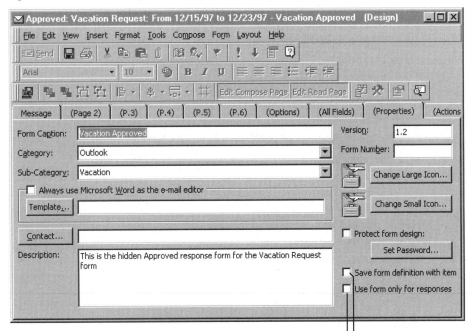

Select this check box after you are sure the Reply form is working correctly.

When this check box is selected, the form is included with the item.

# Publish Reply Forms

For Reply forms to work correctly, they must be available on the user's system. Before you publish the forms, however, it's a good idea to make a backup copy.

▶ **To make a backup copy of a form**

1   With the form in Design mode, click **Save As** on the **File** menu.

2   In the **Save In** box, select the folder where you want to save the form file.

3   In the **File name** box, type a name for the form.

4   Click **Save**.

After you make a backup copy of the form, you can publish it to one of the following forms libraries:

**Organization Forms Library**   Publish the form in this library if you want the form to be available to all users in your organization.

**Personal Forms Library**   Publish the form in this library if you intend to use the form for personal use. The Personal Forms Library is also a good place to publish forms when you want to test them.

**A Folder Forms Library**   Publish the form in a Folder Forms Library if the form is integrated with a folder.

**See Also**   For more information about where to publish forms, see Chapter 13, "Distribute and Maintain Applications."

▶ **To publish a form**

1   On the **Form Design** toolbar, click the **Publish Form As** button.

2   Click **Publish In**, select the forms library you want, and then click **OK**.

3   In the **Form name** box, type a name for the form, and then click **Publish**.

# Test the Forms

After you publish the forms to a forms library, you should run the forms to make sure they work as expected. For example, here's how you publish and test the Vacation Request forms.

▶ **Publish the Vacation Request forms**

1 In the Vacation Request folder, click **New Vacation Request** on the **Compose** menu.

2 On the **Tools** menu, click **Design Outlook Form** to switch to Design mode.

3 On the **Form Design** toolbar, click the **Publish Form As** button.

4 Click **Publish In**.

5 In the **Forms Library** box, click **Personal Forms** and then click **OK**.

6 Click **Publish**.

7 Close the form.

8 On the **Compose** menu, click **New Vacation Approved**, and then repeat steps 2 through 7.

9 On the **Compose** menu, click **New Vacation Denied**, and then repeat steps 2 through 7.

▶ **To test the Vacation Request forms:**

1 On the **Compose** menu, click **New Vacation Request**.

2 Address the form to yourself, and then click the **Send** button.

3 When the Vacation Request item arrives in your Inbox, double-click it to open it.

4 Click the **Approve Vacation** button.

5 Click **Send**.

6 When the Approved Vacation item arrives in your Inbox, double-click it to open it.

# Set the Hidden Properties for the Response Forms

After you publish and test the forms, you select the **Hidden** option for response forms, so the response forms can only be opened as a response to an item. For example, if the **Hidden** check box is selected for the Vacation Approved form and the form is published in the Personal Forms Library, the Vacation Approved form name does not appear in the forms list in the **New Form** dialog box. Users can only open the form when an associated Vacation Request item is selected in the Inbox or when the Vacation Request item is opened in Read mode.

▶ **To set the Hidden property for the Product Idea Response form**

**1** On the **Tools** menu, click **Options**.

**2** Click the **Manage Forms** page, and then click **Manage Forms**.

**3** Note that the upper-right form library box is set to Personal Forms.

**4** In the lower-right library box, click **Vacation Request**, and then click **Properties**.

**5** Select the **Hidden** check box, and then click **OK**.

**6** Repeat steps 4 and 5 for the Vacation Approved and Vacation Denied forms.

**7** Click **Close** and then click **OK**.

## Custom Reply Forms for Users Not on Your Microsoft Exchange System

Sometimes, you may want to create forms that are used between your company and another company over the Internet. For example, let's assume you have a Legal Approval form and Legal Approval Response form and you want to use the forms between your company and an attorney's office. Also assume that the attorney has Outlook, but is not on your Microsoft Exchange system. For this scenario to work correctly, the attorney must have both the Legal Approval Response form installed on her system—either in the Organization Forms or Personal Forms Library.

**Note**  If the Reply form specified by an action is not available on the user's system, Outlook opens the standard Message form in its place.

**See Also**  For more information about where to publish forms, see Chapter 13, "Distribute and Maintain Applications."

# Reply to Folder Actions for Post Forms

When creating applications with Post forms, you can create custom actions so users can reply to items in a folder using custom forms, rather than the standard Post form. In this section, we use the Training Management application for examples of how to implement Reply to Folder actions for Post forms.

▶ **To open the Training Management folder**

- In the Folder List, expand the **Building Microsoft Outlook 97 Applications** folder, and then expand the **3. Building Blocks** folder. Then click the **Training Management** folder.

# Overview of the Training Management Application

The Training Management application enables training personnel to create an entire course catalog in the Training Management folder. To create the catalog, administrators first post Course Catalog Entry items in the folder. Course Catalog Entry items contain a general description of the course. After Course Catalog Entry items have been posted, training administrators can post Course Offering items as responses to the Course Catalog Entry items, as shown in Figure 7.13. After students complete a course, they can post an Evaluation item as a response to the Course Offering item.

**Figure 7.13   The Training Management folder**

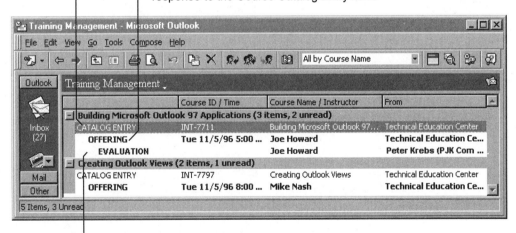

First, the administrator posts a Course Catalog Entry item in the folder.

The Course Offering item is posted as a response to the Course Catalog Entry item.

The Evaluation item is posted as a response to the Course Offering item.

The Training Management application contains the following forms:

**Course Catalog Entry form**   This form enables the administrator to post an item that contains general information about a course, such as the Course ID, cost, name, target audience, and course description. The **Read** page of the form enables an administrator to view the course offering information and to open a Course Offering response item.

**Figure 7.14   The Read page of the Course Catalog Entry form**

┌─ The Course Catalog Entry form contains the original item.

  ┌─ The training administrator clicks here
    to create a response to the original item.

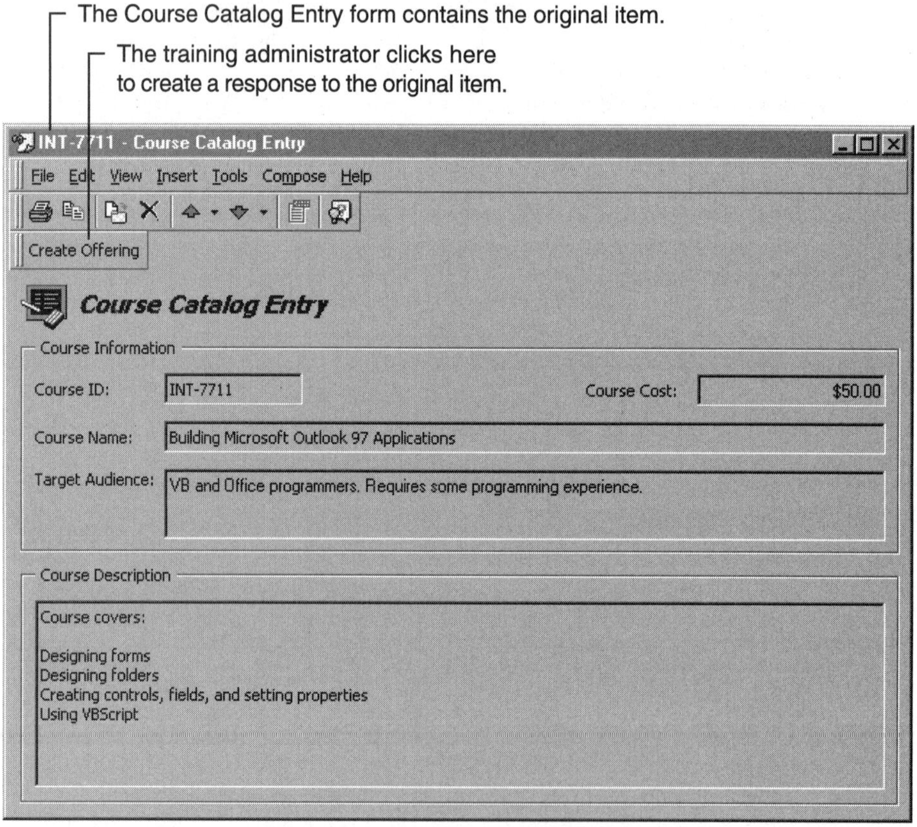

**Course Offering Form**   The Course Offering form enables an administrator post a Course Offering item in the Training Management folder. The Course Offering item, which contains specifics about the course such as class time and instructor, is posted as a response to the Course Catalog Entry item. The **Read** page of the Course Offering form shows two custom buttons: a **Signup** button that lets students register for a class and a **Course Evaluation** button that lets students post a course evaluation in the Training Management folder.

**Figure 7.15   The Compose page of the Course Offering form**

The administrator clicks here to post the Course Offering
Response item in the Training Management folder.

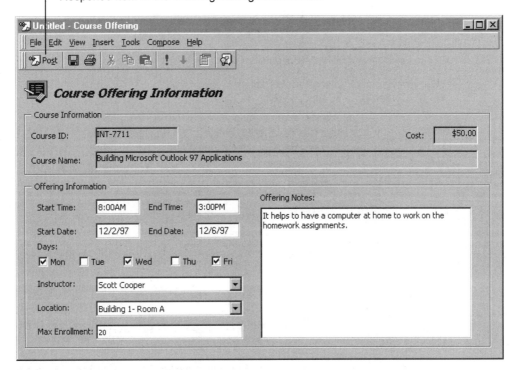

**Signup form**   This form enables a student to send a Signup item to the Course
Registration folder. We won't cover this part of the application in this section.

**Evaluation form**   This form enables students to post an Evaluation item as a response
to a Course Offering item. We won't cover this part of the application in this section.

In the rest of this section, we look at the custom actions of the Course Catalog Entry
form. First, we examine how the actions work in the folder. Then we look at how the
fields are copied from the Course Catalog Entry form to the Course Offering form.
Finally, we look at how response items are organized in a custom view in the Training
Management folder.

# Actions for the Course Catalog Entry Form

Now let's take a look at the **Actions** page for the Course Catalog Entry form, as
shown in Figure 7.16.

▶ **To view the Actions page of the Course Catalog Entry form**

1   On the **Compose** menu of the Training Management folder, click **New Course Catalog Entry**.

2   On the Course Catalog Entry form **Tools** menu , click **Design Outlook Form**.

3   Click the **Actions** page, as shown in Figure 7.16.

**Figure 7.16   The Actions page for the Course Catalog Entry form**

The Reply to Folder action is not enabled
for the Course Catalog Entry form.

The Create Offering action is a custom action that
causes a **Create Offering** command button to be placed
on the **Read** page of the Course Catalog Entry form.

The **Actions** page

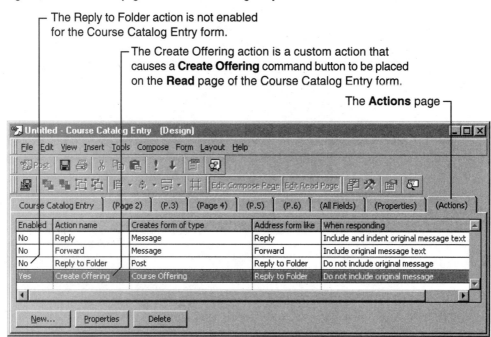

## Make the Reply to Folder Action Unavailable

Here is a simple rule to remember:

**Rule**   If you create a custom Reply to Folder action for a form, set the Enabled option to No for the standard Reply to Folder so the action is not available.

As shown in Figure 7.16, the **Reply to Folder** command is not available for the Course Catalog Entry form. This is done to prevent the user from posting standard Post form items in the Training Management folder. You can also do this for the Reply and Forward actions.

▶ **To make the Reply to Folder action unavailable**

1   On the **Actions** page, double-click the **Reply to Folder** action.

2   Clear the **Enabled** check box.

# New Post to Folder Actions

With new Post to Folder actions, you can specify that custom command buttons and menu commands are added to the form. The menu commands or buttons, when clicked, open a custom form that enables the user to post a response item to the folder. For example, the Course Catalog Entry form has a custom Course Offering action. When an administrator opens a Course Catalog Entry item in his Inbox, he can click the **Course Offering** button as shown in Figure 7.17.

**Figure 7.17   The Create Offering button is added to the Read page of the Course Catalog Entry form. When clicked, it opens the Compose page of the Course Offering form.**

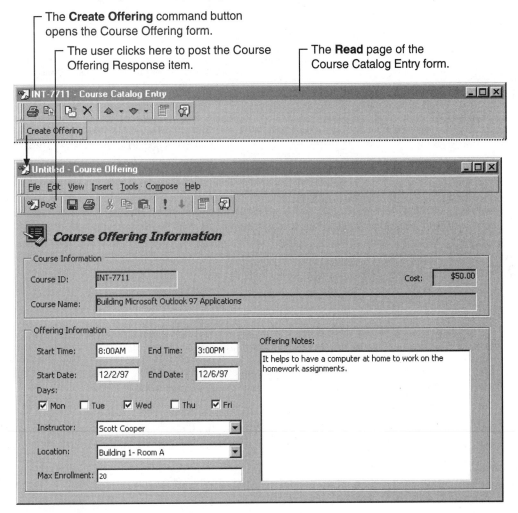

— The **Create Offering** command button opens the Course Offering form.

— The user clicks here to post the Course Offering Response item.

— The **Read** page of the Course Catalog Entry form.

# The Create Offering Action

Now let's take a look at the options that make up the Create Offering action, as shown in Figure 7.18.

▶ **To view the Course Offering action**

- On the **Actions** page, double-click the **Create Offering** action.

**Figure 7.18   The properties for the Create Offering action**

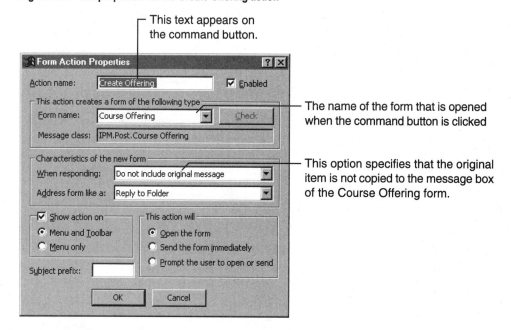

┌ This text appears on
  the command button.

The name of the form that is opened
when the command button is clicked

This option specifies that the original
item is not copied to the message box
of the Course Offering form.

## Action Name

On Post forms, the Action Name option defines the name of the menu command and action button that open the associated Reply to folder form.

The custom **Create Offering** command button appears on the **Read** page of the Course Catalog Entry form. The custom menu command appears in two places:

- On the **Compose** menu on the Outlook toolbar when an item created with the associated form is selected in a folder. For example, the **Create Offering** command appears on the **Compose** menu when a Course Catalog Entry item is selected in the Inbox.

- On the **Compose** menu of the **Read** page of the Course Catalog Entry form.

## Form Name and Message Class

The form name is the name of the form that opens when the command button or menu command is clicked. The message class, the internal identifier for the form, is automatically supplied for you in the **Message class** box. The **Form name** box contains the names of the forms published in the current folder, so you see the Training Management forms in the **Form name** box.

▶ **To specify a form name**

- Do one of the following:

  - In the **Form name** box, type a form name, and then click **Check** to search for the form.

    If Outlook cannot find the form, you see a message box that explains that Outlook can't find the form. If this happens, you should create the Response form before you specify the **Form name** option. After you create the Response form and publish it in a forms library, you can then return to the original form and click the name of the Response form in the **Form name** box.

  - In the **Form name** box, click a form name to specify the form that is activated when the user clicks an action menu command or command button.

  - In the **Form name** box, click **Forms** to open the **New Form** dialog box. In the first box, click the library, and then in the box below it double-click the form you want.

## Characteristics of the New Form

Under **Characteristics of the new form**, you specify how values from the original item are copied to the Response item.

### When Responding

When creating actions, remember that the original message can only be copied only to the message box of the Response item. So, if the Response form does not have a message box, as is the case with the Course Offering form, then the message cannot be copied.

**Rule**  If the Response form does not have a message box, then specify **Do not include original message** in the **When responding** box.

Generally with Post forms you should be very careful about including the original message, especially if the message is very large.

### Address Form Like A

For Post forms, you always choose **Reply to Folder** for the **Address form like a** option. **Reply to Folder** sets up the response form so the Post To field of the Response form contains the active folder address, the Conversation field contains the subject of the original item, and the Subject field is empty.

### Show Action On

Most of the time, you can specify the default **Menu and Toolbar** option. However, there may be times when you want to place action buttons in a custom location on the form. To do this, you can add a command button to the form, and then create a procedure for the command button to open the Response form when the command button is clicked.

**See Also**  For more information about creating procedures for forms, see Chapter 9, "Use Visual Basic Scripting Edition with Outlook."

### This Action Will

For the Course Catalog Entry form, when the Create Offering action is initiated, it opens the Course Offering form. For most Reply to Folder actions, you specify **Open the form** in the **This action will** box.

### Subject Prefix

When the **Reply to Folder** option is selected in the **Address form like a** box, the Subject field of the Response item is cleared. So, in most cases, you leave the **Subject Prefix** box blank when **Reply to Folder** is selected.

# How Field Values Are Copied to the Response Form

Earlier in this chapter, we learned that values from shared fields—those fields that are common between the original item and the Response item—are copied from the original item to the Response item.

When the **Reply to Folder** option is selected in the **Address form like a** box for an action, the same principles apply. Values from shared fields are copied from the original item to the Response item. However, there is one exception.

**Important**  When the **Reply to Folder** option is selected in the **Address form like a** box, the value from the Subject field is not copied from the original item to the Response item. Instead, the value of the Subject field of the original item is copied to the Conversation field of the Response item and the Subject field in the Response item is blank.

In Figure 7.19 there is no Subject field visible on either form. Instead the Subject field is hidden on (Page 2) and bound to the CourseID field, so when a form is opened, the value of the CourseID field appears in the title bar of the form. That's because the value in the item's Subject field always appears in the title bar of the form. Also, there is no message box on either form, so the original item is not copied to the Response item.

When the Create Offering action is started, as shown in Figure 7.19, the values in these fields are copied from the Course Catalog Entry form to the Course Offering form.

- CourseID
- CourseCost
- CourseName

**Figure 7.19   Values between fields common to both the original and Response form are copied to the Response form.**

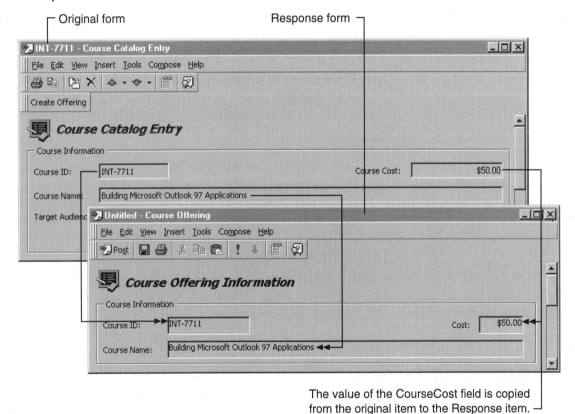

The value of the CourseCost field is copied from the original item to the Response item.

**Rule**   To make sure field values are copied between the original form and the Response form, use the same fields for both forms. For example, for the Training Management application, the CourseID, CourseCost, and CourseName fields are used for both the Course Catalog Entry form and the Course Offering form.

# Create Response Forms

Generally, I recommend that you create all Response forms for an application before you create form actions. For example, for the Training Management application, you create the Course Catalog Entry form, and then you create the Course Offering form. After you've created the Course Offering form, you then return to the Course Catalog Entry form and create a Create Offering action that specifies the Course Offering form as the **Form name** option.

In some cases, the Response form is very similar to the original form so you can use the original form as a template. Other times, its quicker to start from scratch. In the case of the Course Offering Response form, either approach can be used.

# Publish the Forms to the Folder Forms Library

When you create actions for a form, you must make sure that the forms that are opened as a result of the action are published in the Folder Forms Library. Before you publish the forms, however, it's a good idea to make a backup copy of them.

▶ **To make a backup copy of a form**

1  With the form in Design mode, click **Save As** on the **File** menu.

2  In the **Save in** box, select the folder where you want to save the form file.

3  In the **File name** box, type a name for the form.

4  Click **Save**.

▶ **To publish a form in the Folder Forms Library**

1  On the **Form Design** toolbar, click the **Publish Form As** button.

2  If the text next to the **Publish In** button does not reflect the active folder, click **Publish In**, select the Folder Forms Library you want, and then click **OK**.

3  Click **Publish**.

# Test the Forms

After you create actions and custom forms to respond to the actions, you should run the forms to make sure they work as expected. For example, here is a quick way to test the forms and their actions in the Training Management application.

▶ **To test the forms in the Training Management application**

1   In the Folder List, click the **Training Management** folder.

2   On the **Compose** menu, click **New Course Catalog Entry**.

3   Fill in the Course Catalog Entry form, and then click **Post**.

4   In the **Training Management** folder, double-click the Course Catalog Entry item you just posted.

5   Click the **Create Offering** button.

6   Fill in the Course Offering form, and then click **Post**.

    The Course Offering item is posted as a response to the Course Catalog Entry item. As such, it is indented in the folder.

7   Optionally, you can double-click the Course Offering item, and then click **Create Evaluation** or **Signup** on the form.

    The Signup form is a Message form that routes course registration information to a course administrator or public folder. If you like, you can Signup send the message to your Inbox as a test. The Course Evaluation form is a custom Response form that posts a Response Evaluation item in the Training Management folder.

# Set the Hidden Property for Response Forms

After you publish and test forms, you set the **Hidden** property for the response forms. For example, the following procedure sets the **Hidden** property for the response forms in the Training Management folder.

▶ **To set the Hidden property for the Training Management Response forms**

1   In the Folder List, right-click the Training Management folder, and then click **Properties** on the shortcut menu.

2   Click the **Forms** page, and then click **Manage**.

3   In the lower-right box, click **Course Offering**, and then click **Properties**.

4   Select the **Hidden** check box, and then click **OK**.

5   In the lower-right box, click **Course Evaluation**, and then click **Properties**.

6   Select the **Hidden** check box, and then click **OK**.

7   In the lower-right box, click **SignUp**, and then click **Properties**.

8   Select the **Hidden** check box, and then click **OK**.

9   Click **Close**, and then click **OK**.

# CHAPTER 8

# Folders

## In This Chapter

A Quick Reminder About Planning   225
Create or Select a Folder   225
Publish Forms in the Folder   228
Design Folder Views   232
Set General Properties   256
Test Forms and Views   257
Copy the Folder to Public Folders   257
Set Administration Properties   258
Set Permissions   260
Design Rules   262
Test and Release the Folder   268

With Outlook, you can create a wide variety of folders to help users share, organize, and track information in your organization. Here are just a few examples:

- **Discussion folders that provide a public forum for users to submit, share, and respond to ideas and information**   For example, you can create a discussion folder for posting job openings, job candidate information, and interview responses for a candidate. Or you can create a Technical Users Group folder, such as the HTML folder at Microsoft where writers and designers can post, read, and share information and solutions to problems.

- **Reference folders that provide a place to store and organize information**   For example, you can create a Product Specification Library that stores Microsoft Word documents. In addition, you can create a Reference Library that stores Web addresses or a Project Library that stores a variety of materials such as data sheets, PowerPoint presentations, Visual Basic prototypes, or Microsoft Excel workbooks.

- **Tracking folders that enable users to record and review information that is constantly updated**  For example, you can create an application such as the sample Help Desk application, so users and help desk technicians can schedule appointments and track the status of help desk requests.

This chapter takes an in-depth look at creating public folders, discusses how to manage forms, and looks at creating custom views. It also cover how to set folder permissions and create rules for a folder. In this chapter, the folder design process is broken into steps. Each step is clearly marked with a numbered graphic block. Within each step, you can find detailed information that helps you to complete the step.

For the majority of examples in this chapter, the sample Classified Ads folder is used, as shown in Figure 8.1.

▶ **To open the Classified Ads folder**

- In the Folder List, expand the **Building Microsoft Outlook 97 Applications** folder, expand the **3. Building Blocks** folder, and then click the **Classified Ads** folder.

**Figure 8.1  The Classified Ads folder**

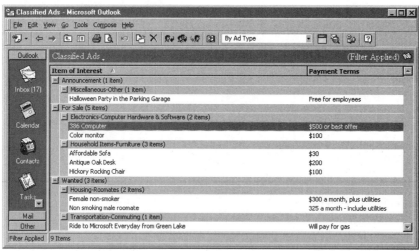

# A Quick Reminder About Planning

To create folders that meet the needs of your users, it helps to first plan them. While planning processes differ with each organization and application, there are general steps you can follow when planning a public folder:

- Determine who will plan, design, and implement the folder.

- Identify folder users and their needs.

- Create a design plan that identifies the problems to be solved and how the folder will solve them. The design plan should include preliminary graphics of form windows or views to be created.

# Create or Select a Folder

With Outlook, you can design a folder by using one of three methods.

| Method | Use when |
| --- | --- |
| Create a new folder from scratch | You cannot find an existing folder in your organization that closely matches the folder you want to create. In this case, it's quicker to start from scratch. |
| Modify an existing folder that is in public use | You want to make minor changes to a folder, such as adding permissions or a view. |
| Copy the design of an existing folder to a new folder, and then modify the new folder | You want to create a new folder based on the design of an existing folder. Or you want to make changes to an existing folder and those changes will disrupt users' work. |

# Choose Where to Design the New Folder

If the method of folder design you choose requires that you create a new folder, you can create the folder in Public Folders, your Outlook Mailbox, or Personal Folders. The location determines whether the folder is public or private and determines the design properties you can set for the folder.

Designing a new folder in a personal folder is highly recommended. In a personal folder, you can create forms and design views, and then test them to make sure they work as expected. After you create forms and design views, you or the administrator can copy the folder to Public Folders where you can complete the design of the folder by setting permissions and administration properties.

The following table shows the attributes that you can set in each folder location.

| Option | In a personal folder | In a mailbox folder | In a public folder |
|---|---|---|---|
| Copy or install forms | x | x | x |
| Design views | x | x | x |
| Designate the types of items allowed in the folder | | | x |
| Set permissions | | | x |
| Set administration properties | some | some | all |
| Define rules | | | x |

# Create a Folder from Scratch

One way to design a folder is to create a new folder. After you create the folder, you can follow the design process outlined in this chapter, beginning with Step 2, "Publish Forms in the Folder."

▶ **To create a folder**

1  In the Folder List, right-click a personal folder you want to create a folder in, and then click **Create Subfolder** on the shortcut menu.

2  In the **Name** box, enter a name for the folder.

3  In the **Folder contains** box, do one of the following:

   • Click **Mail Items** to create a folder that will contain items created with Message, Post, or Office Document forms.

   • Click **Appointment Items**, **Contact Items**, **Journal Items**, **Note Items**, or **Task Items** to create a folder that will contain items of the associated type. For example, if you click **Appointment Items**, Outlook creates a Calendar folder.

4  In the **Description** box, type a description for the form.

5  Clear the **Create a shortcut to this folder in the Outlook Bar** check box.

6  Click **OK**.

# Directly Modify a Folder

If a folder is in public use, it's best to directly modify the folder only if the changes are minor and will not disrupt users' work. Minor changes include adding permissions, adding a view, or changing a folder contact.

To make more significant changes such as modifying forms or rules, copy the design of the folder to another folder, modify the design, as described in "Copy a Folder Design" below, and then copy the modified design back to the original folder.

**Note**   To modify a folder, you must have owner permissions for the folder. To check your permissions for a folder, right-click the folder, and then click **Properties** on the shortcut menu. You can view your permissions on the **Permissions** page.

▶ **To directly modify a folder**

1   In the Folder List, right-click the folder, and then click **Properties** on the shortcut menu.

2   In the **Properties** dialog box, make the changes you want to the folder, and then click **OK**.

# Copy a Folder Design

To create or modify a folder, you can copy the design of an existing folder to a new folder. You can then customize the design of the new folder.

Copying a folder design involves copying design components, such as forms and views, from one folder to another. When a folder design is copied, the folder permissions and rules are always maintained, regardless of whether the folder design is copied to or copied from a folder in a personal folder or a public folder.

When Outlook copies the design to a folder, it merges the design components of the source folder with design components of the destination folder. If two properties conflict—for example, the permissions for a user in the source folder are different from the permissions in the destination folder—the properties in the destination folder take precedence. This ensures that none of the design components in the destination folder are overwritten.

**Note**   To modify a folder, you must have owner permissions for the folder. To check your permissions for a folder, right-click the folder, and then click **Properties** on the shortcut menu. You can view your permissions on the **Permissions** page. To copy permissions, rules, forms, and views, you must have owner permissions for the folder.

▶ **To copy a folder design**

**1** In the Folder List, click the folder you want to copy the design to.

**2** On the **File** menu, point to **Folder**, and then click **Copy Folder Design**.

**3** In the **Copy design from this folder** box, select the folder you want to copy the design from.

**4** Under **Copy design of**, select one or more of the following.

| To | Select |
| --- | --- |
| Copy permissions from the source folder | **Permissions** |
| Copy the rules associated with the source folder | **Rules** |
| Copy the description of the source folder | **Description** |
| Copy forms and views that are stored in the source folder | **Forms & Views** |

**5** Click **OK**.

# Publish Forms in the Folder

Not all folders require custom forms. But for those folders that do, you must first design the forms, and then publish them in a Folder Forms Library. When you publish a form in a Folder Forms Library, you accomplish two things:

- You make the form available in the folder, so it can be opened by users to compose and view items in the folder.

- You expose the form properties, such as form name, description, and menu commands, in Outlook.

▶ **To publish a form in a Folder Forms Library**

**1** First, the form must be in Design mode. To switch a form from Run mode to Design mode, click **Design Outlook Form** on the **Tools** menu.

**2** After you make changes to a form, click the **Publish Form As** button on the **Form Design** toolbar.

**3** In the **Form name** box, type the name for the form.

To change the location (library) where the form is published, click **Publish In**, and then select the folder where you want to publish the form.

**4** Click **Publish**.

**See Also**   For more information about creating and publishing forms, see Chapter 5, "Forms."

# Manage Forms

With the **Forms** page of the folder **Properties** dialog box, as shown in Figure 8.2, you can see the forms that are published in a Folder Forms Library. In addition, you can specify the types of items that can be submitted in the folder. You can also use the **Forms** page to access the Forms Manager. With the Forms Manager, you can copy and delete forms, and view form properties.

▶ **To view the Forms page**

1  In the Folder List, right-click the folder, and then click **Properties** on the shortcut menu.

2  Click the **Forms** page.

**Figure 8.2   The Forms page shows the forms that are published in the Folder Forms Library.**

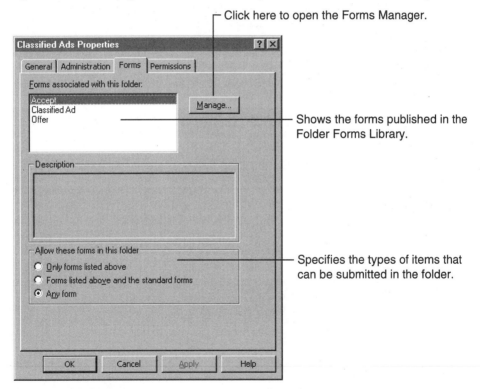

Click here to open the Forms Manager.

Shows the forms published in the Folder Forms Library.

Specifies the types of items that can be submitted in the folder.

**Tip**   You can also access the Forms Manager by clicking **Options** on the Outlook **Tools** menu. Click the **Manage Forms** tab, and then click **Manage Forms**.

## Specify the Types of Items Allowed in the Folder

In many folders, you may want to control the types of items that can be submitted. For example, in the Classified Ads folder, you want to prevent the user from submitting standard post items to the folder because they are out of context and do not appear correctly in the custom views created for the folder.

▶ **To specify the types of items allowed in the folder**

- On the **Forms** page, under **Allow these forms in this folder**, click one of the following.

| To specify that | Click |
|---|---|
| Only items created with the forms specified in the **Forms associated with this folder** box can be submitted in the folder | **Only forms listed above** |
| Only items created with the forms in the **Forms associated with this folder** box and standard Post and Message forms can be submitted in the folder | **Forms listed above and the standard forms** |
| Any type of item can be submitted in the folder | **Any form** |

## Copy and Delete Forms or Set the Hidden Property for a Form

You can use the Forms Manager, as shown in Figure 8.3, to copy and delete forms and to view form properties.

▶ **To open the Forms Manager**

- On the **Forms** page, click **Manage**.

**Figure 8.3   The Forms Manager dialog box**

Click here to select the
source forms library for
a Copy operation.

Shows forms in the selected forms library.

Shows the active folder.

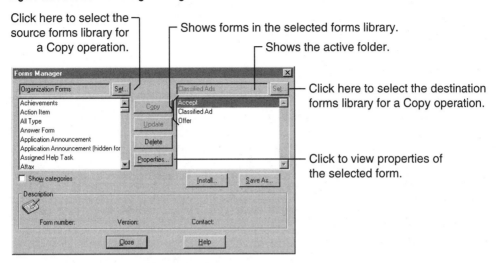

Click here to select the destination
forms library for a Copy operation.

Click to view properties of
the selected form.

If the form that you want to use already exists in your organization and is published in a forms library, you can copy it to the forms library of the folder you're designing. By default, the left box in the **Forms Manager** dialog box shows the contents of the Organization Forms Library and the right box shows the contents of the active Folder Forms Library. The left box is the source forms library from which you can copy forms. The right box is the destination forms library where you copy the forms to. You can easily change the libraries shown in these boxes.

▶ **To change the library in the left or right box of Forms Manager**

1   Choose **Set** for the box that contains the library you want to change.

2   Do one of the following:

- In the **Forms Library** box, click the library you want.

- In the **Folder Forms Library** box, click the folder you want.

▸ **To copy a form to a folder**

• In the left box, click the form you want to copy, and then click **Copy**.

▸ **To delete a form**

• In the right box, click the form you want to delete, and then click **Delete**.

## View Forms Properties or Set the Hidden Property for a Form

With the **Properties** dialog box, you can view a form's properties, and you can set the **Hidden** property for a form. When you select the **Hidden** property for a form, you specify that the form's associated menu command is not visible in the Outlook user interface, so users can only create response items with the form or view items with the form. In addition, forms published in the Personal Forms Library or the Organization Forms Library with the **Hidden** property selected are not visible to the user in the **New Form** dialog box.

▸ **To view the properties of a form**

• In the right box, click the form whose properties you want to view, and then click **Properties**.

▸ **To set the Hidden property for a form**

1  In the right-hand box, click the form that you want to set the **Hidden** property for, and then click **Properties**.

2  Select the **Hidden** check box, and then click **OK**.

**Important**   The **Install** and **Save As** buttons are not valid for Outlook forms. They are intended for use with forms created for Microsoft Exchange Client.

# Design Folder Views

To help users organize and manage the information stored in folders, you can create folder views. With views, users can organize and view the same information in different ways within the folder. With Outlook, you can create table, timeline, card, day/week/month, and icon view types.

This chapter focuses on the most commonly used type of view, the table view. When creating table views, you work with the following view features of Outlook:

• **Columns**   As shown in Figure 8.4, columns show values for a particular field in an item under the column heading.

- **Groups**   With groups, you can create categories of items that share a common field value. As shown in Figure 8.4, items in the By Category view are grouped by the type of ad. Groups can be expanded or collapsed.

- **Sort**   You can sort the items in a group based on the criteria you specify. For example, you can sort items by the date received, by field values, or alphabetically.

- **Filter**   With Outlook filters, you create criteria that specifies the items to be shown in the folder. For example, in Figure 8.4, the filter applied to the folder specifies that only items created with the CreateAd form are shown in the folder.

- **Format**   With the **Format** dialog box, you can specify fonts, grid lines, and in-cell editing for a folder. With in-cell editing, users can change information in a cell in the folder.

**Figure 8.4   The view chosen by the user determines how items are organized in the folder.**

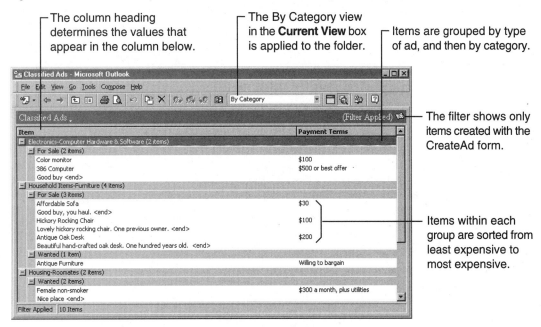

The column heading determines the values that appear in the column below.

The By Category view in the **Current View** box is applied to the folder.

Items are grouped by type of ad, and then by category.

The filter shows only items created with the CreateAd form.

Items within each group are sorted from least expensive to most expensive.

# Create a New View

Each view you create is given a name that appears in the **Current View** box on the **Standard** toolbar, as shown in the preceding illustration in Figure 8.4. When the view name is clicked in the **Current View** box, the view is applied to the folder and the items in the folder are arranged according to the criteria specified in the view.

▶ **To create a new view**

1   On the **View** menu, click **Define Views**.

2   Click **New**.

3   In the **Name of new view** box, type a name.

4   In the **Type of view** box, click the type of view you want.

5   Click **OK** twice.

6   Click **Apply View**.

## Show Only the Views Created for the Folder

For each folder you create, Outlook provides several standard views in the **Current View** box. In many cases, these views are not relevant to your folder, so you can remove them from the **Current View** box. If you want to remove the standard views from the **Current View** box, and show only the custom views you create, you can select the **Show only the views created for this folder** check box, as shown in Figure 8.5.

▶ **To show only the custom views created for the folder**

1   On the **View** menu, click **Define Views**.

2   Select the **Show only those views created for only this folder** check box.

3   Click **Close**.

**Figure 8.5   The Show Only Those Views Created For Only This Folder check box specifies that the standard views are not shown in the Current View box on the Standard toolbar.**

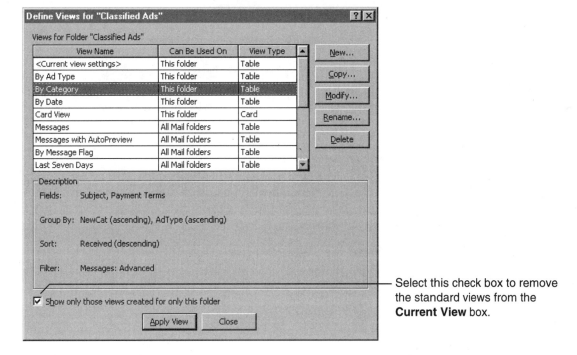

Select this check box to remove the standard views from the **Current View** box.

# Create Columns

With Outlook, you can create columns by dragging fields from the Field Chooser to the column heading row. When you add a column to a view, the column shows the value of the field for each of the items in the view, as shown in Figure 8.6.

**Figure 8.6   Columns for the By Ad Type view in the Classified Ads folder**

┌ Under this column heading, you      ┌ Under this column heading, you
  see the values from the Subject        see the values from the Payment
  field of each item.                     Terms field of each item.

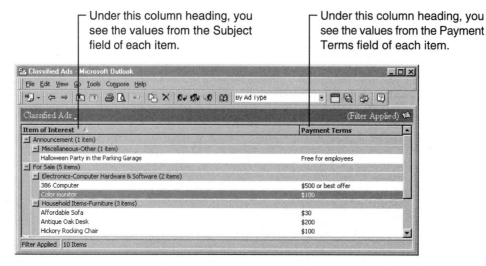

▶ **To add a column to a view**

**1** On the **View** menu, click **Field Chooser**.

**2** In the **Field Set** box in the **Field Chooser**, click the field set you want to choose fields from.

**3** Drag the field you want as the new column heading to the column heading row, as shown in Figure 8.7. Use the double-arrow marker to position the new column heading in the column heading row.

**Figure 8.7   The Payment Terms field is added to the column heading row.**

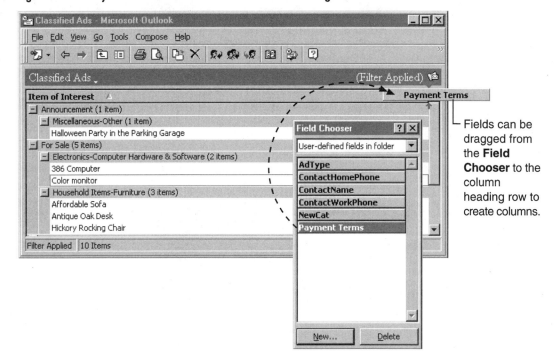

Fields can be dragged from the **Field Chooser** to the column heading row to create columns.

▶ **To remove a column from a view**

• Drag the column heading away from the column heading row until an **X** appears through the column heading, and then release the mouse button.

## Format Columns

By default, a column heading has the same label as the field on which it is based. For example, the Payment Terms column heading is identical to the Payment Terms field. In some cases, however, you may want to change the column heading label so it is different than the field name. Such is the case with the Item of Interest column heading in the By Ad Type view.

On the Classified Ads form, the Subject field on the form is labeled Item of Interest, as shown in Figure 8.8. In this case, the Subject field is used for the form because the Subject field provides the unique ability to display its value in the caption on the form window. Much as the label for a field can be changed on the form, the label can also be changed in the column heading of the view. For example, for the By Ad Type view, as shown earlier in Figures 8.6 and 8.7, the column heading for the Subject field is Item Of Interest. This is accomplished by changing the label for the field in the **Format Columns** dialog box, as shown in Figure 8.8.

**Figure 8.8   The Subject field is labeled Item of Interest. The value of the field appears in the window caption.**

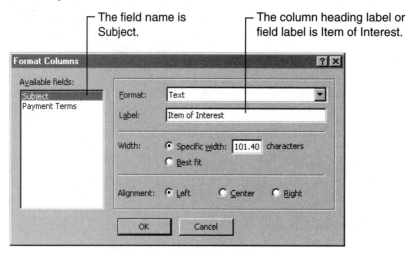

**To change the format properties of a column**

1   Right-click the column heading you want to format, and then click **Format Columns** on the shortcut menu.

2   In the **Available fields** box, click the field you want to format, and then make the changes you want.

3   Click **OK**.

## Create Combination Columns

In some cases, you may want to add Combination fields to a view. To help demonstrate the point, this section shows you an example of a Volunteer Registration application. Note that this application is merely an example and is not included in the Building Microsoft Outlook 97 Applications folder.

With the fields on the Volunteer Registration form, as shown in Figure 8.9, a user can enter his or her first name, last name, address, city, and postal code in separate fields.

**Figure 8.9   The Volunteer Registration form**

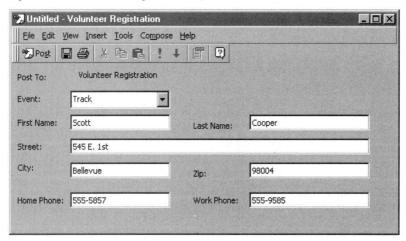

Now, assume you want to create a column in the Volunteer Registration view that combines the VolunteerFirstName and VolunteerLastName field values and shows them in a single Name column, as shown in Figure 8.10. To do this, you create a combination column.

**Figure 8.10   The Volunteer Registration folder**

The Name column combines values from the VolunteerFirstName and VolunteerLastName fields.

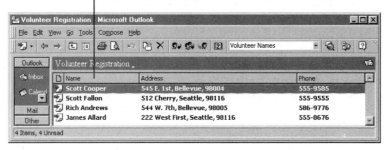

## Create a Combination Column That Combines Text Fragments

There are two kinds of combination fields you can create: those that combine text fragments and those that show the value of the first non-empty field. This section shows you how to create a combination column that combines text fragments. The next section shows you to create a combination column that shows only the value of the first non-empty field.

▶ **To create a combination column**

1 On the **View** menu, click **Field Chooser**.

2 Click **New**.

3 In the **Name** box, type a name.

4 In the **Type** box, click **Combination**.

5 Click **Edit**.

6 Click **Field** to add the fields you want to combine, and the click **OK** twice.

7 From the **Field Chooser**, drag the field you want as the new column heading to the column heading row. Use the double-arrow marker to position the new column heading in the column heading row.

In some cases, you may want to change the label of the combination column so it is different from the field name. In addition, you may want to change the formula specified for the combination column. To do this, you use the **Format Columns** dialog box, as shown in Figure 8.11.

▶ **To change a combination column label or formula**

1 Right-click the column heading, and then click **Format Columns** on the shortcut menu.

2 In the **Available fields** box, select the field whose properties you want to set, and do one or both of the following:

   • To change the formula, click the button next to the **Formula** box.

   • To change the column label, change the text in the **Label** box.

3 Click **OK**.

**Figure 8.11  The format properties for the Name column in the Volunteer Registration folder**

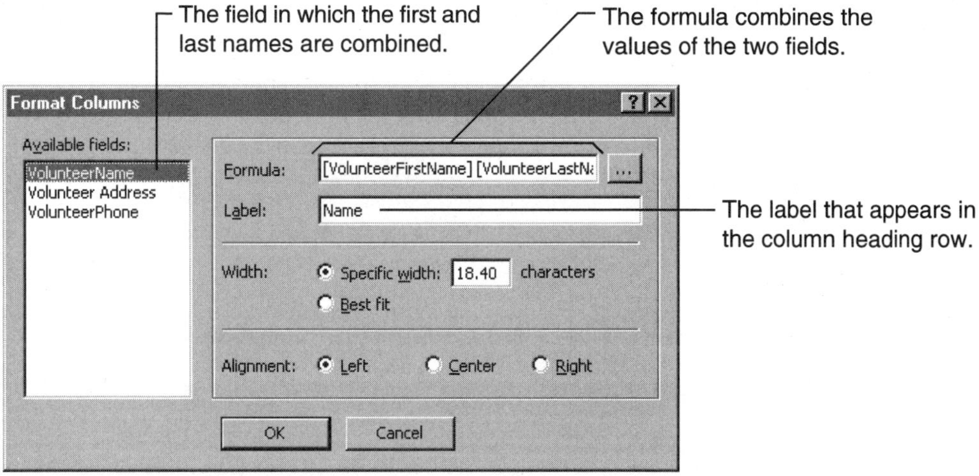

The field in which the first and last names are combined.

The formula combines the values of the two fields.

The label that appears in the column heading row.

## Create a Combination Column That Shows Only the Value of the First Non-Empty Field

In some cases, you may want to create a column that shows only the value of the first non-empty field in the item. For example, you may want to create a combination column if you have multiple item types in the folder, and the items have fields with similar values but different field names. Assume you have documents and standard post items in a folder and you want to create an Author column. Rather than creating a From column for post items and an Author column for document items, you can create an Author/From field, and then click the **Showing only the first non-empty field, ignoring subsequent ones** option.

▶ **To create a combination column that shows only the value of the first non-empty field**

1  On the **View** menu, click **Field Chooser**.

2  Click **New**.

3  In the **Name** box, type a name.

4  In the **Type** box, click **Combination**.

5  Click **Edit**.

6  Click **Showing only the first non-empty field, ignoring subsequent ones**.

7  Click **Field** to add the fields you want to combine, and then click **OK** twice.

8  From the **Field Chooser**, drag the field you want as the new column heading to the column heading row. Use the double-arrow marker to position the new column heading in the column heading row.

# Create Formula Columns

For some views, you may want to show different field values in the folder. For example, in the sample Training Management folder, as shown in Figure 8.12, the Course ID/Time and Course Name/Instructor columns are formula columns. In the Course ID/Time column, the value of the CourseID field is shown in the column if the item is a Catalog Entry item. If the item is a Course Offering item, the value of the StartTime field is shown in the column.

**Figure 8.12   The formula for the Course ID/Time column shows a different field value for each message class.**

The value from the CourseID field is shown for a Catalog Entry item.

The value from the StartTime field is shown for the Course Offering item.

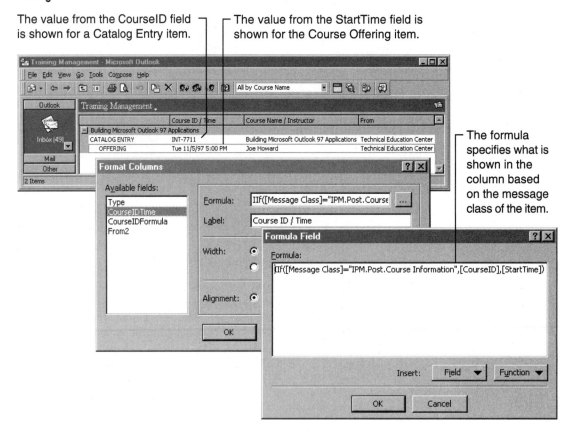

The formula specifies what is shown in the column based on the message class of the item.

▶ **To create a formula column**

1  On the **View** menu, click **Field Chooser**.

2  Click **New**.

3  In the **Name** box, type a name.

4  In the **Type** box, click **Formula**.

5  Click **Edit**.

6  In the **Formula** box, specify the formula you want for the column, and then click **OK** twice.

7  From the **Field Chooser**, drag the field you want as the new column heading to the column heading row. Use the double-arrow marker to position the new column heading in the column heading row.

You may want to change the label of the formula column so it reflects the field values shown in the column. In addition, you may want to change the formula specified for the column.

▶ **To change a formula column label or formula**

1  Right-click the column heading, and then click **Format Columns** on the shortcut menu.

2  In the **Available fields** box, select the field whose properties you want to set, and do one or both of the following:

   • To change the formula, click the button next to the **Formula** box.

   • To change the column label, change the text in the **Label** box.

3  Click **OK**.

Part III   Building Blocks of Applications

# Group Items

Groups provide a convenient way to organize items that have the same field values in a folder. For example, in the By Ad Type view in the Classified Ads folder, items are grouped by ad type, and then by category. So items that have a "For Sale" value in the AdType field, as shown in Figure 8.13, are grouped together. In addition, items that have an "Electronics-Computer Hardware & Software" value in the Category field are grouped together.

**Figure 8.13   The Classified Ads form**

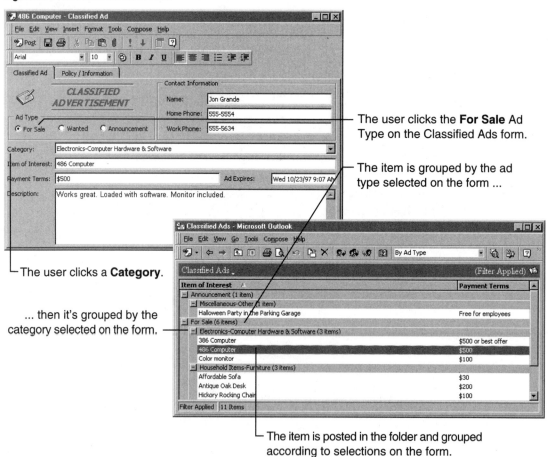

The user clicks the **For Sale** Ad Type on the Classified Ads form.

The item is grouped by the ad type selected on the form ...

The user clicks a **Category**.

... then it's grouped by the category selected on the form.

The item is posted in the folder and grouped according to selections on the form.

**244**   Building Microsoft Outlook 97 Applications

▶ **To group items**

1 On the **View** menu, click **Group By**.

2 In the **Select available fields from** box, click the field set that contains the field you want to group by.

3 Under **Group items by**, click the field you want to group items by.

4 Optionally, you can click the **Show field in view** check box. This option shows the field in the view above the column heading.

5 Click **Ascending** or **Descending**. When **Ascending** is selected, the groups are arranged alphabetically, starting with "A" at the top.

6 To group items into further subsets, click a field in the next available **Then by** box, as shown in Figure 8.14.

7 Click **OK**.

**Figure 8.14   The Group By dialog box for the By Ad Type view**

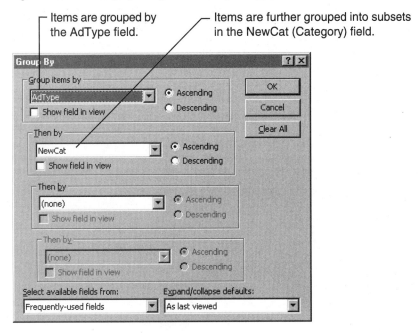

Items are grouped by the AdType field.

Items are further grouped into subsets in the NewCat (Category) field.

## Show or Hide the Group By Box

An easy way to create groups for a view is to show the Group By Box, and then drag column headings to the Group By Box. You can then hide the Group By Box.

▶ **To create items by using the Group By Box**

1  On the **View** menu, click **Group By Box**. The Group By Box appears above the column heading area.

2  Drag the fields you want to group by from the Field Chooser, or from the column heading row, to the Group By Box above the column heading row.

3  After you create the groups you want, click **Group By Box** on the **View** menu to hide the Group By Box.

# Sort Items

Sorting items provides a convenient way to organize information within a group. For example, you can sort items in a group by the date the items were received, or you can sort items alphabetically. When you specify a field to sort by, you can specify ascending or descending order. Ascending order sorts items in alphabetical order, with the oldest date (or the lowest value) at the top of the list. Descending order sorts items in alphabetical order, with the most recent date (or highest value) at the top of the list. Figure 8.15 shows the items in the By Ad Type view sorted by Subject. Remember that the label for the Subject field is changed in the column heading from Subject to Item of Interest.

**Figure 8.15   Items in each group are sorted alphabetically by Subject in the ItemOf Interest column.**

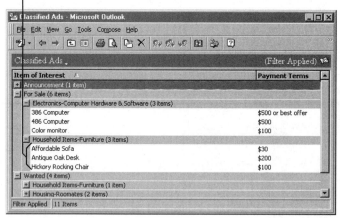

▶ **To sort items**

**1**  On the **View** menu, click **Sort**.

**2**  In the **Select available fields from** box, click the category of fields that contains the field you want to sort by.

**3**  Under **Sort items by**, click the field you want to sort items by.

**4**  Click either **Ascending** or **Descending** to choose the sort order.

**5**  To sort items into further subsets, click a field in the next available **Then by** box, as shown in Figure 8.16.

**6**  Click **OK**.

**Figure 8.16   Items are sorted alphabetically by the value in the Subject field.**

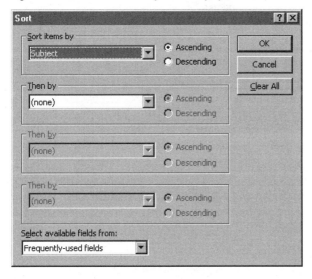

# Group by Conversation, Sort by Conversation Index

Conversation and Conversation Index are unique properties that you can use to create views for discussion folders so people can view the history of responses to an item, also known as a *conversation thread*. For this section, the Product Ideas folder covered in Chapter 3, "Customize Built-In Modules," is used to provide an example of grouping by Conversation and sorting by Conversation Index.

## Grouping by Conversation

Conversation is a unique property that is inherited from the Subject field. For example, if you submit a standard post item to a folder, the Conversation field of the item is set to the value of the Subject field. Therefore, any responses made to the item automatically inherit the value of the Conversation field. As shown in Figure 8.17, the items in the Product Idea folder are grouped by Product Category, and then by Conversation.

**Figure 8.17  Items are grouped by Product Category, and then by Conversation. They are sorted by Conversation Index.**

Items are grouped by Product
Category, and then by Conversation.

Items within each group are sorted by Conversation
Index. Response items are indented.

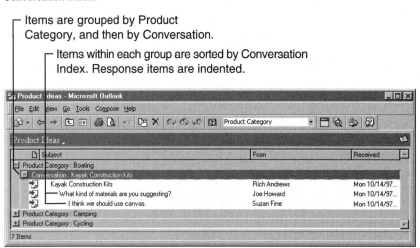

▶ **To group items by Conversation**

1  On the **View** menu, click **Group By**.

2  In the **Select available fields from** box, click **Frequently-used fields**.

3  Under **Group items by**, click the field that you want to group items by.

4  In the **Then by** box, click **Conversation**, as shown in Figure 8.18.

5  Click **OK**.

**Figure 8.18   Items are grouped by Product Category, and then by Conversation.**

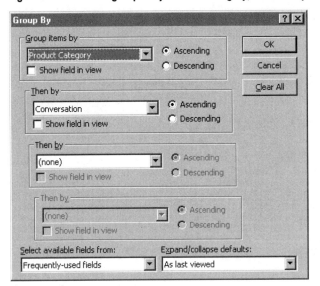

## Sorting by Conversation Index

The Conversation Index property is Outlook's way of keeping track of responses. When you sort by Conversation Index, the responses to each item are indented from, and follow directly after, the original item. In this way, users can track the history of responses to an item, as shown earlier in Figure 8.17.

▶ **To sort items by Conversation Index**

1   On the **View** menu, click **Sort**.

2   Under **Sort items by**, click **Conversation Index**, as shown in Figure 8.19.

3   Click **OK**.

**Figure 8.19   Items are sorted by Conversation Index, so response items are indented and follow the original item.**

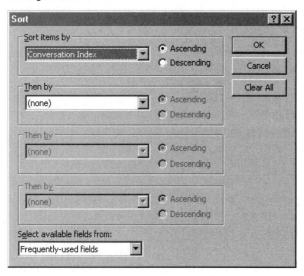

# Filter Items

Filters provide a way to quickly and easily find information in a folder. When a filter is applied in a view, only the items that meet the filter conditions show in the folder. For example, as shown in Figure 8.20, the filter created for the By Ad Type view shows only items created with the CreateAd form (IPM.Post.CreateAd) in the folder.

**Figure 8.20   The filter for the By Ad Type view shows only items created with the CreateAd form (IPM.Post.CreateAd) in the folder.**

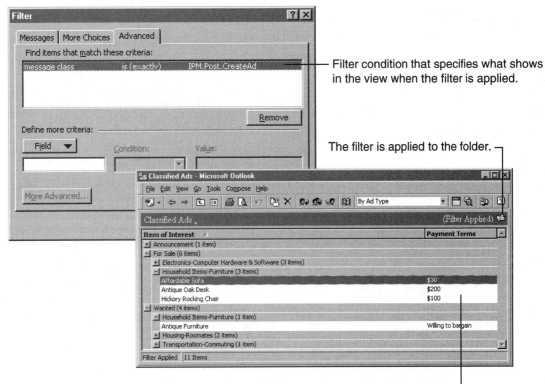

Filter condition that specifies what shows in the view when the filter is applied.

The filter is applied to the folder.

Only items created with the CreateAd form show in the folder.

Filters consist of a condition or set of conditions that determine what items are shown in a folder. For example, a condition may be *From:Jim Hance*. Conditions can have multiple arguments. For example, *From:Jim Hance, Don Funk*. Here are a few simple guidelines to follow when creating conditions:

- Multiple conditions are AND values. For example, the condition *From:Jim Hance;Subject:GG&G* is true if the From field of the incoming item contains "Jim Hance" and the Subject field contains "GG&G."

- Multiple arguments within a condition are OR values. For example, the condition *From:Jim Hance;Karl Buhl, Don Funk;Max Benson* is true if the From field contains any of the names included in the expression.

# Specify Simple Filter Conditions

In some cases, you may want to filter messages that meet specific criteria. For example, you may want to filter all incoming messages from a particular user or about a particular subject.

▶ **To filter on simple message properties**

1  On the **View** menu, click **Filter**.

2  On the **Messages** page, specify the properties you want for the filter. For example, to create a message that shows only messages from a particular person, click **From**, and then double-click the person's name in the list.

3  Click **OK**.

# Specify Advanced Filter Conditions

On the **Advanced** page, you can create a wide variety of filter conditions. For example, you can specify that only items with a specific message class show in the view. In addition, you can specify that only items with a specific value in a field show in the view.

## Filter on Message Class

When you filter on message class, you specify that only items created with a particular form are visible in the folder. For example, in the By Ad Type view in the Classified Ads folder, only items created with the CreateAd form show in the view.

▶ **To filter on message class**

1  On the **View** menu, click **Filter**.

2  Click the **Advanced** page.

3  Click **Field**, point to **All Mail fields**, and then click **Message Class**.

4  In the **Condition** box, click **is (exactly)**.

5  In the **Value** box, type the message class, as shown in Figure 8.21.

6  Click **Add to List**.

7  Click **OK**.

Figure 8.21   The condition for the filter in the By Ad Type view specifies that only items with the message class IPM.Post.CreateAd show in the folder.

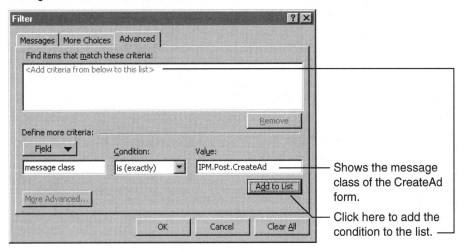

Shows the message class of the CreateAd form.

Click here to add the condition to the list.

## Filter on Field Values

You can create a filter that shows only items that have a specific value in a field. For example, as shown in Figure 8.22, the conditions for the filter specify that only items created with the CreateAd form that have the value "For Sale" in the AdType field and "Transportation-Cars" in the NewCat field show in the view.

Figure 8.22   Advanced filter conditions for the Ad Type view

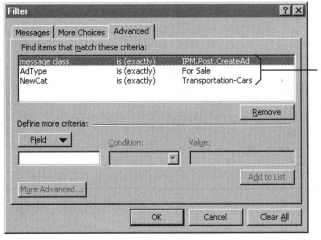

These conditions specify to show only items created with the CreateAd form that have the value For Sale in the AdType field and Transportation-Cars in the NewCat field.

▶ **To filter on a field value**

**1**  On the **View** menu, click **Filter**.

**2**  Click the **Advanced** page.

**3**  Click **Field**, point to the field set you want, and then click the field you want.

**4**  Do one of the following:

- To filter on a single field value, click **is (exactly)** in the **Condition** box, and then type the value you want in the **Value** box.

- To filter on multiple values in a field, click **contains** in the **Condition** box, and then type the values you want separated by a comma in the **Value** box.

**5**  Click **Add to List**.

# Format Views

By using the **Format View** dialog box, you can change the fonts in the view, specify grid lines for the view, specify if group headings are shaded, and turn on in-cell editing so users can enter and edit information in the cells in the folder, as shown in Figure 8.23.

**Figure 8.23   Format options for the By Ad Type view**

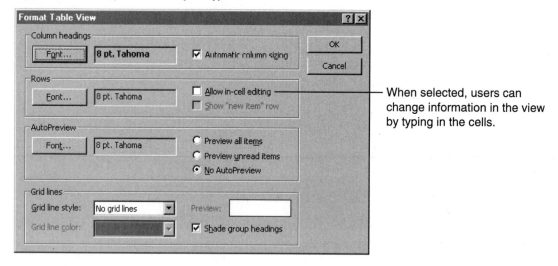

When selected, users can change information in the view by typing in the cells.

▸ **To format a view**

1   In the **Current View** box, switch to the view you want to change.

2   On the **View** menu, click **Format View**.

3   Select the options you want, and then click **OK**.

# Save View Settings

After you make changes to a view, you can save the view by clicking the **Current View** box and pressing ENTER. If the view has not been modified, or it has been previously saved and not modified since, the **Save View Settings** dialog box does not appear. To force the **Save View Settings** dialog box to appear, resize a column heading, click the **Current View** box, and then press ENTER.

▸ **To save view settings**

1   Click the **Current View** box, and then press ENTER.

2   Click **Update the view** *current view name* **with the current view settings**, as shown in Figure 8.24.

3   Click **OK**.

Figure 8.24   **The Save View Settings dialog box appears when you click the Current View box and press ENTER after making changes to a view.**

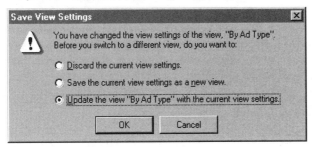

# Set General Properties

On the **General** page of the **Properties** dialog box, as shown in Figure 8.25, you can specify the default form that appears when a user creates a new item in a folder. For example, for the Classified Ads folder, the Classified Ads form appears when the user clicks the **New Post in This Folder** command on the **Compose** menu.

**Figure 8.25   The When Posting To This Folder, Use: option specifies that the Classified Ads form appears when the New Post in This Folder command is clicked.**

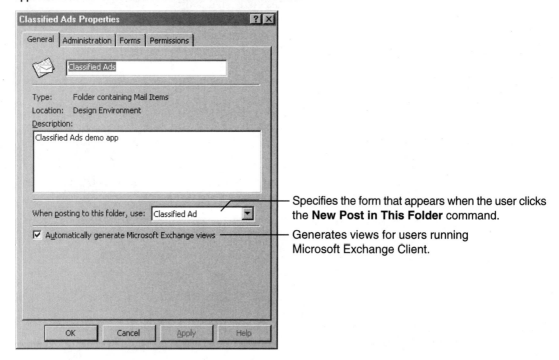

Specifies the form that appears when the user clicks the **New Post in This Folder** command.

Generates views for users running Microsoft Exchange Client.

▶ **To set general properties**

1   In the Folder List, right-click the folder you want to set properties for, and then click **Properties** on the shortcut menu.

2   Click the **General** page.

▶ **To specify the form that appears when the user clicks the New Post in This Folder command**

•   In the **When posting to this folder, use:** box, click the form you want to appear when the user clicks the **New Post in This Folder** command.

   If you do not want a custom form to appear, click **Post** in the **When posting to this folder, use:** box.

▶ **To automatically generate Microsoft Exchange views**

- If your organization uses both Microsoft Exchange Client and Outlook, select the **Automatically generate Microsoft Exchange views** check box. This option generates Microsoft Exchange views for the folder so the views can be seen by users of Microsoft Exchange Client.

**Note**   This property is only available for Outlook table views.

# Test Forms and Views

After you publish forms and define views for the folder, you need to test them to make sure they work as expected.

- To test the forms, open the folder in which the forms are published, and then click the menu commands that are associated with the form on the *Compose* menu. In the form, enter the information you want, and then click the **Post** button. After posting the item in the folder, double-click it to open it and make sure it shows information correctly in the form. You should test each form in the folder.

- To test views, open the folder you want to test, and then click each of the views in the **Current View** box on the **Standard** toolbar. If the folder has multiple forms, you should post several types of items in the folder before testing the views.

When you finish testing the forms and views, you can delete the test items you posted in the folder.

# Copy the Folder to Public Folders

After adding forms, defining views, and testing their functionality, you are ready to copy your folder to Public Folders. You can then complete the folder design by designating types of items allowed in the folder, setting permissions, setting administration properties, and specifying rules. This step is only necessary if you started the folder design process with a personal folder or a mailbox folder, and not in a public folder.

Depending on the policies of your organization, you may not have permission to add a folder to Public Folders. You may be required to hand off the folder to your administrator who then copies the folder and completes the design task according to your specifications. Or, you may be given permissions to copy your folder to a specific public folder and then complete the task yourself. See your administrator for specific instructions.

▶ **To copy the folder to a new location**

1   In the Folder List, right-click the folder, and then click **Copy** "*folder name*" on the shortcut menu.

2   Click the public folder you want to copy the folder to, and then click **OK**.

# Set Administration Properties

After you copy a folder to public folder, it's a good idea to restrict access to the folder while you set folder permissions and test the folder. To restrict access to the folder, you can use the **This folder is available to** option on the **Administration** page, as shown in Figure 8.26.

▶ **To restrict access to the folder**

1   In the Folder List, right-click the folder, and then click **Properties** on the shortcut menu.

2   Click the **Administration** page.

3   Click **Owners only**.

**Figure 8.26   Administration options for the Classified Ads folder**

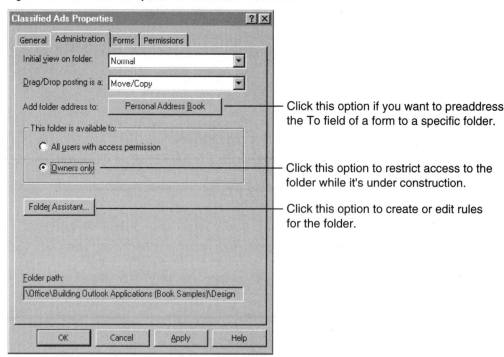

## Initial View on Folder

You use this option to specify the folder view you want to display when the user first opens the folder. By default, this view is the Messages view.

## Drag/Drop Posting Is A

You use this option to specify how Outlook formats items that are dragged to a folder. You can specify that the drag/drop operation formats the posted item in one of the following ways:

- **Move/Copy**  This option specifies that when an item is dragged to a folder, Outlook does not reformat the item. For example, if Eric Lang drags an item from his Inbox from Clair Hector to the Employee Feedback folder, the item that appears in the Employee Feedback folder is shown as sent by Clair Hector.

- **Forward**  This option specifies that when an item is dragged to a folder, Outlook reformats the item to show that is has been forwarded by the user who dragged it to the folder. For example, if Eric Lang drags an Inbox item from Clair Hector to the Employee Feedback folder, the item in the Employee Feedback folder appears as though it has been forwarded by Eric Lang.

## Add Folder Address to Personal Address Book

You use this option to preaddress forms. When you click the **Personal Address Book** button, the folder address is automatically added to your Personal Address Book. You can then use the folder address in your Personal Address Book to preaddress a Message form to a folder or to create a rule that automatically forwards items to the folder.

**Tip**  Another way to make the folder address available for preaddressing a form is to ask your administrator to add the folder address to the Global Address Book. You can then select the folder name from the Global Address Book to preaddress a form.

**See Also**  For more information about preaddressing a Message form to a folder address, see "To Field" in Chapter 6, "Controls, Fields, and Properties."

## This Folder Is Available To

You use this option to make a folder unavailable while it's under construction.

You can click **Owners only** if you are modifying or creating a folder design. This gives only those people with the Owner role permission to access the folder. After the folder is tested and is ready for general use, you can click **All users with access permission** and make the folder available for public use.

**Tip**  The **Owners only** option prevents access to the specified folder, but does not prevent access to subfolders. This way, users can post items in a subfolder while the parent folder is disabled.

### Folder Assistant

You can click the **Folder Assistant** button to create rules that automatically process incoming folder items. Rules are described in more detail in "Design Rules" later in this chapter.

# Set Permissions

You assign permissions to users to define the functions they can perform in the folder. You determine who can view and use the folder by adding the user names, distribution list names, or public folder names to the **Name** box on the **Permissions** page. After the names are added to the **Name** box, you can assign roles to define the permissions for each user or distribution list, as shown in Figure 8.27.

**Figure 8.27   Permissions for the Classified Ads folder**

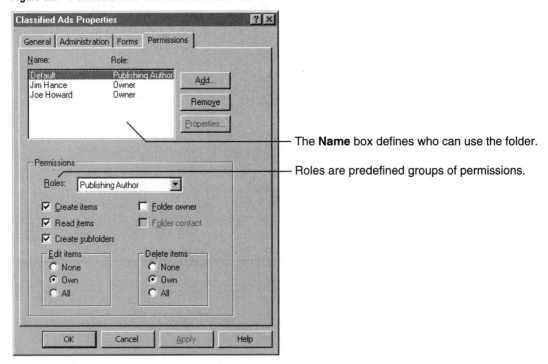

The **Name** box defines who can use the folder.

Roles are predefined groups of permissions.

▶ **To open the Permissions page**

1   In the Folder List, right-click the folder you want to set permissions for, and then click **Properties** on the shortcut menu.

2   Click the **Permissions** page.

## Modify the Name List

The names in the **Name** box determine who can view and use the folder. If you create the folder, you are automatically given owner permissions for the folder. With owner permissions, you can add users to, and remove users from, the **Name** box. You can also change permissions for selected users.

One name in the **Name** box is Default. The permissions defined for Default are granted to all users who have access to the folder. If you want to give a particular user permissions other than Default, add the user name to the **Name** box, and then set permissions for that user.

When you test the folder, it's a good idea to set the Default permissions to None, and then grant access to a limited number of users. When you are sure that everything is working correctly in the folder, you can change the Default permissions and add names to the **Name** box.

You can remove any name from the **Name** box except Default and, if you are the sole owner of the folder, your name. If you remove Default or your name, they will reappear the next time you view the **Permissions** page.

## About Distribution Lists

Distribution lists provide a convenient way to assign permissions to a group of users. For example, rather than enter 50 names in the **Name** box, you can enter the distribution list name to assign permissions to all users on the list.

▶ **To add a user, distribution list, or folder name to the Name box**

1  On the **Permissions** page, click **Add**.

2  Click the user, distribution list, or folder you want to add, and then click **Add**.

3  Click **OK**.

**Note**  Permissions can be set for folders in your Mailbox. Permissions cannot be set in personal folders.

## Assign Roles

When you set permissions for a user, you define the functions they can perform within the folder. You can set permissions by using predefined roles or by using custom roles:

• **Predefined Roles**  Predefined groups of permissions that are available from the **Roles** box.

• **Custom Roles**  Permissions you set for the user that do not match any of the predefined roles.

▶ **To assign roles to users**

1  In the **Name** box, click the user name you want to set permissions for.

2  In the **Roles** box, click a role for the user.

3  The following table lists the roles and the predefined permissions that are assigned to each role.

| Role | Description |
| --- | --- |
| Owner | Create, read, modify, and delete all items and files and create subfolders. As the folder owner, you can change permissions others have for the folder. |
| Publishing Editor | Create, read, modify, and delete all items and files and create subfolders. |
| Editor | Create, read, modify, and delete all items and files. |
| Publishing Author | Create and read items and files, create subfolders, and modify and delete items and files you create. |
| Author | Create and read items and files, and modify and delete items and files you create. |
| Reviewer | Read items and files only. |
| Contributor | Create items and files only. The user cannot open the folder. |
| Custom | Perform activities defined by the folder owner. |
| None | The user cannot open the folder. |

▶ **To assign a custom Role**

1  In the **Name** box, click the user name whose permissions you want to set.

2  In the **Roles** box, click the role that most closely resembles the permissions you want to grant to the user.

3  Under **Permissions**, select the options you want. If the permissions do not match a role, you see **Custom** in the **Roles** box. If the permissions match a role, the role will show in the **Roles** box.

# Design Rules

Rules automatically process items as they arrive in a folder. A rule consists of two parts: A set of conditions that are applied to an incoming item, and the actions that are taken if the conditions are met, as shown in Figure 8.28.

**Figure 8.28   Rules for the Training Management folder**

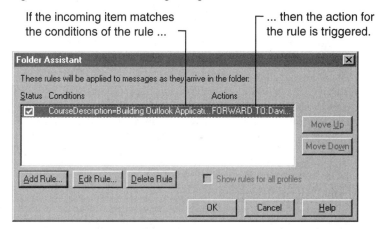

If the incoming item matches
the conditions of the rule ...

... then the action for
the rule is triggered.

You can use rules to:

- Specify that specific types of items are automatically returned to the sender.
- Automatically delete items based on the specified conditions.
- Automatically reply to specific kinds of items with a reply template.
- Automatically forward specific types of items to another folder or user.

▶ **To create rules**

1   In the Folder List, right-click the folder, and then click **Properties** on the shortcut menu.

2   Click the **Administration** tab, and then click **Folder Assistant**.

# Specifying Conditions of a Rule

The conditions of a rule identify the items that are to be processed by the rule. These conditions can range from very simple to relatively advanced. An example of a simple condition is *From:James Allard*. This condition states that if an item is submitted to the folder and the item is from James Allard, then a specified action is taken. A more advanced set of conditions is *Only Messages That Do Not Match This Criteria; From:James Allard;Joe Howard;Scott Cooper*. These conditions state that if the items submitted to the folder are not from James Allard, Joe Howard, or Scott Cooper, then a specified action is taken.

# Rules Syntax

Before you create rules, there are a few fundamental concepts you need to know:

- A rule consists of conditions and a corresponding action. A rule can have one condition or multiple conditions. For example, *From:James Allard* is a single condition and *From:James Allard;Subject:GG&G* are two conditions. Each condition is delimited by a semicolon. A condition can consist of an argument or multiple arguments. For example, *From:James Allard* is a condition with a single argument and *From:James Allard; Joe Howard* is a condition with multiple arguments.

- Multiple conditions within a rule are AND values. For example, the condition *From:James Allard;Subject:GG&G* is true if the From field of the incoming items contains "James Allard" and the Subject field contains "GG&G."

- Multiple arguments within a condition are OR values. For example, the condition *From:James Allard;Joe Howard;Max Benson* is true if the From field of the incoming item contains any one of the names included in the expression.

# Specifying Simple Conditions

With simple conditions, you can specify conditions based on the contents of the From, Sent, To, Subject, and Message fields of an incoming item.

▸ **To specify simple conditions**

1  From the **Folder Assistant** dialog box, click **Add Rule**, or select the rule you want and then click **Edit Rule**.

2  Under **When a message arrives that meets the following conditions**, type the criteria in the associated boxes.

## Specifying Advanced Conditions

With the **Advanced** dialog box, you can specify a wide range of conditions, including conditions based on values in user-defined fields in the folder.

▶ **To specify advanced conditions**

1  In the **Folder Assistant** dialog box, click **Add Rule**, or select the rule you want and then click **Edit Rule**.

2  Click **Advanced**.

3  Type the criteria in the appropriate boxes.

## Specifying That a Rule Applies to Items That Do Not Match the Conditions

You can create rules that take actions if conditions are met and rules that take actions if the conditions are not met.

▶ **To specify that a rule applies only to items that do not match the conditions**

• In the **Advanced** dialog box, click the **Only items that do not match these conditions** check box.

## Specifying Conditions with User-defined Fields

In some cases, you may want to create conditions based on user-defined fields in the folder. For example, for the Training Management folder, you may want to create a rule that forwards a Course Offering item to a distribution list when a Course Offering item that pertains to a specific subject is posted in the folder.

▶ **To specify custom fields as conditions**

1  In the **Advanced** dialog box, under **Show properties of**, do one of the following.

| To | Click |
| --- | --- |
| Show custom fields of the currently selected forms | **Selected forms**, click **Forms**, and then select the forms you want. |
| Show the standard document fields | **Document** |
| Show the custom fields of the currently selected folder | **Folder:** *folder name* |

2  Under **Properties**, select the check box of the property that you want to use to create a condition.

3  In the list or text boxes to the right of the check boxes, do one or more of the following:

- If the field to the right of the selected check box is a text box, you can type one or more values in the text box. For example, if you want to create a rule that forwards Training Management items that have the value "Building Microsoft Outlook 97 Applications" in the CourseDescription field, then type **Building Microsoft Outlook 97 Applications** in the text box to its right, as shown in Figure 8.29 . If you specify multiple values in the text boxes, separate the values with a semicolon.

- If a drop-down list box and a text box are to the right of the check box, click the value in the list box first. Then type or click the criteria in the box to its right.

4  Click **OK**.

**Figure 8.29  With Advanced properties, you can build conditions based on specific field values in a field.**

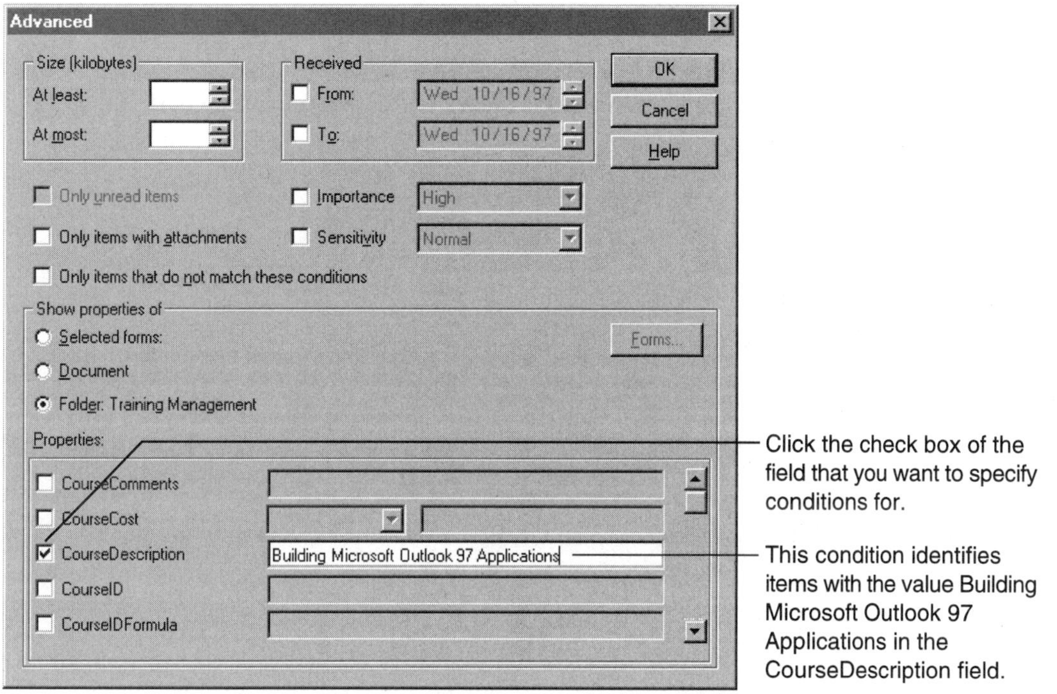

Click the check box of the field that you want to specify conditions for.

This condition identifies items with the value Building Microsoft Outlook 97 Applications in the CourseDescription field.

# Specifying Actions for a Rule

Actions occur when the conditions of a rule are met.

▸ **To specify an action**

- In the **Edit Rule** dialog box, under **Perform these actions**, do one of the following.

| To | Click |
|---|---|
| Return the item to the sender if the conditions of the rule are met | **Return to Sender** |
| Delete the item if the conditions of the rule are met | **Delete** |
| Specify the Reply message that is sent if the conditions of the rule are not met | Click **Reply with**, click **Template**, and then fill out the message box of the form with the Reply message you want to send. |
| Forward an item if the conditions of the rule are not met | Click **Forward**, click **To**, and then select the user name, distribution list, or folder. |

**See Also**   For more information about specifying actions, see Chapter 7, "Actions."

# Test and Release the Folder

After you create or modify a folder, you should pilot test it with a few users. When testing the folder, you and the users involved in the pilot test should compose, submit, and open items in the folder and check views, permissions, and rules to make sure they work as planned.

When you're sure the folder is working properly, you can open the **Administration** page in the folder **Properties** dialog box and make the folder available to the general public.

▸ **To make the folder available to all users with access permission**

1  In the Folder List, right-click the folder, and then click **Properties** on the shortcut menu.

2  Click the **Administration** page.

3  Click **All users with access permission**.

4  Click **OK**.

If you plan to replicate the folder application between servers, define replication settings and test the folder on a small scale before replicating it between a large number of servers.

When the folder is ready for public use, send out an announcement to the users who will be using the folder to let them know the folder is available. You can include a link to the folder in your announcement message so users can easily find the folder.

| For more information about | See |
| --- | --- |
| Setting permissions | "Set Permissions" earlier in this chapter. |
| Distributing and maintaining folders | Chapter 13, "Distribute and Maintain Applications." |
| Replicating folders | The Microsoft Exchange Server documentation. |

# Beyond the Basics

## Contents

Chapter 9   Use Visual Basic Scripting Edition with Outlook   273

Chapter 10   The Business Card Request Application   331

Chapter 11   The Help Desk Application   385

Chapter 12   The Document Tracking Application   427

Chapter 13   Distribute and Maintain Applications   475

# Use Visual Basic Scripting Edition with Outlook

## In This Chapter

The Outlook Script Editor   274

How to Open an Item That Contains VBScript   277

Help and Web Sites   277

Object Libraries   282

Object Models   284

The Application Object   291

The NameSpace Object   294

The Outlook Window (Explorer Object)   295

The Folders Collection Object   296

The MAPIFolder Object   297

The Items Collection Object   300

The Item Object   302

The Inspector Object   307

The Pages Collection Object   308

The Page Object   309

The Controls Collection Object   309

The Control Object   311

The UserProperties Collection Object   313

The Recipients Collection Object   315

Events   316

A Quick Tutorial—the Library Order Application   325

Automation   329

By using Microsoft Visual Basic Scripting Edition (VBScript) in Outlook, you can create procedures that control Outlook folders, forms, items, pages, properties, actions, events, and controls. For example, with Visual Basic Scripting Edition, you can create procedures that use code to create and send or post items. You can also use Visual Basic Scripting Edition to modify Outlook events. For example, you can modify the Write event of a Post form so that it automatically sends a notification message to a distribution list when a new item is posted in a folder. You can also use Visual Basic Scripting Edition to write information from an Outlook item to a database, or you can display information from a database in an Outlook item. In addition, you can use Visual Basic Scripting Edition to automate processes. For example, you can create a procedure for a Bulk Mailer Announcement form that automatically addresses an announcement item to all users in a specified Contacts folder.

This chapter is designed to give you the fundamental skills and knowledge you need to create industrial strength applications by using Visual Basic Scripting Edition. This chapter covers how to use Visual Basic Scripting Edition to:

- Reference a folder collection or a folder in the Folder List.
- Create, open, send, and post standard and custom items.
- Open and close standard and custom forms.
- Set and change field values in items.
- Hide or show a form page.
- Change the properties of a control on a page.
- Specify the recipients of an item.
- Modify Outlook events.

# The Outlook Script Editor

With the Script Editor, which is available for each form, you can add procedures to forms to control an Outlook application or another application such as Microsoft Word or Microsoft Excel. In addition, you can create procedures to control Outlook folders, forms, and items, and controls and properties in items. For example, you can create a procedure to automatically set a folder as the active folder, and then create and post an item in the folder. Or, you can create a procedure that creates a collection of items in a folder based on a specified filter, and then changes a field value for each item in the collection.

▶ **To view the Outlook Script Editor**

1   In Inbox, click **New Mail Message** on the **Compose** menu.

2   On the **Tools** menu, click **Design Outlook Form**.

3   On the **Form Design** toolbar, click **View Code**.

# An Introduction to Using the Script Editor

As an introduction to using the Script Editor, this section describes how to add code to the PropertyChange event to show a message whenever you change a standard field value on a Mail Message form. The PropertyChange event is triggered any time you change a standard field value on the form. For example, if you change the standard **Importance** or **Sensitivity** options on a Message form, the PropertyChange event is triggered because a field value has been changed.

▶ **To create and test a PropertyChange event**

1   On the Script Editor **Script** menu, click **Event**.

2   In the **Events** box, double-click **PropertyChange**.

3   Add the code you want, as shown in Figure 9.1.

4   On the Script Editor **Script** menu, click **Run**.

5   On the form **Tools** menu, click **Design Outlook Form**.

6   Click the **Options** page, and then click a different value in the **Importance** box.

7   Click **OK** to close the message.

**Figure 9.1   The PropertyChange event in the Script Editor**

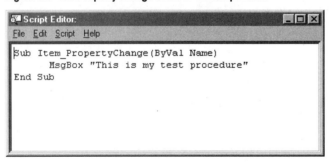

```
Sub Item_PropertyChange(ByVal Name)
     MsgBox "This is my test procedure"
End Sub
```

# Editing Code with the Script Editor

When you create procedures for a form, you can keep the form in Run mode while you edit the code in the Script Editor window.

▶ **To edit code while in Run mode**

1   On the Script Editor **Script** menu, click **Stop**.

2   For the **MsgBox** text in the Script Editor window, as shown in the preceding Figure 9.1, type: **This is my new test procedure**.

3   On the Script Editor **Script** menu, click **Run**.

4   On the form **Options** page, click a different value in the **Importance** box.

5   Click **OK** to close the message.

6   On the Script Editor **Script** menu, click **Stop**.

You can now edit the code again if you want.

# Checking Code Syntax

After you create a procedure, you can run it in the Script Editor window to check for syntax errors.

▶ **To check for syntax errors**

• On the Script Editor **Script** menu, click **Run**. The Script Editor checks the syntax of the code and shows a message if it discovers an error.

# Jumping to a Line of Code

When you test procedures, you sometimes see an error message that references a line of code. The Script Editor provides a way to jump to a particular line of code.

▶ **To jump to a line of code**

1   On the Script Editor **Edit** menu, click **Go To**.

2   In the **Line Number** box, type the line number, and then click **OK**.

# Searching and Replacing Text

The Script Editor does not provide a way to search for and replace text. To perform this task, you can use Microsoft WordPad.

▶ **To use WordPad to search and replace text**

1 Click the **Start** button on the taskbar, and then click **Run**.

2 Type **WordPad**, and then click **OK**.

3 Select the code you want to change in the Script Editor, and then click **Cut** on the **Edit** menu.

4 Click the WordPad window, and then click **Paste** on the **WordPad** toolbar.

5 On the WordPad **Edit** menu, click **Replace**, and then select the options you want.

6 When you are done, copy the modified code back to the Script Editor window.

# How to Open an Item That Contains VBScript

When designing and editing forms, you can prevent Visual Basic Scripting Edition (VBScript) code from executing when you open a form, by holding down the SHIFT key when you select the form. For example, to open a form in your Personal Forms Library, click **Choose Form** on the Outlook **Compose** menu, click **Personal Forms**, and then hold down the SHIFT key and double-click the form you want to open.

The form opens but the VBScript code does not execute. This method helps to ensure that values are not inadvertently written to the fields in the form when the Open event is fired when the form opens. It also helps to ensure that the fields do not contain unwanted data in them when you publish the form.

# Help and Web Sites

In the 1. Help and Web Sites folder in the Building Microsoft Outlook 97 Applications folder, you can find folders containing items that make it possible to install Help files or to visit Web sites. These Help files and Web sites can assist you in your Visual Basic Scripting Edition programming tasks. Here is an overview of the Web sites and Help available:

• **http://www.microsoft.com/vbscript/**   The Microsoft Visual Basic Scripting Edition Web site. If you are using Microsoft Internet Explorer version 3.0, you can get to this site by opening the 1. Help and Web Sites folder in the Building Microsoft Outlook 97 Applications folder. You can then open the Web Sites folder and double-click the Microsoft Visual Basic Scripting Edition item.

- **http://www.microsoft.com/outlook/**  The Microsoft Outlook Web Site. This site contains Visual Basic Scripting Edition samples, form samples, and valuable tips and techniques for creating Outlook applications. If you are using Microsoft Internet Explorer 3.0, you can get to this site by opening the 1. Help and Web Sites folder in the Building Microsoft Outlook 97 Applications folder. You can then open the Web Sites folder and double-click the Microsoft Outlook item.

- **Microsoft Outlook Visual Basic Help**  This Help file includes the Outlook object model and descriptions of supported Outlook objects, methods, properties, constants, and events. If you don't have Microsoft Outlook Visual Basic Help installed, you need to install it now.

▶ **To install Microsoft Outlook Visual Basic Help**

1  In the Folder List, open the **Building Microsoft Outlook 97 Applications** folder, and then open the **1. Help and Web Sites** folder.

2  Open the **Outlook Visual Basic Help** folder.

3  Double-click the **Outlook Visual Basic Help** item in the folder, and then follow the instructions in the item.

- **Microsoft Outlook Forms Help**  This Help file contains comprehensive information about creating forms. In addition, it contains up-to-date information about the supported methods and properties for controls in Outlook. If you don't have Microsoft Outlook Forms Help installed, you need to install it now.

▶ **To install Microsoft Outlook Forms Help**

1  In the Folder List, open the **Building Microsoft Outlook 97 Applications** folder, and then open the **1. Help and Web Sites** folder.

2  Open the **Outlook Forms Help** folder.

3  Double-click the **Outlook Forms Help** item in the folder, and then follow the instructions in the item.

- **The VBScript Folder**  This folder contains sample items that you can open to view and run Visual Basic Scripting Edition code snippets.

▶ **To open the VBScript folder**

1  In the Folder List, open the **Building Microsoft Outlook 97 Applications** folder, and then open the **4. Beyond the Basics** folder.

2  Open the **VBScript** folder, and then open the **VBScript Samples** folder.

3  Double-click the item you want to open, and then click a command button to execute the sample procedure.

4  To view the sample code, click **Design Outlook Form** on the **Tools** menu, and then on the **Form Design** toolbar, click **View Code**.

# Microsoft Outlook Visual Basic Help

You can use the Microsoft Outlook Visual Basic Help file to view the methods and properties for each object, as shown in Figure 9.2.

▶ **To use Microsoft Outlook Visual Basic Help**

1   On the Script Editor **Help** menu, click **Microsoft Outlook Object Library Help**.

2   Click the **Contents** page.

3   Double-click **Objects**, and then double-click the object you want.

**Figure 9.2   Help for the Application object**

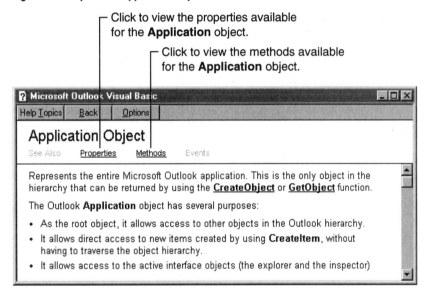

Click to view the properties available
for the **Application** object.

Click to view the methods available
for the **Application** object.

# A Caution About Microsoft Outlook Visual Basic Help

The code examples in Microsoft Outlook Visual Basic Help (Vbaoutl.hlp) were written for Visual Basic for Applications. The code examples will run in Visual Basic Scripting Edition with slight modifications. For example, the code example for the **GetNameSpace** method in the Microsoft Outlook Visual Basic Help file is as follows:

```
Set MyOlApp = CreateObject ("Outlook.Application")
Set OlNameSpace = MyOlApp.GetNameSpace("MAPI")
```

To make this work in Visual Basic Scripting Edition, you must change the code as follows:

```
Set MyNameSpace = Application.GetNameSpace("MAPI")
```

The code example for the **GetDefaultFolder** method in the Microsoft Outlook Visual Basic Help file is as follows:

```
Set MyCalendar = OlNameSpace.GetDefaultFolder(OlFolderCalendar)
```

▶ **To modify the preceding example and test it in a form**

1   On the Outlook **Compose** menu, click **New Mail Message**.

2   On the **Tools** menu, click **Design Outlook Form**.

3   On the **Form Design** toolbar, click **Control Toolbox**.

4   Resize the **Message** control on the form to make room for a CommandButton control.

5   Drag a **CommandButton** control to the form. By default, the CommandButton control is given the name CommandButton1.

6   On the **Form Design** toolbar, click **View Code**.

7   Add the following code to the Script Editor window to create the CommandButton1_Click procedure:

```
Sub CommandButton1_Click
    Set MyNameSpace = Application.GetNameSpace("MAPI")
    Set MyCalendar = MyNameSpace.GetDefaultFolder(9)
    MyCalendar.Display
End Sub
```

7   On the form **Tools** menu, click **Design Outlook Form**.

8   Click **CommandButton1**.

**Important**   When you automate Microsoft Outlook by using Visual Basic Scripting Edition, you must use the numeric values that the constants represent, rather than the constants as described in Microsoft Outlook Visual Basic Help. Notice that in the `set myCalendar = MyNameSpace.GetDefaultFolder(9)` statement in the preceding example, the numeric value is specified rather than the constant, as shown in the example in the Microsoft Outlook Visual Basic Help file.

▶ **To view the numeric values for Outlook constants**

1   On the Script Editor **Help** menu, click **Microsoft Outlook Object Library Help**.

2   Click the **Index** page.

3   In the **Index** list, double-click **constants**.

4   In the **Topics** box, double-click **Microsoft Outlook Constants**.

Many examples in Microsoft Outlook Visual Basic Help assume the object has been already set, as shown in this example:

```
Set MyInspector = MyOlApp.ActiveInspector
MsgBox "The active item is " & MyInspector.CurrentItem.Subject
```

▶ **To modify and test this example**

1   In the Script Editor window, replace the existing CommandButton1_Click procedure with the following:

```
Sub CommandButton1_Click
    Set MyInspector = Application.ActiveInspector
    MsgBox "The active item is " & MyInspector.CurrentItem.Subject
End Sub
```

2   Type your name in the **Subject** box of the form.

3   Click **CommandButton1**.

4   Click **OK** to close the message.

# The Implied Item Object

When you reference the active item in Outlook, the **Item** object is implied. As such, you do not need to set the **Item** object when referencing the active item. For example, to set the value of an active item's Subject field, you can use the following statement:

```
Item.Subject = "This is a test"
```

You can also leave out the reference to the item, as shown in this example:

```
Subject = "This is a test"
```

▶ **To test this example**

1   In the Script Editor window, replace the current CommandButton1_Click procedure with the following:

```
Sub CommandButton1_Click
    Subject = "The item is implied."
End Sub
```

2   Click **CommandButton1**.

3   In the **Subject** box of the form, you now see **The item is implied**.

# Object Libraries

An object library is a file with an .olb file name extension that provides information to programs such as Visual Basic Scripting Edition and Visual Basic for Applications about available objects. For example, the Microsoft Outlook 8.0 Object Library (Msoutl8.olb) contains the methods, events, properties, and constants that can be used to program the available objects.

When you use Visual Basic Scripting Edition in Outlook, there are two primary object libraries that you use:

- **The Microsoft Outlook 8.0 Object Library**   This library contains the objects, methods, events, and properties for almost all the objects that you work with in Outlook, with the exception of the **Page** object, the **Controls** collection object, and the **Control** object.

- **The Microsoft Forms 2.0 Object Library**   This library contains the objects, methods, properties, and constants that you use to work with a **Page** object, a **Controls** collection object, and a **Control** object.

To view the objects available in the Microsoft Outlook 8.0 Object Library and the Microsoft Forms 2.0 Object Library, you can use the Help files described earlier in this chapter, or you can use an object browser.

# Using an Object Browser

An object browser shows the objects, properties, methods, events, and constants available from object libraries. Outlook does not provide an object browser, but you can use the Microsoft Excel 97 Object Browser or the Visual Basic or Visual C++ Developer Studio Object Browser in its place.

▶ **To use the Microsoft Excel 97 Object Browser**

1   On the **File** menu, click **New**.

2   On the **General** page, double-click **Workbook**.

3   On the **Tools** menu, point to **Macro**, and then click **Visual Basic Editor**.

4   On the **View** menu, click **Object Browser**.

## Setting a Reference to the Outlook Object Library

To view the Outlook 8.0 Object Library in the Microsoft Excel 97 Object Browser, you must first set a reference to it.

▸ **To set a reference to the Outlook 8.0 Object Library**

1   On the **Tools** menu, click **References**.

2   In the **Available References** box, select the check box next to **Microsoft Outlook 8.0 Object Library**.

   If the Microsoft Outlook 8.0 Object Library option does not appear, click **Browse**, and then locate Msoutl8.olb. By default, this file is located in the C:\Program Files \Microsoft Office\Office folder. Double-click **Msoutl8.olb** and then click **OK**.

3   Click **OK**.

# Moving Around in an Object Browser

With an object browser, you can browse through all available objects in the Microsoft Outlook 8.0 Object Library and the Microsoft Forms 2.0 Object Library and see their properties, methods, and events, as shown in Figure 9.3. In addition, you can view the constants that are available in the object library and get Help for any component in the library.

▸ **To select an object library in an object browser**

•   To view the Microsoft Outlook 8.0 Object Library, click **Outlook** in the **Project/Library** box.

•   To view the Microsoft Forms 2.0 Object Library, click **MSForms** in the **Project/Library** box.

▶ **To move around in an object browser**

**1**  In the **Project/Library** box, click **Outlook**.

**2**  In the **Classes** box, click an object to view the methods and properties for the object.

**3**  In the **Members of** box, click a method or property to view further details, as shown in Figure 9.3.

**Figure 9.3   The Microsoft Excel 97 Object Browser**

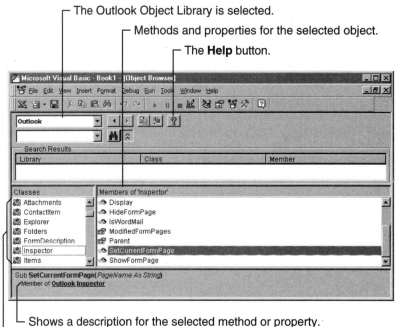

┌ The Outlook Object Library is selected.

        ┌ Methods and properties for the selected object.

              ┌ The **Help** button.

└ Shows a description for the selected method or property.

└ Select an object in the **Classes** box.

# Object Models

An object model provides a visual representation of the hierarchical structure and relationship of objects in an object library, as shown in Figure 9.4. As such, they provide a way for you to quickly see how an object library is designed.

▶ **To view the Microsoft Outlook object model**

1  On the Script Editor **Help** menu, click **Microsoft Outlook Object Library Help**.

2  Click the **Index** page.

3  In the **Index** list, double-click **object hierarchy**.

4  In the **Topics** box, double-click **Microsoft Outlook Objects**.

**Figure 9.4  The Microsoft Outlook object model**

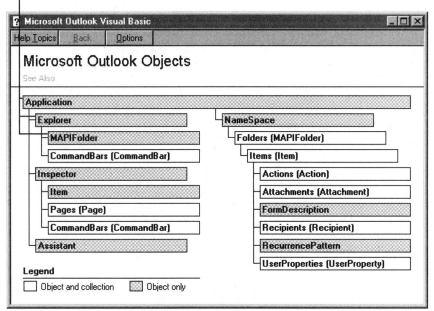

▶ **To view the Microsoft Forms 2.0 object model**

1  On the **Help** menu of the Microsoft Excel 97 Object Browser, click **Contents and Index**, and then click the **Index** tab.

2  Type **object models**, and then double-click **Microsoft Forms**.

3  Double-click **Object Model Overview**.

# Using the Object Hierarchy

In an object library, all objects have a unique set of methods and properties. Properties are attributes of the object that define the object. Methods are actions that can be performed on an object.

To use the object model, you must often move down through the object hierarchy to reference the particular object you want. For example, assume you want to display the Outlook window, which is represented by the **Explorer** object. Since the **Application** object sits at the top of the hierarchy, you must first reference the **Application** object before you reference the **Explorer** object.

In the following procedure, the **ActiveExplorer** method of the **Application** object is used to return the currently active Outlook window (the **Explorer** object). The **Display** method of the **Explorer** object is then used to show the Outlook window on the desktop.

```
Sub CommandButton1_Click
    Set MyExplorer = Application.ActiveExplorer
    MyExplorer.Display
End Sub
```

▸ **To test the code samples in this chapter**

1  Add a CommandButton control to the form, if you haven't already, and then name the button **CommandButton1**.

2  Type the sample code in the Script Editor window.

3  Exit Design mode by clicking **Design Outlook Form** on the form **Tools** menu, and then click **CommandButton1**.

4  Repeat steps 2 and 3 for each code sample you want to test.

The following example moves further down the object hierarchy and returns a **Folder** object. It then uses the **Name** property of the **Folder** object to display the name of the folder in a message.

```
Sub CommandButton1_Click
    Set MyFolder = Application.ActiveExplorer.CurrentFolder
    MsgBox MyFolder.Name
End Sub
```

# Getting and Setting Properties

This section covers how you either get or set the properties of an object. To get or set a property, you must reference both the object name and the property name.

## Getting an Object Property

In certain cases, you want to get the properties of an object. The following procedure retrieves the text in the message box of an item and shows it in a message. Before you click CommandButton1, type some text in the message box of the form.

```
Sub CommandButton1_Click
    BodyText = Item.Body
    MsgBox BodyText
End Sub
```

**Tip**   Notice in the preceding example that the active item is referenced without moving through the object hierarchy. In this case, the item is implied, as discussed in "The Implied Item Object" earlier in this chapter.

## Setting an Object Property

In this example, the body text of the item is set.

```
Sub CommandButton1_Click
    Item.Body = "This text appears in the message box."
End Sub
```

# Using Variables

Variable names follow the standard rules for naming anything in Microsoft Visual Basic Scripting Edition. A variable name:

- Must begin with an alphabetic character.
- Cannot contain an embedded period.
- Must not exceed 255 characters.
- Must be unique in the scope in which it's declared.

Generally, when you declare a variable within a procedure, only code within that procedure can reference or change the value of that variable; it has *local* scope and is known as a *procedure-level* variable. When you declare a variable outside a procedure, you make it recognizable to all the procedures in your script; it has *script-level* scope and is known as a *script-level* variable.

When you're using variables in Visual Basic Scripting Edition, the following limitations apply:

- There can be no more than 127 procedure-level variables (arrays count as a single variable).
- Each script is limited to no more than 127 script-level variables.

The length of time a variable exists is called its *lifetime*. A script-level variable's lifetime extends from the time it's declared until the time the script is finished running. A local variable's lifetime begins when its declaration statement is encountered as the procedure begins, and it ends when the procedure concludes. Local variables are ideal as temporary storage space while a procedure is running. You can have local variables with the same name in different procedures, because each variable is recognized only by the procedure in which it's declared.

A variable's scope is determined by where you declare the variable. At a script level, the lifetime of a variable is always the same; it exists while the script is running. At a procedure level, a variable exists only while the procedure is running; when the procedure exits, the variable is destroyed.

# Using the Variant Data Type

Microsoft Visual Basic Scripting Edition in Outlook uses only the **Variant** data type; a special kind of data type that can contain different types of information, depending on how the value is used. The **Variant** data type can contain either numeric or string information. The **Variant** data type behaves as a number when it's used in a numeric context and as a string when it's used in a string context. If you're working with data that resembles numeric data, Visual Basic Scripting Edition treats it as such and processes it accordingly. If you're working with data that's string data, Visual Basic Scripting Edition treats the data as a string. Numbers enclosed in quotation marks are treated as strings.

The **Variant** data type can make distinctions about the specific nature of numeric information, such as information that represents a date or time. When used with other date or time data, the result is always expressed as a date or a time. The **Variant** data type can contain numeric information ranging in size from **Boolean** values to huge floating-point numbers. These various categories of information that can be contained in a **Variant** data type are called *subtypes*. Usually you can put the type of data you want in a **Variant**, and it will most likely behave in a way that's suited to the data it contains.

# Assigning Objects to Variables

When assigning variables, you assign object variables in a slightly different way than for other variables. For example, if a variable is shared between procedures, you declare the variable as a script-level variable. In this procedure, the ItemChanged variable is declared as a script-level variable. ItemChanged is set to **True** whenever a standard property is changed in an item.

```
Dim ItemChanged    ' Script-level variable.

Sub Item_PropertyChange(ByVal Name)
   ItemChanged = True
End Sub
```

An object variable is a variable that is used to refer to an object. As shown in the following example, you don't need to declare the variable. Instead, you use the **Set** statement to assign an object to a variable. The first line of code in this example assigns the object variable to the newly created item. Once you've set an object, you can then use the object's methods and properties to control the object. This example creates a new mail item, and then displays the item.

```
Sub CommandButton1_Click
   Set MyItem = Application.CreateItem(0)
   MyItem.Display
End Sub
```

# Referencing Collections and Single Objects

Some objects in Outlook are collection objects, while others are single objects. For example, all the items in a folder can be contained in an **Items** collection object. However, a single item in an **Items** collection object may be represented by a **MailItem** object or a **PostItem** object.

The following code uses the **Items** property to reference the collection of items in your Inbox. It then shows the number of items in the **Items** collection object.

```
Sub CommandButton1_Click
   Set MyFolder = Application.GetNameSpace("MAPI").GetDefaultFolder(6)
   Set MyItems = MyFolder.Items
   MsgBox MyItems.Count
End Sub
```

In the next example, the items in the **Items** collection object are referenced by index number. In this case, the code iterates through the **Items** collection and shows the text in the Message field for the three oldest items in the your Inbox.

```
Sub CommandButton1_Click
   Set MyFolder = Application.GetNameSpace("MAPI").GetDefaultFolder(6)
   Set MyItems = MyFolder.Items
   For i = 1 to 3
      MsgBox MyFolder.Items(i).Subject
   Next
End Sub
```

After you set a collection object, you can reference objects in the collection by index, as shown in the preceding example, or by name. For example, to reference an item in an **Items** collection by name, you specify the value of the Subject field.

Before you run this example, do the following:

Click **New Mail Message** on the Outlook **Compose** menu. Address the message to yourself, and type **VBScript Test** in the **Subject** box. Click **Send**. Add the code in the example to the Script Editor, and then click **CommandButton1**.

```
Sub CommandButton1_Click
    Set MyFolder = Application.GetNameSpace("MAPI").GetDefaultFolder(6)
    Set MyItems = MyFolder.Items
    Set MyItem = MyItems("VBScript Test")
    MyItem.Display
End Sub
```

Generally, you don't reference an item in an **Items** collection by name. However, you almost always reference a field property in a **UserProperties** collection by name, as shown in this example that sets the name of the user-defined field called Customer Name to James Allard.

Before you run this example, do the following:

Make sure the form is in Design mode, and then click **Field Chooser** on the **Form Design** toolbar. In the Field Chooser, click **New**, type **Customer Name** in the **Name** box, and then click **OK**. Drag the **Customer Name** field from the Field Chooser to the form. Add the code in the example to the Script Editor. Click **Design Outlook Form** on the **Tools** menu to switch to Run mode, and then click **CommandButton1**.

```
Sub CommandButton1_Click
    UserProperties.Find("Customer Name").Value = "James Allard"
End Sub
```

# Troubleshooting

The Script Editor does not provide tools for debugging a form, so here are a few suggestions as workarounds:

- **Use a MsgBox to return values in procedures.** For example, to view the message class of a form, you can use the following code:

```
Sub CommandButton1_Click
    MsgBox FormDescription.MessageClass
End Sub
```

- **Use the PropertyChange or Click procedure to test code.** When you add code to a PropertyChange or Click procedure, you can immediately test the procedure without publishing the form.

- **Use the Run command in the Script Editor to check code syntax.**
- **Use the Shift key.** While opening a form, hold down the SHIFT key to start the form without executing the code in the form. This often provides a way to open a form that has code that executes when the Open event is triggered.

# The Application Object

The **Application** object sits at the top of the object model and represents the entire Microsoft Outlook application.

The Outlook **Application** object has several purposes:

- As the root object, it enables you to reference other objects in the Outlook object hierarchy.
- It provides methods such as **CreateItem** and **CreateObject** so that you can create new items and reference them without moving through the object hierarchy.
- It provides methods for directly referencing the active Outlook window or form.

**See Also**   For a complete list and description of the methods and properties for the **Application** object, see Microsoft Outlook Visual Basic Help.

# Application Object Methods

This section covers the **ActiveExplorer**, **CreateItem**, **CreateObject**, and **GetNameSpace** methods.

## Returning the Active Window

You can use the **ActiveExplorer** method of the **Application** object to return the active Outlook window.

The following example sets the **MyExplorer** object to the currently active Outlook window, and then displays the window on the desktop when the CommandButton1 control is clicked. To make this example work, add a CommandButton1 control to the form, and then add the example code to the Script Editor.

```
Sub CommandButton1_Click
    Set MyExplorer = Application.ActiveExplorer
    MyExplorer.Display
End Sub
```

## Creating a Standard Item

You can use the **CreateItem** method of the **Application** object to create and return Outlook standard items, such as a message item, a post item, or an appointment item.

This example creates a message item and shows it when CommandButton1 is clicked.

```
Sub CommandButton1_Click
    Set MyItem = Application.CreateItem(0)
    MyItem.Display
End Sub
```

The following table lists the numeric values that you use as arguments for the **CreateItem** method.

| Type of item | Value |
|---|---|
| Mail message | 0 |
| Appointment | 1 |
| Contact | 2 |
| Task | 3 |
| Journal | 4 |
| Note | 5 |
| Post | 6 |

**See Also**   For more information about creating custom items, see "Items Collection Methods" later in this chapter.

## Creating an Automation Object

You can use the **CreateObject** method of the **Application** object to create Automation objects, such as Microsoft Excel, Microsoft Access, or Microsoft Word objects.

This example is taken from the Document Tracking application, which is covered in Chapter 12. It uses the **CreateObject** method to create a database engine automation object. It then calls the FieldValues procedure that writes the values from the item to the Microsoft Access 97 database.

**See Also**   For more information about this procedure and how it's used, see Chapter 12, "The Document Tracking Application."

**Important**   Data Access Objects (DAO) will only work if the user has Microsoft Office 97 (not stand-alone Outlook) installed. In addition, the user must install "Data Access Objects for Visual Basic" (DAO 3.5) during Office 97 Setup.

```
Sub AddNewDatabaseRecord
   DbOpenTable = 1
   On Error Resume Next
   Set Dbe = Item.Application.CreateObject("DAO.DBEngine.35")
   If Err.Number <> 0 Then
      Msgbox Err.Description & " -- Some functions may not work correctly" & Chr(13) &
      ➥"Please make sure that DAO 3.0 or greater is installed on this machine."
      Exit Sub
   End If
   Set MyDb = Dbe.Workspaces(0).OpenDatabase("C:\My Documents\Document Tracking.mdb")
   Set Rs = MyDb.OpenRecordset("Tracking Information", DbOpenTable)
   Rs.AddNew
   Rs("Status") = Item.Status
   Call FieldValues
   Rs.Update
   Rs.MoveLast
   Rs.Close
   MyDb.Close
End Sub
```

**Note**   The **CreateObject** method is unique to Outlook's implementation of Visual Basic Scripting Edition.

## Returning a MAPI NameSpace Object

You can use the **GetNameSpace("MAPI")** method of the **Application** object to return the MAPI message store.

In this example, the **GetNameSpace** method returns the **NameSpace** object. The **CurrentUser** property of the **NameSpace** object is then used to show your name in a message box.

```
Sub CommandButton1_Click
   Set MyNameSpace = Application.GetNameSpace("MAPI")
   MsgBox MyNameSpace.CurrentUser
End Sub
```

**Important**   The only data source currently supported is MAPI, which allows access to all Outlook data stored in MAPI. For this reason, the **GetNameSpace** method must always appear in Outlook as **GetNameSpace("MAPI")**.

# The NameSpace Object

In Outlook, the **NameSpace** object represents the MAPI message store. The **NameSpace** object provides methods for logging on to or logging off Outlook, referencing a default folder, and returning objects directly by ID. In addition, the **NameSpace** object provides access to a variety of methods and properties that are not available with the **Application** object.

**See Also**   For a complete list and description of the methods and properties for the **NameSpace** object, see Microsoft Outlook Visual Basic Help.

# NameSpace Object Methods

This section covers the **GetDefaultFolder** method of the **NameSpace** object.

## Returning a Default Folder

You can use the **GetDefaultFolder** method of the **NameSpace** object to directly access the default folder—also known as the Mailbox. To reference a folder in the Mailbox, you must specify a numeric value as the argument in the **GetDefaultFolder** method. The following table lists these numeric values.

| Folder | Value |
| --- | --- |
| Deleted Items | 3 |
| Outbox | 4 |
| Sent Items | 5 |
| Inbox | 6 |
| Calendar | 9 |
| Contacts | 10 |
| Journal | 11 |
| Notes | 12 |
| Tasks | 13 |

This example uses the **GetDefaultFolder** method of the **NameSpace** object to return the Contacts folder and then show it.

```
Sub CommandButton1_Click
    Set MyFolder = Application.GetNameSpace("MAPI").GetDefaultFolder(10)
    MyFolder.Display
End Sub
```

# Properties of the NameSpace Object

The **NameSpace** object provides two properties that you use quite often. These are the **CurrentUser** and **Folders** properties.

## Returning the Name of the Current User

You can use the **CurrentUser** property of the **NameSpace** object to return the name of the currently logged-on user.

This example shows the current user's name in the message box when the CommandButton1 control is pressed.

```
Sub CommandButton1_Click
    Set MyNameSpace = Application.GetNameSpace("MAPI")
    MsgBox MyNameSpace.CurrentUser
End Sub
```

## Referencing a Folder Collection

You can use the **Folders** property of the **NameSpace** object to reference the collection of folders in the MAPI name space.

This example references the highest level folders in the Folder List and then shows the count in a message.

```
Sub CommandButton1_Click
    Set MyNameSpace = Application.GetNameSpace("MAPI")
    Set MyFolders = MyNameSpace.Folders
    MsgBox MyFolders.Count
End Sub
```

# The Outlook Window (Explorer Object)

The Outlook window is represented by the **Explorer** object. The following sections cover some of the methods and properties for the **Explorer** object.

**See Also**   For a complete list and description of the methods and properties for the **Explorer** object, see Microsoft Outlook Visual Basic Help.

# Explorer Methods

This section covers the **Display** method of the **Explorer** object.

### Showing the Active Outlook Window

You can use the **Display** method of the **Explorer** object to show the active Outlook window.

This example returns the active Outlook window, and then shows it on the desktop.

```
Sub CommandButton1_Click
    Set MyExplorer = Application.ActiveExplorer
    MyExplorer.Display
End Sub
```

# Explorer Properties

This section explains how to use the **CurrentFolder** property.

### Returning the Active Folder

You can use the **CurrentFolder** property of the **Explorer** object to return the active folder in the Outlook window.

This example shows the name of the active folder in the message box when the CommandButton1 control is clicked.

```
Sub CommandButton1_Click
    Set MyExplorer = Application.ActiveExplorer
    MsgBox MyExplorer.CurrentFolder
End Sub
```

# The Folders Collection Object

The Outlook 8.0 Object Library provides two folder objects: a **Folders** collection object and a **MAPIFolder** object. The **Folders** collection object represents multiple folders. The **MAPIFolder** object, covered later in this chapter, represents a single folder.

The **Folders** collection object, which can contain one or multiple folders, is always referenced from the **NameSpace** object.

**See Also**   For a complete list and description of the methods and properties for the **Folders** collection object, see Microsoft Outlook Visual Basic Help.

# Folders Collection Methods

This section covers the **Add** and **Item** methods of the **Folders** collection object.

## Adding a Folder to the Folder List

You can use the **Add** method of the **Folders** collection object to add a folder to the Folder List.

This example uses the **Add** method of the **Folders** collection object to add a folder called My New Folder to the Building Microsoft Outlook 97 Applications personal folder.

```
Sub CommandButton1_Click
   Set MyNameSpace = Application.GetNameSpace("MAPI")
   Set MyFolder = MyNameSpace.Folders("Building Microsoft Outlook 97 Applications")
   Set MyNewFolder = MyFolder.Folders.Add("My New Folder")
End Sub
```

## Iterating Through a Collection of Folders

You can use the **Item** method of the **Folders** collection object to iterate through a collection of folders.

This example uses the **Item** method of the **Folders** collection object to return My New Folder and then display it. It also uses the **Count** property of the **Folders** collection object to return the number of folder items in the folders collection.

```
Sub CommandButton1_Click
   Set MyNameSpace = Application.GetNameSpace("MAPI")
   Set MyFolders = MyNameSpace.Folders("Building Microsoft Outlook 97 Applications")
   Set MyCollection = MyFolders.Folders
   For i = 1 to MyCollection.Count
      Set MyFolder = MyCollection.Item(i)
      MsgBox MyFolder.Name
   Next
End Sub
```

**Note**   When moving through a collection of folders or items, the folders or items are ordered in the collection based upon the date they are received in the folder.

# The MAPIFolder Object

The **MAPIFolder** object represents a single Outlook folder. A **MAPIFolder** object can contain other **MAPIFolder** objects, as well as Outlook items. This section explains how to move through the Folder List by using the **MAPIFolder** object and its **Folders** property.

**See Also**   For a complete list and description of the methods and properties for the **MAPIFolder** object, see Microsoft Outlook Visual Basic Help.

# MAPIFolder Object Methods

This section covers the **CopyTo** and **Display** methods of the **MAPIFolder** object.

## Copying a Folder

You can use the **CopyTo** method of the **MAPIFolder** object to create a copy of a folder in another folder.

This example copies the Notes folder to Inbox.

```
Sub CommandButton1_Click
    Set MyNameSpace = Application.GetNameSpace("MAPI")
    Set MyInboxFolder = MyNameSpace.GetDefaultFolder(6)
    Set MyCurrentFolder = MyNameSpace.GetDefaultFolder(12)
    Set MyNewFolder = MyCurrentFolder.CopyTo(MyInboxFolder)
End Sub
```

## Displaying a Folder

You can use the **Display** method of the **MAPIFolder** object to display the folder represented by the **MAPIFolder** object.

```
Sub CommandButton1_Click
    Set MyNameSpace = Application.GetNameSpace("MAPI")
    Set MyFolder = MyNameSpace.Folders("Public Folders")
    MyFolder.Display
End Sub
```

# MAPIFolder Object Properties

This section covers the **Folders** and **Items** properties. The **Folders** property is useful for accessing a folder in the Folder List. The **Items** property is useful for retrieving a collection of items in the folder.

## Referencing a Folder in the Folder List

You can use the **Folders** property with the **MAPIFolder** object to return another **MAPIFolder** object.

In this procedure, the **Folders** property is used to move through the various branches of the Public Folders list.

```
Sub CommandButton1_Click
    Set MyNameSpace = Application.GetNameSpace("MAPI")
    Set MyFolder = MyNameSpace.Folders("Building Microsoft Outlook 97 Applications")
    Set BeyondFolder = MyFolder.Folders("4. Beyond the Basics")
    Set VBScriptFolder = BeyondFolder.Folders("VBScript")
    MsgBox VBScriptFolder.Name
End Sub
```

# Iterating Through a Collection of Items in a Folder

You can use the **Items** property of the **MAPIFolder** object to return a collection of items in the folder.

The following example uses the **Items** property of the **MAPIFolder** object to return the collection of items in the Inbox folder. It then shows the Subject value of the first five items in the **Items** collection. The items in the **Items** collection are ordered by date received, so the oldest items show first in the collection.

```
Sub CommandButton1_Click
    Set MyNameSpace = Application.GetNameSpace("MAPI")
    Set MyInboxFolder = MyNameSpace.GetDefaultFolder(6)
    Set MyItems = MyInboxFolder.Items
    For i = 1 to 5
        Set MyItem = MyItems(i)
        Msgbox MyItem.Subject
    Next
End Sub
```

# The EntryID and StoreID Properties

The **EntryID** and **StoreID** properties of the **MAPIFolder** object can be used to identify a folder in Outlook. These properties are useful when you are working with multiple-folder applications.

This example sets the value of the entry ID for the Folder field to the entry ID of the folder and the value of the entry ID for the Store field to the store ID.

Before you run this example, do the following:

Make sure the form is in Design mode, and then click **Field Chooser** on the **Form Design** toolbar. In the Field Chooser, click **New**, type **Entry ID for Folder** in the **Name** box, and then click **OK**. Drag the **Entry ID for Folder** field from the Field Chooser to the form. In the Field Chooser, click **New**, type **Entry ID for Store** in the **Name** box, and then click **OK**. Drag the **Entry ID for Store** field from the Field Chooser to the form. Add the code in the example to the Script Editor. Click **Design Outlook Form** on the **Tools** menu to switch to Run mode, and then click **CommandButton1**.

```
Sub CommandButton1_Click
    Set MyFolder = Application.ActiveExplorer.CurrentFolder
    UserProperties.Find("Entry ID for Folder") = MyFolder.EntryID
    UserProperties.Find("Entry ID for Store") = MyFolder.StoreID
End Sub
```

# The Items Collection Object

Items are the discrete packages of information represented by a mail message, a post item, a contact item, a journal item, a meeting request, a note, or a task item. You use the **Items** property to return the **Items** collection of a **MAPIFolder** object. The single item object is represented by the following objects: **JournalItem**, **MailItem**, **MeetingRequestItem**, **NoteItem**, **PostItem**, **RemoteItem**, **ReportItem**, **TaskItem**, and **TaskRequestItem**. This section covers some of the methods and properties of the **Items** collection object. The next section covers the methods and properties of a single item object.

**See Also**  For a complete list and description of the methods and properties for the **Items** collection object, see Microsoft Outlook Visual Basic Help.

## Items Collection Methods

This section covers the **Add**, **Find**, and **Restrict** methods of the **Items** collection object.

### Creating a Custom Item

With Outlook, there are two basic methods of creating items. Standard items such as message items (IPM.Note), post items (IPM.Post), and contact items (IPM.Contact) are created by using the **CreateItem** method of the **Application** object, as discussed earlier in this chapter.

To create custom items, however, such as an IPM.Post.Product Idea item, you use the **Add** method of the **Items** collection object. For example, to create a Product Idea item (IPM.Post.Product Idea) for the Products Ideas folder, you must first return the **Items** collection object, and then use the **Add** method of the **Items** collection object to add the new item to the folder collection.

**Important**  Before you can create a custom item, the form associated with the item must exist in the Folder Forms Library that the item is created from. For example, to create a Product Idea item, the Product Idea form must exist in the Product Ideas Folder Forms Library.

The following example references the Product Ideas folder and then creates a Product Idea item and displays it. Note that the Product Idea form exists in the Product Ideas Folder Forms Library.

```
Sub CommandButton1_Click
    Set MyNameSpace = Application.GetNameSpace("MAPI")
    Set BuildFolder = MyNameSpace.Folders("Building Microsoft Outlook 97 Applications")
    Set QuickFolder = BuildFolder.Folders("2. Quick Guide")
    Set ProductIdeasFolder = QuickFolder.Folders("Product Ideas")
    Set MyItems = ProductIdeasFolder.Items
    Set MyItem = MyItems.Add("IPM.Post.Product Idea")
    MyItem.Subject = "VBScript Test"
    MyItem.Body = "This is a test"
    MyItem.Display
End Sub
```

**Important**   Notice in the preceding procedure that the **Body** property of the single item object corresponds with the Message field on the form. For more details about the properties of standard items, see "Properties of the MailItem and PostItem Objects" later in this chapter.

## Finding an Item in a Folder

You can use the **Find** method of the **Items** collection object to find an item in a folder based on the conditions that you specify.

This example uses the **Find** method of the **Items** collection object to return the first item in the Product Ideas folder with the value "Boating" in the Product Category field.

```
Sub CommandButton1_Click
    Set MyNameSpace = Application.GetNameSpace("MAPI")
    Set BuildFolder = MyNameSpace.Folders("Building Microsoft Outlook 97 Applications")
    Set QuickFolder = BuildFolder.Folders("2. Quick Guide")
    Set ProductIdeasFolder = QuickFolder.Folders("Product Ideas")
    Set MyItem = ProductIdeasFolder.Items.Find("[Product Category] = 'Boating'")
    MyItem.Display
End Sub
```

## Creating a Filtered Collection of Items from a Folder

You can use the **Restrict** method of the **Items** collection object to create filters that return only those items in a folder that match the conditions you specify.

This example returns the collection of items from the Product Ideas folder, and then creates a filtered collection of only items with the value "Boating" in the Product Category field.

```
Sub CommandButton1_Click
    Set MyNameSpace = Application.GetNameSpace("MAPI")
    Set BuildFolder = MyNameSpace.Folders("Building Microsoft Outlook 97 Applications")
    Set QuickFolder = BuildFolder.Folders("2. Quick Guide")
    Set ProductIdeasFolder = QuickFolder.Folders("Product Ideas")
    Set MyItems = ProductIdeasFolder.Items
    Set MyFilter = MyItems.Restrict("[Product Category] = 'Boating'")
    MsgBox MyFilter.Count
End Sub
```

# Properties of the Items Collection Object

This section explains how to use the **Count** property.

## Returning the Count of Items in the Items Collection

You can use the **Count** property of the **Items** collection object to return the number of items in the **Items** collection. This provides an easy way to loop through collections to process a large number of items, as shown in the previous example.

This example returns the number of items in your Inbox and shows the number in a message box.

```
Sub CommandButton1_Click
    Set MyFolder = Item.Application.GetNameSpace("MAPI").GetDefaultFolder(6)
    Set MyItems = MyFolder.Items
    MsgBox "You have " & MyItems.Count & " items in your Inbox."
End Sub
```

# The Item Object

The single item object is represented by the various standard item types provided in Outlook. These include the following objects:

- **MailItem** object—a mail message item
- **AppointmentItem** object—an appointment item
- **ContactItem** object—a contact item
- **TaskItem** object—a task item
- **JournalItem** object—a journal item
- **NoteItem** object—a note item
- **PostItem** object—a post item

**Important**   When a custom item is created, that item has the methods and properties of the item upon which is it based. For example, an item with the message class IPM.Post.Product Idea uses the methods and properties of the **PostItem** object. If you create an item with the message class IPM.Note.Orders, you use the **NoteItem** object.

**See Also**   For more information about how to create a standard item, see "Creating a Standard Item" in "Application Object Methods" earlier in this chapter. For more information about how to create a custom item, see "Creating a Custom Item" in the preceding "Items Collection Methods."

# Methods of the PostItem Object

The **PostItem** object provides a variety of methods that you can use to control the actions of an item. This section covers the **Copy**, **Move**, **Display**, and **Post** methods.

## Copying and Moving an Item

You can use the **Copy** method of the **PostItem** object to create a copy of an item. You can then use the **Move** method to move the copied item to a new location.

This example returns the first item in the Product Ideas folder with the value "Boating" in the Product Category field. It then uses the **Copy** method to create a copy of the item returned from the Product Ideas folder. The **Move** method is then used to move the copied item from the Product Ideas folder to the Inbox.

```
Sub CommandButton1_Click
    Set MyNameSpace = Application.GetNameSpace("MAPI")
    Set BuildFolder = MyNameSpace.Folders("Building Microsoft Outlook 97 Applications")
    Set QuickFolder = BuildFolder.Folders("2. Quick Guide")
    Set ProductIdeasFolder = QuickFolder.Folders("Product Ideas")
    Set MyItem = ProductIdeasFolder.Items.Find("[Product Category] = 'Boating'")
    Set MyCopiedItem = MyItem.Copy
    Set DestinationFolder = MyNameSpace.GetDefaultFolder(6)
    MyCopiedItem.Move DestinationFolder
End Sub
```

## Creating and Displaying a Custom Post Item

You can use the **Display** method of the **PostItem** object to display an item on the desktop. As discussed earlier, you use the **Add** method of the **Items** collection object to create a new custom post item.

This example returns the Product Ideas folder, and then creates a new custom **PostItem** object by using the **Add** method of the **Items** collection object. It then displays the item in the Product Ideas form. If you click the **Post** button on the form, the item is posted in the Product Ideas folder.

```
Sub CommandButton1_Click
    Set MyNameSpace = Application.GetNameSpace("MAPI")
    Set BuildFolder = MyNameSpace.Folders("Building Microsoft Outlook 97 Applications")
    Set QuickFolder = BuildFolder.Folders("2. Quick Guide")
    Set ProductIdeasFolder = QuickFolder.Folders("Product Ideas")
    Set MyItem = ProductIdeasFolder.Items.Add("IPM.Post.Product Idea")
    MyItem.Subject = "This is a test."
    MyItem.Body = "This is Message text."
    MyItem.Display
End Sub
```

## Posting an Item

You can use the **Post** method of the **PostItem** object to post an item in a folder.

The following example sets the folder to the Product Ideas folder. It then creates a new item with the message class IPM.Post Product Idea, which is added to the Product Ideas **Items** collection. In this procedure, the object returned to MyItem by the **Add** method is a **PostItem** object. The **Subject** and **Body** properties of the MyItem object are set, and then the item is posted to the Product Ideas folder. To run this example, use the names of the folders in your Folder List.

```
Sub CommandButton1_Click
    Set MyNameSpace = Application.GetNameSpace("MAPI")
    Set BuildFolder = MyNameSpace.Folders("Building Microsoft Outlook 97 Applications")
    Set QuickFolder = BuildFolder.Folders("2. Quick Guide")
    Set ProductIdeasFolder = QuickFolder.Folders("Product Ideas")
    Set MyItem = ProductIdeasFolder.Items.Add("IPM.Post.Product Idea")
    MyItem.Subject = "This is a test of the Post method."
    MyItem.Body = "This is Message text."
    MyItem.Post
End Sub
```

# Methods of the MailItem Object

This section covers the **Send**, **Reply**, and **Close** methods of the **MailItem** object.

## Sending a Message

You can use the **Send** method of the **MailItem** object to send a message to a recipient.

This example creates a mail message item, sets the Subject and message Body fields, and then sets the To field to your name. It then uses the **Send** method to send the item to the specified recipient.

```
Sub CommandButton1_Click
    Set MyItem = Application.CreateItem(0)
    MyItem.Subject = "This is a test"
    MyItem.Body = "This is Message Body text."
    MyItem.To = Application.GetNameSpace("MAPI").CurrentUser
    MyItem.Send
End Sub
```

## Replying to a Message

You can use the **Reply** method of a **MailItem** object to return a reply item.

This example creates a reply item based on the current item, and then returns the reply item, which is represented by the MyReply object. The reply item is then displayed. To run this example, you must first put a CommandButton1 control on the **Read** page of a Mail Message form. Exit Design mode and send the item to your Inbox, and then open the item in the Inbox and click **CommandButton1**. The reply item is displayed.

```
Sub CommandButton1_Click
    Set MyFolder = Application.GetNameSpace("MAPI").GetDefaultFolder(6)
    Set MyItem = MyFolder.Items.Item(1)
    Set MyReply = MyItem.Reply
    MyReply.Display
End Sub
```

## Closing an Item

You can use the **Close** method of the **MailItem** object to close an item. When you close the item, you also close the item's associated form.

This example closes the current item when CommandButton1 is clicked.

```
Sub CommandButton1_Click
    Item.Close(2)
End Sub
```

You can use one of the following arguments with the **Close** method.

| Save option | Value |
| --- | --- |
| Save all changes without prompting | 0 |
| Discard all changes without prompting | 1 |
| Prompt to save or discard all changes | 2 |

# Properties of the MailItem and PostItem Objects

This section covers the **Body**, **GetInspector**, **To**, and **SenderName** properties of the **MailItem** and **PostItem** objects.

## Setting the Message Text of an Item

You can use the **Body** property of a **MailItem** object or a **PostItem** object to specify the text that appears in the Message control of a mail message.

The following example creates a reply item, enters text in the Message control of the reply item, and then sends the form. To run this example, you must first put a CommandButton1 control on the **Read** page of a Mail Message form. Then switch to Run mode and send the item to your Inbox. Open the item in the Inbox, and then click **CommandButton1**. The reply item appears.

```
Sub CommandButton1_Click
    Set MyReply = Item.Reply
    MyReply.Body = "It rains a lot here. "
    MyReply.Display
End Sub
```

**Note**   The **Body** property does not support Rich Text Format (RTF).

## Using GetInspector to Reference the Form

You can use the **GetInspector** property of the **MailItem** object to reference the form associated with an item. You can then reference the page on the form, and then the controls on the page.

This example uses the **GetInspector** property of the **MailItem** object to return the form associated with the item. It references the **Message** page on the form, and then sets the **Visible** property of the TextBox1 control to **False**.

Before you run this example, do the following:

If you don't have a TextBox1 control on the form, click **Design Outlook Form** on the **Tools** menu to switch to Design mode, and then drag a TextBox control from the Control Toolbox to the form. Click **Design Outlook Form** to switch to Run mode, and then click **CommandButton1** to hide the TextBox1 control.

```
Sub CommandButton1_Click
    Set MyPage = GetInspector.ModifiedFormPages("Message")
    MyPage.TextBox1.Visible = False
End Sub
```

## Setting the To Field of an Item

You can use the **To** property of the **MailItem** object to set the value of a To field.

This example creates a new item, and then sets the To field and Subject field values of the item.

```
Sub CommandButton1_Click
    Set MyItem = Application.CreateItem(0)
    MyItem.To = "James Allard"
    MyItem.Subject = "How to set the To field"
    MyItem.Display
End Sub
```

## Getting the Sender Name of an Item

You can use the **SenderName** property of the **MailItem** object to return the name of the person who sent the message. This example gets the first item in the Inbox and sets the Recip variable to the value of the **SenderName** property. It then creates a new message item and sets its To field to the value of the Recip variable. When the item is displayed, the value of the **SenderName** property shows in the **To** box of the form.

```
Sub CommandButton1_Click
    Set MyFolder = Application.GetNameSpace("MAPI").GetDefaultFolder(6)
    Set MyItem = MyFolder.Items(1)
    Recip = MyItem.SenderName
    Set MyNewItem = Application.CreateItem(0)
    MyNewItem.To = Recip
    MyNewItem.Display
End Sub
```

**Note**  In the preceding example, the name in the To field is not resolved. To resolve a name, the name must be added to the **Recipients** collection object. For more information, see "The Recipients Collection Object" later in this chapter.

# The Inspector Object

Forms in the Outlook object model are referenced by the **Inspector** object. This section covers only some of the methods and properties of the **Inspector** object.

**See Also**  For a complete list and description of the methods and properties for the **Inspector** object, see Microsoft Outlook Visual Basic Help.

# Methods of the Inspector Object

This section covers the **SetCurrentFormPage**, **HideFormPage**, and **ShowFormPage** methods of the **Inspector** object.

## Setting the Current Form Page

You can use the **SetCurrentFormPage** method of the **Inspector** object to set the current form page of a form.

This example shows the **Options** page as the current form page when you click the CommandButton1 control.

```
Sub CommandButton1_Click
    Set MyInspector = Item.GetInspector
    MyInspector.SetCurrentFormPage("Options")
End Sub
```

## Hiding and Showing a Form Page

You can use the **HideFormPage** method of the **Inspector** object to hide a form page.

In this example, the **Options** page of the Message form is hidden.

```
Sub CommandButton1_Click
    Set MyInspector = Item.GetInspector
    MyInspector.HideFormPage("Options")
End Sub
```

To show a form page, you use the **ShowFormPage** method of the **Inspector** object. Replace the preceding code with this code, and then click **CommandButton1** to show the **Options** page.

```
Sub CommandButton1_Click
    Set MyInspector = Item.GetInspector
    MyInspector.ShowFormPage("Options")
End Sub
```

# Properties of the Inspector Object

This section covers the **ModifiedFormPages** property of the **Inspector** object. The **ModifiedFormPages** property returns the entire collection of pages for a form. The **Pages** collection object is covered in more detail in the next section.

## Referencing a Form Page and Its Controls

You can use the **ModifiedFormPages** property of the **Inspector** object to return the **Pages** collection that represents the pages on a form that have been modified. Note that standard pages on a form, such as a **Message** page, are also included in the collection. You must use the **Pages** collection object to switch to the page, which then allows you to gain access to controls on the page.

The following example uses the **ModifiedFormPages** property of the **Inspector** object to return the **Inspector** object page in the **Pages** collection object. It then uses the **Controls** property of the **Page** object to reference the ToggleButton1 control. When the toggle button is down, the Label2 control is visible. When the toggle button is up, the Label2 control is not visible.

Before you run this example, do the following:

Switch to Design mode and drag a ToggleButton control from the Control Toolbox to the **Message** page of the form. Then drag a Label control from the Control Toolbox to the **Message** page. This example assumes that the Label control is named Label2. If it's not, change the name by right-clicking the Label control, and then click **Properties** on the shortcut menu. Click the **Display** tab, type **Label2** in the **Name** box, and then click **OK**. Note that the procedure uses ToggleButton1_Click instead of CommandButton1_Click. To run the example, click **Design Outlook Form** on the **Tools** menu to switch to Run mode, and then click **ToggleButton1**.

```
Sub ToggleButton1_Click
    Set MyPage = Item.GetInspector.ModifiedFormPages("Message")
    Set MyControl = MyPage.ToggleButton1
    If MyControl.Value = True Then
       MyPage.Label2.Visible = True
    Else
       MyPage.Label2.Visible = False
    End If
End Sub
```

# The Pages Collection Object

To reference a page or controls on a page, you use the **ModifiedFormPages** property of the **Inspector** object to reference the **Pages** collection object, and then reference the individual page by name or number.

This procedure uses the **ModifiedFormPages** property of the **Inspector** object to return the number of modified form pages in the **Pages** collection. Note that the pages are not added to the collection until the page is clicked at design time.

```
Sub CommandButton1_Click
    Set PagesCollection = Item.GetInspector.ModifiedFormPages
    MsgBox "The number of modified form pages in the Pages collection is " &
    ➥PagesCollection.Count & "."
End Sub
```

# The Page Object

**Important**   The **Page** object is contained in the Microsoft Forms 2.0 Object Library. To view the methods and properties for the **Page** object, use the Microsoft Excel 97 Object Browser.

You can use the **ModifiedFormPages** property to return the **Pages** collection from an **Inspector** object. You use **ModifiedFormPages(index)**, where index is the name or index number, to return a single page from a **Pages** collection.

This example references the **Message** page, and then references the CommandButton1 control on the page. When clicked, the CommandButton1 control moves to the left.

```
Sub CommandButton1_Click
    Set MyPage = GetInspector.ModifiedFormPages("Message")
    Set MyControl = MyPage.CommandButton1
    MyControl.Left = MyControl.Left + 20
End Sub
```

# The Controls Collection Object

To access controls on Outlook forms, you use the **Controls** collection object. The **Controls** collection object contains the collection of controls on a form page. To access an individual control in the **Controls** collection, you use the index value of the control or the name of the control. The **Controls** collection object is contained in the Microsoft Forms 2.0 Object Library. This section discusses how to reference control collections and controls on a form.

## Methods of the Controls Collection Object

**Important**   The **Controls** collection object is contained in the Microsoft Forms 2.0 Object Library. To view the methods and properties for the **Controls** collection object, use the Microsoft Excel 97 Object Browser.

The **Controls** collection object offers a variety of methods that enable you to manipulate the controls on a form. For example, you can use the **Move** method to move all the controls on a page. Or you can use the **SendToBack** method to send the controls in the **Controls** collection to the back layer of the page.

You can use the **Controls** property to return the **Controls** collection from a **Page** object. You use **Controls(index)**, where index is the name or index number, to return a control from a **Controls** collection.

### Adding a Control to the Form Page

You can use the **Add** method of the **Controls** collection object to add a control to the form.

This example uses the **Add** method to add a new CommandButton control to the **Message** page to the right of the CommandButton1 control.

```
Sub CommandButton1_Click
    Set MyPage = GetInspector.ModifiedFormPages("Message")
    Set MyControl = MyPage.Controls.Add("Forms.CommandButton.1")
    MyControl.Left = MyPage.CommandButton1.Left + 150
    MyControl.Top = MyPage.CommandButton1.Top
    MyControl.Width = 50
    MyControl.Height = 20
    MyControl.Caption = "New Button"
End Sub
```

**See Also**   For more information about using the **Add** method of the **Controls** collection object, see Microsoft Outlook Forms Help.

# Properties of the Controls Collection Object

The **Controls** collection object provides only the **Count** property. With the **Count** property, you can use the **For Each...Next** statement to loop through the controls in a collection.

This example returns the collection of controls on the **Test** page. It then displays the name of each control contained on the page. To test this example, rename a custom page "Test," and then add several controls to the page.

```
Sub CommandButton1_Click
    Set Page = Item.GetInspector.ModifiedFormPages("Test")
    Set MyControls = Page.Controls
    For i = 0 to MyControls.Count - 1
        MsgBox MyControls(i).Name
    Next
End Sub
```

**Important**   Notice that the **For Each...Next** statement starts at 0. You must use 0 to reference the first item in the collection. However, Outlook returns a count of 3. Therefore, you must specify the *Count -1* argument for the **For Each...Next** statement in Outlook. Also, Visual Basic Scripting Edition in Outlook supports only the **For Each...Next** statement.

# The Control Object

**Important**   The **Control** object and the individual control objects, such as CheckBox and TextBox, are contained in the Microsoft Forms 2.0 Object Library. To view the methods and properties for the **Controls** collection object, use the Microsoft Excel 97 Object Browser. For an up-to-date reference of the supported methods and properties for controls, see "Control Reference Help" in Microsoft Outlook Forms Help. To access Microsoft Outlook Forms Help, click **Microsoft Outlook Forms Help** on the Outlook **Help** menu. If this menu is not available, see "Help and Web Sites" earlier in this chapter.

In the Visual Basic Forms object model, the control objects are generically represented by a **Control** object. Further, they are individually represented by the objects that represent the names of the individual control components, such as **TextBox**, **CheckBox**, and so on. As discussed in the preceding section, to reference a control, use the **Controls** property to return the **Controls** collection from a **Page** object, and then use **Controls(index)**, where index is the name or index number, to return a control from a **Controls** collection.

# Properties of Control Objects

The properties available for a control will differ for each type of control. This section covers the **Value** property for the CheckBox control and the **Enabled** property for the TextBox control.

## Setting the Enabled Property of a Control

This example uses a CheckBox control called CheckBox1 and a TextBox control called TextBox1. When the CheckBox1 control is clicked, the procedure evaluates the state of CheckBox1. If the value of CheckBox1 is **True**, then TextBox1 is enabled; otherwise, it is not enabled.

Before you run this example, do the following:

With the form in Design mode, drag a CheckBox control from the Control Toolbox to the **Message** page of the form. If you don't have a TextBox control named TextBox1 already on the form, drag a TextBox control to the form. This example assumes it's named TextBox1. Switch the form to Run mode and then click **CheckBox1** to enable or disable the TextBox1 control.

```
Sub CheckBox1_Click
    Set MyPage = Item.GetInspector.ModifiedFormPages("Message")
    Set MyControls = MyPage.Controls
    If MyControls("CheckBox1").Value = True Then
        MyControls("TextBox1").Enabled = True
    Else
        MyControls("TextBox1").Enabled = False
    End If
End Sub
```

# Setting the PossibleValues Property of a ComboBox or ListBox

Rather than use the **AddItem** method to add items to a ListBox or ComboBox control, you can use the **PossibleValues** property. Note that the **PossibleValues** property is an undocumented property.

In this example, the **PossibleValues** property is used to add the values Red, Green, and Blue to the ComboBox1 control when CommandButton1 is clicked.

```
Sub CommandButton1_Click
    Set MyPage = Item.GetInspector.ModifiedFormPages("Message")
    MyPage.ComboBox1.PossibleValues = "Red;Green;Blue"
End Sub
```

# Resizing a Control Vertically and Horizontally

Quite often, you want controls on a form to adjust horizontally and vertically when the form is resized. To do this, you must set an invisible property called **LayoutFlags**. This example sets the **LayoutFlags** property for the TextBox1 control when you click CommandButton1.

To run this example, do the following:

In Design mode, add a TextBox1 control to the **P.2** page of a form. Resize the TextBox1 control so that its bottom border is near the bottom border of the form and its right border is near the right border of the form. (Don't obscure the CommandButton1 control.) Add the following code for the CommandButton1 control. Switch to Run mode, resize the form, and notice what happens. Then click **CommandButton1** and resize the form. After the **LayoutFlags** property is set, the controls adjust to the size of the form.

```
Sub CommandButton1_Click
    Item.GetInspector.ModifiedFormPages("P.2").TextBox1.LayoutFlags = 68
End Sub
```

After you set the **LayoutFlags** property, you can delete the procedure from the Script
Editor.

## Resizing a Control Vertically

Quite often, you want controls on the form to vertically resize when the form is
vertically resized. To do this, you set the **LayoutFlags** property to 65.

To run this example, do the following:

Delete the TextBox1 control from the **P.2** page and then add a new TextBox1 control.
Resize the TextBox1 control so that its bottom border is near the bottom border of the
form. (Don't obscure the CommandButton1 control.) Add the following code for the
CommandButton1 control. Switch to Run mode, and resize the form vertically. Then
click **CommandButton1**, and vertically resize the form again.

```
Sub CommandButton1_Click
    Item.GetInspector.ModifiedFormPages("P.2").TextBox1.LayoutFlags = 65
End Sub
```

After you set the **LayoutFlags** property, you can delete the procedure from the Script
Editor.

## Binding a Control to a Field at Run Time

You can use the **ItemProperty** property to bind a control to a field at run time.

To run this example, do the following:

Add a new TextBox1 control (or use the existing one if it's already on the form) to the
**P.2** page of the form. Add the following code for the CommandButton1 control.
Switch to Run mode, click the **Message** page, and type **Test** in the **Subject** box. Then
click **CommandButton1**. Notice the value in the **Subject** box appears in the
TextBox1 control because the control is now bound to the Subject field.

```
Sub CommandButton1_Click
    Item.GetInspector.ModifiedFormPages("P.2").TextBox1.ItemProperty = "Subject"
End Sub
```

# The UserProperties Collection Object

The **UserProperties** collection object represents the custom fields contained in an
item. To return a collection of user-defined fields for an item, you can use the
**UserProperties** method of the **MailItem** object, the **PostItem** object, and so on. The
**UserProperty** object represents a single field in the item.

**See Also**   For a complete list and description of the properties and methods for the
**UserProperties** collection object, see Microsoft Outlook Visual Basic Help.

**Note**   Standard properties in Outlook, such as **Subject**, **To**, and **Body**, are properties of the
individual item object. For more information, see "Properties of the MailItem and PostItem
Objects" earlier in this chapter.

# Methods of the UserProperties Collection Object

This section covers the **Find** method of the **UserProperties** collection object.

## Getting the Value of a User Property

You can use the **Find** method of the **UserProperties** collection object to get the value
of a user-defined field in an item.

The following example uses the **Find** method of the **UserProperties** collection object
to return the value of the Customer Name field when the CommandButton1 control is
clicked.

Before you run this example, do the following:

Drag the Customer Name field you created earlier in this chapter to the **Message** page
of the form. If you didn't create a Customer Name field, do so now by clicking **New**
in the Field Chooser, typing **Customer Name**, and then clicking **OK**. Click the **All
Fields** tab on the form, and then in the **Value** cell for **Customer Name**, type **James
Allard**. Click the **Message** page, and then click **CommandButton1**.

```
Sub CommandButton1_Click
    MsgBox "The value of the Customer Name field is " &
    ➥UserProperties.Find("Customer Name").Value & "."
End Sub
```

## Setting the Value of a User Property

You can also use the **Find** method of the **UserProperties** collection object to set the
value of a field.

This examples uses the **Find** method of the **UserProperties** collection object to set
the value of the Customer Name field, and the ComboBox control to which it is
bound, to the value "Scott Cooper."

```
Sub CommandButton1_Click
    UserProperties.Find("Customer Name") = "Scott Cooper"
End Sub
```

# The Recipients Collection Object

The **Recipients** collection object represents the names that appear in the To field of the **MailItem**, **MeetingRequestItem**, and **TaskRequestItem** objects.

This section covers the **Add** and **ResolveAll** methods of the **Recipients** collection object.

**See Also**   For a complete list and description of the properties and methods for the **Recipients** collection object and the **Recipient** object, see Microsoft Outlook Visual Basic Help.

## Adding Recipients to the Collection

You can use the **Add** method of the **Recipients** collection object to add recipient names to the **Recipients** collection.

This example creates a new message item, and then uses the **Recipients** property of the **MailItem** object to return the **Recipients** collection object which, in this case, is empty. It then adds two names to the **Recipients** collection object, uses the **ResolveAll** method to resolve the recipient names, and then displays the Message form.

For this example, you can replace the names "David Goodhand" and "Rich Andrews" with names of people in your organization.

```
Sub AddRecipientsToCollection_Click
    Set MyItem = Application.CreateItem(0)
    Set MyRecipient = MyItem.Recipients
    MyRecipient.Add("David Goodhand")
    MyRecipient.Add("Rich Andrews")
    MyRecipient.ResolveAll
    MyItem.Display
End Sub
```

## Automatically Addressing an Item to All Contacts in a Contacts Folder

This example uses the **Add** method and the **ResolveAll** method to show how you can use the **Recipients** collection object to create a procedure that enables you to automatically address a message to all the users in the Contacts folder in your Mailbox. In this procedure, the Contact's e-mail addresses are added to the **Recipients** collection object.

```
Sub CommandButton1_Click
    Set MyNameSpace = Application.GetNameSpace("MAPI")
    Set MyFolder = MyNameSpace.GetDefaultFolder(10)
    Set MyItems = MyFolder.Items
    Set MySendItem = Application.CreateItem(0)
    Set MyRecipients = MySendItem.Recipients
    MyCount = MyItems.Count
    For i = 1 To MyCount
        If MyItems(i).EMaillAddress > " " Then
            MyRecipients.Add MyItems(i).EMaillAddress
            MsgBox MyItems(i).EMaillAddress
        End If
    Next
    MyRecipients.ResolveAll
    MySendItem.Display
End Sub
```

# Events

By using the Script Editor, you can add code to Outlook events to modify the behavior of the event. For example, for the Open event, you can add code to specify the current form page, or you can add code to write data from a database into a ComboBox control. For the Click event, you can create a procedure that creates a custom item, includes an attachment to the current item, and then posts the item in a folder. In addition to modifying events, you can prevent events from occurring.

▶ **To add or modify an event**

1   With the form in Design mode, click **View Code** on the **Form Design** toolbar.

2   On the Script Editor **Script** menu, click **Event**.

3   In the **Events** box, double-click the event you want.

With an event procedure, the word *Item* refers to the current Outlook item associated with the form. For example, the following Item_PropertyChange procedure sets the value of the Subject field in the item when the value in the **Sensitivity** box on the **Options** page is changed.

```
Sub Item_PropertyChange(ByVal PropertyName)
   Select Case PropertyName
      Case "Sensitivity"
         Item.Subject = "The sensitivity value has changed."
   End Select
End Sub
```

▶ **To test the preceding example code**

1   On the Outlook **Compose** menu, click **New Mail Message**.

2   On the form **Tools** menu, click **Design Outlook Form**.

3   On the **Form Design** toolbar, click **View Code**.

4   Add the preceding sample code to the Script Editor window.

5   On the form **Tools** menu, click **Design Outlook Form**.

6   Click the **Options** page, and then click a new value in the **Sensitivity** box.

7   Click the **Message** page.

   The text is now added to the **Subject** box.

# The Firing Sequence of Events

When an Outlook form is opened to compose an item or to read an item, events are fired in the following sequence.

## When You Create a New Item

When you create a new item, the Item_Open event is fired. In Outlook, you generally create a new item by opening a form. However, for certain folders such as the Tasks folder, you can create a new item by clicking the **New Item** row in the folder. In either case, the Item_Open event is fired.

## When You Send an Item

When you send an item, the Item_Send event is fired, followed by the Item_Write event, and the Item_Close event.

**Note**   The message class, IPM.Note, is used for sending items.

## When You Post or Save an Item

In Outlook, posting an item performs the same task as saving an item. When you post or save an item, the Item_Write event is fired. There are several cases in which an Item_Write event may occur. For example, a post item is created and the **Post** button is clicked on the form; a contact item is created and the **Save and Close** button is clicked on the form; a task item is created by clicking the **New Item** row, and then the item is saved when the user clicks outside the **New Item** row.

When you post or save an item, the Item_Write event is fired, followed by the Item_Close event.

### When You Open an Existing Item

In Outlook, an item can be opened in a couple of ways. If the item exists in a view that allows in-cell editing, the item can be opened simply by clicking the item in the view. In addition, an existing item can also be opened by double-clicking the item and viewing it in a form. When either case occurs, the Item_Read event is fired, followed by the Item_Open event.

### When You Close an Item

When you close an item, the Item_Close event is fired. If changes have been made to the item when you attempt to close it, you are asked if you want to save the item. If you click **Yes**, the Item_Write event is fired, followed by the Item_Close event.

# Preventing Events from Firing

In some cases, you may want to prevent events from occurring. For example, for a Reply event, you may want to add code that opens a custom form rather than the default Message form. To do this, you must first prevent the default behavior from occurring. To prevent the default behavior from occurring, you assign **False** to the function value.

This example prevents the standard Reply event from occurring in a Mail Message form. Instead, it opens a custom Orders form when the **Reply** button is pressed.

```
Function Item_Reply(ByVal Response)
    Item_Reply = False
    Set MyFolder = Application.GetNameSpace("MAPI").GetDefaultFolder(6)
    Set MyItem = MyFolder.Items.Add("IPM.Note.Orders")
    MyItem.To = Item.To
    MyItem.Subject = "RE: " & MyItem.Subject
    MyItem.Display
End Function
```

Events that can be interrupted include Item_Close, Item_CustomAction, Item_Forward, Item_Open, Item_Reply, Item_ReplyAll, Item_Send, and Item_Write.

# The Click Event

The Click event occurs when a user clicks a control, such as a command button, on a form. You can create as many Click procedures as you have controls on the form.

**Important**   The Click event is the only Visual Basic Scripting Edition control event supported in Outlook.

▶ **To create a Click event procedure**

- In the Script Editor, type the name of the control that you are creating the Click event for, followed by an underscore character (_) and the word "Click."

This example creates an item and displays the standard Message form when the CommandButton1 control is clicked on the form.

```
Sub CommandButton1_Click
    Set MyItem = Application.CreateItem(0)
    MyItem.Subject = "This is a test."
    MyItem.To = "David Goodhand"
    MyItem.Display
End Sub
```

**See Also**   For more information about working with controls, see "The Controls Collection Object" and "The Control Object" earlier in this chapter.

# The Close Event

The Close event occurs when the form associated with the item is being closed. When the Close event occurs, the form is still open on the desktop. You can prevent the form from closing by setting the function value to **False**.

The following example shows the code used in the Close event for the Document Tracking form in the Document Tracking application, which is covered in Chapter 12. In this code sample, if the value of the NewItemCreated variable is **True**, then the SendNotification procedure is called. The SendNotification procedure sends a notification message to users to indicate that a new item has been posted in the Document Tracking folder.

```
Function Item_Close()
    If NewItemCreated = True Then
        Call SendNotification
        NewItemCreated = False
    End If
End Function
```

**See Also**   For more information about how this event works, see "The Item_Close Event Procedure" in Chapter 12, "The Document Tracking Application."

# The CustomAction Event

The CustomAction event occurs when a custom action defined in the form is carried out. You define custom actions on the **Action** page of a form by creating a new action. When a CustomAction event is fired, both the name of the custom action being carried out and the newly created response item are passed to the CustomAction event. You can prevent the custom action from occurring by setting the function value to **False**.

This example shows a CustomAction event procedure that is used in the Assigned Help Task form in the Help Desk application, which is covered in Chapter 11. In this case, the Discussion action is created at design time with the form **Action Properties** dialog box. The action is triggered when the user clicks the **Discussion** button on the Assigned Help Task form.

```
Function Item_CustomAction(ByVal MyAction, ByVal MyResponse)
   Select Case MyAction.Name
      Case "Discussion"
         MyResponse.Body = "For more information about this ticket,
         ↦double-click the link." & Chr(10)
         MyResponse.Display
   End Select
End Function
```

To trigger an action from a command button, you can use the **Execute** method of the **Action** object. For example, when the **Discussion** button is pressed on the Assigned Help Task form, the custom Discussion action is triggered.

```
Sub Discussion_Click
   Item.Save
   Item.Actions("Discussion").Execute
End Sub
```

**See Also**  For more information about how this event works, see "Create a Task Discussion Item" in Chapter 11, "The Help Desk Application."

**Tip**  You can also use the CustomAction event as a custom method. For example, you can set the CustomAction event to **False** so that the response form is not loaded. You can then add code to the CustomAction event procedure to accomplish the task you want. For example, you can add code to the CustomAction event to automatically create an announcement message and send it to a distribution list.

# The CustomPropertyChange Event

The CustomPropertyChange event occurs when the value changes in one of the item's user-defined fields. The field name is passed to the procedure, so you can create a **Select Case** statement to determine which field value has changed.

The following example is used in the Document Tracking application in Chapter 12. In this example, the field name is passed as an argument to the FieldName parameter. The **Select Case** statement is then used to evaluate the field that is changed. In this example, the Format Other field is linked to the Format Other check box. If the field is Format Other and its value is **True**, then the OtherComments text box is enabled. If the value of the Format Other field is **False**, then the OtherComments text box is cleared, and the text box is not enabled.

```
Sub Item_CustomPropertyChange(ByVal FieldName)
    ItemChanged = True
    Select Case FieldName
        Case "Format Other"
            Set MyPage = Item.GetInspector.ModifiedFormPages("Production Information")
            Set MyOtherComments = MyPage.Controls("OtherComments")
            If Item.UserProperties.Find("Format Other").Value = True Then
                MyOtherComments.Enabled = True
            Else
                MyOtherComments.Enabled = False
                Item.UserProperties.Find("Other Comments").Value = ""
            End If
    End Select
End Sub
```

**See Also**   For more information about this example, see "The Item_CustomPropertyChange Event Procedure" in Chapter 12, "The Document Tracking Application."

# The Forward Event

The Forward event occurs when the user initiates the Forward action on a form—usually by clicking the **Forward** button. You can prevent the default Forward behavior from occurring by setting the function value to **False**.

In this example, the Forward event is prevented from firing if the message is confidential.

```
Function Item_Forward(ByVal MyForwardItem)
    If Item.Sensitivity = 3 Then
        MsgBox "This message is confidential and cannot be forwarded."
        Item_Forward = False
    End If
End Function
```

# The Open Event

The Open event occurs when an Outlook form is opened to either compose an item or read an item. When the Open event occurs, the form is initialized but not yet displayed. You can prevent the form from opening by setting the function value to **False**.

The following example checks the **ReceivedTime** property of a message to determine if the form is in Compose or Read mode. If the **ReceivedTime** property is not set, then the **Message** page is shown. If the **ReceivedTime** property is set, then the **Options** page is shown, so that the person processing the order can view the order.

Before you run this example, do the following:

Add this example code to the Script Editor window, and then click **Publish Form As** on the **Form Design** toolbar. In the **Name** box, type **TestEvent** and publish the form to the Personal Forms Library. On the Outlook **Compose** menu, click **Choose Form**, and then select the **TestEvent** form in the Personal Forms Library. Notice the **Message** page is shown. Now address the form to yourself and click **Send**. Then double-click the sent item in your Inbox. Notice that the **Options** page is shown.

```
Function Item_Open()
    If Item.ReceivedTime <> "1/1/4501" Then
        Item.GetInspector.SetCurrentFormPage("Options")
        Item.GetInspector.HideFormPage("Message")
    Else
        Item.GetInspector.SetCurrentFormPage("Message")
        Item.GetInspector.HideFormPage("Options")
    End If
End Function
```

**Important**  Notice in the preceding example that the **If** statement checks to see if the ReceivedTime field is set to "1/1/4501." In Outlook, Date fields that show "None" in the field will return a value of "1/1/4501."

# The PropertyChange Event

The PropertyChange event occurs when one of the item's standard fields, such as Subject, To, Importance, or Sensitivity is changed. The field name is passed to the procedure, so you can use the **Select Case** statement to determine which field value has changed.

In this example, a message box shows the value of the Importance or Sensitivity field if the values in the fields are changed. To test this example, add the following code to the Script Editor, exit Design mode, and then change the values of the **Importance** and **Sensitivity** boxes on the **Options** page.

```
Sub Item_PropertyChange(ByVal FieldName)
    Select Case FieldName
        Case "Importance"
            MsgBox "The value of the Importance field is " & Item.Importance & "."
        Case "Sensitivity"
            MsgBox "The value of the Sensitivity field is " & Item.Sensitivity & "."
    End Select
End Sub
```

# The Read Event

The Read event occurs when an existing Outlook item is opened for editing by a user. The Read event differs from the Open event in that the Read event occurs whenever a user selects the item in a view that supports in-cell editing, as well as when the item is being opened in an inspector. The Read event is fired before the Open event.

In this example, the value of the Date Opened user-defined field is set when the submitted item is first opened.

Before you run this example, do the following:

Click **New** in the Field Chooser, and then type **Date Opened** in the **Name** box. In the **Type** box, click **Date/Time**, and then click **OK**. Drag the Date Opened field to the **Message** page, and then click **Edit Read Page** on the **Form Design** toolbar. Resize the Message control to make room for the Date Opened control, and then drag the Date Opened field from the Field Chooser to the **Read** page. Click **Publish Form As** and publish the form in your Personal Forms Library. Then, on the Outlook **Compose** menu, click **Choose Form**, and select the form. Address the form to yourself and click **Send**. Double-click the sent item in your Inbox. Notice that the current date is now in the Date Opened field.

```
Function Item_Read()
    If Item.UserProperties.Find("Date Opened").Value = "1/1/4501" Then
        Item.UserProperties.Find("Date Opened").Value = Now
    End If
End Function
```

# The Reply Event

The Reply event occurs when a user clicks the **Reply** button on the form. When the Reply event occurs, the newly created reply item is passed to the procedure. You can prevent the item from being sent by setting the function value to **False**.

This example prevents the standard Reply event from occurring, and creates an item with a custom Task form. It then copies the values from the item's Subject and To fields to the task response item.

```
Function Item_Reply(ByVal Response)
    Item_Reply = False
    Set MyFolder = Application.GetNameSpace("MAPI").GetDefaultFolder(13)
    Set MyItem = MyFolder.Items.Add("IPM.Task.Test")
    MyItem.To = Item.To
    MyItem.Subject = "RE: " & MyItem.Subject
    MyItem.Display
End Function
```

# The ReplyAll Event

The ReplyAll event occurs when a user clicks the **ReplyAll** command on a form. When a user clicks **ReplyAll**, the response is sent to the sender and to all recipients in the **To** and **Cc** boxes on the form. You can prevent the item from being sent by setting the function value to **False**.

The following example reminds the user that he or she is replying to all the original recipients of an item and makes it possible for the user to cancel the action.

```
Function Item_ReplyAll (ByVal MyResponse)
    MyResult = MsgBox("Do you really want to send this reply to all the
    ➥recipients in the To and Cc boxes? ", 289, "Flame Protector")
    If MyResult = 1 Then
        Item_ReplyAll = True
    Else
        Item_ReplyAll = False
    End If
End Function
```

# The Send Event

The Send event occurs when a user sends an item. You can prevent the item from being sent by setting the function value to **False**. If you prevent the event from occurring, the form remains open.

This example automatically sets the expiration date on the item when the item is sent.

```
Function Item_Send()
    Item.ExpiryTime = Date + 7
End Function
```

# The Write Event

The Write event occurs when the user either sends, posts, or saves an item.

You can prevent an item from being saved by setting the function value to **False**. Quite often, you can include code that writes to external objects such as databases or spreadsheets when the Write event is fired.

This example is taken from Chapter 12, "The Document Tracking Application," and shows how the Item_Write event is used to create or update a database record. For the Document Tracking form, the Item_Write event calls the AddNewDatabaseRecord procedure if a database record for the item has not been created. If the item has been created and the item is changed, the procedure calls the UpdateDatabaseRecord procedure.

```
Function Item_Write()
    If Item.UserProperties.Find("Database Record Created") = "No" Then
        Call AddNewDatabaseRecord
        Item.UserProperties.Find("Database Record Created") = "Yes"
    Else
        If ItemChanged = True Then
            Call UpdateDatabaseRecord
        End If
    End If
End Function
```

**See Also**   For more information, see "The Item_Write Event Procedure" in
Chapter 12, "The Document Tracking Application."

# A Quick Tutorial — the Library Order Application

So far, this chapter has covered a sampling of the objects and methods in Visual Basic
Scripting Edition. Now, let's look at how Outlook objects, methods, and properties
can be applied in the Library Order application. This application is designed to be
simple in order to demonstrate how Visual Basic Scripting Edition can be used to
build and enhance applications.

To run this application, you must have the Building Microsoft Outlook 97
Applications.pst file installed on your system.

# Overview

The Library Order application consists of a Library Materials Order message form, a
Library Materials post form, and a Library Orders folder. To submit a Library
Materials item, you open the Library Materials Order form from your Personal Forms
Library. The Open event of the Library Materials Order form, as shown in the
following example, sets the Library Orders folder as the active folder, and then opens
the Library Materials form. It then closes the Library Materials Order item, which is
never visible.

## The Item_Open Event of the Library Materials Order Form

The Item_Open event of the Library Materials Order form contains code, as shown in
the following example, that sets the Library Orders folder as the active folder, and
then creates and display the Library Order item. It then closes the Library Materials
Order form. The Library Materials Order form is never visible to the user.

```
Function Item_Open()
    Set MyNameSpace = Application.GetNameSpace("MAPI")
    Set BuildFolder = MyNameSpace.Folders("Building Microsoft Outlook 97 Applications")
    Set BeyondFolder = BuildFolder.Folders("4. Beyond the Basics")
    Set VBScriptFolder = BeyondFolder.Folders("VBScript")
    Set LibraryOrdersFolder = VBScriptFolder.Folders("Library Orders")
    Set MyItems = LibraryOrdersFolder.Items
    Set MyItem = MyItems.Add("IPM.Post.Library Materials")
    MyItem.Display
    Item.Close 1
End Function
```

## The Library Materials Post Form

When the Library Materials post form opens, as shown in Figure 9.5, you can select the Book Category and Book Name fields, and then click the **Submit Book Order** button to post the item to the Library Orders folder.

**Figure 9.5   The Library Materials post form**

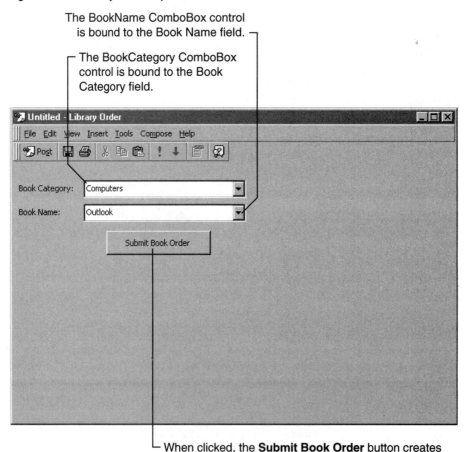

The BookName ComboBox control is bound to the Book Name field.

The BookCategory ComboBox control is bound to the Book Category field.

When clicked, the **Submit Book Order** button creates an item and posts it in the Library Orders folder.

# The CustomPropertyChange Event

The CustomPropertyChange event of the Library Orders form is passed the name of the user-defined field when a value in the field is changed.

This procedure determines if the changed field is the Book Category field. If so, it calls the ChangeBookNameValues procedure.

```
Sub Item_CustomPropertyChange(ByVal MyPropertyName)
    Select Case MyPropertyName
        Case "Book Category"
        Call ChangeBookNameValues
    End Select
End Sub
```

# The ChangeBookNameValues Procedure

The ChangeBookNameValues procedure returns the **Orders** page so you can gain access to the controls on it. It then checks the value of the Book Category field. If the field value is "Computers," it loads one list of values into the BookName control. If the value is "Gardening," it loads a different list.

```
' Changes the values in the Book Name field when the Book Category field changes.
Sub ChangeBookNameValues
    Set Page = Item.GetInspector.ModifiedFormPages("Orders")
    Set MyControl = Page.Controls("BookName")
    Select Case Item.UserProperties.Find("Book Category").Value
    Case "Computers"
        MyControl.Clear
        MyControl.AddItem "Outlook"
        MyControl.AddItem "Windows 95"
        MyControl.AddItem "DOS"
        MyControl.ListIndex = 0
    Case "Gardening"
        MyControl.Clear
        MyControl.AddItem "Roses"
        MyControl.AddItem "Tools"
        MyControl.AddItem "Shrubs"
        MyControl.ListIndex = 0
    End Select
End Sub
```

# The SubmitBookOrder_Click Procedure

For the SubmitBookOrder_Click procedure, the **Post** method of the **PostItem** object is carried out.

```
' Post an order in the Library Orders folder.
Sub SubmitBookOrder_Click
    Item.Post
End Sub
```

## Setting Up the Library Order Application

To set up this application, you must copy the Library Materials Order form from the Library Orders Folder Forms Library to your Personal Forms Library.

▶ **To copy the Library Materials Order form**

1   On the Outlook **Tools** menu, click **Options**.

2   Click the **Manage Forms** page.

3   Click **Manage Forms**.

4   Next to the left-hand **Forms** box, click **Set**.

5   In the **Folder Forms Library** box, select the **Library Orders** folder. It's located in the VBScript folder in the 4. Beyond the Basics folder in the Building Microsoft Outlook 97 Applications folder.

6   Click **OK**.

7   The right-hand **Forms** box should be set to **Personal Forms**. (If it's not, click the **Set** button, and change the setting to the Personal Forms Library.)

8   In the right-hand box in the **Forms Manager**, click **Library Materials Order**, and then click **Copy**.

The Library Materials Order form is now copied to your Personal Forms Library.

## Running the Library Orders Application

Now you can run the Library Orders application and test it by submitting a sample book order.

▶ **To run the Library Orders application**

1   On the Outlook **Compose** menu, click **Choose Form**, and then click **Library Materials Order** in the Personal Forms Library.

2   In the **Book Category** box, click **Gardening**.

3   In the **Book Name** box, click **Roses**, and then click **Submit Book Order**.

The Library Order application also consists of the Library Orders folder. In this case, the Library Orders folder is a folder in the VBScript personal folder. However, for a real application, create this folder in Public Folders.

# Automation

In addition to using Visual Basic Scripting Edition to program Outlook objects, you can use it to program Outlook objects remotely. You use Automation when you want to control an entire session. For example, you may want to automatically send a message from within a Visual Basic or Microsoft Excel application.

To automate Outlook from another application, such as Visual Basic or Microsoft Excel, you must first reference the Microsoft Outlook 8.0 Object Library. You can then use the **GetObject** function to automate a session that's already running, or the **CreateObject** function to open a new Outlook session. After the Outlook **Application** object is returned, you can then write code that uses the objects, properties, methods, and constants in the Outlook 8.0 Object Library.

This example creates a mail item from a Microsoft Excel 97 worksheet when the MailSalesReport button is clicked.

```
Sub MailSalesReport_Click
    Set MyOlApp = CreateObject("Outlook.Application")
    Set MyItem = MyOlApp.CreateItem(OlMailItem)
    MyItem.Subject = "Sales Results - " & Now()
    MyItem.Body = " Click the icon to open the Sales Results." & Chr(13)
    Set MyAttachments = MyItem.Attachments
    MyAttachments.Add "C:\My Documents\005.doc", OlByReference, 1, "4th Quarter 1996
    ➥Results Chart"
    MyItem.To = "Sales"
    MyItem.Display
End Sub
```

**Note**  As shown in the preceding example, the constants in the Outlook 8.0 Object Library are valid when used in Visual Basic or Visual Basic for Applications.

**Important**  If you use Automation to control Outlook, you cannot write event procedures to respond to the events supported by Outlook items.

# CHAPTER 10

# The Business Card Request Application

**In This Chapter**
Overview of the Business Card Request Application   332
Create the Business Card Requests Folder   335
Preaddress a Message Form   336
Design the Form   336
Create Views   376
Set Permissions   380
Test the Application   381
Send the Form to the Administrator   381
Check the Form for Viruses and Harmful Code   382
Release the Application   383

The Business Card Request application covered in this chapter provides a good example of the kinds of processes that you can streamline with Outlook applications. It can also serve as a template for other similar request processes in your organization, such as copier services requests, audio/visual equipment requests, or move requests. In the course of designing the Business Card Request application, we cover some important design concepts, such as how to:

- Preaddress a Message form to a public folder.

- Create separate layouts for **Compose** and **Read** pages.

- Use Visual Basic Scripting Edition to hide and show a page based on whether the form is submitted or not.

- Use Visual Basic Scripting Edition to create a delivery notification message.

- Create a folder view that groups request items into Request Pending or Request Processed groups.

- Submit the Business Card Request form to an administrator who checks the form for harmful macros and viruses and then publishes the form in the Organization Forms Library.

# Overview of the Business Card Request Application

The Business Card Request application consists of the following components:

**The Business Card Requests folder**   The Business Card Requests folder, as shown in Figure 10.1, contains Business Card Request items. Items in the folder are grouped by their request status.

**Figure 10.1   The Business Card Requests folder**

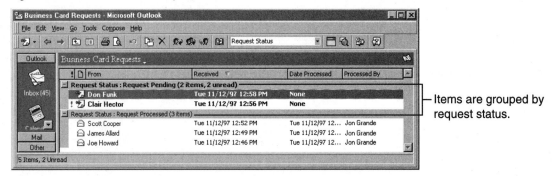

Items are grouped by request status.

**The Business Card Request form**   The Compose window of the Business Card Request form, as shown in Figure 10.2, lets users create and submit a Business Card Request to the Business Card Requests folder.

**Figure 10.2   The Compose window of the Business Card Request form**

┌ The To field is preaddressed to the
└ Business Card Requests folder.

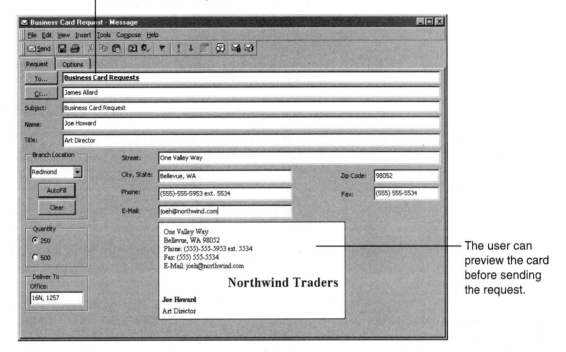

The user can
preview the card
before sending
the request.

When the administrator who is responsible for processing the Business Card Request double-clicks the submitted request in the Business Card Requests folder, she sees the **Read** page of the Business Card Request form. With the controls on the **Status** page of the form, the administrator updates the status of the request and sends a confirmation to the user, as shown in Figure 10.3.

**Figure 10.3   The Status page on the Read page of the Business Card Request form**

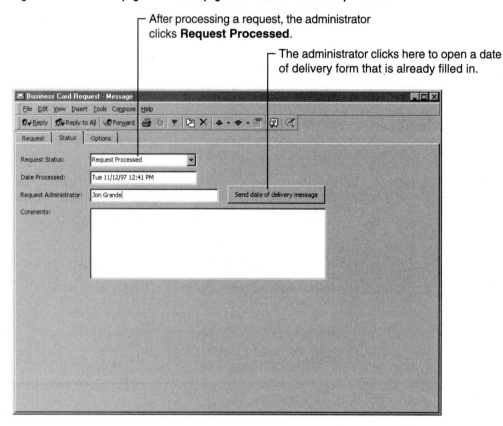

┌ After processing a request, the administrator
  clicks **Request Processed**.

┌ The administrator clicks here to open a date
  of delivery form that is already filled in.

**Custom views**   The Business Card Requests folder provides two custom views. The Request Status view, as shown in Figure 10.1, indicates which request are processed. Processed orders are in one group, unprocessed orders are in the other. The By Requester Name view groups request items by the From field, so users can easily find their request in the folder by searching for their name.

**Permissions**   Business Card Request administrators are given Editor permissions so they can edit items in the folder, while the general public is given Contributor permissions so they can submit items in the folder, but cannot change them after they are submitted. Application designers are given Owner permissions.

**VBScript**   The Business Card Request form contains several procedures written with Visual Basic Scripting Edition, which automate the request process. One procedure automatically fills in the address boxes on the Business Card Request form when the user clicks the **AutoFill** button. Another procedure automatically fills in the text of the delivery notification item that is sent to the requester.

# Create the Business Card Requests Folder

In earlier chapters, you started your applications in a personal folder. For the Business Card Request application, however, you create the folder in Public Folders so you can publish the public folder address to your Personal Address Book. Later you use this address to preaddress the Business Card Request form to the Business Card Requests public folder.

▶ **To create the Business Card Requests folder**

1   In the Folder List, click Public Folders, right-click the folder you want to create the Business Card Requests folder in, and then click **Create Subfolder** on the shortcut menu.

2   In the **Name** box, type **Business Card Requests**

3   In the **Description** box, type: **This folder contains submitted business card requests and shows if a request is pending or processed**.

4   Click **OK**.

# Publish the Folder Address and Restrict Access to the Folder

You use the **Administration** page of the **Properties** dialog box to publish the folder address to your Personal Address Book. Later, when you design the Business Card Request form, you preaddress the form by specifying the Business Card Requests folder in the To box of the form. You also select the **Owners only** option to prevent users from opening the folder while it's under construction.

▶ **To publish the folder address to your Personal Address Book**

1   In the Folder List, right-click the Business Card Requests folder, and then click **Properties** on the shortcut menu.

2   Click the **Administration** page, and then click **Personal Address Book**.

   Although you don't receive confirmation, the folder address is published to your Personal Address Book.

3   Keep the **Properties** dialog box open.

▶ **To prevent users from opening the folder**

- On the **Administration** page, click **Owners only** and then click **OK**.

# Preaddress a Message Form

To start the form design process, you preaddress a Message form to the Business Card Requests folder you just published in your Personal Address Book. With this method, you can be sure Business Card Request items always arrive in the intended folder. And it makes it easy for users to submit requests because all they need to do is fill in the form and then click the **Send** button.

**Important**  To preaddress the form, you must be in Run mode.

▶ **To preaddress the form to the Business Card Requests folder**

1  On the **Compose** menu, click **New Mail Message**.

2  Click the **To** button.

3  In the **Show names from the** box, click **Personal Address Book**.

4  Under **Type Name or Select from List**, click **Business Card Request**.

5  Click **To**, and then click **OK**.

# Design the Form

Now you switch to design mode and add controls and fields to create the Business Card Request form.

▶ **To switch to design mode**

- On the form **Tools** menu, click **Design Outlook Form**.

# Edit the Compose Page

When you design a form, you start by editing the **Compose** page. For the **Compose** page of the Business Card Request form, you change the name of the **Message** page to **Request**, and then you add controls to the page. When you're done, the **Compose** page looks like the illustration in Figure 10.4.

Figure 10.4   The Compose page of the Business Card Request form

The **Message** page is renamed **Request**.

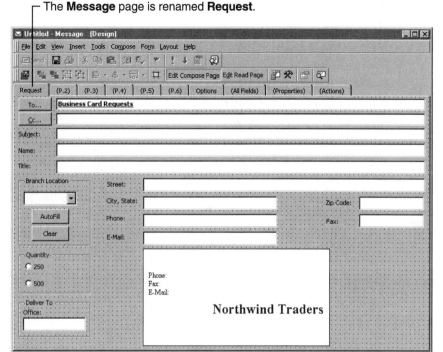

## Rename the Message Page

When you've completed the Business Card Request form, the form will have two pages. A **Request** page the user fills out and sends to the Business Card Requests folder and a **Status** page the administrator uses to indicate a request has been processed. For now, we'll focus on the **Request** page.

▸ **To rename the Message page**

1   On the form, click the **Message** page.

2   On the **Form** menu, click **Rename Page**.

3   In the **Page name** box, type **Request** and then click **OK**.

## Set the Initial Value of the Subject Field

The Business Card Request form is used for only one purpose, so you set the initial value of the Subject field to Business Card Request.

▸ **To set the initial value of the Subject field**

1   Right-click the **Subject** control, and then click **Properties** on the shortcut menu.

2   Click the **Value** page.

3   Select the **Set the initial value of this field to** check box, and then type **Business Card Request**

4   Click **OK**.

## Remove the Message Control

You don't use the Message control on the Business Card Request form, so you remove it, as shown in Figure 10.5.

▸ **To remove the Message control**

•   Click the Message control, and then press the DEL key.

**Figure 10.5   The selected Message control on the Request page**

Click the Message control and then delete it. ⌐

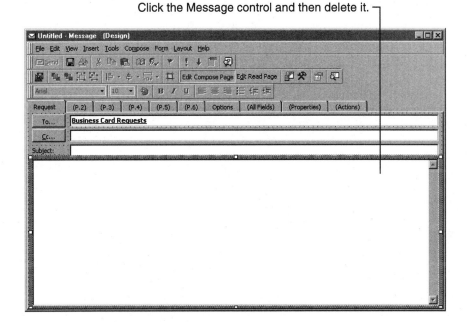

## Add the BusinessCardName Control

The BusinessCardName control is a TextBox control you add to the form by dragging the control from the Control Toolbox. After you add a TextBox control, you set its display properties to name the control. For this application, we'll set the exact sizes for the Top, Left, and Height properties of the controls. The Width property is up to you. You can use the illustrations provided in this chapter as a guideline.

▶ **To add the BusinessCardName control and set its Display properties**

1  On the **Form Design** toolbar, click the **Control Toolbox** button.

2  Drag a TextBox control from the Control Toolbox to the form.

3  Right-click the control, and then click **Properties** on the shortcut menu.

4  On the **Display** page, set the following properties.

| Property | Setting |
| --- | --- |
| **Name** | BusinessCardName |
| **Top** | 82 |
| **Left** | 76 |
| **Height** | 24 |
| **Width** | *User-defined* |
| **Resize with form** | Selected |

When you've finished setting properties, leave the **Properties** dialog box open.

## Bind the BusinessCardName Control to the BusinessCardName Field

Now you switch to the **Value** page of the **Properties** dialog box and create a field called BusinessCardName. When you create the field, the BusinessCardName control is automatically bound to the BusinessCardName field. At run time, users enter information in the BusinessCardName control. The information in the control is saved to the BusinessCardName field.

▶ **To create a field called BusinessCardName**

1  In the **Properties** dialog box, click the **Value** page.

2  Click **New**.

3  In the **Name** box, type **BusinessCardName**, and then click **OK**.

4  Leave the Properties dialog box open.

## Set Validation Properties

You set Validation properties for the BusinessCardName field so users can't send the form unless there is text in the BusinessCardName field.

▶ **To set Validation properties**

1   Click the **Validation** page.

2   Select the **A value is required for this field** check box, and then click **OK**.

## Add a Label for the Name Field

You add a label for the BusinessCardName control so users know what to type into the control.

1   Drag a Label control from the Control Toolbox to the form.

2   Click the Label control, and then type **Name:**

3   Resize the label and position it on the form as shown in Figure 10.6.

**Figure 10.6   The BusinessCardName control and its label**

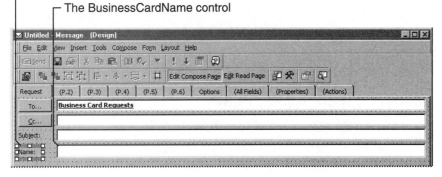

## Add the BusinessCardTitle Control

Now you add another TextBox control to the form. This control serves as the BusinessCardTitle control.

▶ **To add the BusinessCardTitle control**

1   Drag a TextBox control from the Control Toolbox to the form.

2   Right-click the control, and then click **Properties** on the shortcut menu.

## Bind the Control to the BusinessCardTitle Field

Now you create a field called BusinessCardTitle that you bind the control to. Then you switch to the **Display** page and set Display properties for the control.

▶ **To create a field called BusinessCardTitle**

1  In the **Properties** dialog box, click the **Value** page.

2  Click **New**.

3  In the **Name** box, type **BusinessCardTitle**, and then click **OK**.

4  Click the **Display** tab, and then set the following properties.

| Property | Setting |
|---|---|
| **Name** | BusinessCardTitle |
| **Top** | 112 |
| **Left** | 76 |
| **Height** | 24 |
| **Width** | *User-defined* |
| **Resize with form** | Selected |

5  Click **OK**.

## Add a Label for the BusinessCardTitle Control

Now you add a label for the BusinessCardTitle control.

1  Drag a Label control from the Control Toolbox to the form.

2  Click the Label control, and then type **Title:**

3  Resize the label and position it on the form as shown in Figure 10.7.

**Figure 10.7   The BusinessCardTitle control and its label**

— The label for the BusinessCardTitle control

— The BusinessCardTitle control

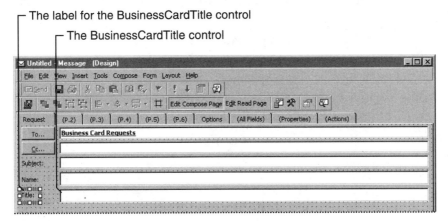

# Add the BusinessCardStreet Control

1  Add a TextBox control to the form.

2  Right-click the control, and then click **Properties** on the shortcut menu.

3  On the **Value** page, click **New**.

4  In the **Name** box, type **BusinessCardStreet**, and then click **OK**.

5  On the **Validation** page, select the **A value is required for this field** check box, and then click **OK**.

6  On the **Display** page, set the properties as shown in the following table:

| Property: | Setting: |
| --- | --- |
| **Name** | BusinessCardStreet |
| **Top** | 143 |
| **Left** | 207 |
| **Height** | 24 |
| **Width** | *User-defined* |
| **Resize with form** | Selected |

7  Click **OK**.

8  Drag a Label control from the Control Toolbox to the form.

9  Click the Label control, and then type **Street:**

10  Resize and position the label as needed.

## Add the BusinessCardCityState Control

**1** Add a TextBox control to the form.

**2** Right-click the control, and then click **Properties** on the shortcut menu.

**3** On the **Value** page, click **New**, type **BusinessCardCityState** in the **Name** box, and then click **OK**.

**4** On the **Validation** page, select the **A value is required for this field** check box.

**5** On the **Display** page, set the properties as shown in the following table:

| Property: | Setting: |
|---|---|
| **Name** | BusinessCardCityState |
| **Top** | 175 |
| **Left** | 207 |
| **Height** | 24 |
| **Width** | *User-defined* |

**6** Click **OK**.

**7** Drag a Label control from the Control Toolbox to the form.

**8** Click the Label control, and then type **City, State:**

**9** Resize and position the label as needed.

## Add the BusinessCardZipCode Control

**1** Add a TextBox control to the form.

**2** Right-click the control, and then click **Properties** on the shortcut menu.

**3** On the **Value** page, click **New**, type **BusinessCardZipCode** in the **Name** box, and then click **OK**.

**4** On the **Validation** page, select the **A value is required for this field** check box, and then click **OK**.

**5** On the **Display** page, set the properties as shown in the following table.

| Property | Setting |
| --- | --- |
| Name | BusinessCardZipCode |
| Top | 175 |
| Left | 553 |
| Height | 24 |
| Width | *User-defined* |
| Resize with form | Selected |

**6** Click **OK**.

**7** Drag a Label control from the Control Toolbox to the form.

**8** Click the Label control, and then type **Zip Code:**

**9** Resize and position the label as needed.

## Add the BusinessCardPhone Control

1   Add a TextBox control to the form.

2   Right-click the control, and then click **Properties** on the shortcut menu.

3   On the **Value** page, click **New**.

4   In the **Name** box, type **BusinessCardPhone**, and then click **OK**.

5   On the **Validation** page, select the **A value is required for this field** check box, and then click **OK**.

6   On the **Display** page, set the properties as shown in the following table:

| Property | Setting |
| --- | --- |
| Name | BusinessCardPhone |
| Top | 206 |
| Left | 207 |
| Height | 24 |
| Width | *User-defined* |

7   Click **OK**.

8   Drag a Label control from the Control Toolbox to the form.

9   Click the Label control, and then type **Phone:**

10   Resize and position the label as needed.

# Add the BusinessCardFax Control

**1** Add a TextBox control to the form.

**2** Right-click the control, and then click **Properties** on the shortcut menu.

**3** On the **Value** page, click **New**.

**4** In the **Name** box, type **BusinessCardFax**, and then click **OK**.

**5** On the **Display** page, set the properties as shown in the following table:

| Property | Setting |
| --- | --- |
| **Name** | BusinessCardFax |
| **Top** | 206 |
| **Left** | 553 |
| **Height** | 24 |
| **Width** | *User-defined* |
| **Resize with form** | Selected |

**6** Click **OK**.

**7** Drag a Label control from the Control Toolbox to the form.

**8** Click the Label control, and then type **Fax:**

**9** Resize and position the label as needed.

## Add the BusinessCardEMail Control

1   Add a TextBox control to the form.

2   Right-click the control, and then click **Properties** on the shortcut menu.

3   On the **Value** page, click **New**.

4   In the **Name** box, type **BusinessCardEMail**, and then click **OK**.

5   On the **Display** page, set the properties as shown in the following table:

| Property | Setting |
|---|---|
| Name | BusinessCardEMail |
| Top | 237 |
| Left | 207 |
| Height | 24 |
| Width | *User-defined* |
| Resize with form | Selected |

6   Click **OK**.

7   Drag a Label control from the Control Toolbox to the form.

8   Click the Label control, and then type **E-Mail:**

9   Resize and position the label.

Your form should now look like the form shown in Figure 10.8.

**Figure 10.8   The Business Card Request form with the address controls added to the form**

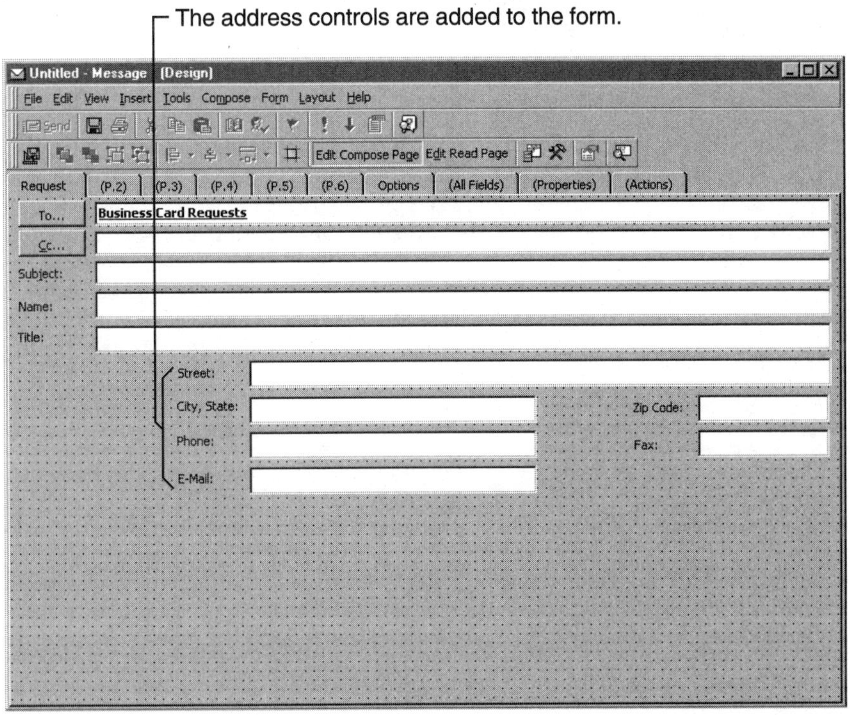

The address controls are added to the form.

# Add the BusinessCardBranchLocation Control

The BusinessCardBranchLocation control is a Frame control that contains other controls.

▸ **To add the BusinessCardBranchLocation control**

1   Add a Frame control to the form.

2   Right-click the control, and then click **Properties** on the shortcut menu.

3   On the **Display** page, set the properties as shown in the following table:

| Property: | Setting: |
| --- | --- |
| **Name** | BusinessCardBranchLocation |
| **Caption** | Branch Location |
| **Top** | 141 |
| **Left** | 8 |
| **Height** | 122 |
| **Width** | user-defined |

4   Click **OK**.

5   Resize and position the control.

# Add the BusinessCardBranch Control

The BusinessCardBranch control is a ComboBox control that shows a list of branch locations at run time.

▶ **To add the BusinessCardBranch control**

1  Drag a ComboBox control into the BusinessCardBranchLocation frame.

2  Right-click the control, and then click **Properties** on the shortcut menu.

3  On the **Value** page, click **New**.

4  In the **Name** box, type **BusinessCardBranch**, and then click **OK**.

5  In the **List Type** box, click **Droplist**.

6  In the **Possible values** box, type: **Bellevue; Redmond; Seattle**

7  In the **Initial Value** box, type **Redmond**.

8  Click the **Display** page, and then set the following properties.

| Property | Setting |
|---|---|
| **Name** | BusinessCardBranch |
| **Top** | 18 |
| **Left** | 7 |
| **Height** | 24 |
| **Width** | *User-defined* |

9  Click **OK**.

# Add the AutoFill Control

The AutoFill control is a CommandButton control. Later in this chapter, you create a procedure for this control that automatically loads address values into the address boxes based on the value in the BusinessCardBranchLocation field.

▶ **To add the AutoFill control**

1  Drag a CommandButton control into the BusinessCardBranchLocation frame.

2  Right-click the control, and then click **Properties** on the shortcut menu.

3  On the **Display** page, set the following properties.

| Property | Setting |
| --- | --- |
| Name | AutoFill |
| Caption | AutoFill |
| Top | 49 |
| Left | 22 |
| Height | 26 |
| Width | *User-defined* |

4  Click **OK**.

# Add the Clear Control

The Clear control is also a CommandButton control. Later in this chapter, you create a procedure for this control that clears the values in the address boxes.

▶ **To add the Clear control**

1  Drag a CommandButton control into the BusinessCardBranchLocation frame.

2  Right-click the CommandButton control, and then click **Properties** on the shortcut menu.

3  On the **Display** page, set the following properties.

| Property | Setting |
| --- | --- |
| Name | Clear |
| Caption | Clear |
| Top | 79 |
| Left | 22 |
| Height | 26 |
| Width | *User-defined* |

4  Click **OK**.

Your form should now look like the form shown in Figure 10.9.

**Figure 10.9   The BusinessCardBranchLocation frame is added to the form.**

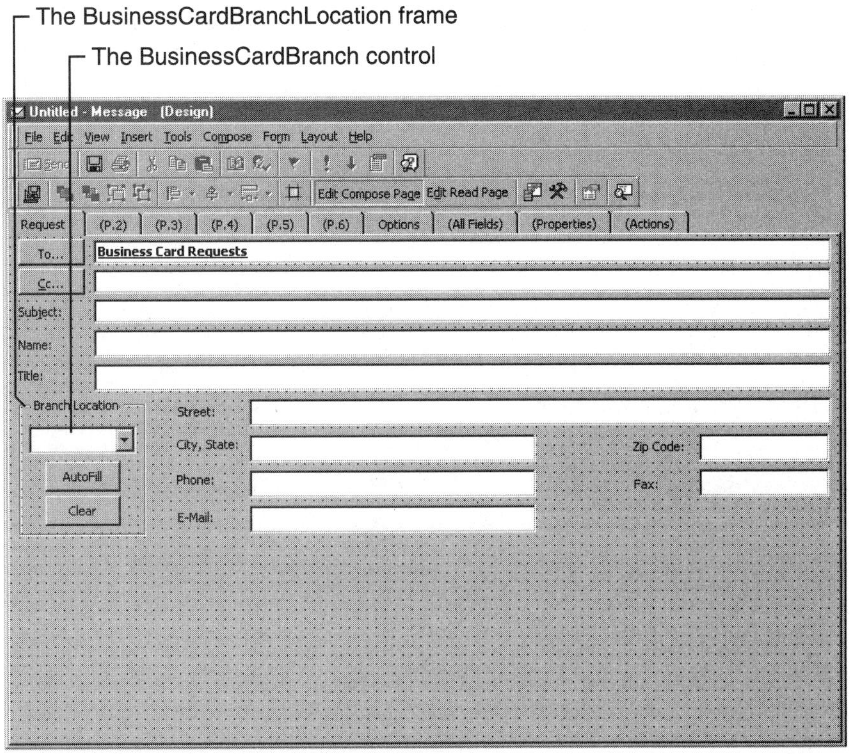

The BusinessCardBranchLocation frame

The BusinessCardBranch control

## Add the Quantity Control

The Quantity control is a Frame control that will contain option buttons.

▶ **To add the Quantity control**

1   Add a Frame control to the form.

2   Right-click the control, and then click **Properties** on the shortcut menu.

3   On the **Display** page, set the following properties.

| Property | Setting |
|----------|---------|
| **Name** | Quantity |
| **Caption** | Quantity |
| **Top** | 271 |
| **Left** | 8 |
| **Height** | 76 |
| **Width** | *User-defined* |

4   Click **OK**.

# Add the CardQuantity1 Control

The CardQuantity1 control is an OptionButton control that the user clicks to specify an order of 250 business cards.

▸ **To add the CardQuantity1 control**

1  Drag an OptionButton control into the Quantity frame.

2  Right-click the OptionButton control, and then click **Properties** on the shortcut menu.

3  On the **Value** page, click **New**.

4  In the **Name** box, type **CardQuantity**, and then click **OK**.

5  In the **Value** box, type **250**.

6  On the **Display** page, set the following properties.

| Property | Setting |
|----------|---------|
| Name | CardQuantity1 |
| Caption | 250 |
| Top | 8 |
| Left | 8 |
| Height | 24 |
| Width | *User-defined* |

7  Click **OK**.

8  Right-click the CardQuantity1 control, and then click **Advanced Properties** on the shortcut menu.

9  Click the **Value** cell, and then type **True**.

10  Close the **Advanced Properties** dialog box.

# Add the CardQuantity2 Control

The CardQuantity2 control is an OptionButton control that the user clicks to specify an order of 500 business cards. When you add this OptionButton control to the frame, the OptionButton control is automatically bound to the CardQuantity field.

▶ **To add the CardQuantity2 control**

1   Drag an OptionButton control into the Quantity frame.

2   Right-click the OptionButton control, and then click **Properties** on the shortcut menu.

3   On the **Value** page, type **500** in the **Value** box.

4   On the **Display** page, set the following properties.

| Property | Setting |
| --- | --- |
| **Name** | CardQuantity2 |
| **Caption** | 500 |
| **Top** | 38 |
| **Left** | 8 |
| **Height** | 24 |
| **Width** | *User-defined* |

5   Click **OK**.

## Add the DeliverTo Control

The DeliverTo control is a Frame control that will contain a TextBox control that users type their office location into.

▶ **To add the DeliverTo control**

1   Add a Frame control to the form.

2   Right-click the control, and then click **Properties** on the shortcut menu.

3   On the **Display** page, set the following properties.

| Property | Setting |
| --- | --- |
| **Name** | DeliverTo |
| **Caption** | Deliver To |
| **Top** | 355 |
| **Left** | 8 |
| **Height** | 68 |
| **Width** | *User-defined* |

4   Click **OK**.

## Add the BusinessCardOffice Control

1  Drag a TextBox control into the DeliverTo frame.

2  Right-click the TextBox control, and then click **Properties** on the shortcut menu.

3  On the **Value** page, click **New**.

4  In the **Name** box, type **BusinessCardOffice**, and then click **OK**.

5  On the **Display** page, set the following properties.

| Property | Setting |
|----------|---------|
| **Name** | BusinessCardOffice |
| **Top** | 25 |
| **Left** | 6 |
| **Height** | 24 |
| **Width** | 97 |

6  Click **OK**.

7  Drag a Label control to the form. Don't drag it into the Deliver To frame yet.

8  Click the Label control, and then type **Office:**

9  Make the label small enough to fit into the Deliver To frame, and then drag the label into the Deliver To frame.

Your form should now look like the form shown in Figure 10.10.

**Figure 10.10   The Business Card Request form with the address controls added to the form.**

The CardQuantity1 and CardQuantity2 controls

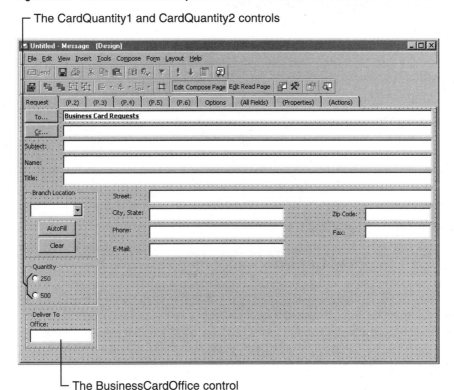

The BusinessCardOffice control

# Add the BusinessCardImage Control

**1**   Add an Image control to the form.

**2**   Right-click the control, and then click **Properties** on the shortcut menu.

**3**   On the **Display** page, set the following properties.

| Property | Setting |
|---|---|
| **Name** | BusinessCardImage |
| **Top** | 264 |
| **Left** | 207 |
| **Height** | 171 |
| **Width** | *User-defined* |
| **Background color** | Window |

**4**   Click **OK**.

# Add the CardAddress Control

The CardAddress control is a TextBox control that reflects the values that the user types in the address boxes in the upper portion of the Business Card Request form. When the user changes a value in one of the address fields, the value is automatically updated in the CardAddress control. To accomplish this, you create a formula for the CardAddress control that automatically changes the value in the label when a value in one of the address fields changes.

▶ **To add the CardAddress control**

**1**   Drag a TextBox control on top of the BusinessCardImage control.

**2**   Right-click the TextBox control, and then click **Properties** on the shortcut menu.

**3**   On the **Value** page, click **New**.

**4**   In the **Name** box, type **CardAddress**, and then click **OK**.

**5**   Click **Edit**, and then in the **Formula** box, type the formula, as shown in Figure 10.11, and then click **OK**.

**6**   Click **Calculate this formula automatically**.

Figure 10.11  Formula for the CardAddress field

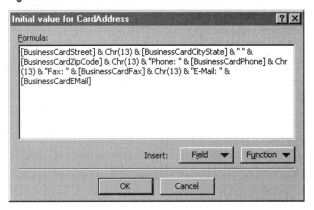

**Initial value for CardAddress**                                    [?] [X]

**Formula:**

[BusinessCardStreet] & Chr(13) & [BusinessCardCityState] & " " &
[BusinessCardZipCode] & Chr(13) & "Phone: " & [BusinessCardPhone] & Chr
(13) & "Fax: " & [BusinessCardFax] & Chr(13) & "E-Mail: " &
[BusinessCardEMail]

Insert:   Field ▼    Function ▼

OK        Cancel

**7** On the **Display** page, set the following properties for the control.

| Property | Setting |
| --- | --- |
| Name | CardAddress |
| Top | 271 |
| Left | 215 |
| Height | 79 |
| Width | *User-defined* |
| Font | 9 pt. Times New Roman |
| Foreground color | Window Text |
| Background color | Window |
| Read-only | Selected |
| Sunken | Cleared |
| Multi-line | Selected |

**8** Click **OK**.

## Add the CardName Control

The CardName control is a Label control that reflects the values that the user types in the **Name** box in the upper portion of the Business Card Request form. When the user types in the **Name** box, the CardName field is automatically updated. To accomplish this, you create a formula for the CardName field that automatically changes the value in the field when a value in **Name** box changes.

▸ **To add the CardName control**

1   Drag a Label control on top of the BusinessCardImage control.

2   Right-click the Label control, and then click **Properties** on the shortcut menu.

3   On the **Value** page, click **New**.

4   In the **Name** box, type **CardName**, and then click **OK**.

5   In the **Initial Value** box, type: **[BusinessCardName]**

6   Click **Calculate this formula automatically**.

7   On the **Display** page, set the following properties.

| Property | Setting |
|---|---|
| **Name** | CardName |
| **Top** | 394 |
| **Left** | 217 |
| **Height** | 15 |
| **Width** | *User-defined* |
| **Font** | 9 pt. Times New Roman Bold |
| **Foreground color** | Window Text |
| **Background color** | Window |

8   Click **OK**.

# Add the CardTitle Control

The CardTitle control is a Label control that shows the value on the business card that the user types in the **Title** box. When the user makes changes to the **Title** box, the changes are automatically reflected in the CardTitle control. The CardTitle control is bound to the Title field that you created earlier in this chapter. In addition, you create an expression for the CardTitle field so that the value of the field is automatically updated when the user changes the value in the Title control.

▶ **To add the CardTitle control**

1   Drag a Label control on top of the BusinessCardImage control.

2   Right-click the Label control, and then click **Properties** on the shortcut menu.

3   On the **Value** page, click **New**.

4   In the **Name** box, type **CardTitle**, and then click **OK**.

5   In the **Initial Value** box, type: **[BusinessCardTitle]**

6   Click **Calculate this formula automatically**.

7   On the **Display** page, set the following properties.

| Property | Setting |
|---|---|
| **Name** | CardTitle |
| **Font** | 9 pt. Times New Roman |
| **Top** | 414 |
| **Left** | 217 |
| **Height** | 15 |
| **Width** | *User-defined* |
| **Foreground color** | Window Text |
| **Background color** | Window |

8   Click **OK**.

# Add the CompanyLogo Control

The CompanyLogo control is a Label control that shows the company name. The CompanyLogo control is not bound to a field.

Part IV   Beyond the Basics

▶ **To add the CompanyLogo control**

1  Drag a Label control on top of the CardImage control, as shown in Figure 10.12.

2  Right-click the Label control, and then click **Properties** on the shortcut menu.

3  On the **Display** page, set the following properties.

| Property | Setting |
|---|---|
| **Name** | CompanyLogo |
| **Caption** | Northwind Traders |
| **Top** | 356 |
| **Left** | 329 |
| **Height** | 31 |
| **Width** | 203 |
| **Font** | 18 pt. Times New Roman Bold |
| **Foreground color** | Window Text |
| **Background color** | Window |

4  Click **OK**.

**Figure 10.12   The CardAddress, CardName, and CardTitle controls are added to the form.**

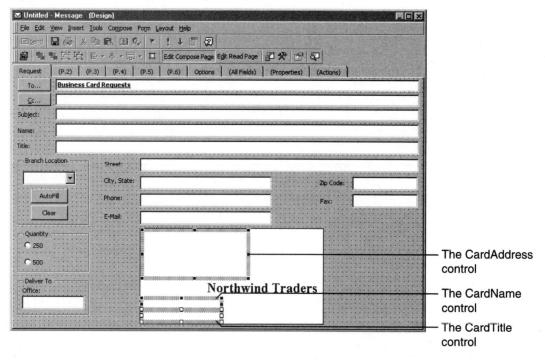

## Set the Tab Order for the Compose Page

There are a few nuances to setting the tab order that are worth noting. Label controls can be tabbed to at design time, but are skipped over at run time. So you don't need to worry about Label controls in the **Tab Order** dialog box. Also Frame controls have their own tab order for controls in the frame.

▶ **To set the tab order**

1   On the **Layout** menu, click **Tab Order**.

2   In the **Tab Order** box, make sure that the controls are listed in the following relative order. If Label controls are located between the controls below, that's OK. Outlook does not tab to Label controls at run time.

BusinessCardName, BusinessCardTitle, BusinessCardStreet, BusinessCardCityState, BusinessCardZipCode, BusinessCardPhone, BusinessCardFax, BusinessCardEMail, BusinessCardBranchLocation, Quantity, DeliverTo.

# Test the Compose Page Layout

Before you design the **Read** page of the form, it's a good idea to view the layout of the **Compose** page in Run mode.

▶ **To test the layout**

• On the **Tools** menu, click **Design Outlook Form**.

# Edit the Read Page

Now you will edit the **Read** page.

• On the **Tools** menu, click **Design Outlook Form** to switch to Design mode.

To design the **Read** page, you delete the Message control on the **Read** page, and then copy the controls from the **Compose** page.

▶ **To switch to the Read page and delete the Message control**

1   On the **Form Design** toolbar, click the **Edit Read Page** button.

2   Click the Message control, and then press DEL.

## Copy Controls from the Compose Page

Now you switch back to the **Compose** page.

▶ **To copy controls from the Compose page**

1  On the **Form Design** toolbar, click the **Edit Compose Page** button.

2  On the **Edit** menu, click **Select All**.

3  Hold down the CTRL key, and click the following controls in the header area so that they are not selected, as shown in Figure 10.13.

4  On the **Standard** toolbar, click the **Copy** button.

5  On the **Form Design** toolbar, click the **Edit Read Page** button.

6  On the **Standard** toolbar, click the **Paste** button.

7  Reposition the controls so they fit correctly on the page. The fit is a little tight. However, at run time, there will be ample room on the form because the **Form Design** toolbar is not shown.

**Figure 10.13   The header fields are not selected.**

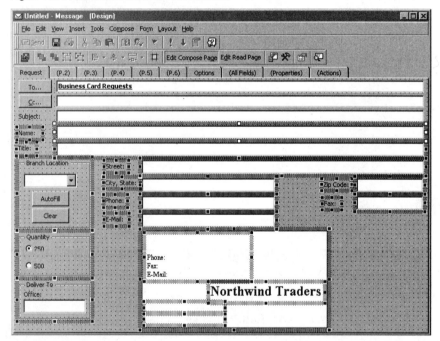

## Add the Status Page to the Form

Now you add the **Status** page to the form. The **Status** page is used by the Business Card Request administrator to indicate the order has been processed and to send a notification to the requester that their business cards will arrive in two weeks.

▶ **To name the Status page**

1   Click the **(P.2)** page.

2   On the **Form** menu, click **Separate Read Layout**.

3   On the **Form** menu, click **Rename Page**.

4   Type **Status** in the **Page name** box, and then click **OK**.

5   On the **Form Design** toolbar, click the **Edit Read Page** button.

# Add the BusinessCardRequestStatus Control

The BusinessCardRequestStatus control is a ComboBox control. With this control, the administrator can select a Request Pending or Request Processed value to indicate the status of the request.

▶ **To add the BusinessCardRequestStatus control**

1   Drag a ComboBox control to the form.

2   Right-click the control, and then click **Properties** on the shortcut menu.

3   On the **Value** page, click **New**.

4   In the **Name** box, type **BusinessCardRequestStatus**, and then click **OK**.

5   In the **List Type** box, click **Droplist**.

6   In the **Possible values** box, type **Request Pending; Request Processed**.

7   In the **Initial Value** box, type **Request Pending**.

8   On the **Display** page, set the following properties.

| Property | Setting |
| --- | --- |
| **Name** | BusinessCardRequestStatus |
| **Top** | 16 |
| **Left** | 132 |
| **Height** | 24 |
| **Width** | *User-defined* |

9   Click **OK**.

# Add the BusinessCardDateProcessed Control

At run time, when the administrator clicks **Request Processed** in the BusinessCardRequestStatus control, the current date is shown in the BusinessCardDateProcessed control.

▶ **To add the BusinessCardDateProcessed control**

1  Add a TextBox control to the form.

2  Right-click the control, and then click **Properties** on the shortcut menu.

3  On the **Value** page, click **New**.

4  In the **Name** box, type **BusinessCardDateProcessed**, and then click **Date/Time** in the **Type** box.

5  Click **OK**.

6  On the **Display** page, set the following properties.

| Property | Setting |
|----------|---------|
| **Name** | BusinessCardDateProcessed1 |
| **Top** | 47 |
| **Left** | 132 |
| **Height** | 24 |
| **Width** | 196 |

7  Click **OK**.

8  Drag a Label control from the Control Toolbox to the form.

9  Click the Label control, and then type: **Date Processed:**

10  Resize and position the label as needed.

## Add the BusinessCardRequestAdministrator Control

At run time, when the administrator clicks **Request Processed** in the BusinessCardRequestStatus control, the administrator's name shows in BusinessCardDateProcessed control.

▶ **To add the BusinessCardRequestAdministrator control**

1  Add a TextBox control to the form.

2  Right-click the control, and then click **Properties** on the shortcut menu.

3  On the **Value** page, click **New**.

4  In the **Name** box, type **BusinessCardRequestAdministrator**, and then click **OK**.

**5** On the **Display** page, set the following properties.

| Property | Setting |
| --- | --- |
| Name | BusinessCardRequestAdministrator |
| Top | 78 |
| Left | 132 |
| Height | 24 |
| Width | 235 |

**6** Click **OK**.

**7** Drag a Label control from the Control Toolbox to the form.

**8** Click the Label control, and then type **Request Administrator:**

**9** Resize and position the label as needed.

## Add the SendDeliveryMessage Control

The SendDeliveryMessage control is a CommandButton control that you will create a Click procedure for later in this chapter.

▶ **To add the SendDeliveryMessage control**

**1** Drag a CommandButton control to the form.

**2** Right-click the control, and then click **Properties** on the shortcut menu.

**3** On the **Display** page, set the following properties.

| Property | Setting |
| --- | --- |
| Name | SendDeliveryMessage |
| Caption | Send date of delivery message |
| Top | 72 |
| Left | 384 |
| Height | 32 |
| Width | *User-defined* |

**4** Click **OK**.

# Add the BusinessCardComments Control

With the BusinessCardComments control, the administrator can enter comments about the request if necessary.

▶ **To add the BusinessCardComments control**

1  Add a TextBox control to the form.

2  Right-click the control, and then click **Properties** on the shortcut menu.

3  On the **Value** page, click **New**.

4  In the **Name** box, type **BusinessCardComments**, and then click **OK**.

5  On the **Display** page, set the following properties.

| Property | Setting |
| --- | --- |
| Name | BusinessCardComments |
| Top | 112 |
| Left | 132 |
| Height | 125 |
| Width | *User-defined* |
| Resize with form | Selected |
| Multi-line | Selected |

6  Click **OK**.

7  Drag a Label control from the Control Toolbox to the form.

8  Click the Label control, and then type **Comments:**

9  Resize and position the label as shown in Figure 10.14.

10  When you're finished, the **Status** page should look like the illustration in Figure 10.14.

**Figure 10.14   The finished layout of the Status page**

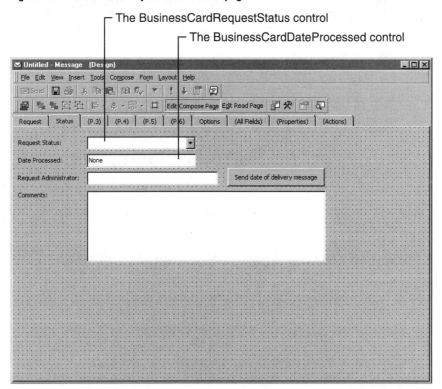

**Tip**   To view the layout of the **Read** page, you must publish the form, create a Business Card Request, send it, and then open it in the Business Card Requests folder. If you click **Design Outlook Form** on the **Tools** menu at this time, the **Compose** page is shown. You can view the **Read** page later in the chapter when you test the application.

# Make a Backup Copy of the Form Before Proceeding

Before you go any further, it's a good idea to make a backup copy of the form.

▶ **To make a backup copy of the form**

1   On the **File** menu, click **Save As**.

2   In the **Save in** box, click a folder in which to save the form.

3   In the **Name** box, type **Business Card Request**, and then click **Save**.

# Create Procedures for the Form By Using the Script Editor

With the Outlook Script Editor, you create procedures for the form by using Visual Basic Scripting Edition.

## Create a Procedure for the AutoFill Command Button

To help users complete the Business Card Request form and to ensure consistency in business card requests, you create an AutoFill_Click procedure that automatically fills in the values in the address boxes on the form when the user clicks the AutoFill button. Before loading the values into the address fields on the form, the AutoFill procedure finds the value of the BusinessCardBranch field, and then loads the set of address values based on that BusinessCardBranchLocationList field value.

▶ **To create the AutoFill_Click procedure**

**1** On the **Form Design** toolbar, click the **View Code** button.

**2** Add the following procedure to the Script Editor window. (You can copy this sample code from the Business Card Request form on the companion CD.) Feel free to substitute your own address value in the procedure.

```
'loads the values in the address boxes based on the value in the
Branch Location box.
Sub AutoFill_Click
    Select Case Item.UserProperties.Find("BusinessCardBranch").Value
        Case "Redmond"
            Item.UserProperties.Find("BusinessCardStreet").Value =
            ➡"One Valley Way"
            Item.UserProperties.Find("BusinessCardCityState").Value =
            ➡"Redmond, WA"
            Item.UserProperties.Find("BusinessCardZipCode").Value =
            ➡"98052"
            Item.UserProperties.Find("BusinessCardFax").Value =
            ➡"(555) 555-5534"
        Case "Bellevue"
            Item.UserProperties.Find("BusinessCardStreet").Value =
            ➡"10 State St."
            Item.UserProperties.Find("BusinessCardCityState").Value =
            ➡"Bellevue, WA"
            Item.UserProperties.Find("BusinessCardZipCode").Value =
            ➡"98115"
            Item.UserProperties.Find("BusinessCardFax").Value =
            ➡"(555) 555-5535"
        Case "Seattle"
            Item.UserProperties.Find("BusinessCardStreet").Value =
            ➡"1 Beach Dr."
            Item.UserProperties.Find("BusinessCardCityState").Value =
            ➡"Seattle, WA"
            Item.UserProperties.Find("BusinessCardZipCode").Value =
            ➡"98116"
                Item.UserProperties.Find("BusinessCardFax").Value =
            ➡"(555) 555-5536"
        End select
End Sub
```

▶ **To test the AutoFill procedure**

1   On the **Tools** menu, click **Design Outlook Form**.

2   In the **Branch Location** box, click a value, and then click **AutoFill**.

3   Repeat for each value in the **Branch Location** box.

4   When you're finished testing, click **Design Outlook Form** on the **Tools** menu to switch to Design mode.

## Create a Procedure for the Clear Command Button

The Clear_Click procedure clears the values from the address fields. With the **Clear** button, users can automatically remove values if they make a mistake with the **AutoFill** button.

▶ **To create the Clear_Click procedure**

1   On the **Form Design** toolbar, click the **View Code** button.

2   Add the following procedure to the Script Editor window.

```
'clears the values in the address boxes.
Sub Clear_Click
    Item.UserProperties.Find("BusinessCardStreet").Value = ""
    Item.UserProperties.Find("BusinessCardCityState").Value = ""
    Item.UserProperties.Find("BusinessCardZipCode").Value = ""
    Item.UserProperties.Find("BusinessCardFax").Value = ""
End Sub
```

▶ **To test the Clear procedure**

1   On the **Tools** menu, click **Design Outlook Form**.

2   In the **Branch Location** box, click a value, and then click **AutoFill**.

3   Click **Clear**.

4   Repeat steps 1–3 for each value in the **Branch Location** box.

5   When you're finished testing, click **Design Outlook Form** on the **Tools** menu to switch to Design mode.

## Create a Procedure for the SendDeliveryMessage Command Button

When clicked, the **SendDeliveryMessage** button on the **Status** page opens a Message form that is addressed to the requester. The text in the **Subject** box of the message informs the user that the business cards will arrive in two weeks.

▶ **To create the SendDeliveryMessage procedure**

1  On the **Form Design** toolbar, click the **View Code** button.

2  Add the following procedure to the Script Editor Window.

```
'creates a message item that tells the user their cards will be ready
'in about two weeks.
Sub SendDeliveryMessage_Click
    AdminName = Application.GetNameSpace("MAPI").CurrentUser
    Set MyItem = Application.CreateItem(0)
    MyItem.To = Item.SenderName
    MyItem.Subject = "Your business card request has been processed.
    ➥ Your cards will be delivered in about two weeks."
    MyItem.Body = "If you have questions, feel free to contact me."
    MyItem.Display
End Sub
```

Because the SendDeliveryMessage control is located on the **Read** page, you must submit a Business Card Request item to the Business Card Requests folder, and then open the item to test the procedure. You will test this procedure later in this chapter.

# Add Code to the CustomPropertyChange Event

The **CustomPropertyChange** event is an Outlook event that occurs when the user changes a value on the Business Card Request form. In this case, you add code to the **CustomPropertyChange** event to determine the field value that has changed. If the field is the Request Status field and the value of the field is Request Processed, then the Request Administrator and Date Processed fields are automatically filled in.

▶ **To add code to the CustomPropertyChange event**

1  On the **Script** menu of the **Script Editor**, click **Event**.

2  In the **Events** box, double-click **CustomPropertyChange**.

3  Change the **Name** value in parentheses to **myFieldName** as shown in the first line of code in the following sample. Then add the following code.

```
'if Request Processed is selected in the Request Status box, the Date
'Processed and Request Administrator boxes are automatically filled in
Sub Item_CustomPropertyChange(ByVal myFieldName)
    If myFieldName = "BusinessCardRequestStatus" and
    ➥Item.UserProperties.Find("BusinessCardRequestStatus") = "Request Processed" then
        Item.UserProperties.Find("BusinessCardDateProcessed") = Now
        AdminName = Application.GetNameSpace("MAPI").CurrentUser
        Item.UserProperties.Find("BusinessCardRequestAdministrator").Value = AdminName
    Else
        Item.UserProperties.Find("BusinessCardDateProcessed").Value = "1/1/4501"
        Item.Userproperties.Find("BusinessCardRequestAdministrator").Value = ""
    End If
End Sub
```

Because the controls involved in this procedure are located on the **Read** page, you must submit a Business Card Request item to the Business Card Requests folder, and then open the item to test the procedure. You will test this procedure later in this chapter.

## Add Code to the Open Event

The **Open** event is an Outlook event that occurs when users open the Business Card Request form to compose or read an item. In this case, you add code to the **Open** event to hide the **Status** page if the user opens the form to compose a business card request. When a submitted Business Card Request item is opened, the **Status** page is displayed.

▸ **To add code to the Open event**

1   On the **Script** menu of the **Script Editor**, click **Event**.

2   In the **Events** box, double-click **Open**.

3   Add the following code.

```
'hides the Status page when the user opens the form to compose an
item.
Function Item_Open()
    Set MyInspector = Item.GetInspector
        If Item.SenderName = "" then
            MyInspector.HideFormPage("Status")
        Else
            MyInspector.ShowFormPage("Status")
        End if
End Function
```

# Set Form Properties

Now you set the Form Properties for the Business Card Request form.

▸ **To set Form Properties:**

•   Click the form (**Properties**) page, and then set the following properties.

| Property | Setting |
| --- | --- |
| **Form caption** | |
| **Contact** | *Your name* |
| **Description** | Use this form to send a business card request to the Business Card Requests folder. |
| **Version** | 1.0 |
| **Form Number** | 1-1 |

# Make a Backup Copy of the Form

It's always a good idea to make a backup copy of the form before you publish it.

▶ **To save the Business Card Request form**

1   On the **File** menu, click **Save As**.

2   In the **Save in** box, click a folder in which to save the form.

3   In the **Name** box, type **Business Card Request**, and then click **Save**.

# Publish the Form

It's quite likely that you will not be able to publish the form to the Organization Forms Library because you don't have administrator permissions. Instead, you can publish it to your Personal Forms Library. You can then open the form and send a business card request to the Business Card Requests folder to test the forms. In addition to the Personal Forms Library, you also publish the form in the Business Card Requests Folder Forms Library. This provides a convenient way for an administrator to create a Business Card Request item because a New Business Card Request command is added to the **Compose** menu of the folder.

▶ **To publish the form to your Personal Forms Library**

1   On the **Form Design** toolbar, click the **Publish Form As** button.

2   In the **From name** box, type **Business Card Request**, and then click **Publish**.

▶ **To publish the form to the Business Card Request Folder Forms Library**

1   On the **Form Design** toolbar, click the **Publish Form As** button.

2   Click **Publish In**.

3   In the **Folder Forms Library** list, click the Business Card Requests folder, and then click **OK**.

4   Click **Publish**.

**Tip**   In the Business Card Requests folder, click the **Compose** menu. Note that **the New Business Card Request command** is added to the menu. Outlook automatically adds the menu command when you publish the form in the Business Card Request Folder Forms Library.

# Create Views

The Create Request Status view groups items by the Request Pending or Request Processed value in the Request Status field. Items in each group are then sorted by the date they were received. When an administrator opens an item and completes the order, he selects **Request Processed** in the **Request Status** box. The item is then moved to the Request Processed group.

# Create the Request Status View

The Request Status view, as shown in Figure 10.15, groups items by the Request Pending or Request Processed value in the BusinessCardRequestStatus field. Items in each group are then sorted by date processed. If there is not a date in the DateProcessed field, items are sorted by date received.

**Figure 10.15   The Request Status view in the Business Card Requests folder**

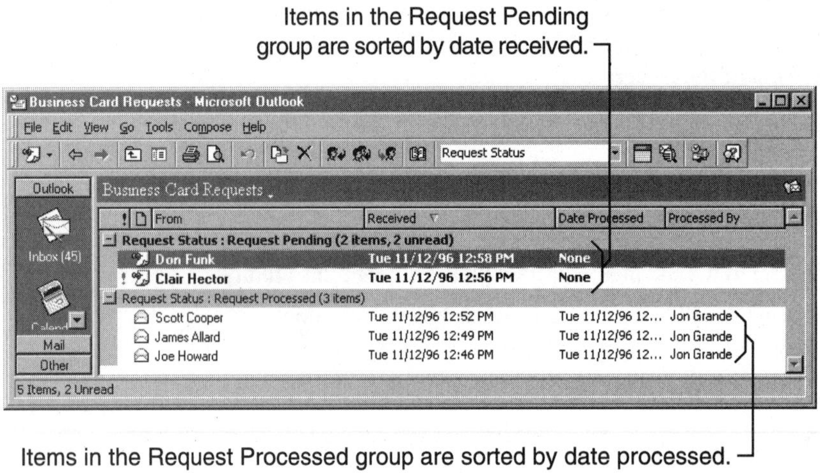

Items in the Request Pending group are sorted by date received.

Items in the Request Processed group are sorted by date processed.

▶ **To create the By Request Status view**

1  In the Folder List, click the Business Card Requests folder.

2  On the **View** menu, click **Define Views**.

3  Click **New**.

4  In the **Name of new view** box, type **Request Status**.

5  Click **OK** twice, and then click **Apply View**.

# Remove Columns

Now you remove the fields that aren't necessary for the Request Status view.

▶ **To remove fields**

•  Drag the Flag Status, Attachments, and Subject column headings, as shown in
Figure 10.16, away from the column heading row until an X appears through the
column heading; then release the mouse button.

**Figure 10.16   Drag the Flag Status, Attachments , and Subject column headings from the
column heading row.**

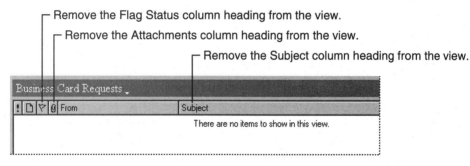

Remove the Flag Status column heading from the view.

Remove the Attachments column heading from the view.

Remove the Subject column heading from the view.

# Add Columns

Now you add columns to the Request Status view.

▶ **To add a column to a view**

1  On the **View** menu, click **Field Chooser**.

2  In the top box in the Field Chooser, click the **Business Card Request field** set.

3  Drag the BusinessCardDateProcessed field from the Field Chooser to the column heading row and drop it to the right of the Received column heading.

4  Right-click the BusinessCardDateProcessed column heading, and then click **Format Columns** on the shortcut menu.

5  In the **Label** box, type **Date Processed**, and then click **OK**.

6  Drag the BusinessCardRequestAdministrator field from the Field Chooser to column heading row and drop it to the right of the BusinessCardDateProcessed column heading.

7  Right-click the BusinessCardRequestAdministrator column heading, and then click **Format Columns** on the shortcut menu.

8  In the **Label** box, type **Processed By**, and then click **OK**.

   The column heading should now look similar to the column heading in Figure 10.17. If you want to set the exact width of the columns, right-click the column heading, and then click **Format Columns** on the shortcut menu. Then type the column width in the **Specific width** box.

**Figure 10.17  The column heading row for the Request Status view**

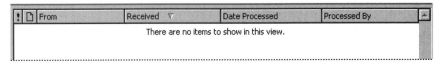

# Group By

Now you group by the BusinessCardRequestStatus field. However, before you group items, you add the BusinessCardRequestStatus field as a column. Next you format the column to change the label to Request Processed, then you remove the column. You cannot directly format a group label, so this method provides a handy alternative.

▶ **To format the BusinessCardRequestStatus field**

1  From the Field Chooser, drag the BusinessCardRequestStatus field to the column heading row. It really doesn't matter where you put the column heading at this time.

**2**  Right-click the BusinessCardRequestStatus column heading, and then click **Format Columns** on the shortcut menu.

**3**  In the **Label** field, type **Request Status**.

**4**  Click **OK**.

▶ **To group by BusinessCardRequestStatus**

**1**  On the **View** menu, click **Group By Box**.

An area with the text **Drag a column header here to group by that column** appears above the Column Heading row.

**2**  Drag the Request Status column heading into the **Drag a column header here to group by that column** area.

**3**  On the **View** menu, click **Group By Box**.

## Sort By

- Click the Date Processed column heading, so items in each group are listed in order according to date processed.

## Save the Request Status View

**1**  Click the **Current View** box, and then press ENTER.

**2**  Click **Update the view "Request Status" with the current settings**, and then click **OK**.

# Create the By Requester Name View

The By Requester Name view, as shown in Figure 10.18, shows request items sorted in ascending order by the requester's name, so a user's request is easy to find in the folder.

**Figure 10.18   The By Requester Name view**

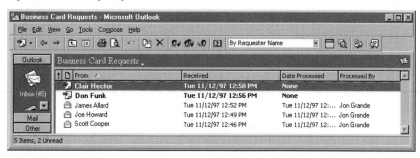

▶ **To create the By Requester Name view**

1  On the **View** menu, click **Define Views**.

2  Click **Request Status**, and then click **Copy**.

3  In the **Name of new view** box, type **By Requester Name**, and then click **OK**.

4  Click **Group By**.

5  In the **Group items by** box, click **(none)**, click **OK** twice, and then click **Apply View**.

6  Click the From column heading so the arrow points up, as shown in the preceding illustration in Figure 10.18.

## Save the By Requester Name View

1  Click the **Current View** box, and then press ENTER.

2  Click **Update the view "By Requester Name" with the current settings**, and then click **OK**.

# Set Permissions

For the Business Card Requests folder, you give the general public, represented by the **Default** name in the **Permissions** dialog box, a Contributor role so users can send items to the folder. However, after an item is submitted in the folder, users cannot change items. You then give those people who are responsible for processing business card requests an Editor role so they can edit and save items in the folder. In addition, you give those people who are responsible for designing and maintaining the folder Owner permissions, so they can make any necessary changes to the folder.

▶ **To set permissions for the Business Card Requests folder**

1  In the Folder List, right-click the Business Card Requests folder, and then click **Properties** on the shortcut menu.

2  Click the **Permissions** tab.

3  Set the following permissions for the folder.

| Name | Role | Assign To |
|------|------|-----------|
| Default | Contributor | General users who will submit business card requests |
| Business Card Request administrators | Editor | Administrators who are responsible for processing business card request orders |
| Application designers or system administrators | Owner | People responsible for maintaining and designing applications |

**See Also**   For more information about setting permissions, see "Set Permissions" in Chapter 8, "Folders."

# Test the Application

Now it's a good idea to test the application to make sure it's working as expected.

▶ **To test the application**

1  On the **<Compose>** menu, click **Choose Form**.

2  Click **Personal Forms**, and then double-click **Business Card Request**.

3  Fill in the form, and then click **Send**.

4  In the Folder List, click the Business Card Requests folder.

5  Double-click the Business Card Request item you just sent to the folder.

6  Click **Enable Macros**.

7  Click the **Status** page.

8  In the **Request Status** box, click **Request Processed**.

9  Click **Send date of delivery message**, and then click the **Send** button to send the form.

10  Close the Business Card Request form. When asked if you want to save the changes, click **Yes**.

11  In the **Current View** box, click **By Requester Name**.

12  Repeat Steps 1–10 several times to make sure the application is working correctly.

# Send the Form to the Administrator

When you are sure the application is working as expected, you create a message and attach the form as a file attachment in the message. The administrator is responsible for checking the form for harmful macros and viruses. If the form is clean, the administrator clears the **Save form definition with item** option on the **Properties** page of the form, and then publishes the form to the Organization Forms Library where it can be opened by all users on the Microsoft Exchange system.

▶ **To send the attached form**

1   On the **Compose** menu, click **New Mail Message**.

2   Fill in the To field with the name of the administrator.

3   In the Message box, type the following:

**Please check this form for viruses and harmful macros. If none are found, clear the Save form definition with item option on the Properties page of the form, and then publish the form to the Organization Forms Library.**

4   On the **Insert** menu, click **File**, and then open the folder in which you saved the Business Card Request.oft file earlier in the chapter.

5   Double-click the Business Card Request.oft file.

6   Click **Send**.

# Check the Form for Viruses and Harmful Code

If you are the administrator, you open the form, and then save the file attachment. You then check the form for viruses and harmful macros. If none exist, you clear the **Save form definition with item** option, and then publish the form to the Organization Forms Library.

▶ **To check a form that has been sent to you**

1   Save the form file to a folder, and then run a virus-checking tool on the form.

2   When you are certain the form is virus-free, hold down the SHIFT key and then double-click the form .oft file.

   **Important**  When you hold down the SHIFT key when opening a form, you prevent any code from executing when the form opens.

3   In the Folder List, select the folder where you want to open the form, and then click **OK**.

4   On the **Tools** menu, click **Design Outlook Form**.

5   Click the **Properties** page.

6   Clear the **Save form definition with item** check box.

▶ **To publish the form**

1   On the **Form Design** toolbar, click the **Publish Form As** button.

2   Click **Publish In**.

3   In the **Forms Library** box, click **Organization Forms**, and then click **OK**.

4   Click **Publish**.

5   On the **Form Design** toolbar, click the **Publish Form As** button.

6   Click **Publish In**.

7   In the **Folder Forms Library** box, click **Public Folders**, and then locate and click the Business Card Requests folder.

8   Click **OK**.

9   Click **Publish**.

# Release the Application

Before you release the application, it's a good idea to test the folder one more time. When you're sure the application is working as expected, you set the **Initial View on Folder** property to Request Status and you make the folder available by clicking the **All users with access permission** option.

▶ **To set administration properties**

1   In the Folder List, right-click the Business Card Requests folder, and then click **Properties**.

2   Click the **Administration** tab.

3   In the **Initial View on folder** box, click **Request Status**.

4   Click **All users with access permission**.

Now that the folder is ready to use, send a message to your co-workers to notify them that the application is available. You might want to include a shortcut to the folder in your message to make it easy for your co-workers to find the folder.

# CHAPTER 11

# The Help Desk Application

## In This Chapter

Overview of the Help Desk Application   385

Set Up the Application   392

The Help Request Form   398

The Assigned Help Task Form   407

One of the best ways to learn how to design Microsoft Outlook applications is to take a look at the sample applications in Outlook. In this chapter, we'll take a look at the sample Help Desk application. There are several reasons for examining the Help Desk application. It showcases most of the design techniques that you use when creating applications. It shows you how to create an application that consists of multiple forms and folders. And, it shows you how to create an application that creates and stores a variety of item types, including custom tasks, posts, and messages.

To introduce the Help Desk application and its components, we'll walk through the Help Request process to demonstrate how Outlook can be used to automate a process in your organization. Then we'll take a look at how to set up the Help Desk application in your organization. After you set up the application, we'll explore some of the design techniques that are implemented in this application.

# Overview of the Help Desk Application

The Help Desk application provides users with an easy way to submit a request for technical assistance to your organization's Help Desk group. In addition, the application makes it possible for Help Desk personnel to assign, organize, track, collaborate on, and resolve Help Desk requests. Perhaps the easiest way to explain how the Help Desk application works is to walk you through the entire Help Request process from beginning to end.

**The user opens the Help Request form.**   The Help Request form is a Message form published in the Organization Forms Library and the Help Desk Folder Forms Library. To open the Help Request form, as shown in Figure 11.1, users click **Choose Form** on the **Compose** menu, and then select the **Help Request** form. The form is preaddressed to the Help Request folder, so the user does not need to specify the folder address to submit the request. The user simply fills in the request and clicks the **Send** button.

Figure 11.1   The Compose page of the Help Request form

The user clicks the **Send** button to send the request.
The hidden To field is preaddressed to the Help Desk folder.

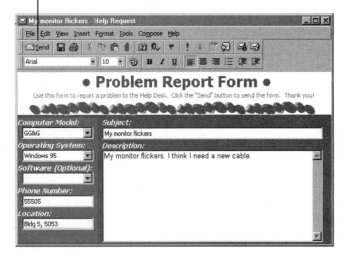

**The Help Request form arrives in the Help Desk folder,** as shown in Figure 11.2.

**Figure 11.2   The Help Desk folder**

A Help Request item in the Help Desk folder

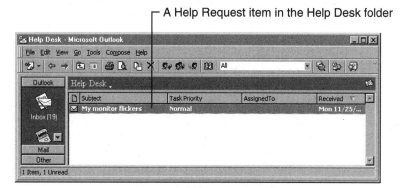

**A Help Desk administrator opens the Help Request form in the Help Desk folder,** as shown in Figure 11.3.

**Figure 11.3   The Read page of the Help Request form**

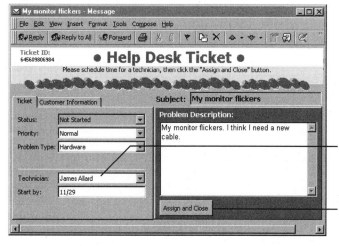

The technician's name is copied to the To field of the message item that notifies the technician that a task is assigned to him.

When clicked, this button triggers a procedure that creates an Assigned Help Task item in the Assigned Help Task folder.

**The administrator clicks the Assign and Close button.**   When the Help Desk administrator clicks the **Assign and Close** button on the Help Request form, three things happen:

- Information in the item is written from the Help Request form to the newly created Assigned Help Task item. This item is created and saved in the Assigned Help Tasks folder, as shown in Figure 11.4.

**Figure 11.4   The Assigned Help Tasks folder**

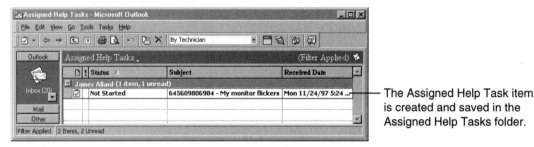

The Assigned Help Task item is created and saved in the Assigned Help Tasks folder.

- The administrator sees a prompt that asks him if he wants to delete or save the Help Request. Based on his choice, the request is saved or deleted from the Help Desk folder.

- A message is created and sent to the Inbox of the technician assigned to the request. When the message is created, the Assigned Help Task item just created and saved in the Assigned Help Tasks folder is inserted as an attachment in the message, as shown in Figure 11.5.

**Figure 11.5   The Read page of the Help Request form**

The message is addressed to the assigned technician.

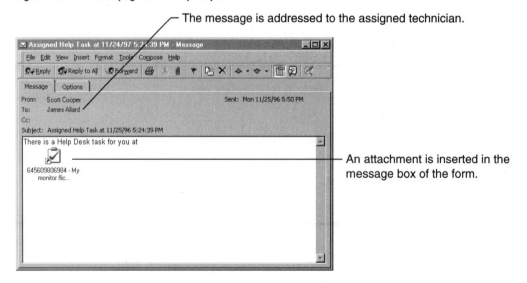

An attachment is inserted in the message box of the form.

**The assigned technician double-clicks the attachment in the message.**   When the technician double-clicks the attachment in the message, the Assigned Help Task item opens, as shown in Figure 11.6.

**Figure 11.6   The Read page of the Assigned Help Task form**

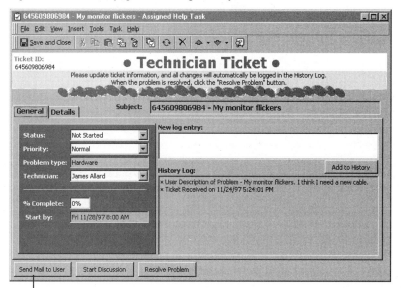

The technician can click the **Send Mail to User** button to open the Correspondence Mail form.

**The technician can send correspondence mail to the user to get more information.**   In many cases, the technician requires additional information to resolve the request. To send mail to the user, the technician clicks the **Send Mail to User** button to show the Correspondence Mail form, as shown in Figure 11.7.

**Figure 11.7   The Compose page of the Correspondence Mail form**

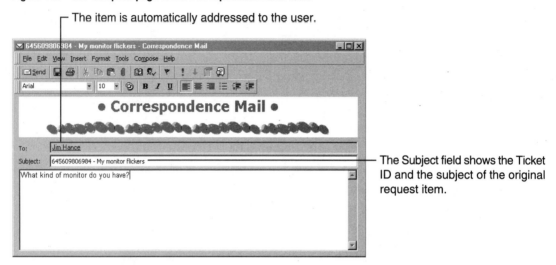

─ The item is automatically addressed to the user.

─ The Subject field shows the Ticket ID and the subject of the original request item.

**The technician can click the Start Discussion button to start an online conversation about the request.**   If the technician experiences problems resolving the request, she clicks the **Start Discussion** button to open the Task Discussion form, as shown in Figure 11.8. The technician can then post a Discussion item (or post) to the folder. Other technicians can review the post and post their own suggestions or solutions to the problem.

**Figure 11.8   The Compose page of the Task Discussion form. The Discussion item is posted in the Assigned Help Tasks folder.**

The technician clicks the **Post** button to post the Task Discussion item to the Assigned Help Task folder.

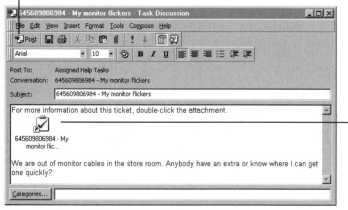

An attachment to the Assigned Help Task item is included in the message box.

**When the problem is solved, the technician clicks the Resolve Problem button** on the Assigned Help Task form to send a message to the user saying that the Help Request is resolved. The task is then shown as completed in the Assigned Help Tasks folder, as shown in Figure 11.9.

**Figure 11.9   The resolved task in the Assigned Help Tasks folder**

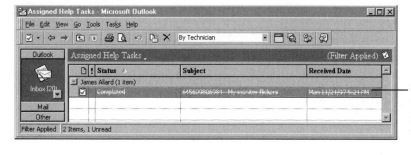

When the Assigned Help Task item is resolved, a strikethrough line appears through the item in the view.

# Set Up the Application

Before you can run the Help Desk application, you must customize the application so it works in your environment. For example, you must copy the Help Desk Application folder to Public Folders and then publish the folder address. In addition, you must set the address in the To field of the Help Request form to the Help Requests folder. You also add the names of your organization's Help Desk technicians to the form.

## Copy the Help Desk Folder to Public Folders

To make the Help Desk application available to users in your organization, you copy the Help Desk folder from the Building Microsoft Outlook 97 Applications folder to Public Folders. Before you copy the folder, however, make sure you have owner permission in the folder where you want to copy the folder.

▶ **To check your permission for a folder**

1  In the Folder List, right-click the folder you want to check, and then click **Properties** on the shortcut menu.

2  Click the **Permission** tab.

3  If you have owner permission for the folder, you should see your name in the list with the owner role assigned.

4  If you do not have owner permission for the folder you want to copy the folder to, see your administrator.

▶ **To copy the Help Desk folder to Public Folders**

1  In the Folder List, expand the Building Microsoft Outlook 97 Applications folder, and then expand the Beyond the Basics folder.

2  Right-click the Help Desk Application folder, and then click **Copy "Help Desk Application"** on the shortcut menu.

3  Double-click the folder you want to copy the Help Desk folder to.

## Publish the Folder Address and Restrict Folder Access

For the Help Desk application to operate properly, you must preaddress the Help Request form with the address of the Help Requests folder. Before you can do this, however, you must publish the folder address to your Personal Address Book. You can also ask your administrator to publish the folder in the Global Address Book. It's much easier and faster, however, to publish the folder address to your Personal Address Book.

▶ **To publish the Help Desk folder address to your Personal Address Book**

1 In the Folder List, right-click the Help Desk Application folder, and then click **Properties** on the shortcut menu.

2 Click the **Administration** tab, and then click **Personal Address Book**.

The Help Desk folder address is now available in your Personal Address Book. This enables you to set the To field of the Help Request form to this address. First, however, you restrict user access to the folder while you work on it.

▶ **To prevent users from opening the folder**

• On the **Administration** page, click **Owners Only** under **This folder is available to**, and then click **OK**.

# Set Permissions

With Outlook, you can define flexible permissions for folders. For example, for the Help Desk folder, you give general users contributor permission so they can submit items to the folder but cannot change items after they are submitted. You give the Help Desk administrator and technicians editor permission so they can edit and create items in the folder. And you give the Help Desk manager and application designers owner permission so they can maintain the folder.

## Set Permissions for the Help Desk Folder

▶ **To set permissions for the Help Desk folder**

1 In the Folder List, right-click the Help Desk folder, and then click **Properties** on the shortcut menu.

2 Click the **Permissions** tab, and then set the permissions as shown in the following table. When you are done, click **OK**.

| Name | Role | Description | Assign to |
| --- | --- | --- | --- |
| Default | Contributor | Can submit items to the folder, but cannot open or edit items in the folder. | General users who submit Help Request items. |
| *Help Desk technicians* | Editor | Can create, read, and edit all items. | Help Desk technicians or administrators responsible for assigning the Help Request task. |
| *Help Desk manager* | Owner | All permissions. | Managers who supervise Help Desk technicians. |
| *Application designers or system administrators* | Owner | All permissions. | People responsible for maintaining and designing applications. |

## Set Permissions for the Assigned Help Tasks Folder

For the Assigned Help Tasks folder, you restrict access to Help Desk administrators, technicians, and managers only.

▸ **To set permissions for the Assigned Help Tasks folder**

1   In the Folder List, right-click the Assigned Help Tasks folder, and the click **Properties** on the shortcut menu.

2   Click the **Permissions** tab, and then set the permissions as shown in the following table. When you are done, click **OK**.

| Name | Role | Description | Assign to |
|------|------|-------------|-----------|
| Default | None | General users cannot access the folder. | |
| *Help Desk technicians* | Editor | Can create, read, and edit all items. | Help Desk technicians or administrators responsible for assigning the Help Request task. |
| *Help Desk manager* | Owner | All permissions. | Managers who supervise Help Desk technicians. |
| *Application designers or system administrators* | Owner | All permissions. | People responsible for maintaining and designing applications. |

# Customize the Help Request Form for Your Organization

Now that the folders are set up, you customize the Help Request form to your environment. First, you preaddress the To field of the form to the Help Request folder address you published to your Personal Address Book. Then you add the names of the technicians to the AssignedTo field. When you are done, you publish the form to the Personal Forms Library and the Help Desk Folder Forms Library. After you thoroughly test the application, you can submit the Help Request form to your administrator who can then publish the Help Request form in the Organization Forms Library. You can then delete the temporary form you published in your Personal Forms Library.

## Preaddress the Help Request Form

Now you set the initial value of the To field in the Help Request form to the Help Requests folder. In this way, when users open the form, they can submit a Help Request to the public folder without worrying about or knowing the folder address. To preaddress the form, you must go back and forth between Run and Design mode.

▶ **To preaddress the Help Request form**

1  In the Folder List, click the Help Desk folder.

2  On the **Compose** menu, click **New Help Requests**.

3  On the form **Tools** menu, click **Design Outlook Form** to switch to Design mode.

4  Click the **Message** tab.

5  On the **Form** menu, click **Display This Page**.

6  On the form **Tools** menu, click **Design Outlook Form** to switch to Run mode.

7  In the **To** box, delete the current entry, and then click the **To** button.

8  In the **Show names from the** box, click **Personal Address Book**.

9  In the list, double-click **Help Desk**, and then click **OK**.

10  On the form **Tools** menu, click **Design Outlook Form** to switch to Design mode.

11  On the **Form** menu, click **Display This Page** to clear the options so the page is once again hidden at run time.

## Specify the Technician Names in the AssignedTo Field

Next, you set the names that appear in the **Technician** box on the **Read** page of the Help Request form. This control, as shown in Figure 11.10, is actually named AssignedTo and is bound to the AssignedTo field.

**Figure 11.10   The AssignedTo control on the Read page of the Help Request form**

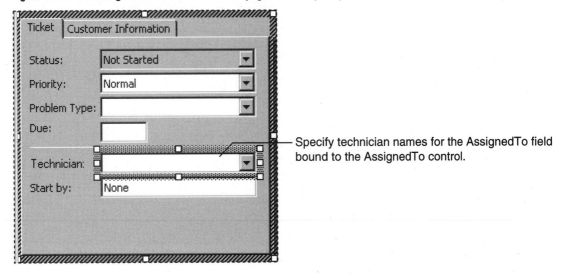

Specify technician names for the AssignedTo field bound to the AssignedTo control.

▶ **To specify the names in the AssignedTo field**

1  Right-click the AssignedTo control—shown as the **Technician** box on the form—and then click **Properties** on the shortcut menu.

2  Click the **Value** tab.

3  In the **Possible values** box, type the full names of the technicians whose names you want available in the **Technician** box at run time.

The names you type in the **Possible values** box, as shown in Figure 11.11, are the names used to address messages sent to technicians to notify them that tasks are assigned to them. So make sure the names you enter in the **Possible values** box are names that resolve when copied to the To field of a message.

**Figure 11.11   The names of the technicians are possible values in the AssignedTo field.**

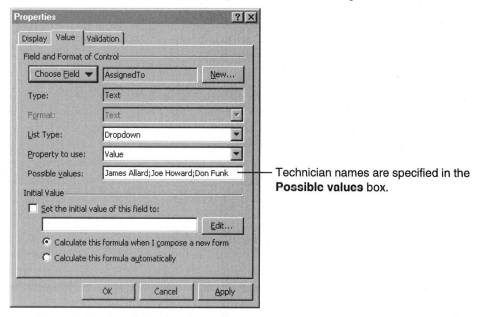

Technician names are specified in the **Possible values** box.

▶ **To make a backup copy of the Help Request form**

1  On the form's **Properties** page, clear the **Save form definition with item** check box.

2  On the form **File** menu, click **Save As**.

3  In the **Save in** box, select a folder.

4  In the **File name** box, type **Help Request**, and then click **Save**.

Later, you will use this form to send to the administrator.

▶ **To publish the form in the Personal Forms Library**

- On the **Form Design** toolbar, click **Publish Form As**, and then click **Publish**.

▶ **To publish the form in the Help Desk Folder Forms Library**

1 On the **Form Design** toolbar, click the **Publish As** button, and then click **Publish in**.

2 Double-click the **Help Desk** folder in Public Folders.

3 Click the **Publish** button.

If you don't publish the customized form to the Help Desk Folder Forms Library, the names of the technicians do not appear in the **Technician** box. Instead, the old Help Request form in the Help Desk Folder Form Library opens when you double-click a submitted item in the Help Desk folder.

# Test the Application

Now that the application is set up, you test it to make sure the application works as planned.

▶ **To test the Help Desk application**

1 On the **Compose** menu, click **Choose Form**, and then double-click the **Help Request** form.

2 Fill in the Help Request form, and then click **Send**.

3 In the Folder List, open the Help Desk folder, and then double-click the item you just sent to open it.

4 In the **Technician** box, make sure the names you added to the list are available. Type your name, and then click the **Assign and Close** button.

5 Open your Inbox and double-click the Assigned Help Task item that just arrived.

6 In the message box, double-click the attachment.

7 Click the **Send Mail to User** button, type a message in the message box, and then click **Send**.

8 Click the **Start Discussion** button, type a message in the message box, and then click **Post**.

9 Click the **Resolve Problem** button, and then click **Yes**.

You should now have a good idea of how this application works. Let's move on to take an in-depth look at some of the design techniques used in the Help Desk application.

# The Help Request Form

The Help Desk application provides a common Outlook groupware scenario. In the Help Desk application, Assigned Help Task items are saved in the Assigned Help Tasks folder. However, unless a Help Desk technician opens the Assigned Help Tasks folder, he has no idea that a new task has been assigned to him. To solve this problem, the Submit_Click procedure is added to the Help Request form. The Submit_Click procedure is triggered when the Help Desk administrator clicks the **Assign and Close** button. The Submit_Click procedure automatically creates and saves an Assigned Help Task item in the Assigned Help Tasks folder. The procedure then sends a message to the assigned technician's Inbox to notify her that she has an Assigned Help Task item. A shortcut to the Assigned Help Task item is included in the message, so when the message arrives in the technician's Inbox, she can click the shortcut to view the item.

In addition to the technique just described, we'll explore several other useful techniques in this section, including how to:

- Assign script-level variables.

- Determine the Compose mode or Read mode of an item.

- Create a unique Ticket ID.

- Automatically create a custom Assigned Help Task item and post it in the Assigned Help Tasks folder.

- Automatically send a message to the technician who is assigned an item and include a shortcut to the Assigned Help Task item in the message.

▶ **To view the code in the Help Request form**

1   Open the Help Desk folder.

2   On the **Compose** menu, click **New Help Request**.

3   On the **Tools** menu, click **Design Outlook Form**.

4   On the **Form Design** toolbar, click the **View Code** button.

# Assign Script-Level Variables

In the Help Request code, as shown in this example, several script-level variables are declared at the top of the Script Editor window. These variables are used among procedures that create the Ticket ID value for the Help Request item.

```
'*********************************************************************
'* Help Request code
'* Functions/Procedures:
'* Standard Events:
'* Item_Open()
'* Item_CustomPropertyChange(ByVal String)
'*
'* Helpers:
'*     ChangeProblemType()
'*     TrimUserName()
'*     CreateDateAsNumber()
'*********************************************************************
Dim UserName          ' Script level variables used for the Ticket ID.
Dim Trimmed
Dim Munged
Dim TicketID
```

# Determine If the Help Request Form Is in Compose Mode or Read Mode

In many of the applications you create, you need to determine if the form is in Compose mode or Read mode. To determine if a Message form is in Compose mode or Read mode, you can add a statement to the Item_Open event to get the **SenderName** property of an item. As shown in the following example, if the **SenderName** property is equal to "", then the form is in Compose mode and the code to create the TicketID value is executed.

```
'*********************************************************************
'* Procedure:  Item_Open()
'* Description:  Upon open, save the current folder location (because it
'*        may change later by the user). Also, set a flag if the form
'*        is in Read mode or Compose mode (by checking the
'*        SenderName property).
'*********************************************************************
Sub Item_Open()
   Dim MyDate
   Dim NowID

   If (Item.SenderName = "") Then     ' If item is in Compose mode, create the ID.
      UserName = Application.GetNameSpace("MAPI").CurrentUser

      ' Trim the user name of spaces.
      Trimmed = TrimUserName(UserName)

      NowID = Now
      ' Get date as numbers only.
      MyDate = CreateDateAsNumber(NowID)

      ' Set the Ticket ID for this item.
      TicketID = MyDate & Trimmed

      Item.UserProperties.Find("TicketID").Value = TicketID

      Item.BillingInformation = TicketID
   End If
End Sub
```

# Create a Unique Ticket ID for Each Item

To create a unique Ticket ID for each item, as shown in Figure 11.12, the Item_Open event calls two functions: the **TrimUserName** function and the **CreateDateAsNumber** function.

**Figure 11.12   A unique Ticket ID is created for each Help Request.**

┌─ The Ticket ID

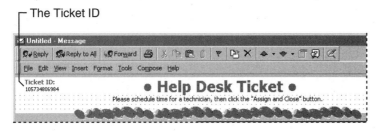

# The TrimUserName Function

When a Help Request item is opened in Compose mode, the code in the Item_Open event gets the **CurrentUser** property and passes it to the TrimUserName function. The TrimUserName function converts the name into a numeric value and returns it to the Trimmed variable, as shown in this example.

```
'*********************************************************************
'* Procedure:  TrimUserName(ByVal UserName)
'* Description:  Trims the user name so that it can be used in the
'*        Ticket ID.
'*********************************************************************
Function TrimUserName(ByVal UserName)
    Dim Counter         ' Declare variables.
    Dim AscName
    Dim KeepChar
    Dim KeepName
    Dim DiscardChar
    Dim RightName
    Temp = ""
    KeepName = ""

    For li = 0 To 2    ' For first three letters of user name.
        CharName = Mid(UCase(UserName), li + 1, 1)

        AscName = Asc(CharName)

        If ((AscName >= 48) and (AscName <= 57)) or ((AscName >= 65)
    ➥and (AscName <=90)) Then
            KeepName = KeepName + CStr(AscName)
        End If
    Next

    RightName = Right(KeepName, 6)
    TrimUserName = RightName
End Function
```

## The CreateDateAsNumber Function

The code in the Item_Open event also gets the **Now** property. This property returns
the current date and passes it to the CreateDateAsNumber function. The
CreateDateAsNumber function converts the date to a numeric value and returns the
value to the MyDate variable. The values of Trimmed and MyDate are then combined
in the Item_Open event code to form the Ticket ID value. The BillingInformation field
of the item is then set to the value of the Ticket ID.

```
'************************************************************************
'* Procedure:  CreateDateAsNumber(ByVal NowID)
'* Description:  Manipulates the date so that it can be used in the
'*       Ticket ID.
'************************************************************************
Function CreateDateAsNumber(ByVal NowID)
    For li = 0 To 16     ' For all 17 characters of the date stamp.
        CharName = Mid(UCase(NowID), li + 1, 1)
        AscName = Asc(CharName)
        If ((AscName >= 48) and (AscName <= 57)) Then
            KeepName = KeepName + CStr(CharName)
        End If
    Next
    RightID = Right(KeepName, 6)

    CreateDateAsNumber = RightID
End Function
```

# Automatically Create and Save an Assigned Help Task Item

On the **Read** page of the Help Request form, you see an **Assign and Close** button, as
shown in Figure 11.13. When this button is clicked, it triggers the Submit_Click
procedure. This procedure performs several tasks that follow.

**Figure 11.13   The Assign and Close button triggers the Submit_Click procedure that creates and saves an Assigned Help Task item in the Assigned Help Tasks folder.**

└ The **Assign and Close** button triggers the SubmitClick procedure.

- Sets the active folder as the Assigned Help Tasks folder, and then creates an Assigned Help Task item.

- Copies the necessary values from the Help Request item to the Assigned Help Task item.

- Sets the value of the item Importance field to **!** if the value of the Task Priority field is not "Normal."

- Saves the Assigned Help Task item in the Assigned Help Tasks folder.

- Creates a message, inserts a shortcut to the Assigned Help Task item in the message box of the message, and then sends the message to the assigned Help Desk technician.

In this section, we'll take a look at the Submit_Click procedure and discuss the techniques used in this procedure. Many of these techniques, once mastered, can be used in a variety of other applications.

## Set the Active Folder as the Assigned Help Tasks Folder

One of the problems you face in creating Outlook applications with multiple folders is setting the active folder. For example, with the Help Desk application, you open the Help Request item in the Help Desk folder and then create an Assigned Help Task item and save it in the Assigned Help Tasks folder. To do this, you must set the Assigned Help Tasks folder as the active folder. The fastest and easiest way to do this is to use the **Parent** property of the Help Request item to return the active folder, which, in this case, is the Help Desk folder. You then use the **Parent** property of the Help Desk folder to return the Help Desk Application folder. As shown in this example, you can then set the active folder as the Assigned Help Tasks folder.

**Important**  To create a custom item such as **IPM.Task.Assigned Help Task**, you must set the folder that contains the form as the active folder. In addition, the form associated with the item you want to create must be contained in the Folder Forms Library for that folder. You then use the **Add** method of the **Items Collection** object to create the item.

```
'***********************************************************************
'* Procedure:  Submit_Click
'* Description:  When the Submit button is clicked, copy all fields
'*         into the Task item, and finally delete this item.
'***********************************************************************
Sub Submit_Click
    If Item.UserProperties.Find("AssignedTo").Value = "" Then
        Temp = MsgBox("Please enter a technician before trying to assign a
        ➡task.",0,"Create Task")
    Else
        Assign = MsgBox("This will create a task in the Assigned Tasks folder,
        ➡delete this item, and send mail to the technician indicating that
        ➡they have a task to complete.",1,"Create Task")
    If Assign = 1 Then
        Set HelpDeskFolder = Item.Parent
        Set HelpDeskAppFolder = HelpDeskFolder.Parent
        Set TaskFolder = HelpDeskAppFolder.Folders("Assigned Help Tasks")
        Set AssignedItem = TaskFolder.Items.Add("IPM.Task.Assigned Help Task")
```

# Copy Values from the Help Desk Item to the Assigned Help Task Item

After the Submit_Click procedure creates the Assigned Help Task item, it copies the necessary values from the Help Desk item to the Assigned Help Task item. Notice that, in some cases, the field from the original item is actually different from the field in the new item. For example, in the first line of code in this example, the value of the Computer Model field of the current item (the Help Request item) is copied to the Computer Brand and Model field of the Assigned Help Task item. To get or set the value of a custom field, you must use the **Find** method of the **UserProperties** object.

```
Submit_Click    (continued)
        ' Populate the Assigned Help Task form with all the corresponding
        ' fields in this item.
        AssignedItem.UserProperties.Find("Computer Brand and Model").Value =
        ➥Item.UserProperties.Find("Computer Model").Value
        AssignedItem.UserProperties.Find("Problem Type").Value =
        ➥Item.UserProperties.Find("Problem Type").Value
        AssignedItem.UserProperties.Find("Phone").Value =
        ➥Item.UserProperties.Find("Phone Number").Value
        AssignedItem.UserProperties.Find("Computer OS").Value =
        ➥Item.UserProperties.Find("Operating System").Value
        AssignedItem.UserProperties.Find("Ticket ID").Value =
        ➥Item.UserProperties.Find("TicketID").Value
        AssignedItem.Subject =
        ➥Item.UserProperties.Find("TicketID").Value & " - " & Item.Subject
        AssignedItem.UserProperties.Find("Description").Value = Item.Body
        AssignedItem.UserProperties.Find("Technician Name").Value =
        ➥Item.UserProperties.Find("AssignedTo").Value
        AssignedItem.UserProperties.Find("Received Date").Value = Item.SentOn
        AssignedItem.UserProperties.Find("Computer Software").Value =
        ➥Item.UserProperties.Find("Software").Value
        AssignedItem.UserProperties.Find("From User").Value = Item.SenderName
        AssignedItem.UserProperties.Find("User Location").Value =
        ➥Item.UserProperties.Find("Request Location").Value
        AssignedItem.UserProperties.Find("Task Priority").Value =
        ➥Item.UserProperties.Find("Task Priority").Value
        AssignedItem.UserProperties.Find("AssignedOn").Value =
        ➥Item.UserProperties.Find("Start by").Value
```

## Set the Importance Property of the Assigned Task Item

The following code provides an example of how you set standard property values and custom properties values in an item. In this example, the **Find** method and the **Value** property are used in the **Select Case** statement to get the value of the user-defined Task Priority field. When the property is a standard property of the item, as is the case in this example where **Importance** is a standard property of the **TaskItem** object, you can set the value without using the **Find** method or the **Value** property.

```
Submit_Click    (continued)
    ' If Task Priority is something other than Normal, set the
    ' Importance icon to !.
    Select Case Item.UserProperties.Find("Task Priority").Value

    Case "Normal"
        AssignedItem.Importance = 1
    Case Else
        AssignedItem.Importance = 2
    End Select
```

## Save the Assigned Help Task Item

After the Submit_Click procedure copies information from the Help Request item to the Assigned Help Task item and then sets the **Importance** property of the Assigned Help Task item, it saves the item in the Assigned Help Tasks folder.

```
Submit_Click    (continued)
    AssignedItem.Save
```

## Create a Message, Insert a Shortcut to the Assigned Help Task Item in the Message, and Send

After the Assigned Help Task item is saved, the Submit_Click procedure creates a message. In this case, the message is a standard **MailItem** object, so there is no need to worry about setting the active folder. However, remember that when creating standard items, you must use the numeric value of the item rather than the constant. In this example, the `Application.CreateItem(0)` statement creates a standard message item. After the item is created, the Subject and Body text are set for the item. The To field of the item is then set to the technician's name specified in the AssignedTo field of the Help Desk item. Finally, the saved Assigned Help Task item is inserted as a shortcut in the message box of the message. The item is then sent to the technician's Inbox, and the Help Desk administrator is given the option to save or delete the submitted Help Request in the Help Request folder.

```
Submit_Click    (continued)
     Set myItem = Application.CreateItem(0)
     MyItem.Subject = "Assigned Help Task at " & Now()
     MyItem.Body = "There is a Help Desk task for you at " & chr(13)

     On Error Resume Next
     MyItem.To = Item.UserProperties.Find("AssignedTo").Value

     Set MyAttachments = MyItem.Attachments
     MyAttachments.Add AssignedItem, 4
     MyItem.Send
     If err Then
        MsgBox("The Mail did not send because the technician was not recognized")
     End If

     Item.Delete     ' After everything was submitted, delete this item.

        End If
    End If
End Sub
```

# The Assigned Help Task Form

The Assigned Help Task form is a custom form based on the standard Task form.
When creating forms for tracking applications, the Task form often serves as good
starting point, as you'll see in this chapter and in Chapter 12, "The Document
Tracking Application." The Task form, and the Task items created with it, have
built-in fields and functionality for tracking the progress of a task. For example, the
Task form has a Status field and a % Complete field. In addition, when a task is
complete, a line is drawn through the item in the folder indicating the task is complete.

Perhaps most important, however, the Task form makes it easy to update and save
Task items because the Task form has a **Save and Close** button, which is used to
submit new items, and to update existing items. As a result, the user is never confused
about whether he should save or post an item.

The Assigned Help Task form appears when you double-click an Assigned Help Task item in the Assigned Help Tasks folder. With the **Read** page of this form, as shown in Figure 11.14, a Help Desk technician can send mail to a user, post a Discussion item to the Assigned Help Tasks folder, or indicate that the Help Task is resolved.

**Figure 11.14  The Read page of the Assigned Help Task form**

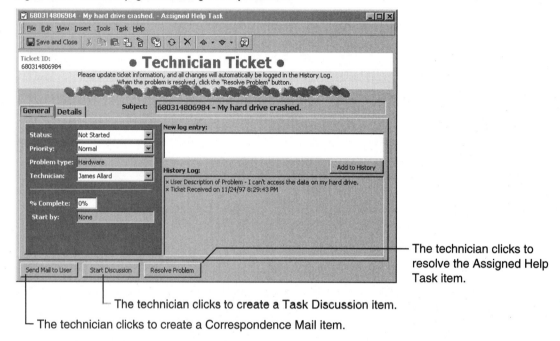

The technician clicks to resolve the Assigned Help Task item.

The technician clicks to create a Task Discussion item.

The technician clicks to create a Correspondence Mail item.

▶ **To view the code in the Assigned Help Task form**

1  Open the Assigned Help Tasks folder.

2  Double-click an Assigned Help Task item.

3  If an Assigned Help Task item does not exist in the folder, follow the instructions in "Test the Application" earlier in this chapter.

4  On the form **Tools** menu, click **Design Outlook Form**.

5  On the **Form Design** toolbar, click the **View Code** button.

# The Open Event of the Assigned Help Task Item

For the Item_Open event, we'll look at several techniques, including how to:

• Write the initial Help Request information into the History Log.

- Lock controls on the form if the item is resolved.
- Set script-level variables to the original values of the fields. In other procedures, the values of these variables are compared to the current value of the field to determine if the field value has changed.

## Write the Initial Help Request Item into the History Log

At the bottom of the **Read** page of the Assigned Help Task form there is a TextBox control that is bound to the Flag field, as shown in Figure 11.15. The Flag field is used to determine if the form is being opened for the first time.

**Figure 11.15   The TextBox control is bound to the Flag field.**

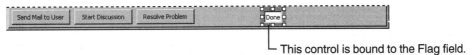

└─ This control is bound to the Flag field.

The initial value of the Flag field is set to Opened, as shown in Figure 11.16.

**Figure 11.16   The Value properties for the Flag field**

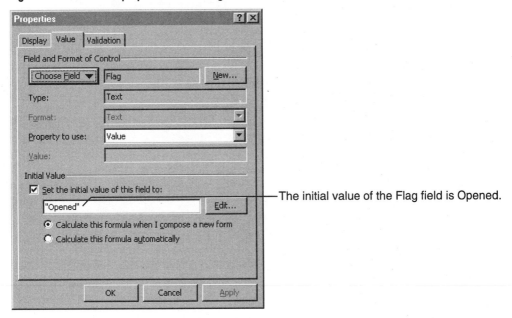

─The initial value of the Flag field is Opened.

The code in the Item_Open event checks the value of the Flag field. If the field value is Opened, then the user description of the problem and the date the item is received is written to the History Text field of the item. The value of the Flag field is then set to Done.

```
'*********************************************************************
'* Procedure:  Item_Open
'* Arguments:
'* Description:  Upon opening, set the History Log to list opening
'*          information. Store the initial values of certain fields
'*          for use in later functions.
'*********************************************************************
Sub Item_Open()
Dim MyPage
Dim Resolved

    Ticket_Resolved = False

    If (Item.UserProperties.Find("Flag").Value = "Opened") Then
        Item.UserProperties.Find("History Text").Value = Chr(164) &
        ➥" Ticket Received on " & Item.UserProperties.Find("Received Date").Value

        If (Item.UserProperties.Find("Description").Value <> "") Then
            Item.UserProperties.Find("History Text").Value = Chr(164) &
            ➥" User Description of Problem - " &
            ➥Item.UserProperties.Find("Description").Value & Chr(10) &
            ➥Item.UserProperties.Find("History Text").Value
        Else
            Item.UserProperties.Find("History Text").Value = Chr(164) &
            ➥" No User Description of Problem" & Chr(10) &
            ➥Item.UserProperties.Find("History Text").Value
        End If

        Item.UserProperties.Find("Flag").Value = "Done"
        Item.Status = 0
    End If
```

## If the Item Is Resolved, Lock the Controls on the Form

When the Help Desk technician clicks the **Resolve Problem** button on the Assigned Help Task form, the status of the item is set to 2, meaning the request is resolved. If the item is resolved, many of the controls on the Assigned Help Task form are locked so they cannot be changed. Notice in the following code example that the **Ticket** page must first be referenced with the `Item.GetInspector.ModifiedFormPages.Add("Ticket")` statement before controls on the page can be referenced.

```
Item_Open    (continued)
   Resolved = Item.Status

   ' Comment this code out if you don't want to lock all values for the
   ' fields when the task is "Resolved".
   If (Resolved = 2) Then              ' 2 = Closed.
      Set MyPage = Item.GetInspector.ModifiedFormPages.Add("Ticket")
      MyPage.Controls("Status").Locked = True
      MyPage.Controls("Priority").Locked = True
      MyPage.Controls("CompletePercent").Locked = True
      MyPage.Controls("NewLogEntry").Locked = True
      MyPage.Controls("TechnicianName").Locked = True
   End If
```

## Set Variables to Store the Initial Information

The Item_Open event stores the original values of the Task Priority, PercentComplete, and Status fields. If these values change, a log entry is made in the History Text field of the form when the user clicks the **Save and Close** button on the Assigned Help Task form. The process of making a log entry in the History Text field is covered in more detail in "The Item_Write Event" later in this chapter.

```
Item_Open    (continued)
' Sets variables to store the initial information.
   Orig_Priority = Item.UserProperties.Find("Task Priority").Value
   Orig_Complete = Item.PercentComplete
   Orig_Status = Item.Status
End Sub
```

# The PropertyChange Event

The PropertyChange event occurs when a change is made to a standard property of an item. For example, the **Status** and **PercentComplete** properties are standard properties of a task. The PropertyChange event for the Assigned Help Task form, as shown in the following example, checks to see whether the PercentComplete or Status fields have been changed. If they have been changed, the Property_Changed field value is set to True. Then if the PercentComplete field value is called, the Set_Complete_Changed procedure is called. If the Status field value is changed, the Set_Status_Changed procedure is called.

When the value of a standard field is changed, the name of the changed field is passed to the PropertyChange event. As shown in this example, you can then use the **Select Case** statement to determine the field that has been changed and to call procedures based on the field that is passed to the event.

```
'************************************************************************
'* Function:   Item_PropertyChange
'* Arguments:
'* Description:  Checks whether any non-user defined task fields
'*        have changed. In this case, Status is the only field affected.
'************************************************************************
Sub Item_PropertyChange(ByVal MyProperty)     ' Checks if Status changed.
    Property_Changed = True

    Select Case MyProperty
       Case "PercentComplete"
          Call Set_Complete_Changed()
       Case "Status"
          Call Set_Status_Changed()
       Case Else
          Property_Changed = False      ' If it wasn't changed, set
    End Select                          ' flag to False.
End Sub
```

# The Set_Status_Changed Procedure

As shown in the following code example, the Set_Status_Changed procedure compares the value of the original Status field value against the current Status field value. If the values are different, the Status_Changed variable is set to True. In addition, if the Status field value is 2, then the PercentComplete field value is set to 100.

```
Sub Set_Status_Changed()
    Dim x        ' Temp variable.
    Dim y        ' Temp variable.

    x = Orig_Status
    y = Item.Status

    Status_Changed = (x <> y)

    If (y = 2) Then
       Item.PercentComplete = "100"
    End If
End Sub
```

# The CustomPropertyChange Event

The CustomPropertyChange event is used to check whether custom field values have
changed. As shown in the following example, if the values of the Task Priority or
Complete Percent fields are changed, the Item_Change flag is set to true and the
respective procedures are called based on the field that is passed as an argument to the
CustomPropertyChange event.

```
'**********************************************************************
'* Function:  Item_CustomPropertyChange()
'* Arguments: MyProperty - String
'* Description:  Checks whether any user-defined fields have changed.
'*        Only Task Priority and Complete Percent are affected.
'**********************************************************************
Sub Item_CustomPropertyChange(ByVal MyProperty)
' This is just the event handler, all code should be elsewhere.

   Item_Changed=True        ' Initially sets the Changed flag.

   Select Case MyProperty
      Case "Complete Percent"
         Call Set_Complete_Changed()
      Case "Task Priority"
         Call Set_Priority_Changed()
      Case Else
         Item_Changed=False               ' If nothing changes, set flag
   End Select                             ' as False.
End Sub
```

## The Set_Priority_Changed Procedure

The Set_Priority_Changed procedure is called from the Item_CustomPropertyChange procedure. The Set_Priority_Changed procedure compares the original value of the field against the new value and sets the value of the Priority_Changed flag based on the results. The Priority_Changed flag is then used in the Write event to determine if the field value is written to the History Log of the Assigned Help Task item.

```
Sub Set_Priority_Changed()
' If the user changes the value of priority,
' flag it as dirty and to be logged.
Dim x           ' Temp variable.
Dim y           ' Temp variable.

    x = Orig_Priority
    y = Item.UserProperties.Find("Task Priority").Value

    ' The following statement...
    Priority_Changed = (x <> y)

    ' ...is equivalent to the next five lines of code:
    ' If x <> y Then
    ' Item.UserProperties.Find("Task Priority").Value = True
    ' Else
    '    Item.UserProperties.Find("Task Priority").Value = False
    ' End If
End Sub
```

# The Item_Write Event

The Item_Write event is triggered when the technician clicks the **Save and Close** button on the Assigned Help Task form. The Item_Write event checks the values of the Item_Changed and Property_Changed flags. Based on the values that changed in the item, it then writes the values to the History Text field of the Assigned Help Task item. The code in the Item_Write event also converts the Status field value into a text version for the History Text field.

```
'****************************************************************
'* Function:  Item_Write()
'* Arguments:
'* Description:  Writes all changed fields into the History Log.
'****************************************************************
Sub Item_Write()
Dim Priority_Conversion

    ' If the status, priority, %complete, or severity changed,
    ' enter these into the log.
    If (Item_Changed or Property_Changed) Then
        LogEntry = ""                    ' Clear the initial LogEntry.
```

```
If (Priority_Changed) Then
    If LogEntry <> "" Then
        LogEntry = LogEntry & ", "    ' Commas in LogEntry after each entry.
    End If

    ' Assign the Task Priority value.
    Select Case Item.UserProperties.Find("Task Priority").Value
        Case "Normal"    ' To display the default Importance icon upon save.
            Item.Importance = 1
        Case Else
            Item.Importance = 2
    End Select

    LogEntry = LogEntry & "Priority Changed to " &
    ➥Item.UserProperties.Find("Task Priority").Value
    Orig_Priority = Item.UserProperties.Find("RPriority").Value
    Priority_Changed = False
End If

If (Complete_Changed) Then       ' Check %Complete.
    If LogEntry <> "" Then
        LogEntry = LogEntry & ", "
    End If
    LogEntry = LogEntry & "%Complete changed to " &
    ➥(Item.PercentComplete) & "%"
    Orig_Complete = Item.PercentComplete
    Complete_Changed = False
End If

If (Status_Changed) Then
    If LogEntry <> "" Then
        LogEntry = LogEntry & ", "
    End If

    If (Orig_Status = 2) Then
        Item.UserProperties.Find("Close Date").Value = "None"
    End If

' Convert the enumerated value of Status into a text
' representation (for the History Log).
Select Case Item.Status
    Case 0
        Status_Conversion = "Not Started"
    Case 1
        Status_Conversion = "In Progress"
    Case 2
        Status_Conversion = "Completed"
    Case 3
        Status_Conversion = "Waiting on Someone Else"
    Case 4
        Status_Conversion = "Deferred"
End Select
```

```
              LogEntry = LogEntry & "Status Changed to " & Status_Conversion

              Orig_Status = Item.Status
              Status_Changed = False
        End If


        MailEntryLog = ""

        If (SentMail_Flag) Then    ' If resolution mail was sent, report in log.
              MailEntryLog = "Resolution mail sent to user on " & Now() &
              ➥Chr(13) & Chr(10)
              SentMail_Flag = False
        End If

        ' Write History Log.
        HistoryLog = Item.UserProperties.Find("History Text").Value
        NewHistoryLog = Now() & ": " &
        ➥Application.GetNameSpace("MAPI").CurrentUser & " - " & LogEntry
        NewHistoryLog = Chr(164) & " " & NewHistoryLog & Chr(10)
        Item.UserProperties.Find("History Text").Value =
        ➥MailEntryLog & NewHistoryLog & HistoryLog

        If (Ticket_Resolved) Then       ' When ticket is resolved.
              Item.UserProperties.Find("History Text").Value = Chr(164) &
              ➥" Ticket closed on " & Now() & Chr(10) &
              ➥Item.UserProperties.Find("History Text").Value
              Ticket_Resolved = False
        End If

        Item_Changed = False
     End If
End Sub
```

# Create a Correspondence Mail Item

If a technician wants to send mail to the user, he can click the **Send Mail to User** button to open the Correspondence Mail form, as shown in Figure 11.17. The Correspondence Mail form is a hidden Message form that is published in the Assigned Help Tasks Folder Forms Library.

**Figure 11.17   The Correspondence Mail form**

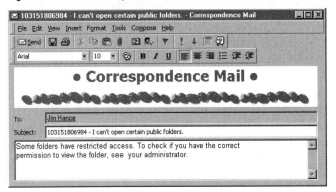

**Important**   You can publish different types of forms—such as Message, Post, Task, or Appointment—in the same Folder Forms Library. For example, the Assigned Help Tasks Folder Forms Library contains a Message form, a Post form, and a Task form.

When the technician clicks the **Send Mail to User** button, he triggers the SendCorrespondence_Click procedure. This procedure demonstrates several very important techniques that are well worth adding to your bag of tricks. For example, this procedure demonstrates how to:

- Use the Item.Parent statement to set the parent folder of the item as the active folder.

- Use the **EntryID** and **StoreID** properties to identify the Assigned Help Task item.

- Use the **GetItemFromID** method to write information from the Correspondence Mail item to the Assigned Help Task item.

## Use the Item.Parent Statement to Identify the Assigned Help Task Folder

In the SendCorrespondence_Click procedure, as shown in the following example, the **Parent** property of the item is used to return the name of the parent folder of the active folder. Using the Item.Parent statement often provides a handy way to set the folder associated with the item as the active folder.

```
'****************************************************************************
'* Procedure:   SendCorrespondence_Click
'* Arguments:
'* Description:  Sends mail to end user. Calls the Correspondence
'*        Mail item and populates with the necessary fields,
'*        then displays the form. EntryID and StoreID contain
'*        address of the Assigned Help Task item.
'****************************************************************************
Sub SendCorrespondence_Click
    ' Stick the Ticket ID into a native field so that it can be "Found"
    ' by the mail form.
    Item.Save
    Set AssignedFolder = Item.Parent
```

## Use the EntryID and StoreID Properties to Identify the Assigned Help Task Item

After the Assigned Help Task folder is set as the active folder, a Correspondence Mail item is created and the several of the field values from the Assigned Help Task item are copied to the Correspondence Mail item, as shown in the following example.

The SendCorrespondence_Click procedure demonstrates how the **EntryID** and **StoreID** properties provide a way to write values between forms in a non-response situation. For example, after the technician opens the Correspondence Mail form and sends a Correspondence Mail item, information from the Correspondence Mail item is written into the History Text field of the Assigned Help Task item. To identify the Assigned Help Task item that the Correspondence Mail form was opened from, the **EntryID** and **StoreID** property values of the Assigned Help Task item are copied to the Correspondence Mail item. After the necessary values are copied from the Assigned Help Task item to the Correspondence Mail item, the item is displayed.

```
Sub SendCorrespondence_Click    (continued)
    Set CorrespondenceItem = AssignedFolder.Items.Add("IPM.Note.Correspondence Mail")
    CorrespondenceItem.To = Item.UserProperties.Find("From User").Value
    CorrespondenceItem.Subject = Item.Subject
    Item.Role = Item.UserProperties.Find("Ticket ID").Value
    CorrespondenceItem.UserProperties.Find("AssignedEntryID").Value =
    ➡Item.EntryID
    CorrespondenceItem.UserProperties.Find("AssignedStoreID").Value =
    ➡Item.Parent.StoreID
    CorrespondenceItem.UserProperties.Find("Ticket ID").Value =
    ➡Item.UserProperties.Find("Ticket ID").Value
    CorrespondenceItem.Display
End Sub
```

## Use the GetItemFromID Method to Write Information from the Correspondence Item to the Assigned Help Task Item

When a Correspondence Mail item is sent, a log entry is written to the History Text field in the Assigned Help Task form. To make this happen, code is added to the Item_Send procedure of the Correspondence Mail form. Remember that the Send_Correspondence_Click procedure copied the **EntryID** and the **StoreID** property values to the Correspondence Mail item. The Item_Send procedure, as shown in the following example, uses the values as arguments in the following statement to return a pointer to the Assigned Help Task item.

```
Set MyItem = MyNameSpace.GetItemFromID(TaskItemID,TaskStoreID)

'*********************************************************************
'* Procedure:  Item_Send()
'* Description:  On Send, find the task that called it and place the body
'*       of the message into the History Log.
'*********************************************************************
Function Item_Send()
    TaskItemID = Item.UserProperties.Find("AssignedEntryID").Value
    TaskStoreID = Item.UserProperties.Find("AssignedStoreID").Value
    Set MyNameSpace = Application.GetNameSpace("MAPI")
    Set MyItem = MyNameSpace.GetItemFromID(TaskItemID,TaskStoreID)
    ' Store message and write it into the log.
    History = MyItem.UserProperties.Find("History Text").Value
    If (Item.Body <> "") Then
        MyItem.UserProperties.Find("History Text").Value =
        ➡ Chr(164) & " " & Now() & ": " &
        ➡ Application.GetNameSpace("MAPI").CurrentUser &
        ➡" - Correspondence Mail sent to User - " & Item.Body &
        ➡Chr(13) & Chr(10) & History
        MyItem.Save
        MyItem.Display
    End If
End Function
```

# Create a Task Discussion Item

The Discussion item portion of the Help Desk application provides a good example of how you can use the **Form Action Properties** dialog box in conjunction with Microsoft Visual Basic Scripting Edition to create a customized response item. In the Assigned Help Task form, the Discussion response action is defined on the **Form Action Properties** dialog box. However, the action is started by the **Start Discussion** button, as shown in Figure 11.18, that triggers a procedure that executes the action.

**Figure 11.18   The Start Discussion button triggers the Discussion action.**

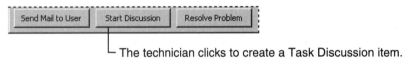

└ The technician clicks to create a Task Discussion item.

In this section, we'll cover three techniques for creating custom responses. We'll cover how to:

- Attach an action defined in the **Form Action Properties** dialog box of the form to a CommandButton control.

- Use the Item_CustomAction event to set properties for a response item.

- Combine posts and tasks in a folder view. In the Assigned Help Tasks folder, Assigned Help Task items (tasks) and Task Discussion items (posts) are combined in a view in this folder.

## Attach a Defined Action to a Command Button

One way to create custom actions for a form is to define the action in the **Form Action Properties** dialog box. Using the **Form Actions Properties** dialog box minimizes the amount of code you need to add to the form to create the Task Discussion response item and provides a quick way to create a custom response. The properties for the Discussion action are set in the **Form Action Properties** dialog box, as shown in Figure 11.19.

▸ **To view the properties for the Discussion action**

1   On the Assigned Help Task form, click the **Actions** tab.

2   Double-click the **Discussion** cell.

**Figure 11.19   The Form Action Properties dialog box for the Discussion action.**

┌─ The **Show action on** check box is cleared.

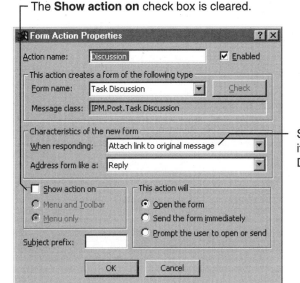

Specifies an attachment to the Assigned Help Task item to appear in the message box of the Task Discussion item

Notice two things about the properties set for the Discussion action. First, the properties specify that an attachment to the original message is included. This means that a shortcut to the Assigned Help Task item appears in the message box of the Task Discussion form. Second, the **Show action on** check box is cleared, so no action button appears on the form. Instead, the **Start Discussion** button is used to initiate the response.

### Add a Command Button to the Form and Create a Procedure to Trigger the Action Defined in the Form Action Properties Dialog Box

To trigger the Discussion action, the **Start Discussion** button is added to the form. As shown in this example, a procedure is created for the Discussion_Click procedure that executes the Discussion action defined in the **Form Action Properties** dialog for the Assigned Help Task form.

```
'*********************************************************************
'* Procedure:  Discussion_Click
'* Arguments:
'* Description:  Starts a discussion on the problem or request in
'*        the Assigned Help Tasks folder.
'*********************************************************************
Sub Discussion_Click
   Item.Save
   Item.Actions("Discussion").Execute
End Sub
```

# Set Properties on the Response Item

Defining a response action in the **Form Action Properties** dialog box is fast and easy, but there are many properties, such as the message text of the response item, that you must set using a different method. To do this, you use the Item_CustomAction event procedure. The Item_CustomAction event occurs any time a custom action is triggered for the form. One important feature of the Item_CustomAction event is that the newly created response item object is passed to the Item_CustomAction event. As a result, you can use this object to set properties on the response item.

As shown in this example, the Task Discussion object, **MyResponse**, is passed to the Item_CustomAction procedure. The **Body** property of the item is then set and the item appears, as shown in Figure 11.20.

```
'************************************************************************
'* Procedure:   Item_CustomAction
'* Arguments:
'* Description:  Executes when a custom action is executed.
'************************************************************************
Function Item_CustomAction(ByVal MyAction, ByVal MyResponse)
   Select Case MyAction.Name
      Case "Discussion"
         MyResponse.Body = "For more information about this ticket,
         ➥double-click the shortcut." & Chr(10)
         MyResponse.Display
   End Select
End Function
```

**Figure 11.20   The Task Discussion item created by the Discussion action**

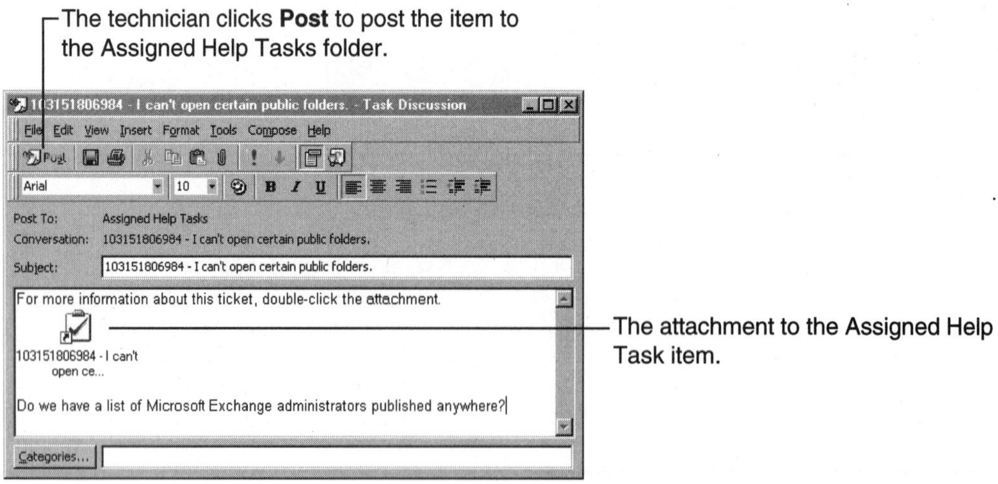

The technician clicks **Post** to post the item to the Assigned Help Tasks folder.

The attachment to the Assigned Help Task item.

## Combine Different Item Types in a View

With Outlook, you can combine a variety of item types in a folder, and then creatively organize them in a view. As shown in Figure 11.21, tasks and posts are combined in the By Discussion Topic view.

▶ **To switch to the By Discussion Topic view**

- In the Folder List, open the Assigned Help Tasks folder, and then click **By Discussion Topic** in the **Current View** box.

**Figure 11.21   The Discussion item (post) is posted as a response to the Assigned Help Task item (task).**

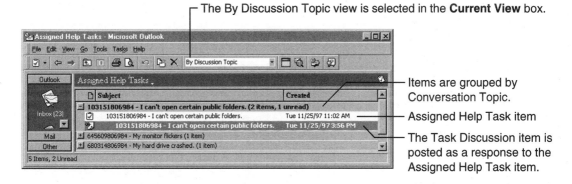

The By Discussion Topic view is selected in the **Current View** box.

Items are grouped by Conversation Topic.

Assigned Help Task item

The Task Discussion item is posted as a response to the Assigned Help Task item.

The By Discussion Topic view groups items by Conversation Topic, and then sorts them by Conversation Index, resulting in a conversation thread, as shown earlier.

▶ **To view the properties for the By Discussion Topic view**

1  On the **View** menu, click **Define Views**.

2  Click the **By Discussion Topic** view, and then click **Modify**.

# Create the Resolve Item

The Resolve process in the Help Desk application serves several purposes. It enables the Help Desk technician to send a Resolved confirmation message to the user. It also automatically marks the task complete and draws a strikethrough line through the task in the Assigned Help Tasks folder.

In this section, we'll cover two techniques for creating custom responses, including how to:

- Automatically create a **MailItem** object.
- Set the standard properties of a task.

## The Resolve_Click Procedure

When the technician clicks the **Resolve Problem** button, the Resolve_Click procedure is triggered. This procedure opens a message box that tells the technician that a message will be sent to the user to indicate the problem is resolved. If the technician clicks **Yes**, the status of the Assigned Help Task item is set to 2 to indicate that the task is complete. In this case, the **Status** property is a standard property of the task. Rather than using the constants as defined in the Outlook Visual Basic Help file, you must use the literal value as shown in the code example. Also notice that the Resolve_Click procedure calls the **Now** function to return the current date and time. This value is then written into the Close Date field. After the Resolve_Click procedure sets values for the Status, Percent Complete, and Close Date fields, it calls the SendMailToUser procedure.

```
'*********************************************************************
'* Procedure:  Resolve_Click
'* Arguments:
'* Description:  When the technician decides to mark the task
'*        as resolved, "Status" and "%Complete" are set to
'*        Closed and 100, respectively, the form is saved,
'*        and mail is sent to the user.
'*********************************************************************
Sub Resolve_Click
    Dim User_Item

    User_Item = MsgBox("This will send a mail message to the user indicating
    ➥that the problem is resolved." & Chr(13) & Chr(10) & Chr(13) & Chr(10) &
    ➥" Would you like to save and close this form?",4,"Completed")

    On Error Resume Next

    If User_Item = 6 Then    ' Item 6 is answer "Yes" to above message box question.
        Item.Status = 2
        Item.PercentComplete = "100"
        Item.UserProperties.Find("Close Date").Value = Now()
        Ticket_Resolved = True
        Call SendMailToUser()
        Item.Save
        Item.Close(0)
    End If
End Sub
```

## The SendMailToUser Procedure

The SendMailToUser procedure creates a standard message. As such, you do not need to set a folder address. The procedure copies the value of the From User field of the Assigned Help Task item to the To field of the message. Then the procedure sets the Subject and Message text of the item and sends the item to the user.

```
'*********************************************************************
'* Procedure:  SendMailToUser()
'* Arguments:
'* Description:  Upon exiting when resolved, this automatically sends
'*       a mail message to the end user, stating the problem is now
'*       resolved.
'*********************************************************************
Sub SendMailToUser()
   Set MyItem = Application.CreateItem(0)    ' Creates native Mail form.
   ' Populate the native fields.
   MyItem.To = Item.UserProperties.Find("From User").Value
   MyItem.Subject = "Problem - resolved"
   MyItem.Body = Item.Subject & " -- Your request was resolved by the
   ↪Help Desk at " & Now() & "."
   MyItem.Send
   SentMail_Flag = True
End Sub
```

## The AddToHistory_Click Procedure

When the **Add to History** button is clicked, the AddToHistory_Click procedure adds
the contents in the New History Log field to the History Text field, as shown in
Figure 11.22.

**Figure 11.22   The Add to History button on the Assigned Help Task form**

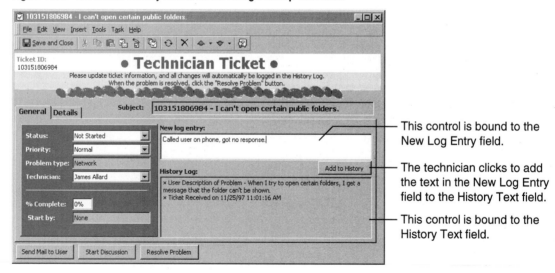

This control is bound to the New Log Entry field.

The technician clicks to add the text in the New Log Entry field to the History Text field.

This control is bound to the History Text field.

As shown in this example, the AddToHistory_Click procedure adds the text in the New Log Entry field to the History Text field. The procedure then clears the contents of the New Log Entry field.

```
'***********************************************************************
'* Procedure:  AddToHistory_Click
'* Arguments:
'* Description:  Each time the "Add to History" button is clicked,
'*        the contents of the New Log Entry field is copied into
'*        the History Log and the New Log Entry field is cleared.
'***********************************************************************
Sub AddToHistory_Click
    Dim HistoryLog          ' Temp for the old History Log.
    Dim NewHistoryLog       ' Temp for the new History Log.
    Dim LogEntry            ' Temp for the new History Log entry line.

    ' If the New Log Entry field is not empty, we need to record the description
    ' in the log and clear out the description.
    If Len(Item.UserProperties.Find("New Log Entry").Value) > 0 Then
        HistoryLog = Item.UserProperties.Find("History Text").Value
        NewHistoryLog = Now() & ": " &
        ➡Application.GetNameSpace("MAPI").CurrentUser & " - " &
        ➡Item.UserProperties.Find("New Log Entry").Value
        NewHistoryLog = NewHistoryLog & Chr(13) & Chr(10)
        Item.UserProperties.Find("History Text").Value =
        ➡Chr(164) & " " & NewHistoryLog & HistoryLog
        Item.UserProperties.Find("New Log Entry").Value = ""
    End If
End Sub
```

# A Suggested Enhancement

Although not covered it in this chapter, a logical enhancement to this application is to create an Appointment folder in the Help Desk Application folder to make it possible for the Help Desk administrator, technicians, and managers to schedule, organize, and track Help Desk appointments. To create this enhancement, you can implement many of the techniques covered in this chapter.

<br>

# The Document Tracking Application

## In This Chapter

Overview of the Document Tracking Application 428

Setting Up the Document Tracking Application 434

Testing the Document Tracking Application 440

The Document Tracking Form 443

The Document Tracking Database 469

Document Tracking Folder Views 470

Releasing the Document Tracking Application 472

The Document Tracking application provides a good example of how you can build Microsoft Outlook applications to streamline a process, enhance group collaboration, and facilitate tracking of information. In most organizations, the process of writing, editing, and releasing marketing materials is a group activity that involves many different phases. For example, in some organizations, including Microsoft, after a writer finishes a document, he or she submits it to a production manager. The production manager is then responsible for assigning tasks such as editing, copy editing, legal approval, part number assignment, Hypertext Markup Language (HTML) conversion, virus checking, and final posting of the document.

The Document Tracking application described in this chapter is used not only to automate the assignment of tasks, but also to track the progress of a document as it moves through the approval and production process. In addition, the Document Tracking application provides a user-friendly and mail-enabled front end to a Microsoft Access 97 database. When a Document Tracking item is saved in the Document Tracking folder, the information in the item is written to a Microsoft Access database. The database can then be used for generating queries and monthly reports.

This chapter covers how to:

- Modify a standard Task form.
- Create Help for a control.
- Build a small-scale application that can be used by a specific workgroup.
- Use Microsoft Visual Basic Scripting Edition to create messages and provide a shortcut to the Document Tracking item in the message.
- Create a Microsoft Access database record when an item is saved in a folder.
- Find the record of an item in a Microsoft Access database and automatically update the record for the user.

# Overview of the Document Tracking Application

The Document Tracking application provides an easy way to submit a document for editing, legal approval, virus checking, and posting. In addition, the Document Tracking application streamlines the process of assigning tasks for the production manager. For example, after a Document Approval item is submitted to the Document Tracking folder, the production manager can click the **Send Edit Request** button on the Document Tracking form to send a task request to an editor. The editor can then use the Document Tracking form to open the submitted document and to indicate he or she has finished the edit. Along the way, the production manager can easily scan the Document Tracking folder to get an overview of the document's progress. Perhaps equally important, each time a change is made to a Document Tracking item, the information in the item is automatically updated in the Microsoft Access Document Tracking database. In this way, production managers can always produce up-to-date status reports from the database.

To demonstrate how the Document Tracking application works, the rest of this section goes through the process of using the Document Tracking application to submit, edit, approve, and post a document.

**A user opens the Marketing Handoff form, which then opens the Document Tracking form.** In this chapter, you can assume that the Document Tracking application is used by a specific group in an organization, rather than an entire organization, so the Marketing Handoff form is installed in the Personal Forms Library. To open the form, the user clicks **Choose Form** on the *Compose* menu, and then clicks the Marketing Handoff form in the Personal Forms Library.

The Marketing Handoff form is never visible to the user, however. In fact, the sole purpose of the Marketing Handoff form is to set the Document Tracking folder as the active folder, and then create and show a Document Tracking item. The Marketing Handoff form is then closed. The invisible Marketing Handoff form is necessary because if you were to open a Document Tracking form from the Personal Forms Library, and then attempt to save the Document Tracking item, the item would be saved in the active folder, which quite often is the Inbox. As a workaround to this problem, code is added to the Item_Open procedure of the Marketing Handoff form to accomplish the task of setting the Document Tracking folder as the active folder, and then creating and showing a Document Tracking item, as shown in Figure 12.1.

**Figure 12.1   The Document Tracking form**

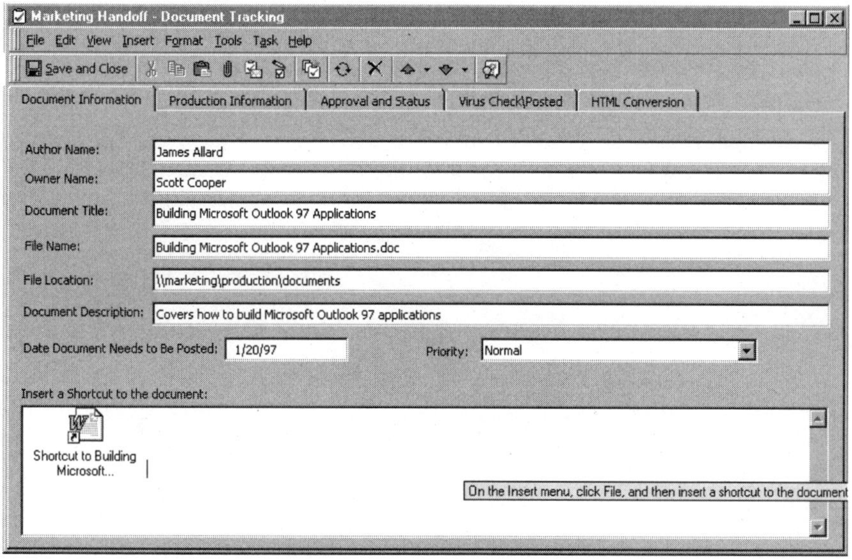

**The user clicks the Save and Close button on the Document Tracking form.**   After the user fills in the Document Tracking form, he or she clicks the **Save and Close** button on the form. This causes three things to happen:

1. A record is created for the item in the Document Tracking database, as shown in Figure 12.2.

**Figure 12.2   The Tracking Information table contains records of Document Tracking items.**

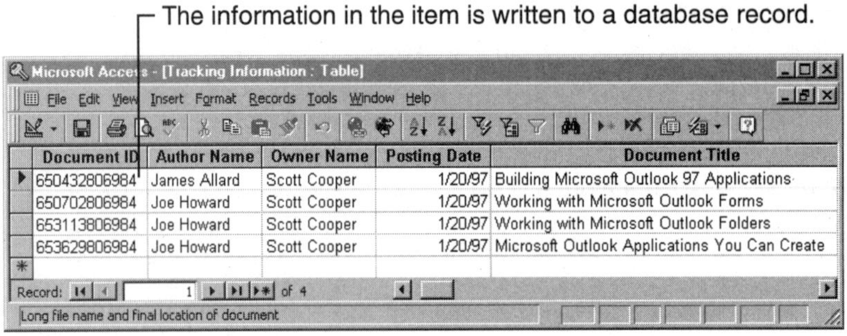

┌ The information in the item is written to a database record.

2. The Document Tracking item is saved in the Document Tracking folder, as shown in Figure 12.3.

**Figure 12.3   The Document Tracking item is saved in the Document Tracking folder.**

┌ The item is saved in the Document Tracking folder.

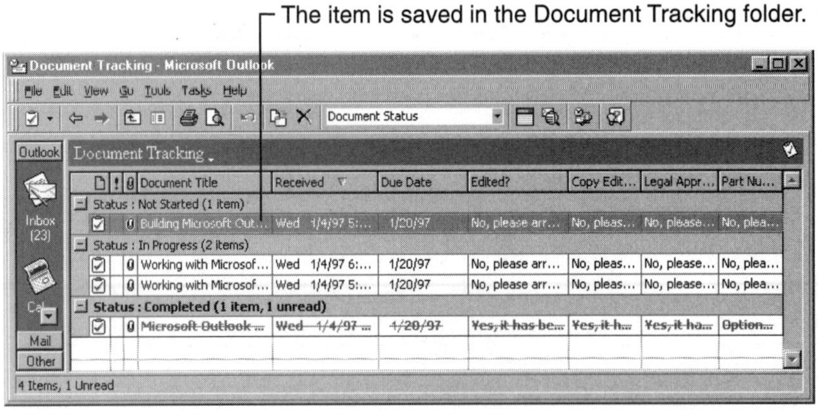

3. A procedure in the Document Tracking form creates a notification message and sends it to the production manager. A shortcut to the Document Tracking item is included in the notification message, as shown in Figure 12.4.

**Figure 12.4   The notification message that is sent when an item is submitted in the Document Tracking folder.**

The production manager double-clicks the icon to open the Document Tracking item in the Document Tracking folder.

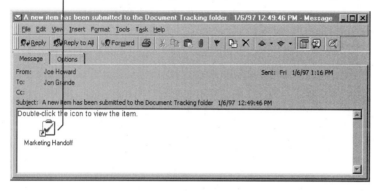

**The production manager opens the item.**   He or she starts the production and approval process by assigning tasks to various people in the organization. To assign tasks, the production manager clicks one of the Send Request buttons on the **Approval and Status** page of the Document Tracking form, as shown in Figure 12.5.

**Figure 12.5   The Approval and Status page of the Document Tracking form**

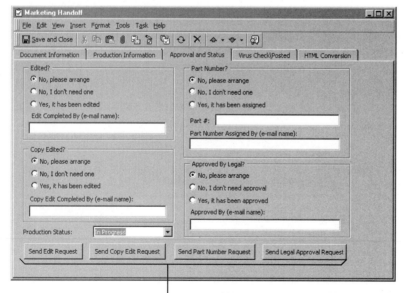

The production manager clicks one of the Send Request buttons to create and send a task request.

For example, when the **Send Edit Request** button is clicked, a message is automatically created that includes a shortcut to the Document Tracking item, as shown in Figure 12.6.

**Figure 12.6   The Edit Request item that is automatically created when the Send Edit Request button is clicked.**

A shortcut to the Document Tracking item is inserted in the message box of the Edit Request item.

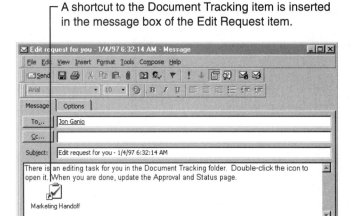

When the message arrives in the editor's Inbox, he or she double-clicks the Task icon in the message box to open the item in the Document Tracking folder. The editor can then double-click the linked document to open and edit it. When the editor finishes editing the document, he or she can update the **Edited** options on the **Approval and Status** page, as shown in Figure 12.7.

**Figure 12.7   Edited options are updated on the Approval and Status page of the Document Tracking form.**

The editor updates the **Edited** options and enters his e-mail name in the **Edit Completed By** box.

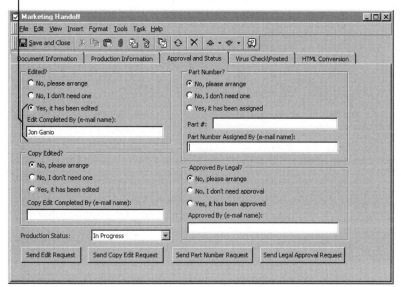

**When the editor saves the item,**  the record is automatically updated in the Document Tracking database.

**When all the necessary tasks are completed**  and the item is posted on the server, the production manager clicks **Completed** in the **Production Status** box on the Document Tracking form. He or she then saves the item in the Document Tracking folder. The item is updated in the database and a line appears through the item in the Document Tracking folder to indicate that the task is complete.

# Setting Up the Document Tracking Application

Before you can run the Document Tracking application, there are a few tasks you must perform to customize the application for your environment. This section explains these tasks.

## Copying the Document Tracking Folder

These instructions assume that you have added the Building Microsoft Outlook 97 Applications personal folder (.pst) file to your Microsoft Exchange system. If you haven't, see "Add the Personal Folder (.PST) File to Outlook" in the Introduction at the beginning of this book.

To make it possible for a variety of people to easily submit, collaborate upon, and track the progress of Document Tracking items, you must make the Document Tracking folder publicly available. To do this, you copy it from the Building Microsoft Outlook 97 Applications personal folder to Public Folders.

**Note**  If you don't have permission to copy the folder to Public Folders, see your administrator.

▶ **To copy the Document Tracking folder**

1   In the Folder List, open the **Building Microsoft Outlook 97 Applications** folder.

2   Open the **4. Beyond the Basics** folder.

3   Right-click the **Document Tracking** folder, and then click **Copy "Document Tracking"** on the shortcut menu.

4   In the **Copy the selected folder to the folder** box, open the **Public Folders** folder, and then double-click the folder you want to copy the Document Tracking folder to.

## Restricting Access to the Folder

To prevent users from opening the folder while you test or modify it, you need to restrict access to it.

▶ **To restrict access to the Document Tracking folder**

1   In the Folder List, right-click the **Document Tracking** folder you just added to Public Folders, and then click **Properties** on the shortcut menu.

2   Click the **Administration** page.

3   Click **Owners only**, and then click **OK**.

# Opening and Modifying the Marketing Handoff Form

The Marketing Handoff form is the form that you publish in the Personal Forms Library of those people who use the application. The Marketing Handoff form does not appear when opened from the Personal Forms Library. Instead, its purpose is to set the Document Tracking folder as the active folder, and then to create a Document Tracking item from that folder.

To modify the Marketing Handoff form, you modify its Open_Click procedure so that the specified Document Tracking folder address matches the folder address of the Document Tracking folder you just added to Public Folders.

▶ **To open the Marketing Handoff form**

1   In the Folder List, right-click the **Document Tracking** folder, and then click **Properties** on the shortcut menu.

2   Click the **Forms** page.

3   Click **Manage**.

4   In the **Forms** box on the right, click **Marketing Handoff**, and then click **Properties**.

5   Clear the **Hidden** check box, and then close all the dialog boxes.

6   Hold down the SHIFT key, and then click **New Marketing Handoff** on the **Tasks** menu.

   When you hold down SHIFT while opening a form, Visual Basic Scripting Edition code in the form is prevented from executing.

## Changing the Folder Address in the Item_Open Procedure

Now you can switch to Design mode and change the address that is specified for the Document Tracking folder in the Item_Open procedure of the Marketing Handoff form.

▶ **To modify the Item_Open procedure**

1   On the **Tools** menu of the Marketing Handoff form, click **Design Outlook Form**.

2   On the **Form Design** toolbar, click **View Code**.

3   Change the code in the Item_Open procedure to set the active folder to the Document Tracking folder address.

For example, assume you copied the Document Tracking folder to the Public Folders\All Public Folders\Marketing folder. You would then modify the Item_Open procedure as shown in this example.

```
Function Item_Open()
    Set MyNameSpace = Application.GetNameSpace("MAPI")
    Set PublicFolders = MyNameSpace.Folders("Public Folders")
    Set AllPublicFolders = PublicFolders.Folders("All Public Folders")
    Set DocumentTrackingFolder = AllPublicFolders.Folders("Marketing")
    Set MyItem = DocumentTrackingFolder.Items.Add("IPM.Task.Document
    ➡Tracking")
    MyItem.Display
    Item.Close 1
End Function
```

4   After you change the code in the Item_Open procedure, click **Run** on the **Script** menu to make that sure you have no syntax errors.

## Making a Backup Copy of the Marketing Handoff Form

At this point, you make a backup copy of the Marketing Handoff form. When you're ready to release the application, you can send a copy of this form to users so they can install it in their Personal Forms Library.

▶ **To save the Marketing Handoff form**

1   On the **File** menu, click **Save As**.

2   In the **Save in** box, click a folder in which to save the form.

3   In the **File name** box, type **Marketing Handoff**, and then click **Save**.

## Publishing the Marketing Handoff Form

Now you can publish the Marketing Handoff form to your Personal Forms Library so you can test the application in your environment.

▶ **To publish the Marketing Handoff form**

1   On the **Form Design** toolbar, click **Publish Form As**.

2   Click **Publish** to publish the form to the Personal Forms Library.

3   Close the Marketing Handoff form.

## Hiding the Marketing Handoff Form

Now you need to reset the **Hidden** property for the Marketing Handoff form in the Document Tracking Folder Forms Library.

▶ **To hide the Marketing Handoff form**

1   In the Folder List, right-click the **Document Tracking** folder, and then click **Properties** on the shortcut menu.

2   Click the **Forms** page.

3   Click **Manage**.

4   In the **Forms** box on the right, click **Marketing Handoff**, and then click **Properties**.

5   Select the **Hidden** check box, and then close all the dialog boxes.

# Copying the Document Tracking Database

Next, you need to copy the Document Tracking database to a new location. The Document Tracking database is attached in an item in the ReadMe and .MDB subfolder in the Document Tracking folder.

The code in the Document Tracking form is currently set up to write to a database called Document Tracking in C:\My Documents. If you want to test the application without modifying the code in the Document Tracking form, save the database to C:\My Documents.

**Important**   The Document Tracking application only works if a user has Microsoft Office 97 (not stand-alone Outlook) installed. In addition, the user must install the "Data Access Objects for Visual Basic" during Setup. To install the "Data Access Objects for Visual Basic," run Office 97 Setup, select the **Data Access** option, and then click **Change Option**. Under **Options**, select **Data Access Objects for Visual Basic**, and then click **OK**.

▶ **To copy the Document Tracking database**

1   In the Folder List, open the **ReadMe and .MDB** folder in the **Document Tracking** folder.

2   Double-click the **ReadMe** item.

3   Right-click the **Document Tracking.mdb** icon, and then click **Save As** on the shortcut menu.

4   Click a folder for the Document Tracking icon, and then click **Open**.

   If you don't want to modify the code while you test the application, save the Document Tracking item in C:\My Documents. Later, when you're sure the application is working as expected, you can move the database to a server and then modify the code in the Document Tracking item so that it points to the database on the server.

5   Click **Save**.

# Opening and Modifying the Document Tracking Form

The Document Tracking form has three procedures that you must modify. These are the SendNotification procedure, the AddNewDatabaseRecord procedure, and the UpdateDatabaseRecord procedure. For the SendNotification procedure, you specify your name as the person who is notified. For the AddNewDatabaseRecord and the UpdateDatabaseRecord procedures, you specify the path of the Document Tracking database that you just copied.

▶ **To open the Document Tracking form**

1   Hold down the SHIFT key, and then click **New Document Tracking** on the **Tasks** menu. It's essential that you hold down the SHIFT key to prevent the Visual Basic Scripting Edition code from executing.

2   On the Document Tracking form **Tools** menu, click **Design Outlook Form**.

3   On the **Form Design** toolbar, click **View Code**.

4   In the Script Editor window, locate the SendNotification procedure. It's the last procedure in the Script Editor.

## Customizing the SendNotification Procedure

If you want to use this feature in the Document Tracking application, uncomment the code. Then replace "Your Name" in the RequestItem.To statement with your e-mail name. Later, when you're ready to release the application for general use, you can change the names to the names of production managers in your organization. For now, however, it's best to use just your name.

```
RequestItem.To = "Your Name"
```

The SendNotification procedure, as shown in the following code example, creates a message item, addresses it to the specified people, attaches a link to the Document Tracking item, and then sends the message. The SendNotification procedure is called from the Item_Closed event if the value of NewItemCreated is **True**.

```
'*********************************************************************
' Procedure: SendNotification
' Description: Called by Item_Close when the Document Tracking item is first
' submitted, this procedure sends a message to the production manager to
' notify him or her that a new item has been submitted in the folder.
'*********************************************************************

Sub SendNotification
    Set DocTrackItem = Application.ActiveInspector.CurrentItem
    DocTrackItem.Save
    Set RequestItem = Application.CreateItem(0)
    RequestItem.Subject = "A new item has been submitted to the Document
    ➥Tracking folder " & Now()
    RequestItem.Body = "Click the icon to view the item. " & Chr(13)
    RequestItem.To = "Jon Grande; Don Funk"
    Set MyAttachments = RequestItem.Attachments
    MyAttachments.Add DocTrackItem, 4
    RequestItem.Send
End Sub
```

After you change the code in the SendNotification procedure, click **Run** on the Script Editor **Script** menu to make sure you have no syntax errors.

## Customizing the AddNewDatabaseRecord and the UpdateDatabaseRecord Procedures

The AddNewDatabaseRecord and UpdateDatabaseRecord procedures point to C:\My Documents\Document Tracking.mdb by default, as shown in this example:

```
Set MyDB = Dbe.Workspaces(0).OpenDatabase("C:\My Documents\Document Tracking.mdb")
```

If you saved the Document Tracking database somewhere other than
C:\My Documents, you must change the path in the AddNewDatabaseRecord and
UpdateDatebaseRecord procedures.

▶ **To modify the code in the Document Tracking form**

1   In the Script Editor window, find the AddNewDatabaseRecord procedure.

2   In the AddNewDatabaseRecord procedure, locate the following line of code, and
then change it to point to the new database location.

```
Set MyDB = Dbe.Workspaces(0).OpenDatabase("C:\My Documents\Document
➥Tracking.mdb")
```

For example, if the database is located in \\Marketing\Production, you modify the
code as follows:

```
Set MyDB = Dbe.Workspaces(0).OpenDatabase("\\Marketing\Production\
➥Document Tracking.mdb")
```

3   In the Script Editor window, locate the UpdateDatabaseRecord procedure, and then
repeat Step 2 in the UpdateDatabaseRecord procedure.

4   On the Script Editor **Script** menu, click **Run** to make sure there are no syntax
errors.

## Publishing the Document Tracking Form

Now you can publish the Document Tracking form to the Document Tracking Folder
Forms Library.

▶ **To publish the Document Tracking form**

1   On the **Form Design** toolbar, click **Publish Form As**.

2   Click **Publish**.

# Testing the Document Tracking Application

You're now ready to test the Document Tracking application to make sure your
changes work. To start, you open the Marketing Handoff form in the Personal Forms
Library.

# Creating a Document Tracking Item

To test the application, you open the Marketing Handoff form in the Personal Forms Library. You fill in the Document Tracking form that is opened by the Marketing Handoff form, and then click the **Save and Close** button. When you save the item, a record is automatically created in the Document Tracking database.

▶ **To create a Document Tracking item and database record**

1   In the Folder List, click **Inbox**. This is most often the active folder when a user opens the Marketing Handoff form.

2   On the **Compose** menu, click **Choose Form**.

3   In the Personal Forms Library, double-click **Marketing Handoff**.

4   Fill in the options on the **Document Information** page.

5   In the **Insert a Shortcut to the document** message box, insert a shortcut by clicking **File** on the **Insert** menu.

6   Fill in the options on the **Production Information** page of the form.

7   On the toolbar, click **Save and Close**.

8   On the Outlook Bar, click the **Other** group, and then select **My Computer**.

9   In the Folder List, select the folder where the Document Tracking database is located.

10   In the list of items, double-click the **Document Tracking** icon to open the database.

11   On the **Tables** page, double-click the **Tracking Information** icon.

Notice that a record is created for the item you just saved in the Document Tracking folder.

12   Close the Tracking Information table.

# Updating a Document Tracking Item and Sending Requests

After a Document Tracking item is submitted, the production and approval process begins. To help understand how this works, you can open the notification message in your Inbox, double-click the Document Tracking icon in the message box of the notification message, and then send an Edit Request item. Then, update the **Production Status** option and save the item.

**Note**  If you didn't change the name in the SendNotification procedure to your e-mail name, a notification message will not appear in your Inbox. If you don't want to modify this procedure, you can simply open the saved Document Tracking item in the Document Tracking folder.

▶ **To update the Document Tracking item and send task requests**

1  On the Outlook Bar, click the **Outlook** group, and then click **Inbox**.

2  Double-click the notification message in your Inbox, and then double-click the icon in the message box of the form.

3  On the Document Tracking form, click the **Approval and Status** page.

4  Click **Send Edit Request**.

5  When the Message form appears, address it to yourself, and then click **Send**.

6  In the Document Tracking form **Production Status** box, click **In Progress**.

7  On the toolbar, click **Save and Close**.

## Testing the Edit Task Request

Now you can play the role of the editor in this production and approval process. You open the Edit Task Request item in your Inbox, and then double-click the linked Document Tracking item. You can then open the document in the Document Tracking item and update the **Approval and Status** page of the Document Tracking form.

▶ **To test the Edit Task Request item**

1  On the Outlook Bar, click **Inbox** in the Outlook group.

2  Double-click the Edit Request item you just sent.

3  Double-click the icon in the message box of the item.

4  When the Document Tracking item opens, double-click the shortcut to the document in the message box. If you are the editor, you can edit the document.

5  Close the document, and then click the **Approval and Status** page.

6  Under **Edited**, click **Yes, it has been edited**, and then type your name in the **Edit Completed By (e-mail name)** box.

7  On the toolbar, click **Save and Close**.

## Checking the Database Record

When you make changes to a Document Tracking item and then save the item, the record for the Document Tracking item is automatically updated in the Document Tracking database. To make sure the record is properly updating, you can reopen the Tracking Information table and make sure your new changes are reflected in the database record.

▶ **To open the Tracking Information table**

1  On the Outlook Bar, click the **Other** group, and then click the folder where the Document Tracking database is located.

2  In the list of items, double-click the **Document Tracking** icon to open the database.

3  On the **Tables** page, double-click the **Tracking Information** icon.

You can see that the changes you made to the Document Tracking item are reflected in the database record.

# The Document Tracking Form

The Document Tracking form is based on the standard Task form. The Task form works well in the Document Tracking application because it makes it possible for users to easily submit and update an item in the folder by clicking the **Save and Close** button on the Document Tracking form. For example, with a Post form, when users open a submitted item, a **Post Reply** button appears on the form. Users can be confused about whether to click the **Post Reply** button on the form or click **Save** on the **File** menu. With the Task form, the **Save and Close** button appears when the form is in Compose mode and Read mode, so this confusion is eliminated.

Also, the Task form that the Document Tracking form is based on does not require a separate layout for composing and reading items, so there is less design work involved in creating the form. Finally, the Task form provides built-in task management features such as the **Status** property. For example, when **Completed** (which is bound to the Status field) is selected in the **Production Status** box on the Document Tracking item, and the item is saved, Outlook draws a line through the task to show it is complete.

This section discusses some of the design techniques and implementations of the Document Tracking form, including how to:

- Hide the standard Task page.

- Write values from the Document Tracking form to a Microsoft Access 97 database.

- Update values in the database when field values are changed in the Document Tracking item.

- Check if values exist in the fields. This is important because if you try to write a field value from a field that is empty, the procedure stops execution.

▶ **To open the Document Tracking form**

1  In the Folder List, click the **Document Tracking** folder.

2  On the **Tasks** menu, click **New Document Tracking**.

3  On the Document Tracking **Tools** menu, click **Design Outlook Form**.

# The Task Page

For the Document Tracking form, the standard **Task** and **Status** pages are hidden at run time. This is done because these standard pages cannot be sufficiently modified to suit the purposes of this application. For example, you can't add or remove controls from standard **Task** pages. As shown in Figure 12.8, the **Task** page label is in parentheses, indicating that it is not visible at run time.

▶ **To hide a page**

- Click the page, and then clear the **Display This Page** option on the **Form** menu.

**Figure 12.8   The Task page is hidden at run time.**

The **Task** page is hidden at run time.

**Marketing Handoff** is specified in the Subject field.
It also appears in the title bar of the form.

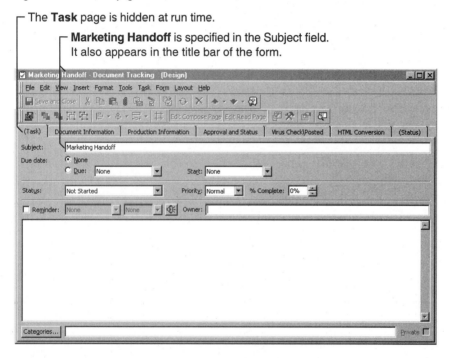

## The Subject Field

Although the **Task** page is hidden at run time, the value of the Subject field, as shown in Figure 12.8, determines the text that appears in the title bar of the form. So the Subject field is set to "Marketing Handoff" to reflect the name the user clicks when opening the form in the **New Form** dialog box. The remainder of the text in the title bar of the form is determined by the text specified for the **Caption** property of the form.

In addition, when a shortcut to a Document Tracking item is attached in an Edit Request item, the text under the shortcut is the **Subject** property value of the item. To set the value of the Subject field, "Document Tracking" is entered into the **Subject** box on the **Task** page of the Document Tracking form.

# The Document Information Page

The **Document Information** page, as shown in Figure 12.9, is the page that's filled in by the author of the document. This section doesn't cover how to add each field. Rather, it discusses how to add several different types of fields and controls, and then explains the properties for them.

**Figure 12.9   The Document Information page**

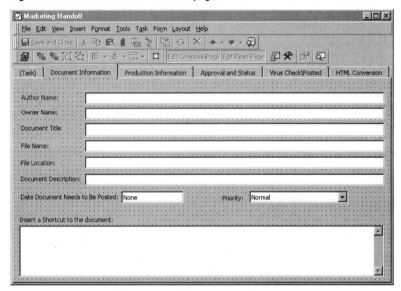

This section discusses the following techniques for the **Document Information** page:

- Using the Field Chooser
- Setting display properties
- Setting validation properties
- Working with Date data type fields
- Working with the standard Priority field
- Using the Message control
- Adding control TipText
- Setting tab order

## Using the Field Chooser to Add Controls and Fields

For creating Text fields, you can save time by using the Field Chooser to create controls and fields. When you use the Field Chooser to create a field, Outlook automatically creates a control and label for the field. When you add the control to the form by dragging the field from the Field Chooser, the field is already bound to the control.

## Setting Display Properties

In most cases, you want TextBox controls to resize when the form is resized. As a general rule, if the right border of the control is next to the right border of the form, you turn on the **Resize with form** option for the control. For the **Document Information** page, the **Resize with form** option is turned on for all controls on the **Document Information** page, with the exception of the DateDocumentNeedsToBe Posted control and the Label controls.

▸ **To set the Resize with Form option**

1  Right-click the control you want to set display properties for, and then click **Properties** on the shortcut menu.

2  On the **Display** page, select the **Resize with form** check box.

## Setting Validation Properties

For the **Document Information** page, the **A value is required for this field** option is turned on for the Author Name, Owner Name, Document Title, File Name, File Location, and Document Description fields. At run time, if a value is not entered in one of these fields, the user sees a message indicating that a field that requires a value is empty.

▸ **To set the A Value is Required for This Field option**

1  Right-click the control you want to set validation properties for, and then click **Properties** on the shortcut menu.

2  On the **Validation** page, select the **A value is required for this field** check box.

**Note**  The "None" value is automatically supplied as the initial value for fields with the Date/Time data type, so the **A value is required for this field** option is not available. For this form, no validation property is required for the Date Document Needs to Be Posted field.

Chapter 12   The Document Tracking Application

## Working with Date Data Type Fields

On the **Document Information** page, the controls are bound to Text fields, with the exception of the Message control, the Label controls, and the DateDocumentNeedsToBePosted control. The field type for the Date Document Needs to Be Posted field is a Date/Time data type. The format is mm/dd/yy.

## Working with the Priority Field

The Priority field is a standard field of a Task item. By default, the Priority field is located on the **Task** page. However, for the Document Tracking form, the **Task** page is hidden at run time. So a standard Priority field is dragged from the Field Chooser to the **Document Information** page.

## Using the Message Control

With Outlook Forms, shortcuts to files can only be inserted in the Message control. In addition, only one Message control can be used per Compose or Read page. For the Document Tracking form, the Message control on the **Task** page of the form is not used. Instead, a Message control is added to the **Document Information** page. At run time, the user inserts a shortcut to the document into the Message control on the **Document Information** page.

## Adding TipText for Controls

For some controls, such as the Message control, you may want to provide TipText Help for controls, as shown in Figure 12.10. With control TipText, the TipText appears when the pointer is positioned over the control at run time. If you click **Design Outlook Form** on the **Tools** menu to switch to Run mode, you can see that TipText Help is provided for the AuthorName, OwnerName, and Message controls.

**Figure 12.10   TipText for the Message control**

▶ **To create TipText Help**

1   Right-click the control, and then click **Advanced Properties** on the shortcut menu.

2   Click the **ControlTipText** cell to select it, and then type the text you want for the control TipText in the text box at the top of the window.

3   Close the Advanced Properties window.

## Setting Tab Order

When designing forms, it's usually best to set the tab order of a page before you move on to the next page. At design time, you can tab through all controls on the page. However, at run time, the user cannot tab to Label controls. Figure 12.11 shows the tab order for the controls on the **Document Information** page.

**Figure 12.11   The tab order for the Document Information page**

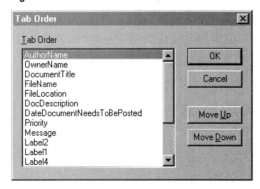

# The Production Information Page

For the **Production Information** page, as shown in Figure 12.12, this section discusses several techniques, including how to:

- Create a unique Document ID.

- Enable or disable a control when a particular field on the form is changed.

- Automatically create a message when the **Send General Correspondence** command button is clicked.

**Figure 12.12   The Production Information page**

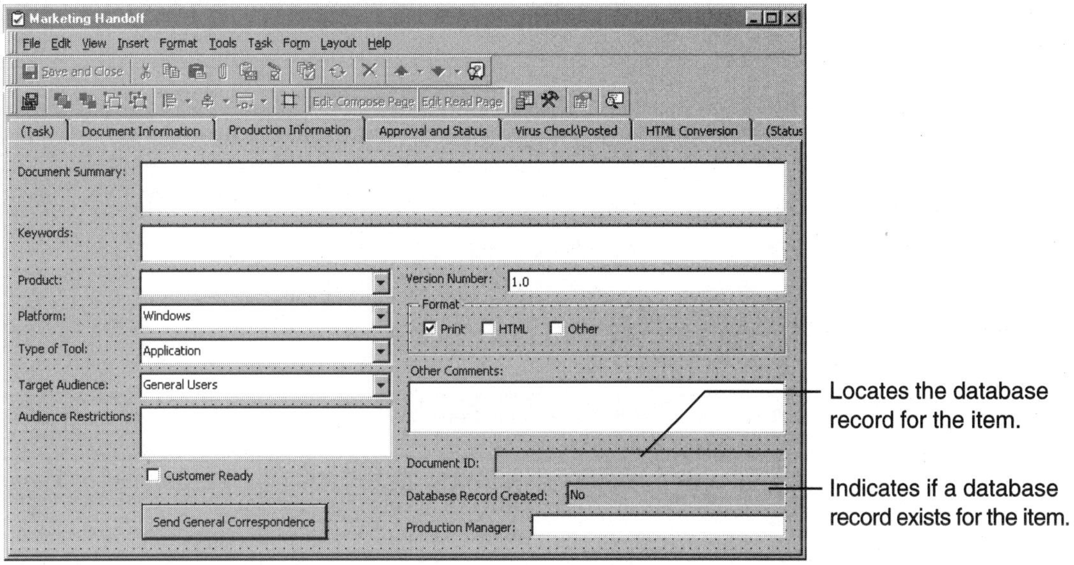

Locates the database
record for the item.

Indicates if a database
record exists for the item.

## Document Summary

There are two things worth noting about the **Document Summary** box. The
**Multi-line** option is selected for this control, which allows users to type multiple lines
of text in the control. In addition, the **Resize with form** option is selected, so the
control automatically resizes when the user resizes the form.

▶ **To set the Multi-line and Resize with Form options**

1   Right-click the control, and then click **Properties** on the shortcut menu.

2   On the **Display** page, select the **Resize with form** and **Multi-line** check boxes.

## Keywords

In the **Keywords** box, users can type keywords that can be used in filters, searches,
and queries to locate an item. For example, an administrator may want to filter all
items in the Document Tracking folder that have the keyword "Outlook" in the
Keywords field.

## The Product, Platform, Type of Tool, and Target Audience Fields

The Product, Platform, Type of Tool, and Target Audience fields all share a common trait. Each is bound to a ComboBox control. As a result, you create these fields by first adding the ComboBox control from the Control Toolbox, and then binding the field to the control. This example explains how the Type of Tool ComboBox control is created and bound.

▶ **To add a ComboBox control and bind it to a field**

1  Drag a ComboBox control from the Control Toolbox to the form.

2  Right-click the ComboBox control, and then click **Properties** on the shortcut menu.

3  On the **Display** page, type **TypeofTool** in the **Name** field.

4  On the **Value** page, click **New**.

5  In the **Name** box, type **Type of Tool**, and then click **OK**.

6  In the **Possible values** box, type the values you want to appear in the **Type of Tool** list at run time. Separate the values with a semicolon, as shown in Figure 12.13.

**Figure 12.13   The Value properties for the Type of Tool field**

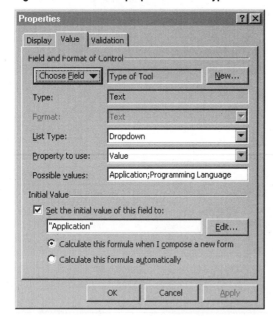

# The Document ID Field

When a Document Tracking item is submitted, a unique Document ID is created for the Document Tracking item. The Document ID uniquely identifies the Document Tracking item, most specifically in the Document Tracking database. When updates are made to the Document Tracking database when an item is changed, the Document ID is used to find the document record in the Document Tracking database. Updates can then be made to the record. Note that the Document ID field is bound to the DocumentID control. The **Read only** option is selected for the DocumentID control.

## Creating the Unique Document ID

To create a unique Document ID for a Document Tracking item, much of the code is borrowed from the Help Desk application covered in Chapter 11, and then modified for the Document Tracking application. When the form is opened, the value of the Database Record Created field is evaluated. If the field value is "No," a unique Document ID is created for the Document Tracking item.

The following script-level variables are declared at the top of the Script Editor window for the procedures involved in creating the Document ID.

```
'***********************************************************************
Dim UserName        ' Script-level variables used for the Document ID.
Dim Trimmed


'***********************************************************************
'* Procedure: Item_Open()
'* Description: Check the value of the Database Record Created field.
'* If the value is "No", create a unique ID.
'***********************************************************************
Sub Item_Open()
   Dim MyDate
   Dim NowID

   If Item.UserProperties.Find("Database Record Created") = "No" Then

      ' If document is new.
      UserName = Application.GetNameSpace("MAPI").CurrentUser

      ' Trim the user name of spaces.
      Trimmed = TrimUserName(UserName)

      NowID = Now
      ' Get date as numbers only.
      MyDate = CreateDateAsNumber(NowID)

      ' Set the ticket ID for this item.
      DocumentID = MyDate & Trimmed

      Item.UserProperties.Find("Document ID").Value = DocumentID

   End If
End Sub
```

**See Also**  For more information about the TrimUserName or CreateDateAsNumber functions, see "Create a Unique Ticket ID for Each Item" in Chapter 11, "The Help Desk Application."

## The Database Record Created Field

The value of the Database Record Created field is set to "Yes" when a database record is created for the Document Tracking item. The value of this field is evaluated during the Item_Write event. The Item_Write event is triggered when a user clicks the **Save and Close** button on the form. In addition, the Item_Write procedure is triggered when a user clicks a command button on the form to send a General Correspondence item or a Request item. In this case, the Item_Write event is triggered because the item must be saved before a shortcut to the item can be included in a message.

If the value of the Database Record Created field is "No," then the AddDatabaseRecord procedure is called, a new record is created, and the Database Record Created field is set to "Yes." Note that the initial value of the Database Record Created field is "No."

In the Item_Write procedure, if the value of the Database Record Created field is "Yes" and the ItemChanged variable is **True**, then the UpdateDatabaseRecord procedure is called. Note also that the DatabaseRecordCreated control, bound to the Database Record Created field, is read-only.

# The Send General Correspondence Command Button

The **Send General Correspondence** command button makes it possible for anyone who is working with a Document Tracking item to a send a message to another user. For example, the production manager may want to send a message to a user to request a more realistic Date Document Needs to Be Posted date. Or an editor may want to send a message to the production manager to notify him or her of a change in the schedule. When the **Send General Correspondence** button is clicked, the item is created and displayed, as shown in Figure 12.14.

**Figure 12.14   The message created when the Send General Correspondence button is clicked.**

A shortcut to the Document Tracking item is included in the General Correspondence item.

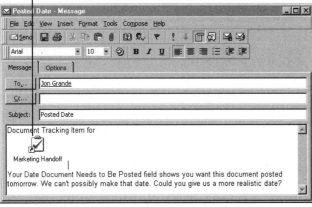

## The SendGeneralCorrespondence_Click Procedure

To add a Click event for a command button, you type **Sub** in the Script Editor window, and then type the name of the CommandButton control followed by **_Click**. As shown in this example, the SendGeneralCorrespondence_Click procedure shows a message box that asks the user if they want to save the item. If the user clicks "Yes" in the message box, then the CorrespondenceMessageLink procedure is called. If the user clicks "No," the CorrespondenceMessage procedure is called.

```
'**********************************************************************
'* Procedure: SendGeneralCorrespondence
'* Description: Ask the user if they want to save the item. If Yes, the
'* item is saved, a database record is created, and a message with a shortcut
'* to the item is created. If No, a message is created.
'**********************************************************************
Sub SendGeneralCorrespondence_Click
    If Item.UserProperties.Find("Database Record Created") = "No" Then
        SaveItem = MsgBox("Do you want to save this item in the folder at this
        ➥time?",3,"Save item")
        If SaveItem = 2 Then
            Exit Sub
        ElseIf SaveItem = 7 Then                ' If No, create message without shortcut.
            Call CorrespondenceMessage
        ElseIf SaveItem = 6 Then                ' If Yes, create message with shortcut.
            Call CorrespondenceMessageLink
        End If
    Else
        Call CorrespondenceMessageLink
    End If
End Sub
```

# The CorrespondenceMessageLink Procedure

The CorrespondenceMessageLink procedure, as shown in this example, sets the
DocTrackItem object to the active item and then saves the item. It then creates a
shortcut to the Document Tracking item in the message box.

```
'**************************************************************************
'* Procedure: CorrespondenceMessageLink
'* Description: Creates a general message item with a shortcut to the
'* Document Tracking item.
'**************************************************************************
Sub CorrespondenceMessageLink
    Set DocTrackItem = Application.ActiveInspector.CurrentItem
    DocTrackItem.Save
    Set CorrespondenceItem = Application.CreateItem(0)
    DocTitle = Item.UserProperties.Find("Document Title").Value
    CorrespondenceItem.Subject = DocTitle
    CorrespondenceItem.Body = "Document Tracking Item for " & DocTitle & Chr(13)
    Set MyAttachments = CorrespondenceItem.Attachments
    MyAttachments.Add DocTrackItem, 4
    CorrespondenceItem.Display
End Sub
```

# The Approval and Status Page

The **Approval and Status** page, as shown in Figure 12.15, is used by various
members of the production team. For example, the production manager can click the
Send Request buttons at the bottom of this page to send edit, copy edit, part number,
or legal approval requests. When the requests are complete, the person who completes
the request uses this page to update the status of the request and to enter his or her
e-mail name. In addition, after the production manager sends out the various request
items, he or she changes the **Production Status** option to **In Progress**. When the
Document Tracking item is saved, the record is updated in the Document Tracking
database.

**Figure 12.15   The Approval and Status page of the Document Tracking form**

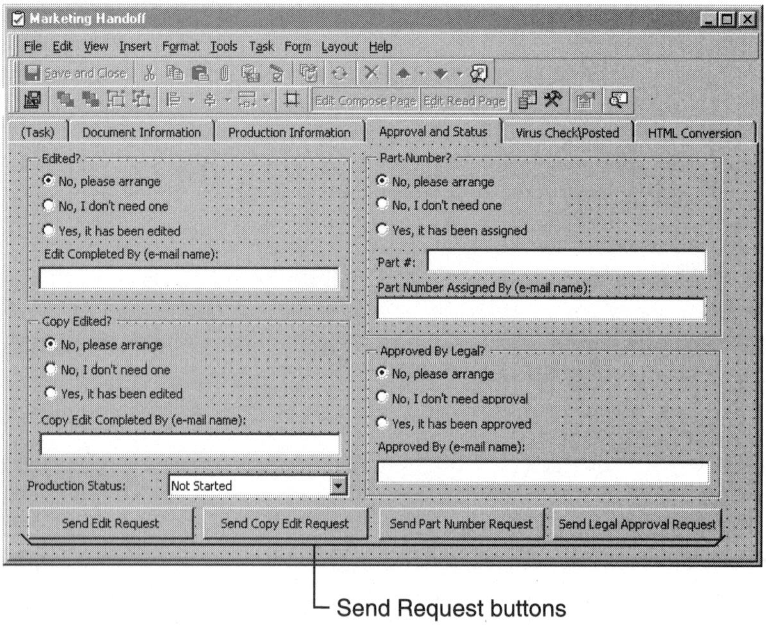

Send Request buttons

# The Edited, Copy Edited, Part Number, and Approved By Legal Group Boxes

Setting properties for OptionButton controls can be tricky. First, you must add the OptionButton control to the form by dragging it from the Control Toolbox. You then bind the option buttons in the group to a common field. For example, each OptionButton control in the **Edited** group is bound to the Edited field. Remember, after you bind the OptionButton control to the field, you must change the **Value** property for the field. As shown in Figure 12.16, the **Value** property of the **Yes, it has been edited** option button is changed to **Yes, it has been edited**.

**Figure 12.16   The Value properties set for the Yes, it has been edited option button.**

The **Yes, it has been edited** option button is bound to the Edited field.

This text appears in views in the Document Tracking folder when the **Yes, it has been edited** option button is clicked.

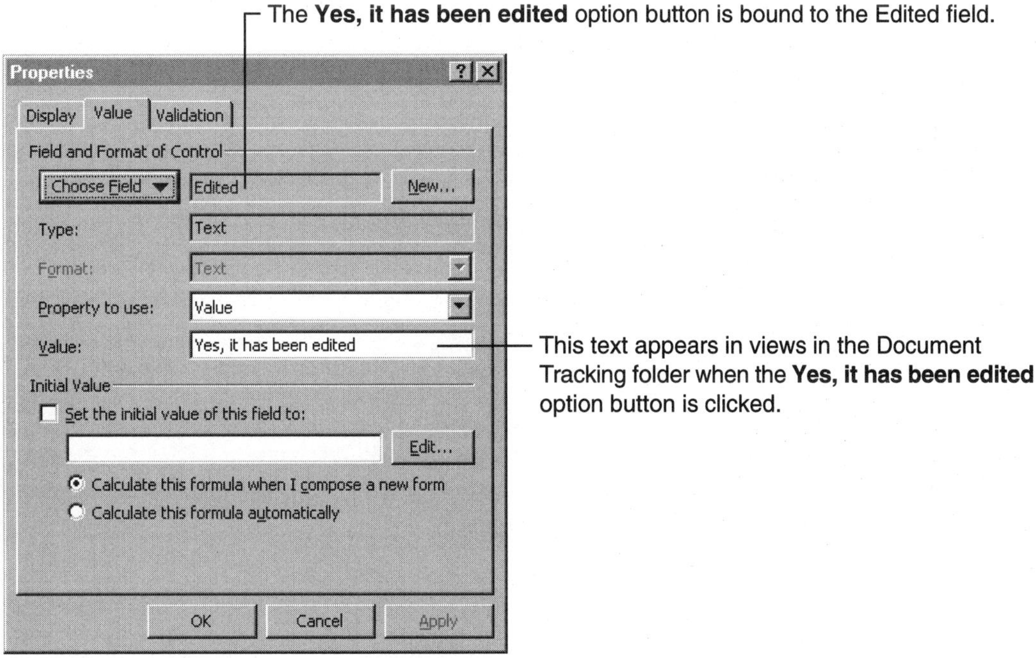

## Production Status

The **Production Status** box is actually the standard Status field. To add the Status field, you click the **All Tasks fields** field set in the Field Chooser, and then drag the Status field to the form. You can then change the label for the control, such as on the **Approval and Status** page.

## The Send Request Command Buttons

At the bottom of the **Approval and Status** page, you can see a series of command buttons. With each of these buttons, the production manager can send a request to another person in the organization. When clicked, each of these buttons creates a message that includes a shortcut to the original Document Tracking item, as shown in Figure 12.17.

Each of the procedures for the Send Request buttons on the **Approval and Status** page are very similar, so this section only covers the SendEditRequest and the SendCopyEditRequest procedures.

**Figure 12.17   The message created when the Send Edit Request button is clicked.**

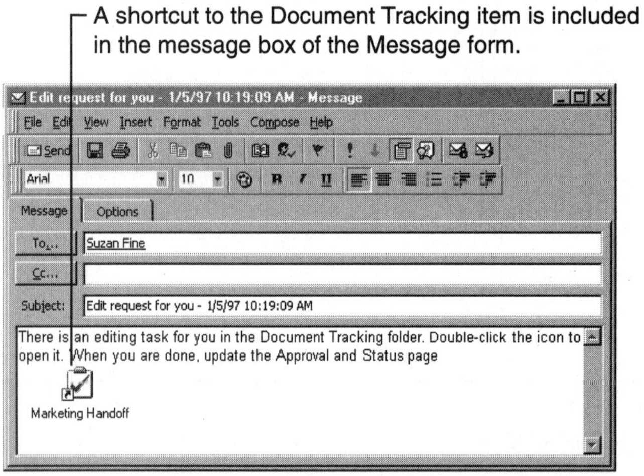

┌─ A shortcut to the Document Tracking item is included
  in the message box of the Message form.

## The SendEditRequest_Click Procedure

When the **Send Edit Request** button is clicked, the SendEditRequest_Click procedure sets the **DocTrackItem** object to the active Document Tracking item. The Document Tracking item is saved, and the **CreateItem** method is used to create a message. The Document Tracking item is then added as a shortcut in the message box of the message.

```
'************************************************************************
' Procedure: SendEditRequest
' Description: Creates a message request for an editor with a shortcut to the
' Document Tracking item in the message box.
'************************************************************************
Sub SendEditRequest_Click
   Set DocTrackItem = Application.ActiveInspector.CurrentItem
   DocTrackItem.Save
   Set RequestItem = Application.CreateItem(0)
   RequestItem.Subject = "Edit request for you - " & Now()
   RequestItem.Body = "There is an editing task for you in the Document Tracking
   ➥folder. Double-click the icon to open it. When you are done, update the Approval
   ➥and Status page." & Chr(13)
   Set MyAttachments = RequestItem.Attachments
   MyAttachments.Add DocTrackItem, 4
   RequestItem.Display
End Sub
```

## The SendCopyEditRequest_Click Procedure

The SendCopyEditRequest_Click procedure is almost identical to the
SendEditRequest_Click procedure. However, notice that the text for the **Subject** and
**Body** properties is changed to reflect the nature of the task request.

```
'************************************************************************
' Procedure: SendCopyEditRequest
' Description: Creates a message request for a copy editor with a shortcut
' to the Document Tracking item in the message box.
'************************************************************************
Sub SendCopyEditRequest_Click
   Set DocTrackItem = Application.ActiveInspector.CurrentItem
   DocTrackItem.Save
   Set RequestItem = Application.CreateItem(0)
   RequestItem.Subject = "Copy edit request for you - " & Now()
   RequestItem.Body = "There is a copyediting task for you in the
   ➥Document Tracking folder. Double-click the icon to open it. When you are done,
   ➥update the Approval and Status page." & Chr(13)
   Set MyAttachments = RequestItem.Attachments
   MyAttachments.Add DocTrackItem, 4
   RequestItem.Display
End Sub
```

# The Virus Check\Posted Page

The **Virus Check\Posted** page, as shown in Figure 12.18, is very similar to the **Approval and Status** page. It is used by the production manager to send a Virus Check Request for print and HTML versions of the document. It is used by people who perform virus checks to update the Virus Check status and to enter their e-mail names. It is also used by the production manager to enter posted information for each version of the form.

**Figure 12.18   The Virus Check\Posted page**

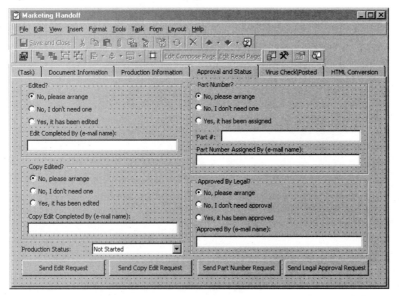

# The HTML Conversion Page

The **HTML Conversion** page, as shown in Figure 12.19, makes it possible for the writer, editor, or production manager to include comments or instructions about converting the document to HTML. Note that the **Resize with form** and **Multi-line** check boxes are selected for this control.

**Figure 12.19   The HTML Conversion page**

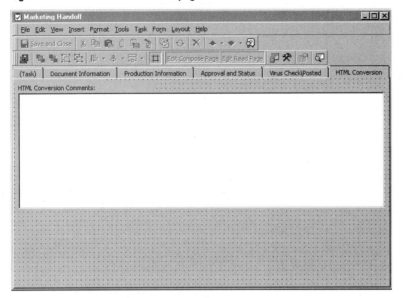

# Script-level Variables

For the Document Tracking form, the following script-level variables are declared at the top of the Script Editor window. The UserName and Trimmed variables are used in the Item_Open procedure and in the TrimUserName and CreateDateAsNumber functions, as discussed earlier in this chapter.

The ItemChanged variable is used to determine if field values on the form have changed. The ItemChanged variable is used in the Item_Write, Item_PropertyChange, and Item_CustomPropertyChange procedures.

The NewItemCreated variable is set in the Item_Write procedure when a new item is first saved in the Document Tracking folder. When the item is closed, the Item_Close event calls the SendNotificationProcedure if NewItemCreated is **True**.

The script-level database variables are used in the AddNewDatabaseRecord and UpdateDatabaseRecord procedures.

```
' Script-level variables used for the document ID.
Dim UserName
Dim Trimmed

' Script-level variable, set in Item_Write event.
' Item_Close calls SendNotification if True.
Dim NewItemCreated

' Script-level variable, set if field values change.
Dim ItemChanged

' Script-level database variables.
Dim Dbe
Dim MyDB
Dim Rs
Dim DbOpenTable
```

# The Item_PropertyChange Event Procedure

The Item_PropertyChange event procedure, as shown in this example, is triggered any time a standard property is changed on the Document Tracking form. On the Document Tracking form, there are two standard fields that are visible and can be changed: the Priority field and the Status field. If a user makes a change to one of these fields after opening the Document Tracking form, then the ItemChanged variable is set to **True**.

```
'**********************************************************************
' Procedure: Item_PropertyChange
' Description: Checks to see if standard field values have changed.
'**********************************************************************
Sub Item_PropertyChange(ByVal Name)
    ItemChanged = True
End Sub
```

# The Item_CustomPropertyChange Event Procedure

The Item_CustomPropertyChange event procedure, as shown in this example, is triggered when a value is changed in a user-defined field on the Document Tracking form. If a user-defined field is changed, the ItemChanged variable is set to **True**.

When the Item_CustomPropertyChange event is triggered, the name of the changed field is passed to the Item_CustomPropertyChange event procedure. As shown in the following code example, the **Select Case** statement is used to determine the field that has changed. In this procedure, if the changed field is the Format Other field and the value of the field is **True**, then the Other Comments control is enabled. If the Format Other field is **False**, the Other Comments control is not enabled.

```
'***********************************************************************
' Procedure: Item_CustomPropertyChange
' Description: Checks to see if field values have changed. If the Format
' Other check box is selected, the Other Comments box is enabled.
'***********************************************************************
Sub Item_CustomPropertyChange(ByVal FieldName)
   ItemChanged = True
   Select Case FieldName
      Case "Format Other"
         Set MyPage = Item.GetInspector.ModifiedFormPages("Production Information")
         Set MyOtherComments = MyPage.Controls("OtherComments")
         If Item.UserProperties.Find("Format Other").Value = True Then
            MyOtherComments.Enabled = True
         Else
            MyOtherComments.Enabled = False
            Item.UserProperties.Find("Other Comments").Value = ""
         End If
   End Select
End Sub
```

# The Item_Write Event Procedure

The Item_Write event procedure is triggered when a user clicks the **Save and Close** button on the Document Tracking form. It's also triggered when a user clicks one of the Send Request command buttons or the **Send General Correspondence** command button. The Item_Write procedure evaluates the Database Record Created field to see if a database record has been created. If the value is "No," the AddNewDatabaseRecord procedure is called. In addition, the NewItemCreated variable is set to **True**. This variable is evaluated during the Item_Close event procedure, as described in the following section.

If the value of the Database Record Created field is "Yes," and the ItemChanged variable is set to **True** (a value has changed in the item), the UpdateDatabaseRecord procedure is called and the record is updated in the database.

```
'***********************************************************************
' Procedure: Item_Write
' Description: If the item is new, then the AddNewDatabaseRecord procedure
' is called. If the item record is in the database, the UpdateDatabaseRecord
' procedure is called if field values have changed (ItemChanged = True).
'***********************************************************************
Function Item_Write()
   If Item.UserProperties.Find("Database Record Created") = "No" Then
      Call AddNewDatabaseRecord
      NewItemCreated = True
      Item.UserProperties.Find("Database Record Created") = "Yes"
   Else
      If ItemChanged = True Then
         Call UpdateDataBaseRecord
      End If
   End If
End Function
```

# The Item_Close Event Procedure

If NewItemCreated is **True**, then the SendNotification procedure is called. As discussed earlier in this chapter, the SendNotification procedure notifies a production manager that a new item is posted in the Document Tracking folder.

```
'************************************************************************
'* Procedure: Item_Close
'* Description: Calls SendNotification if the value of NewItemCreated
'* is True.
'************************************************************************
Function Item_Close()
    If NewItemCreated = True Then
        Call SendNotification
        NewItemCreated = False
    End If
End Function
```

# The AddNewDatabaseRecord Procedure

The AddNewDatabaseRecord procedure is called from the Item_Write procedure if the value of the Database Record Created field is "No." The AddNewDatabaseRecord procedure opens the Document Tracking database, and then writes the value of the Status field that is in the item to the Status field in the database record. Status is handled in this way because it's a field that always has a value selected. Other fields, however, such as Audience Restrictions, may be empty, so the FieldValues procedure is called to handle additional processing of the fields.

**Note**   The AddNewDatabase Record procedure requires that the user has Microsoft Office 97 (not stand-alone Outlook) installed. In addition, the user must install the "Data Access Objects for Visual Basic" during Office 97 Setup. To install the "Data Access Objects for Visual Basic," run Office 97 Setup, select the **Data Access** option, and then click **Change Option**. Under **Options**, select **Data Access Objects for Visual Basic**, and then click **OK**.

```
'**********************************************************************
' Procedure: AddNewDatabaseRecord
' Description: Adds a new record to the Document Tracking database
' for the Document Tracking item.
'**********************************************************************

Sub AddNewDatabaseRecord
    DbOpenTable = 1
    On Error Resume Next
    Set Dbe = Application.CreateObject("DAO.DBEngine.35")
    If Err.Number <> 0 Then
        Msgbox Err.Description & " -- Some functions may not work correctly"
        ➥ & Chr(13) & "Please make sure that DAO 3.5 is installed on this machine"
        Exit Sub
    End If
    Set MyDB = Dbe.Workspaces(0).OpenDatabase("C:\My Documents\Document Tracking.mdb")
    Set Rs = MyDB.OpenRecordset("Tracking Information", DbOpenTable)
    Rs.AddNew
    Rs("Status") = Item.Status
    Call FieldValues
    Rs.Update
    Rs.MoveLast
    Rs.Close
    MyDB.Close
End Sub
```

# The UpdateDatabaseRecord Procedure

The UpdateDatabaseRecord procedure is called from the Item_Write procedure if the value of the Database Record Created field is **True** and the value of the ItemChanged variable is **True**. The UpdateDatebaseRecord procedure uses the **Seek** method to find the record by the value of the Document ID field in the database.

```
'**************************************************************************
' Procedure: UpdateDatabaseRecord
' Description: Adds a new record to the Document Tracking database
' for the Document Tracking item.
'**************************************************************************

Sub UpdateDatabaseRecord

DbOpenTable = 1
On Error Resume Next
Set Dbe = Item.Application.CreateObject("DAO.DBEngine.35")
    If Err.Number <> 0 Then
        Msgbox Err.Description & " -- Some functions may not work correctly" & Chr(13) &
        ➥ "Please make sure that DAO 3.5 is installed on this machine"
        Exit Sub
    End If

    Set MyDB = Dbe.Workspaces(0).OpenDatabase("C:\My Documents\Document Tracking.mdb")
    Set Rs = MyDB.OpenRecordset("Tracking Information", DbOpenTable)

    Rs.Index = "Document ID"            ' Define current index.
    Rs.Seek "=", Item.UserProperties.Find("Document ID").Value
    Rs.Edit
    Rs("Status") = Item.Status
    Call FieldValues
    Rs.Update
    Rs.MoveLast
    Rs.Close
    MyDB.Close
End Sub
```

# The FieldValues Procedure

Not every field value in the Document Tracking item is written to the Document Tracking database, but most of them are. The FieldValues procedure calls the CheckValue procedure for each field whose value is potentially written to the database and passes the CheckValue procedure the name of the form field and the database field.

The FieldValues procedure is called by both the AddNewDatabaseRecord procedure and the UpdateDatabaseRecord procedure.

```
'************************************************************************
' Procedure: FieldValues
' Description: Calls the CheckValue function and passes it the name of the
' form field and the database field.
'************************************************************************

Sub FieldValues
    On Error Resume Next
    CheckValue "Author Name", "Author Name"
    CheckValue "Owner Name", "Owner Name"
    CheckValue "Document ID", "Document ID"
    CheckValue "Document Title", "Document Title"
    CheckValue "Date Document Needs to Be Posted","Posting Date"
    CheckValue "Document Title", "Document Title"
    CheckValue "File Name", "File Name"
    CheckValue "File Location", "File Location"
    CheckValue "Doc Description", "Document Description"
    CheckValue "Doc Summary", "Document Summary"
    CheckValue "Doc Keywords", "Document Keywords"
    CheckValue "Product", "Product"
    CheckValue "Version Number", "Version Number"
    CheckValue "Platform", "Platform"
    CheckValue "Customer Ready", "Customer Ready"
    CheckValue "Type of Tool", "Type of Tool"
    CheckValue "Target Audience", "Target Audience"
    CheckValue "Audience Restrictions", "Audience Restrictions"
    CheckValue "Format Print", "Format Print"
    CheckValue "Format HTML", "Format HTML"
    CheckValue "Format Other", "Format Other"
    CheckValue "Other Comments", "Other Comments"
    CheckValue "Production Manager", "Production Manager"
    CheckValue "Edited", "Edited"
    CheckValue "Edit Completed By", "Edit Completed By"
    CheckValue "Copy Edit","Copy Edit"
    CheckValue "Copy Edit Completed By","Copy Edit Completed By"
    CheckValue "Part Number Status", "Part Number Status"
    CheckValue "Part Number", "Part Number"
    CheckValue "Part Number Assigned By", "Part Number Assigned By"
    CheckValue "Approved By Legal", "Approved By Legal"
    CheckValue "Approved By Legal Name", "Approved By"
    CheckValue "Print Version Virus Check", "Print Version Virus Check"
    CheckValue "Print Virus Checked By", "Print Virus Checked By"
    CheckValue "HTML Version Virus Check","HTML Version Virus Check"
    CheckValue "HTML Virus Checked By","HTML Virus Checked By"
    CheckValue "Print Version Posted","Print Version Posted"
    CheckValue "Print Version Date Posted", "Print Version Date Posted"
    CheckValue "Print Version Posted To Path", "Print Version Posted To Path"
    CheckValue "Print Version Posted By", "Print Version Posted By"
    CheckValue "HTML Version Posted","HTML Version Posted"
    CheckValue "HTML Version Date Posted","HTML Version Date Posted"
    CheckValue "HTML Version Posted To Path","HTML Version Posted To Path"
    CheckValue "HTML Version Posted By", "HTML Version Posted By"
End Sub
```

# The CheckValue Procedure

The CheckValue procedure runs a series of checks on the fields whose values are potentially written to the database. If the field does not contain valid data, the field value is not written to the database.

The CheckValue procedure first checks if the field exists on the form, and then checks to see if the field is empty. It then checks if the field is a Date/Time field. If it's not, the value is written to the database. If it is, the CheckValue procedure checks whether the value of the field is "1/1/4501." In an Outlook Date/Time field, this value represents "None." If the value is not "None," the value is written to the database.

```
'************************************************************************
' Procedure: CheckValue
' Description: Checks the field for valid data. If valid data exists, write
' the field value to the database.
'************************************************************************

Sub CheckValue (ByVal FormField, ByVal DbField)
    If Not UserProperties.Find(FormField) Is Nothing Then
        If UserProperties.Find(FormField).Value <> "" Then
            If IsDate(UserProperties.Find(FormField).Value) Then
                If UserProperties.Find(FormField).Value <> "1/1/4501" Then
                    Rs(DbField) = UserProperties.Find(FormField).Value
                End If
            Else
                Rs(DbField) = UserProperties.Find(FormField).Value
            End If
        End If
    End If
End Sub
```

# The SendNotification Procedure

The SendNotification procedure, as shown in the following code example, automatically notifies the specified people when a Document Tracking item is submitted in the Document Tracking folder. This procedure is called by the Item_Write procedure and creates a message, addresses it to the specified people, attaches a shortcut to the Document Tracking item, and then sends the message.

```
'*******************************************************************
'* Procedure: SendNotification
'* Description: Called by Item_Close when the NewItemCreated variable is
'* True. Sends a message to the production manager to notify her or him
'* that a new item has been submitted in the folder.
'*******************************************************************

Sub SendNotification
    Set DocTrackItem = Application.ActiveInspector.CurrentItem
    DocTrackItem.Save
    Set RequestItem = Application.CreateItem(0)
    RequestItem.Subject = "A new item has been submitted to the
    ➥Document Tracking folder " & Now()
    RequestItem.Body = "Click the icon to view the item. " & Chr(13)
    RequestItem.To = "Peter Krebs"
    Set MyAttachments = RequestItem.Attachments
    MyAttachments.Add DocTrackItem, 4
    RequestItem.Send
End Sub
```

# The Document Tracking Database

The Document Tracking database is a Microsoft Access 97 database that consists of a Tracking Information table. When you release this application for general use, make sure the Document Tracking database is located on a server to which all users have access.

The Document Tracking database is relatively simple and consists of the Tracking Information table, as shown in Figure 12.20. The ID field serves as the primary key and an index is specified for the Document ID field. In the UpdateDatabaseRecord procedure in the Document Tracking form, the Document ID field is defined as the active index and the **Seek** method is used to find the recordset in the database.

**Figure 12.20   The Tracking Information table**

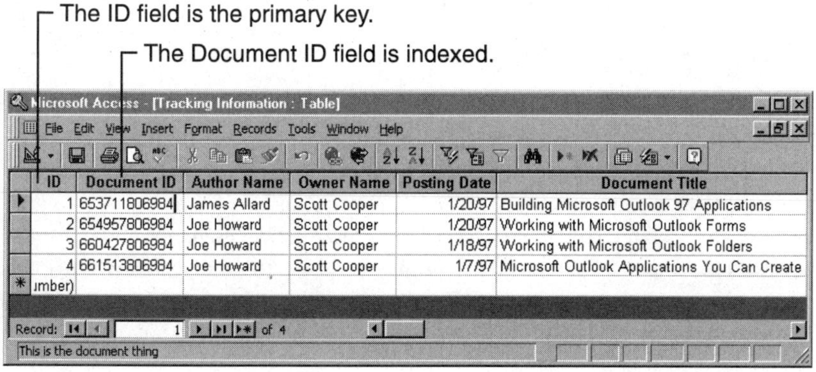

┌─ The ID field is the primary key.
│       ┌─ The Document ID field is indexed.

# Document Tracking Folder Views

The Document Tracking folder consists of two custom views that organize the Document Tracking items: the By Document Status view and the By Production Manager view. For the Document Tracking folder, the **Show only those views created for only this folder** option is selected, as shown in Figure 12.21, so that the standard list of views for a Tasks folder are not available.

**Figure 12.21   The Define Views dialog box**

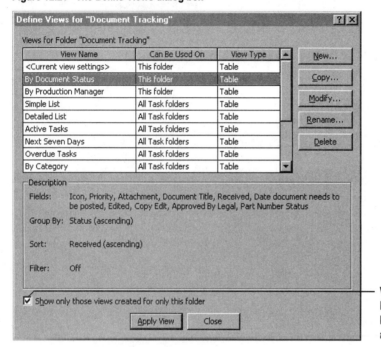

When selected, only the By Document Status and By Production Manager views are available in the **Current View** box.

# The By Document Status View

The By Document Status view groups Document Tracking items by the value in the Status field, as show in Figure 12.22. The By Document Status view makes it possible for production managers to quickly view the tasks that have been accomplished in the document approval and production process. When an item is first saved in the Document Tracking folder, its status is **Not Started**. After a production manager opens the item and sends the various Edit and Part Number requests to others in the organization, he or she changes the status of the Document Tracking item to **In Progress** and then saves the item. As shown in Figure 12.22, completed items have a line through them.

**Figure 12.22   The By Document Status view**

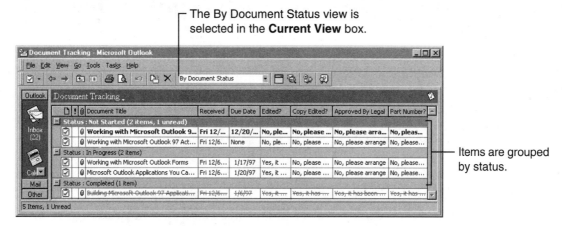

The By Document Status view is selected in the **Current View** box.

Items are grouped by status.

# The By Production Manager View

With the By Production Manager view, production managers can quickly view the progress of documents they are responsible for. As shown in Figure 12.23, items in the By Production Manager view are grouped by the value in the Production Manager field.

**Figure 12.23   The By Production Manager view**

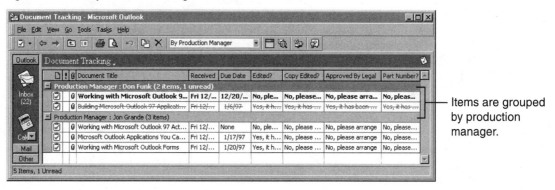

Items are grouped by production manager.

# Releasing the Document Tracking Application

Before you release the Document Tracking application for public use, you must set permissions for the Document Tracking folder, so that those people who use the folder can submit and update items in the folder. You must also distribute the Marketing Handoff form to those users who will participate in the document production process. Those users must then publish the Marketing Handoff form to their Personal Forms Library.

## Setting Permissions

You use the **Properties** dialog box to set permissions for the Document Tracking folder.

▶ **To set permissions for the Document Tracking folder**

1   In the Folder List, right-click the **Document Tracking** folder, and then click **Properties** on the shortcut menu.

2   Click the **Permissions** page.

3   Set the following permissions for the folder.

| Name | Role | Assign to |
|------|------|-----------|
| Default | None | |
| <All participants in the document production process> | Editor | People responsible for submitting documents or updating document tracking items. |
| <Application designers or system administrators> | Owner | People responsible for maintaining and designing applications. |

**See Also**   For more information about setting permissions, see "Set Permissions" in Chapter 8, "Folders."

## Setting Administration Properties

You can then set the Administration properties on the folder so it's available to all users with access permissions.

▶ **To set administration properties**

•   On the **Administration** page of the **Properties** dialog box, click **All users with access permission**, and then click **OK**.

# Distributing a Form for Publishing in a Personal Forms Library

Now you can distribute the Marketing Handoff form to those people who will participate in the document production process.

## Inserting the .OFT Attachment in a Message

To make a form accessible to a specific workgroup, the form must be published in the Personal Forms Library of each person who needs to use the form. The easiest way to send an .oft file is in the message box of a message.

▶ **To insert an .oft attachment in a message**

1   On the form *Compose* menu, click **New Mail Message**.

2   On the **Insert** menu, click **File**.

3   In the **Look in** box, select the folder where you saved the Marketing Handoff .oft file.

4   Under **Insert as**, click **Attachment**, and then click **OK**.

5   In the **To** box, type the names of the people you want to receive the attached .oft file, or click the **To** button and then select the names from the list.

6   In the message box under the attachment, include the instructions listed in the following procedure "To publish the attached form in your Personal Forms Library."

7   Click **Send**.

## Including Instructions About How to Publish the Form

Along with the .oft file, you can include the following instructions that explain to users how to publish the attached form in their Personal Forms Library.

▶ **To publish the attached form in your Personal Forms Library**

1   Double-click the attachment.

2   On the form **File** menu, click **Publish Form As**.

3   Click **Publish In**.

4   In the **Forms Library** box, click **Personal Forms**, and then click **OK**.

5   Click **Publish**.

# Distribute and Maintain Applications

## In This Chapter

Distribute Forms   475

Manage Forms   482

The Forms Cache   485

Form Activation   486

The Switch Forms Utility   486

Distribute Folders   487

The process of distributing and maintaining Microsoft Outlook applications varies with each organization. In some organizations, the application designer develops the application and then submits it to an administrator who is responsible for its distribution, maintenance, and security. In other organizations, the application designer both develops the application and serves as its administrator.

This chapter covers basic concepts and procedures the administrator can use for distributing and maintaining Outlook applications within an organization.

# Distribute Forms

This section provides information, strategies, and instructions for distributing forms in your organization. It covers how to:

- Make forms available in the Organization Forms Library, the Personal Forms Library, or a Folder Forms Library.

- Send a form to an administrator or to another user.

- Distribute forms in a personal folder (.pst) file.

- Make forms available for offline use.

# Make Forms Available in the Organization Forms Library

Most often, the types of forms contained in the Organization Forms Library are general purpose Message forms that you want to make available to the entire organization. The Organization Forms Library is located on Microsoft Exchange Server, so access to the forms in this library is determined by the structure and configuration of your Microsoft Exchange system.

Usually, there are two types of Message forms that you publish in the Organization Forms Library:

- General purpose Message forms, such as the While You Were Out form and Vacation Request form that are used to send messages from one user to another.

- Message forms that make it possible for users to submit information in a public folder. For example, the Business Card Request form covered in Chapter 10 and the Help Request form covered in Chapter 11 are used to send items to a public folder. In other cases, the Message form in the Organization Forms Library is used to set a public folder as the active folder and then create an item in that public folder.

**Note**  Non-Message forms such as Post, Contact, and Task forms are contained in the Folder Forms Library contained within the folder. So if the folder is located in a public folder, the forms contained in the folder's Folder Form Library are made available to all users who have access to the folder.

## Submit the Form to an Administrator

In most organizations, only administrators have permission to publish forms in the Organization Forms Library. As such, application designers who want forms published in the Organization Forms Library must submit the forms to the administrator.

▶ **To submit a form to an administrator**

1  With the form in Design mode, click **Save As** on the **File** menu.

2  In the **Save in** box, click the folder you want to save the form in.

3  In the **File name** box, type the form name.

4  Click **Save**.

The form is saved as an .oft file.

5  On the form's **Compose** menu, click **New Mail Message**.

6  On the **Insert** menu, click **File**.

7  In the **Look in** box, click the folder you saved the .oft file in.

8  On the right side of the dialog box, select the **As attachment** check box, and then click **OK**.

9  In the **To** box, type the administrator's name, or click the **To** button and then select the administrator's name from the list.

10  Click **Send**.

## Check the Form for Viruses and Harmful Code

The administrator is responsible for making sure the form is free of viruses and harmful code.

## Publish the Form

If the administrator finds the form is free of viruses and harmful code, he clears the **Save form definition with item** check box on the **Properties** page of the form and publishes the form in the Organization Forms Library.

▶ **To clear the Save form definition with item check box**

1  With the form in Design mode, click the **Properties** tab.

2  Clear the **Save form definition with item** check box.

▸ **To publish the form in the Organization Forms Library**

1   With the form in Design mode, click the **Publish Form As** button.

2   Click the **Publish In** button.

3   In the **Forms Library** box, click **Organization Forms**, and then click **OK**.

4   Click **Publish**.

# Make Forms Available in the Personal Forms Library

There are three good reasons to publish a form in the Personal Forms Library:

- In many cases, you want to limit the number of people who have access to a form. For example, with the Document Tracking application covered in Chapter 12, you want to limit access to the Document Tracking folder to only those people responsible for submitting and tracking marketing documents. To do this, you publish the Marketing Handoff form in the Personal Forms Library of only the people who use the application.

- In some cases, you may want to publish a form in your Personal Forms Library so you are the only person who can use the form. For example, you may want to create a customized announcement form for communicating with a specific group of customers.

- You want to test a form that will later be published in the Organization Forms Library. In this case, you can test the form in the Personal Forms Library before you submit it to an administrator for publishing in the Organization Forms Library.

## About the Save Form Definition with Item Check Box

If you are distributing forms to users who will install the form in their Personal Forms Libraries or you are publishing a form to your own Personal Forms Library, you should clear the **Save form definition with item** check box.

▸ **To clear the Save form definition with item check box**

1   With the form in Design mode, click the **Properties** tab.

2   Clear the **Save form definition with item** check box.

## Distribute a Form for Publishing in a Personal Forms Library

Quite often, you want to distribute a form to a specific group of users and give them instructions about how to publish the form in their Personal Forms Library. The following instructions describe how to do this.

## Save the Form as an .oft File

First, you save the form as an .oft file so you can distribute it to other users.

▶ **To submit a form to an administrator**

1   With the form in Design mode, select **Save As** on the **File** menu.

2   In the **Save in** box, click the folder you want to save the form in.

3   In the **File name** box, type the form name.

4   Click **Save**.

The form is saved as an .oft file.

## Insert a Form (.oft) File as an Attachment in a Message

To make a form accessible to a specific workgroup, the form must be published in the Personal Forms Library of each person who needs to use the form. The easiest way to do this is to save the form as an .oft file and then insert the .oft file into a message box of a message.

▶ **To insert a form (.oft) file as an attachment in a message**

1   On the form's **Compose** menu, click **New Mail Message**.

2   On the **Insert** menu, click **File**.

3   In the **Look in** box, click the folder you saved the .oft file in.

4   On the right side of the dialog box, select the **As attachment** check box, and then click **OK**.

5   In the **To** box, type the names of the people you want to receive the attached .oft file, or click the **To** button and then select the names from the list.

6   In the message box, include the instructions listed in the following section to publish the attached form in the users' Personal Forms Libraries.

7   Click **Send**.

## Include Instructions About How to Publish the Form

Along with the form (.oft) file, include these instructions that explain to users how to publish the attached form in their Personal Forms Libraries.

▶ **To publish the attached form in a Personal Forms Library**

1   Double-click the attachment.

2   Click **Disable Macros**.

3   On the **File** menu, click the **Publish Form As**.

4   Click **Publish In**.

5   In the **Forms Library** box, click **Personal Forms**, and then click **OK**.

6   Click **Publish**.

## Publish a Form in Your Personal Forms Library

In some cases, you may want to create a form and then publish it in your Personal Forms Library. If the form will be sent to people who do not have the form, you may want to leave the **Save form definition with item** check box selected.

▶ **To publish a form in your Personal Forms Library**

1   On the form's **File** menu, click the **Publish Form As**.

2   Click **Publish In**.

3   In the **Forms Library** box, click **Personal Forms**, and then click **OK**.

4   Click **Publish**.

# Make Forms Available in a Folder Forms Library

Folder Forms Libraries are containers for forms. Each folder contains a unique Folder Forms Library and the library is contained within the folder. As such, a Folder Forms Library can exist on the server or on the user's hard disk, depending on the location of the folder. There are two good reasons for publishing forms to a Folder Forms Library:

• Most often, the forms in a Folder Forms Library are used to post or save information in a folder. Such forms may include a standard or custom Post, Contact, or Task form. However, in some cases, Message forms are installed in the Folder Forms Library so users can send items from the folder. For example, in the Help Desk application covered in Chapter 11, the Correspondence Mail form is located in the Folder Forms Library of the Assigned Help Tasks folder so users can send messages while working in the folder.

• Another reason to publish forms in a Folder Forms Library is to transport the forms in a personal folder (.pst) file. You can use the personal folder file for storing and distributing forms. Making forms available in a personal folder file is described in "Distribute Forms in a Personal Folder (.pst) File" later in this chapter.

## About the Save Form Definition with Item Check Box

By default, the **Save form definition with item** check box is selected only for Message forms. As such, you only need to clear the **Save form definition with item** check box for Message forms that you publish in a Folder Forms Library. For other forms, such as Post, Task, and Contact forms, the **Save form definition with item** check box is cleared.

▶ **To publish a form in a Folder Forms Library**

1  On the form's **File** menu, click the **Publish Form As**.

2  Click the **Publish In** button.

3  In the **Folder Forms Library** box, click the Folder Forms Library that you want to publish the form to, and then click **OK**.

4  Click **Publish**.

# Use the Save Form Definition with Item Check Box to Send a Form to Another User

In some cases, you need to send items using a Message form to users who do not have access to the form associated with the item. For example, you may want to send a Product Announcement form to a customer. To ensure that the item appears in the form it was created with, you select the **Save form definition with item** check box on the **Properties** page of the form when the form is in Design mode. You then publish the form in a forms library, as described earlier in this chapter.

# Distribute Forms in a Personal Folder (.pst) File

If you want to distribute one or more forms using a floppy disk, a CD-ROM, or a network drive, publish the form to the Folder Forms Library of a folder that is located in a personal folder (.pst) file. You can then make a copy of the .pst file and use it for distribution. For more information about distributing a .pst file, see "Distribute a Folder in a Personal Folder (.pst) File" later in this chapter.

# Make Forms Available for Offline Use

Users can set up Outlook so they can work offline with forms and folders.

▶ **To set up Outlook for offline use**

• See offline folder (.ost) file topics in Outlook Help.

When the user sets up her computer for offline use, Outlook creates an .ost file on the user's hard disk. The .ost file contains the following items:

• The default folders in the user's Mailbox.

• Any other folders in the user's Mailbox that are designated as offline folders.

• Folders in the user's Favorites folder that are designated as offline folders.

• Forms that are used to compose and read items in the offline folders.

### How Forms Are Made Available for Offline Use

Any form associated with an item in the user's offline folder file is automatically made available for offline use when the user clicks the **Synchronize** command on the **Tools** menu. When the user clicks **Synchronize**, Outlook searches the items in each offline folder and copies any forms associated with the items to the offline folder (.ost) file (if the forms are not already in the .ost).

For example, suppose a Weekly Schedule item is sent to a user's Inbox, and the user has set up her computer for offline use. When the user synchronizes her offline folders, the Weekly Schedule form, which is the form associated with the Weekly Schedule item, is copied to the user's offline folder file and is available for offline use.

### How Form Conflicts Are Resolved

Changes made to forms while the user is working offline are not transferred back to Microsoft Exchange Server. Any changes made to forms on Microsoft Exchange Server, however, are automatically reflected in the user's .ost file when the user synchronizes folders.

# Make Forms Available for Remote Use

Users in remote locations with dial-up connections to Microsoft Exchange Server can use forms just as if they were connected directly to the server. Before users can work with a dial-up connection, however, they must prepare their computers for dial-up work. The recommended way to work with a dial-up connection is to use offline folders. Users can then work with items in offline folders exactly as they work with items in folders on the server.

# Manage Forms

This section describes how to copy and delete forms and change form properties using the Forms Manager. It also provides some strategies and clever tricks for making changes to forms.

# The Forms Manager

With the Forms Manager, as shown in Figure 13.1, you can copy and delete forms and change form properties.

▶ **To open the Forms Manager**

**1** In the Folder List, right-click the folder that contains the form you want to change.

For the Organization Forms Library or the Personal Forms Library, you can right-click Inbox.

**2** On the shortcut menu, click **Properties**.

**3** Click the **Forms** page, and then click **Manage**.

The Forms Manager shows the forms that are in the active Folder Forms Library in the lower-right box, as shown in Figure 13.1.

**Figure 13.1   The Forms Manager dialog box**

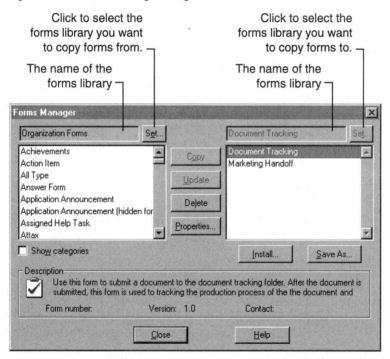

▶ **To copy a form**

**1** Click the left **Set** button to choose the forms library you want to copy forms from.

**2** In the lower-left box, select the forms you want to copy.

**3** Click the right **Set** button to choose the forms library you want to copy forms to.

**4** Click **Copy**.

▶ **To set form properties**

1   In the lower-right box, select the form you want to set properties for.

2   Click **Properties**.

3   Select the options you want.

▶ **To delete a form**

1   In the lower-right box, click the forms you want to delete.

2   Click **Delete**.

**Note**   The **Install** and **Save As** buttons are used to install and save forms developed for Microsoft Exchange Client.

# Modify Forms

Quite often, changing a form can impact another form or folder. When modifying a form, here are some things to consider:

- If a view or rule is based on a particular field, and you remove or modify a field name, the view or rule must be updated to reflect the change.

- If fields are renamed on an existing form, their associated field values in items created using a previous version of the form do not appear on the new form. You'll see a workaround for this later in this chapter.

- If the form contains Microsoft Visual Basic Scripting Edition, any changes you make to the form components, such as the controls or fields, must also be changed in the Script Editor if the components are referenced in script.

- If you add new fields to an existing form, and then publish the modified form in a forms library, and then open old items with the new form, the new fields on the form will be blank or show the initial value for the field if there is one.

## Manage Changes to Forms

Let's assume you make changes to a form in an application that's been in use for several months. Rather than remove the old form, you can keep the old form in the forms library and set its **Hidden** property. This way, users can't create new items with the form, but they can view existing items with the form that the items were created with.

▶ **To set the Hidden property of a form**

**1** In the Folder List, right-click the folder that contains the form you want to change.

For the Organization and Personal Forms Library, you can right-click Inbox.

**2** On the shortcut menu, click **Properties**.

**3** Click the **Forms** tab, and then click **Manage**.

The Forms Manager shows the forms in the active Folder Forms Library in the lower-right box, as shown earlier in Figure 13.1.

**4** Click the right **Set** button to choose the forms library that contains the forms you want to set the **Hidden** property for.

**5** In the lower-right box, click the form you want to set the **Hidden** property for, and then click **Properties**.

**6** Select the **Hidden** check box, and then click **OK**.

**Note** Another way to set the **Hidden** property for a form is to select the **Use form only for responses** check box on the **Properties** page of a form.

# The Forms Cache

The forms cache is a folder located in C:\Windows\Forms that serves as a storage location for forms. The forms cache improves the load time of a form because commonly used forms are loaded from the hard disk rather than downloaded from the server. When a form is activated for the first time, the form definition file is copied from its forms library to the user's C:\Windows\Forms folder. The forms cache keeps a temporary copy of the form definition in a subfolder whose name roughly matches the name of the form.

The form table, Frmcache.dat, also located in C:\Windows\Forms, is used to locate a form and also to prevent multiple instances of the same form from being loaded in the cache. When a form is activated, Outlook checks to see if a form with the same message class is already in the cache. If not, it copies the form definition to the cache. In addition, if a change has been made to a form, Outlook copies the new form definition to the cache.

The size of the forms cache can be determined by the user. To specify the amount of disk space allocated for forms, the user can click **Options** on the **Tools** menu. Then click the **Manage Forms** tab and specify the disk space under **Temporary storage for forms**.

# Form Activation

A form is activated when the user selects a form to compose an item, or when the user performs an operation on a existing item. For example, the user double-clicks an existing item in a folder to open it. Outlook uses the following form caching scheme to activate forms:

- Application Forms Library—Checks for standard forms, such as Note, Post, Standard Default, Contact, and Appointment.

- Cached Forms—Checks for a form in the forms cache.

- Active Folder Library—Checks for a form in the Folder Forms Library of the active folder.

- Personal Forms Library—Checks for the form definition in the Personal Forms Library. If not found, Outlook opens the form.

- Organization Forms Library—Checks the form definition in the Organization Forms Library. If found, Outlook opens the form.

# The Switch Forms Utility

In some cases, you may want to clean the forms cache, especially if you suspect that files in the cache are corrupt or when you suspect a conflict because you have two forms with the same name in the cache. To clean the forms cache, you manually delete all files and subfolders in the C:\Windows\Forms folder with the exception of the C:\Windows\Forms\Configs folder. You can then run the Switch Forms utility to restore the default forms in the forms cache.

▶ **To install Switch Forms**

1   In the Folder List, open the Building Microsoft Outlook 97 Applications folder, and then open the Miscellaneous Applications folder.

2   Open the Switch Forms folder, and then double-click the item in the folder.

3   Double-click the Switchfm.exe icon.

▶ **To manually clean the forms cache**

1   Open Windows Explorer.

2   Open the C:\Windows\Forms folder.

3   Delete all folders in the C:\Windows\Forms folder except the C:\Windows\Forms\Configs folder.

▶ **To run Switch Forms**

1   Click the Windows **Start** button, point to **Programs**, and then click **Switch Forms**.

2   Click **Microsoft Outlook**.

Switch Forms restores Outlook default forms in the forms cache.

# Distribute Folders

After a folder is designed, you can copy it to a Mailbox folder, Personal Folders, or Public Folders.

This section discusses the different methods for making a folder available for use. It also discusses offline folder issues and offers references for archiving and aging folders.

**Important**   Do not attempt to distribute folders using the Outlook Import and Export Wizard. The Import and Export Wizard is designed for importing and exporting data, not distributing folders.

## Make a Folder Available to All Users in Your Organization

You can make a folder available to all users in your organization by creating the folder in or copying the folder to Public Folders. Then it is up to the administrator to determine if the folder is replicated throughout the organization. You or the administrator can set permissions for who can access the folder and to what extent those users can work in the folder.

**Note**   To copy a folder to Public Folders, you are required to have permission to create subfolders for that part of the Microsoft Exchange folder hierarchy.

Based on the policies of your organization, you may not have permission to copy a folder to Public Folders. You may be required to hand off the folder to your administrator who then copies the folder and completes the design tasks according to your specifications. Or you may be given permission to copy your folder to a specific public folder and then complete the task yourself. See your administrator for specific instructions.

▶ **To create a folder in Public Folders**

1   In Public Folders, right-click the folder you want to create the subfolder in, and then click **Create Subfolder** on the shortcut menu.

2   In the **Name** box, type a name for the folder.

3   Select the options you want.

▶ **To copy a folder to Public Folders**

1  In the Folder List, right-click the folder you want to copy, and then click **Copy** on the shortcut menu.

2  Click the public folder you want to copy the folder to, and then click **OK**.

## Set Permissions for the Folder

When you set permissions on the folder, you determine who can access the folder and the functions they can perform in the folder.

▶ **To set permissions for the folder**

1  In the Folder List, right-click the folder you copied to Public Folders, and then click **Properties** on the shortcut menu.

2  Click the **Permissions** page.

3  Set permissions for the folder.

**See Also**  For more information about setting permissions, see "Set Permissions" in Chapter 8, "Folders."

If the folder is replicated to other servers, make sure you set the permissions so that all users who need access to the folder have the appropriate permissions.

# Make a Folder Available for Personal Use

Private folders are stored in the user's Mailbox folder or in a personal folder (.pst) file. There are three good reasons for storing a folder in a personal folder file:

• The user has exclusive rights to the folder. For example, many users keep a list of personal contacts in their Contacts folder in their Mailbox.

• The user can access information in the folder even when not logged on to Microsoft Exchange Server. This can be especially useful for people who travel, because they can access information in a personal folder on their laptop without a live connection to the server.

• The user can easily distribute the folder in a personal folder file. For example, many of the applications in this book were tested in Public Folders. After they were tested in Public Folders, they were copied to the Building Microsoft Outlook 97 Applications folder so they could be distributed in a .pst file.

▶ **To create a folder in your Mailbox or in a personal folder file**

**1** In the Folder List, right-click the Mailbox folder or personal folder you want to create the subfolder in, and then click **Create Subfolder** on the shortcut menu.

**2** In the **Name** box, type a name for the folder.

**3** Select the options you want.

▶ **To copy a folder to your Mailbox or personal folder file**

**1** In the Folder List, right-click the folder you want to copy, and then click **Copy** on the shortcut menu.

**2** Click the Mailbox folder or personal folder you want to copy the folder to, and then click **OK**.

# Distribute a Folder in a Personal Folder (.pst) File

A personal folder (.pst) file provides a convenient way to distribute applications using a floppy disk, a CD-ROM, or a network drive. For example, you can create folders on your Microsoft Exchange system either in public folders or personal folders. When you are ready to distribute the folders, you can create a personal folder file, and then copy the folders to the file.

## Create a Personal Folder File

▶ **To create a personal folder (.pst) file**

**1** On the **Tools** menu, click **Services**.

**2** On the **Services** page, click **Personal Folders**, and then click **Add**.

**3** In the **Available information services** box, click **Personal Folders**, and then click **OK**.

**4** Specify the file name and location for your personal folder file.

**5** Click **Open**.

**6** In the **Name** box, enter a name for the personal folder file.

**7** Select the options you want.

## Copy Folders to a Personal Folder File

▶ **To copy a folder to a personal folder (.pst) file**

**1** In the Folder List, right-click the folder you want to copy, and then click **Copy** on the shortcut menu.

**2** Click the personal folder you want to copy the folder to, and then click **OK**.

### Distribute the Personal Folder File

To distribute the personal folder (.pst) file, in Windows Explorer, copy the .pst file to a floppy disk, a network drive, or a CD-ROM.

### Make an Existing Personal Folder File Available on Your Microsoft Exchange System

▸ **To make an existing personal folder (.pst) file available on your Microsoft Exchange System**

1   On the **File** menu, point to **Open Special Folder**, and then click **Personal Folder**.

2   Specify the location you want, and then double-click the personal folder (.pst) file you want.

The file appears in your Folder List.

# Making Changes to a Folder

If you are responsible for maintaining an application, you are often asked to make modifications to the forms or folder that make up the application. For example, users may ask for enhancements to a form or for additional folder views or permission.

If the changes to the folder are substantial, you should copy the design of the folder to another folder, make the necessary changes to the folder, and then copy the design back to the original folder. If the changes are minor, such as adding a permission or a view, you can modify the folder directly. To make changes to a folder, you must have owner permission for the folder.

**See Also**   For more information about how to modify a folder, see Chapter 8, "Folders."

# Make Folders Available for Offline Use

To work offline or with a dial-up connection, the user should prepare his computer for offline and dial-up work. Once the computer is set up, the task of setting up folders for offline use is simple.

**See Also**   For more information about setting up a computer and Outlook with a dial-up connection or for setting up offline folders, see Outlook Help.

To make a folder available for offline use, the user designates the folder as an offline folder. The following folders can be designated as offline folders:

- Inbox, Outbox, Sent Items, and Deleted Items are the only default Outlook folders in the user's Mailbox that can be made available for offline use.
- Any folder in the user's Mailbox that the user created.
- Any folder in the user's Favorites folder.

## How Folders Are Made Available for Offline Use

When the user sets up his computer for offline use, an offline folder (.ost) file is created on his hard disk. The offline folder file contains a replica of folders he works with offline.

Once the folders are set up for offline use, they must be synchronized by the user so the offline folders contain the same information as the folders on the server. To synchronize folders, the user clicks **Synchronize** on the **Tools** menu.

## How Folders Are Synchronized

While working offline, the contents of both the offline folder and the folder on the server can change. For example, the user may post items in a Contacts folder while offline. At the same time, users connected to the server may also post items to the Contacts folder.

To make sure the contents of offline folders are identical to the contents of folders on the server, the user clicks the **Synchronize** command on the **Tools** menu. Offline folders can be synchronized individually or all at once. When the user synchronizes folders, the changes made in the server folder are reflected in the offline folder, and the changes made in the offline folder are reflected in the server folder.

When a user of offline folders reconnects to Microsoft Exchange Server, changes made in the offline folders are reflected in the folders on the server. However, changes made in the folder on Microsoft Exchange Server while the user was offline are not reflected in the offline folders until the user synchronizes the folders.

## Folder Replication Issues

Replication is the process by which Microsoft Exchange Server keeps folders synchronized that are in different locations. Generally, folder replication is handled by Microsoft Exchange Server administrators and involves careful planning and coordination between site administrators.

If you are an application designer, here are a few issues you should be aware of regarding folder replication:

- If a folder contains critical data that must be refreshed immediately in all locations when new data is received, the folder should not be replicated.

- Replicate applications from a central location. It often makes sense to store all applications on one server and perform all replication and updates to the application from this central location.

- Make sure each site that needs to replicate the application has appropriate permission to support replication.

# Age and Archive a Folder

You can have Outlook automatically remove items of a specified age and transfer them to an archive file. To do this, you must first turn on AutoArchive and then set the AutoArchive properties for each folder you want automatically stored.

| To | See |
|---|---|
| Age and archive a personal folder | Outlook Help |
| Age and archive a public folder | Microsoft Exchange Server documentation |

# Index

## A

actions
  Approve Vacation 201
  Course Catalog Entry form, viewing 214
  Course Offering, viewing 216
  Create Offering, properties 216
  defined, attaching to Command buttons 420
  form, basic characteristics 110
  new Reply 199
  new, creating for the Product Ideas form 84
  Post to Folder, new 215
  Product Idea form, setting 81
  Product Idea Response form, setting 85
  Reply to Folder, making unavailable 214
  specifying for rules 268
  Task Discussion, viewing properties 420
  Vacation Request 198
  Voting buttons, setting automatically 192
Address Form Like A option
  Course Offering form 217
  Message forms 203
addresses
  Business Card Requests folder, publishing 335
  folder, adding to Personal Address Book 162, 259
  Help Desk, publishing to Personal Address
    Book 393
  reply, specifying for Art Approval form 190
Application objects
  creating Automation objects 292
  creating standard Outlook items 291
  defined 291
  Help 279
  methods 291
Approval and Status page
  defined 456
  illustrated 456
  Production Status box 458
  Send Request command buttons 458
  Value properties, setting 457

Art Approval form
  actions, automatically setting for Voting
    buttons 192
  Art Approval folder 188
  creating 189
  options, setting 190
  overview 188
  publishing to the Personal Forms Library 192
  Read page, illustrated 186
  reply address, specifying 190
  reviewing replies 194
  sending procedure 193
  Subject field, setting initial values 189
  testing 193
  To field, preaddressing 189
  Tracking item, specifying storage 191
  Tracking page, illustrated 186
  Vacation Request folders 196
Assign and Close button, Help Request form 402
Assigned Help Task
  code, viewing 408
  CustomPropertyChange event 413
  folder, resolved tasks 391
  folders 388
  form, Item Write event 414
  form, PropertyChange events 411
  form, Read page 408
  form, Resolve Problem option 391
  form, resolved items 410
  form, Set Status Changed procedure 412
  form, TextBox control 409
  item, identifying using Entry ID and Store ID 418
  items, Importance property 406
  items, linking from Message items 406
  items, Open event 408
  items, receiving information from the
    Correspondence item 419
  items, saving 406
  items, values copied from Help Desk item 405
AutoArchive property 492

# B

Beta Contacts application
  releasing 59
  setting administration properties 59
  testing 56
Beta Contacts folder
  copying to Public Folders 57
  creating 35
  illustrated 31
  items, creating 43
  items, deleting 56
  permissions 57
  publishing the Contacts form 55
  specifying Beta Contacts form as the default
    form 56
Beta Participant views
  Beta Agreement Sent, entering dates 46
  columns, adjusting to Best Fit width 41
  creating 40
  fields, adding new 40
  fields, removing 40
  filters, creating 42
  illustrated example 42
Built-in forms
  basic characteristics 104
Business Card Request application
  releasing to other users 383
  sending to the administrator for virus checking 381
  testing 381
  virus checking 382
Business Card Request forms
  administration properties, setting 383
  AutoFill command button, creating 370
  backing up 375
  BusinessCardBranch control, adding 351
  BusinessCardBranchLocation control, adding 350
  BusinessCardCityState control, adding 344
  BusinessCardComments control, adding 368
  BusinessCardDateProcessed control, adding 365
  BusinessCardEMail control, adding 348
  BusinessCardFax control, adding 347
  BusinessCardImage control, adding 358
  BusinessCardName controls, adding 340
  BusinessCardOffice control, adding 356
  BusinessCardPhone control, adding 346
  BusinessCardRequestProcessed control, adding 365
  BusinessCardStreet control, adding 343
  BusinessCardTitle control, adding 341
  BusinessCardZipCode control, adding 345

Business Card Request forms *(continued)*
  CardAddress control, adding 358
  CardQuantity1 control, adding 354
  CardQuantity2 control, adding 354
  CardTitle control, adding 360
  Clear command, creating 372
  Clear control, adding 352
  CompanyLogo control, adding 361
  Compose page, copying controls to the Read
    page 363
  Compose page, editing 336
  Compose page, illustrated example 333
  Compose page, tab order 363
  Compose page, testing the layout 363
  CustomPropertyChange events, adding code 373
  DeliverTo control, adding 355
  Display properties, BusinessCardName controls 340
  Message controls, removing 338
  Message page 337
  Open events, adding code 374
  properties, setting 374
  publishing 375
  Quality control, adding 353
  Read page, editing 363
  Read page, illustrated example 334
  SendDeliveryDate control, adding 367
  SendDeliveryMessage command button, creating 372
  Status page 364
  Subject field, setting the initial value 338
  virus checking 382
Business Card Requests folder
  addresses, publishing to Personal Address Book 335
  creating 335
  design mode, activating 336
  illustrated 332
  Message forms, using in Business Card form design
    process 336
  overview 332
  preaddressing forms 336
buttons
  Approve Vacation 200
  Assign and Close, Help Request form 403
  AutoFill command, creating 370
  Clear command, creating 372
  command, defined actions 420
  Create Offering, Course Catalog Entry form 215
  custom command 199
  Save and Close, Document Tracking form 430
  Send Mail to User 390

buttons *(continued)*
  SendDeliveryMessage command, creating 372
  SendGeneralCorrespondence command 454
  Task Discussion 390
  Voting *See* Voting buttons

# C

Calendar forms
  creating procedure 118
captions, specifying for OptionButton controls 171
CheckBox controls
  binding to fields 173
  Contacts form, adding 53
  defined 172
  initial values, setting 173
  properties, setting for Contacts form 54
Click events 318
Close events 319
collection objects, Microsoft Outlook 289
colors
  background, changing for controls 141
  foreground, changing for controls 141
columns
  adding to views 236
  Beta Participants view, resizing to Best Fit 41
  combination, changing labels or formulas 240
  combination, creating 238–240
  combination, showing only value for first non-empty field 241
  creating 236
  format properties 238
  formulas, creating 242
  heading order, arranging for Product Category view 90
  Potential Beta Participants view, resizing to Best Fit 39
  Product Category view, removing 377
  removing from views 237
  Request Status view, adding 378
Combination fields 149
ComboBox controls
  Contacts form, adding 48
  defined 173
  initial values, setting 174
  labels, Contacts form 51
  list types 174
  properties, setting for Contacts form 49
  values, adding 174

CommandButton controls
  adding 179
  Click procedure, testing 180
  defined 178
  procedures, creating 180
Compose pages
  Approved Vacation form 200
  Business Card Request form, editing 336
  Business Card Request form, illustrated example 333
  Business Card Request, copying controls 363
  Business Card Request, testing the layout 363
  Correspondence Mail form, illustrated 390
  Course Offering form 213
  editing for Product Ideas forms 67–73
  Help Request form 386
  Help Request form, determining 400
  illustrated 120
  Product Ideas form, copying controls to the Read page 74
  Product Ideas form, illustrated example 64
  Product Ideas form, tab order 73
  Product Ideas Response form, editing 78
  Product Ideas Response form, illustrated example 65
  tab order, setting 130
  tab order, setting for the Business Card Request form 363
  Task Discussion form 391
Contacts form
  CheckBox controls, adding 53
  ComboBox controls, adding 48
  creating procedure 117
  customizing overview 46
  opening in Design mode 47
  pages, renaming and displaying 48
  properties, setting 54
  publishing to the Beta Contacts folder 55
  testing at design time 55
  TextBox controls, adding 51
Contacts module
  Beta Contacts form 34
  overview 31
Control object
  methods 311
Control Toolbox
  customizing 124
  showing 123

controls

adding procedures with the Control Toolbox  123

adding to the Document Information page with Field
Chooser  446

Advanced properties  125

advanced Properties window  143

aligning  129

AssignedTo, Help Request form  395

background colors, changing  141

BackStyle properties  144

binding to existing fields  127, 144

BusinessCardBranch, Business Card Request
form  351

BusinessCardBranchLocation, Business Card
Request form  350

BusinessCardCityState, Business Card Request
form  344

BusinessCardComments, Business Card Request
form  368

BusinessCardDateProcessed, Business Card Request
form  365

BusinessCardEMail, Business Card Request
form  348

BusinessCardFax, Business Card Request form  347

BusinessCardImage, Business Card Request
form  358

BusinessCardName, adding to Business Card
Request forms  340

BusinessCardOffice, Business Card Request
form  356

BusinessCardPhone, Business Card Request
form  346

BusinessCardRequestProcessed, Business Card
Request form  365

BusinessCardStreet, Business Card Request
form  343

BusinessCardTitle, Business Card Request
form  341

BusinessCardZipCode, Business Card Request
form  345

CardAddress, Business Card Request form  358

CardQuantity1, Business Card Request form  354

CardQuantity2, Business Card Request form  354

CardTitle, Business Card Request form  360

Categories, removing when creating Product Ideas
form  68

CheckBox  172

Clear, Business Card Request form  352

combination fields  149

controls *(continued)*

ComboBox, adding to Contacts form  48

CommandButton  178

CompanyLogo, Business Card Request form  361

Control Toolbox, customizing  124

Control Toolbox, showing  123

DeliverTo, Business Card Request form  355

display properties, viewing  140

editing on forms  129

foreground colors, changing  141

form, basic characteristics  107

formula fields, creating  152–155

Frame  178

Image  182

Label, binding  168

Label, setting initial values  169

layering  143

ListBox  176

Message, adding labels  72

Message, adjusting when creating Product Ideas
form  68

Message, Document Information page  447

Message, restrictions for usage  165

MultiPage  180

OptionButton  170

Product Category, adding  69

Product Category, aligning  71

Product Category, labeling  71

properties, displaying  125

Quality, Business Card Request form  353

read-only status  132

requiring VBScript  184

selecting on forms  129

SendDeliveryDate, Business Card Request
form  367

sending to back layers  143

sending to front layers  143

setting display properties  140

spacing  130

SpinButton  184

Subject, aligning  71

tab order, setting  130

TabStrip, differences from MultiPage controls  182

TextBox, Assigned Help Task form  409

TipText, creating  130

TipText, Document Information page  447

Controls collection object

methods  310

properties  310

Conversation Index property 249
conversation threads 247
Correspondence Mail form
    Compose page 390
    defined 416
    opening using the Send Mail to User button 416
Course Catalog Entry form
    Actions page, viewing 214
    overview 212
    Read page, illustrated 212
Course Offering form
    action names 216
    Address Form Like A option 217
    backup copies, creating 220
    Compose page 213
    defined 212
    naming 217
    Post to Folder actions 215
    Reply to Folder action 214
    Show Action On option 218
    Subject Prefix option 218
    This Action Will option 218
    When Responding option 217
CustomAction events 319
CustomPropertyChange event
    Assigned Help Task form 413
    defined 320
    Library Order application 326

**D**

databases
    Document Tracking, copying 437
dates
    Beta Agreement Sent, entering in Beta Participants
        view 46
    calculating totals for formulas 154
Design Environment Personal folders
    creating 34
Design mode 116
distribution lists 261
Document Information page
    A Value Is Required for This Field option,
        setting 446
    controls, adding with Field Chooser 446
    Date Document Needs to Be Posted field 447
    defined 445
    Display properties 446
    fields, adding with Field Chooser 446

Document Information page *(continued)*
    illustrated 445
    Message controls 447
    Priority field 447
    Resize With Form property 446
    tab order, setting 448
    TipText for controls 447
    TipText help, creating 448
    Validation properties 446
Document Tracking
    application, Administration properties 472
    application, overview 428
    application, releasing 472
    application, setting up 434–440
    application, testing 440
    Approval and Status page 456
    database record, checking 442
    database record, creating 441
    database, defined 469
    databases, copying 437
    Document Information page 445
    Edit Task Request, testing 442
    folder views 470
    folder, copying to Public Folders 434
    folders, restricting access 434
    form code, modifying 440
    form, AddNewDatabaseRecord procedure 439
    form, Approval and Status page 431
    form, illustrated 429
    form, opening 438, 443
    form, overview 443
    form, procedures that must be modified 438
    form, publishing 440
    form, Save and Close button 430
    form, script-level variables 461
    form, SendNotification procedure 439
    form, Task page 444
    form, UpdateDatabaseRecord procedure 439
    HTML Conversion page 460
    items, creating for Document Tracking testing 441
    items, Send Edit Request button 432
    items, sending task requests 441
    items, Tracking Information table 430
    items, updating 441
    Notification message 431
    Product Information page 448
    Tracking Information table, opening 442
    Virus Check\Posted 460

# E

EntryID properties, Assigned Help Task items  418
events
    adding  316
    Click  318
    Close  319
    CustomAction  319
    CustomPropertyChange, adding code  373
    CustomPropertyChange, Assigned Help Task
        form  413
    CustomPropertyChange, defined  320
    CustomPropertyChange, Library Order
        application  326
    firing sequence  317–318
    firing, preventing  318
    Forward  321
    Item Write, Assigned Help Task form  414
    modifying  316
    Open  321, 374, 408
    overview  316
    PropertyChange  322
    PropertyChange, Assigned Help Task form  411
    PropertyChange, Outlook Script Editor  275
    Read  322
    ReplyAll  323
    Send  324
    testing example  317
    Write  324
Explorer
    methods  295
    object  295
    properties  296

# F

Field Chooser
    adding controls and fields to the Document
        Information page  446
    adding or removing columns  23
    availability for form types  146
    when to use  128
fields
    adding from form to Field List procedure  126
    adding from the Field Chooser  128
    adding new, Potential Beta Participants view  37
    adding to the Document Information page with Field
        Chooser  446
    AssignedTo, Help Request form  396
    automatic calculation of formulas  152

fields *(continued)*
    Beta Agreement Sent, entering dates  46
    binding controls  125, 144
    BusinessCardName, creating  340
    BusinessCardRequestStatus, formatting  378
    BusinessCardTitle, creating  342
    calculating date differences  154
    calculating totals for formulas  153
    Combination, adding to views  238
    Combination, building expressions  150
    Combination, creating procedure  149
    ComboBox, adding and binding to the Product
        Information page  450
    custom, specifying conditions  266
    DataBase Record Created, Product Information
        page  451
    deleting  128
    Document ID, Product Information page  451
    dragging to column heading row  38
    Field Chooser availability for form types  146
    Field Chooser, when to use  127
    Flag  409
    form, basic characteristics  108
    Format box, illustrated  147
    formats, specifying  148
    formula, creating  152–155
    initial values, setting  155
    Message, overview of task capabilities  164
    Potential Beta Participants, creating  36
    Priority, Document Information page  447
    Product Category, removing  88
    requirements for data entry  157
    shared between Vacation Request and Vacation
        Application forms  205
    shared, capabilities  116
    strings, combining  150
    To, setting initial values  161
    types, specifying  148
    user-defined, creating procedure  126, 146
    using to create columns  236
    validating amounts  159
    validation formulas, creating  158
    value strings, combining with text fragments  150
    values, combining  151
    values, comparing with values of other fields  160
    values, copying to the Reply form  205
    values, copying to the Response form  218
    values, filtering  253
    Visual Basic Expression Service  20

filters
  Beta Participants views, creating  42
  By Ad Type view example  251
  conditions  251
  defined  250
  message properties  252
  on field values  253
  on message class  252
Folder Forms Library
  advantages of publishing forms  480
  form publishing procedure  228, 481
  publishing Help Request forms  397
  publishing Reply forms  208
folders
  active, setting to Assigned Help Tasks folder  404
  addresses, adding to Personal Address Book  162, 259
  advantages of personal use  488
  applications  10
  Art Approval, creating  188
  Assigned Help Tasks  388, 394
  automatic archiving  492
  based on built-in modules  10
  Beta Contacts, creating  35
  Beta Contacts, illustrated  31
  Business Card Request, creating  335
  Business Card Request, overview  332
  Business Card Request, preventing users from opening  336
  Business Card Request, setting permissions  380
  choosing where to design  225
  Classified Ads, opening  224
  collection methods  296
  collection object  296
  Contacts module  31
  copying in Mailbox or personal folder file  489
  copying to new locations  257
  copying to Public Folders for distribution to other users  488
  creating from scratch  226
  creating in Mailbox or personal folder file  489
  creating in Public Folders for distribution to other users  487
  custom views, showing  234
  default permissions  261
  Design Environment personal, creating  34
  design recommendations  226
  designs, copying  227
  Discussion  11

folders (continued)
  Document Tracking, copying to Public Folders  434
  Document Tracking, securing  434
  drag/drop posting  259
  Folders Assistant  260
  forms and views, testing  257
  forms cache storage location  485
  General properties, setting  256
  grouping items  244
  Help and Web Sites, contents listed  16–17
  Help and Web Sites, opening  16
  Help Desk, checking permissions  392
  Help Desk, illustrated  387
  Help Desk, setting permissions  393
  initial view  259
  items, specifying  230
  Library Orders  328
  making available for personal use  488
  making available to all users  487
  making available to users with access permissions  268
  making unavailable  259
  materials that can be stored in  12
  methods, designing  225
  Microsoft Exchange views, automatically generating  257
  Microsoft Outlook Web site reference  13
  modifying directly  227
  Name List permissions  261
  names, adding to the Name List  261
  new, creating  34
  permissions, assigning  260
  personal, creating procedure  117
  personal, distributing  489
  personal, making available on Microsoft Exchange system  490
  pilot testing  268
  planning before creating  225
  Potential Beta Participants view, illustrated  32
  preaddressed forms  162
  Product Ideas, copying to Public Folders  92
  Product Ideas, creating  65
  Product Ideas, permissions  92
  Product Ideas, specifying default Product Ideas form for  90
  Properties dialog box  25
  protecting  258
  publishing forms  228
  reference applications  12

folders *(continued)*
    replication 269
    replication issues 491
    restricting access 258
    rules, designing 262–268
    shortcuts, inserting in Message controls 166
    strategies for distributing 487–492
    Synchronize command for establishing offline
      use 491
    Tracking 11
    Training Management, opening 211
    using offline 481
    Vacation Request, opening 196
    VBScript, opening 278
    Volunteer Registration, illustrated 239
Folders collection object 296
Form (Inspector) object
    defined 307
    methods 307
    properties 308
forms
    actions, basic characteristics 110
    activating 486
    advantages of publishing in the Folder Forms
      Library 480
    advantages of publishing in the Personal Forms
      Library 478
    Approved Vacation 200
    Art Approval, overview 188
    Assigned Help Task, illustrated 389
    attached, publication instructions 479
    basic types 101
    Beta Contacts, illustrated 34
    Beta Contacts, specifying as default form 56
    Beta Contacts, testing 56
    built-in modules 9
    Built-in, basic characteristics 104
    cache, manually cleaning 486
    cache, storage location 485
    Calendar, creating procedure 118
    changing the libraries in Forms Manager 231
    checking for viruses and harmful code 477
    components 105–112
    Compose page, basic characteristics 105
    Compose page, illustrated 119
    conflicts, resolving 482
    Contacts, creating procedure 117
    Contacts, customizing 46
    controls, adding 124

forms *(continued)*
    controls, basic characteristics 107
    controls, selecting and editing 129
    copying to folders 232
    Correspondence Mail, illustrated 390
    Course Catalog Entry, Training Management
      application 212
    Course Evaluation, Training Management
      application 213
    Course Offering, Training Management
      application 212
    creating from Outlook templates 119
    debugging suggestions 290
    definitions, saving with items 114
    deleting 232
    disk space, specifying 485
    distributing for publication in the Personal Forms
      Library 473, 478
    distributing in personal folder file 481
    Document Tracking, illustrated 429
    Document Tracking, overview 443
    Field Chooser availability for specific types 146
    fields, basic characteristics 108
    Form Designer 5, 17
    Forms Manager 230
    Help Request, overview 385–391
    Help Request, preaddressing 394
    hiding Message pages 123
    inserting .oft file as attachment in a message 479
    Journal, creating procedure 118
    Library Materials Post 326
    locating and loading using the Frmcache.dat
      table 485
    making available for remote use 482
    managing changes 484
    Marketing Handoff, defined 429
    Marketing Handoff, opening and modifying 435
    message class box 202
    message class, changing 136
    Message, basic characteristics 101
    Message, creating procedure 118
    Message, examples 5
    Message, testing 138
    Microsoft Outlook Web site reference 13
    modifying rules 484
    names, specifying for Course Offering 217
    names, specifying procedure 135
    New Post in This Folder option 256
    Notes, creating procedure 118

forms *(continued)*
  Office Document 8
  Office Document, basic characteristics 103
  Office Document, creating procedure 117
  opening in Design mode 117
  opening process 114
  Outlook Form Designer 99
  Outlook, Help 278
  page, viewing 229
  pages, basic characteristics 106
  Post, basic characteristics 102
  Post, creating procedure 118
  Post, testing 138
  preaddressing 161
  Product Idea Response, Hidden property 209
  Product Ideas, creating 66
  Product Ideas, testing at design time 76
  properties, basic characteristics 109
  properties, setting for Contacts form 54
  properties, setting procedure 133
  properties, viewing 232
  publishing in a Folder Forms Library 228
  publishing tips 136
  publishing to Folder Forms Library procedure 481
  publishing to Organization Forms Library
    procedure 478
  publishing to Personal Forms Library procedure 480
  Read page, basic characteristics 105
  Read page, illustrated 120
  Reply, characteristics 203
  Reply, overview 207
  Response, creating 220
  Save Form Definition With Item option,
    clearing 478, 480
  saving as files 136
  script editing, basic characteristics 111
  sending to other users with Save Form Definition
    With Item option 481
  Separate Read Layout option 121
  setting the Hidden property 232, 485
  Signup, Training Management application 213
  strategies for distributing 475–482
  strategies for managing 482
  submitting to an administrator for publication 477
  Switch Forms utility 486
  Synchronize command for establishing offline
    use 482
  Task Discussion 390

forms *(continued)*
  Tasks, creating procedure 118
  text strings, building 154
  types published in the Organization Forms
    Library 476
  using offline 481
  Vacation Request application 196
  viewing in Run mode 130
  Volunteer Registration, illustrated 239
  While You Were Out 154
Forms Manager
  copying forms 483
  defined 482
  deleting 484
  opening 483
  setting properties 484
formulas
  amount validation 159
  column labels, changing 243
  columns, creating 242–243
  combination columns, changing 240
  comparing field values 160
  date calculation 154
  field, automatic calculation 152
  field, calculating totals 153
  field, creating 152
  validation, creating 158
  Visual Basic Expression Service 21
Forward events 321
Frame controls 178
Frmcache.dat, using to locate and load forms 485

## G

General properties, setting for folders 256
Group By box, displaying 245

## H

help
  Application object 279
  Assigned Help Task folders 388
  control TipText, creating 131
  folders, Microsoft Outlook Web site reference 13
  forms, Microsoft Outlook Web site reference 13
  Help and Web Sites folder, contents listed 16–17
  Help and Web Sites folder, opening 16
  Help Desk folders 387
  Microsoft Forms 2.0, viewing 285
  Microsoft Outlook forms 278

help *(continued)*
    Microsoft Outlook object model, viewing 285
    Microsoft Outlook Visual Basic, caution 279
    Microsoft Outlook Visual Basic, overview 278
    Microsoft Outlook Visual Basic, using 279
    Microsoft Outlook Web site 278
    Microsoft Outlook, overview 15
    Microsoft Visual Basic Scripting Edition Web
      site 277
    Outlook, offline folder file topics 481
    programming tasks in Outlook 276
    Request form 387
    TipText, creating for the Document Information
      page 448
    tutorial, Library Order Application 325
    viewing numeric values for Outlook constants 280
Help Desk
    address, publishing to Personal Address Book 393
    application, copying to Public Folders 392
    application, making available to other users 392
    application, overview 385
    Assigned Help Task form, illustrated 389
    Assigned Help Tasks folder, permissions 394
    Correspondence Mail, illustrated 390
    Folder Forms Library, publishing Help Request
      forms 397
    folder, illustrated 387
    folders, security 393
    items, copying values to Assigned Help Task
      item 405
    permissions, checking 392
    permissions, setting 393
    Request form, preaddressing 394
    Request form, technician names 395
    resolved tasks 391
    Task Discussion form 390
    testing the application 397
Help Request form
    Assign and Close button 403
    Assigned Help Tasks folder 388
    AssignedTo controls 395
    backing up 396
    code, viewing 399
    Compose mode, determining 400
    Compose page 386
    CreateDateAsNumber function 402
    overview 386
    publishing in Help Desk Folder Forms Library 397
    publishing in the Personal Forms Library 397

Help Request form *(continued)*
    Read mode, determining 400
    Read page 387, 388
    Ticket IDs, creating 400
    TrimUserName function 401
    variables, script-level 399
Help Request items
    initial, writing to the History Log 409
    setting active folders to Assigned Help Task
      folders 404
    Ticket ID value 399
    TrimUserName function 401
Hidden property
    Marketing Handoff form 437
    Product Idea Response form 209
    Product Idea Response form, setting 90
    Response forms 221
    setting for forms, overview 232
    setting for forms, procedure 485
HTML Conversion page 460
hyperlinks
    inserting in Message controls 166
    protocols supported for Message controls 167

# I

Image controls 182
Importance property, Assigned Task item 406
initial values
    CheckBox controls, setting 173
    ComboBox controls, setting 174
    Label controls, setting 169
    ListBox controls, setting 177
    OptionButton controls, setting 172
    overview 155
    Product Category field, clearing 79
    Subject field, Business Card Request form 338
    Subject fields, setting overview 163
    To field, setting 161
Inspector object *See* Form (Inspector) object
installation
    Microsoft Outlook Forms Help 278
    Microsoft Outlook Visual Basic Help 17, 278
    Outlook Forms Help folder 16
    Switch Forms utility 486
Item objects
    defined 302
    MailItem object 304
    PostItem object 303

items
    Beta Contacts folder, deleting 56
    Beta Contacts, creating 43
    Correspondence Mail, creating 416
    defined 113
    folders, drag/drop posting 259
    folders, Folder Assistant 260
    folders, grouping 244
    folders, rule conditions 263
    folders, sorting 246
    inserting in Message controls 165
    objects, implied 281
    Product Category view, grouping 89
    Product Category view, sorting 89
    Resolve, creating 423–426
    saving with form definitions 114
    standard Outlook, creating 291
    types, combining in a view 423
Items collection
    creating custom items 300
    Find method 301
    methods 300
    object properties 302
    object, defined 300
    Restrict method 301

**J**

Journal forms, creating procedure 118

**L**

Label controls 168
labels
    BusinessCardName controls Name fields 341
    BusinessCardTitle control, adding 342
    column, changing for formulas 243
    combination columns, changing 240
    ComboBox control, Contacts form 51
    Message control, adding 72
    Product Category, adding 71
    Product Idea, changing 79
    TextBox control, Contacts form 53
layer controls 143
libraries
    opening forms 115
    Organization Forms, example of opening forms 115
Library Order application
    ChangeBookNameValues procedure 327
    CustomPropertyChange event 326

Library Order application *(continued)*
    Library Materials Post form 326
    Library Orders folder 328
    SubmitBookOrder Click procedure 327
    tutorials, overview 325
ListBox controls
    adding values 177
    binding to fields 176
    defined 176
    initial values, setting 177

**M**

MailItem object
    methods 304
    properties 305
MAPIFolder object
    defined 297
    EntryID property 299
    methods 298
    properties 298
    StoreID property 299
Marketing Handoff form
    backing up 436
    defined 429
    hiding 437
    modifying 436
    opening 435
    publishing 436
message class box
    Course Offering form, naming 217
    Vacation Request form, naming 202
Message controls
    file attachments, inserting 165
    folder shortcuts, inserting 166
    guidelines 165
    hyperlinks, inserting 166
    items, inserting 165
    objects, inserting 168
    shortcuts, inserting 165
Message forms
    Address Form Like A option 203
    Art Approval form overview 188
    basic characteristics 101
    creating procedure 118
    opening when creating Art Approval forms 189
    preaddressing 161
    preaddressing to Business Card Request folders 336
    Separate Read Layout option 121

Message forms *(continued)*
  testing in Personal or Organization Forms
    Library 138
  Voting buttons 185–195
  When responding option 203
methods
  Application objects 291
  Control object 311
  Controls collection object 310
  Copy To, MAPIFolder object 298
  Display, MAPIFolder object 298
  Explorer object 296
  Folders collection 296
  Form (Inspector) object 307
  GctItcmFromID 419
  Items collection 300
  MailItem object 304
  MAPIFolder object 298
  NameSpace objects 294
  object library, defined 286
  PostItem object 303
  UserProperties collection object 314
Microsoft Excel 97
  object browser, defined 282
  object browser, illustrated 284
  referencing Outlook Object Library 283
Microsoft Exchange
  folder replication issues 491
  making personal folder files available 490
  Organization Forms Library 476
  views, automatically generating 257
Microsoft Forms 2.0
  Object Library, defined 282
  viewing 285
Microsoft Outlook
  Application object 291
  application tasks that can be accomplished 4
  applications that can be created 5
  collection objects 289
  column heading order, arranging for views 90
  constants, viewing numeric values 280
  design tools 15–26
  events 316–324
  folder applications 10
  Folders collection object 296
  Form (Inspector) object 307
  form caching scheme for activating forms 486
  Form Designer 5, 17
  Forms Help 278

Microsoft Outlook *(continued)*
  Help, offline folder file topics 481
  Help, overview 15
  Implied Item object 281
  Item objects 302
  Items collection object 300
  items, automatically archiving 492
  Library Order application tutorial 325
  MAPIFolder object 297
  Microsoft Excel 97 object browser 282
  NameSpace objects 294
  Object Library 282
  object models, viewing 285
  Page object 309
  Pages collection object 308
  Recipients collection object 315
  reference the object library from Microsoft
    Excel 97 283
  Script Editor 274
  sessions, controlling with Visual Basic and
    Automation 23
  templates, using to create forms 119
  UserProperties Collection Object 313
  using offline 481
  VBScript folder, opening 278
  view features 232
  Visual Basic Help, caution 279
  Visual Basic Help, overview 278
  Visual Basic Help, using 279
  Web sites, overview 15, 278
  Window (Explorer object) 295
Microsoft Visual Basic Scripting Edition
  variants 288
  Web site 277
modules
  built-in 9
  Contacts 31
MultiPage controls
  defined 180
  differences from TabStrip controls 182

**N**

NameSpace objects
  defined 294
  GetDefaultFolder method, returning default
    folders 294
  methods 294
  properties 295

NameSpace objects *(continued)*
   referencing Folder collections  295
   returning CurrentUser name  295
New Post in This Folder option, specifying for
  forms  256
Notes forms, creating procedure  118

# O

object browser
   Microsoft Excel 97, using in Outlook  282
   moving around in  283
   selecting an object library  283
object library
   defined  282
   Folders collection  296
   methods, defined  286
   Microsoft Excel 97 object browser  282
   Microsoft Forms 2.0  282
   Microsoft Outlook  282
   object models  284
   Outlook, referencing from Microsoft Excel 97  283
   properties, defined  286
   selecting in the object browser  283
object models
   defined  284
   Outlook, viewing  285
objects
   Application  291
   Automation  292
   Control  311
   Controls collection  310
   Explorer  295
   Folders collection  296
   Form (Inspector)  307
   Item  302
   Items collection  300
   MAPI NameSpace  293
   MAPIFolder  297
   NameSpace  294
   Page  309
   Pages collection  308
   Recipients collection  315
   UserProperties collection  313
Office Document forms
   basic characteristics  103
   creating procedure  118
   examples  8

OFT attachment, inserting in a message box  473
Open events  321
OptionButton controls
   captions  171
   defined  170
   initial values, setting  172
   value properties, setting  171
Organization Forms Library
   checking forms for viruses and harmful code  477
   form publishing procedure  478
   opening forms example  114
   publishing Reply forms  208
   submitting forms to an administrator for
     publication  477
   types of forms published  476
Outlook Form Designer  99
   Advanced Properties dialog box  19
   advantages of using  18
   defined  5, 17
   Properties dialog box  19
   Script Editor for programming forms  22
   viewing  18
   Visual Basic Expression Service  20
Outlook Script Editor
   editing code in Run mode  276
   Help  276
   Item_PropertyChange event  275
   jumping to lines of code  276
   object library  282
   overview  274
   reference materials  276
   syntax errors, checking  276
   troubleshooting suggestions  290
   variables  287
   viewing  275
   window, basic characteristics  111

# P

Page object  309
pages
   Approval and Status, Document Tracking form  431,
     456
   Contacts form, renaming and displaying  48
   Document Information  445
   form, basic characteristics  106
   hiding at run time  123
   HTML Conversion, Document Tracking form  460
   Message, hiding  122

pages *(continued)*
  Message, renaming for Business Card Request
    form 337
  Product Information 448
  renaming procedure 123
  Separate Read Layout option 122
  showing at run time 123
  Task, Document Tracking form 444
  Virus Check\Posted, Document Tracking form 460
Pages collection object 308
permissions
  Assigned Help Tasks folder, setting 394
  Beta Contacts folder 57
  Business Card Requests folder, setting 380
  custom roles, assigning 261
  default 261
  defined 260
  distribution lists 261
  Document Tracking application 472
  Help Desk folder, checking 392
  Help Desk folder, setting 393
  Name list 261
  page, opening 260
  predefined roles, assigning 261
  Product Ideas folder 92
Personal Address Book
  Business Card Request folder address,
    publishing 335
  folder addresses, adding 162, 259
  Help Desk folder address 393
personal folders, creating 117
Personal Forms Library
  advantages of publishing forms 478
  distributing forms for publication 473
  form publishing procedure 480
  publication instructions for attached forms 479
  publishing Art Approval forms 192
  publishing Help Request forms 397
  publishing Reply forms 208
  publishing the Marketing Handoff form 436
Post forms
  Action Name option 216
  basic characteristics 102
  creating procedure 118
  ideas for using with the Outlook Form Designer 7
  Product Ideas folder, opening in Design mode 67
  Reply to Folder actions 210

Post forms *(continued)*
  Separate Read Layout option 121
  testing in Personal or Organization Forms
    Library 138
PostItem object
  methods 303
  properties 305
Potential Beta Participants view
  columns, headings 37
  columns, resizing to Best Fit 39
  creating 36
  fields, adding new 37
  fields, dragging to column heading row 38
  fields, removing 36
  illustrated 32
  Product Category view 90
  saving 39
procedure-level variables 287
procedures
  AddNewDatabaseRecord 464
  AutoFill Click, creating for Business Card Request
    forms 370
  CheckValue 468
  Clear_Click, creating for Business Card Request
    forms 372
  FieldValue 466
  Item_Close event 464
  Item_CustomPropertyChange 462
  Item_PropertyChange event 462
  Item_Write Event 463
  SendDeliveryMessage, creating for Business Card
    Request forms 372
  SendNotification 468
  UpdateDatabaseRecord 466
Product Category controls
  adding procedure 69
  aligning 71
  defined 69
  labels 71
  properties, setting 69
  read-only status, applying 78, 79
Product Category view
  column heading order, arranging 90
  creating procedure 88
  defined 87
  fields, removing 88
  items, grouping by product category, then by
    conversation 89

Product Category view *(continued)*
   items, sorting by the Conversation Index field 89
   Potential Beta Participants view 90
Product Idea Response form, setting the Hidden
  property 209
Product Ideas
   administration properties, setting 92
   application, overview 62
   application, releasing to other users 92
   application, setting Initial View on Folder
    property 92
   application, testing 91
   folder, copying to Public Folders 92
   folder, creating 65
   folder, illustrated 63
   folder, Product Category view 63
   form, actions 81
   form, aligning controls 71
   form, backing up 84
   form, Compose page editing 67–73
   form, creating new actions 84
   form, illustrated example 64
   form, making Reply to Folder action unavailable 82
   form, opening in Design mode 81
   form, properties 76
   form, publishing 85
   form, Read page editing 73–76
   form, specifying as default for Product Ideas
    folder 90
   form, testing at design time 76
   forms, backing up 77
   forms, creating 66
   forms, publishing 77
   Response form, actions 85
   Response form, backing up 80, 87
   Response form, Compose page editing 78
   Response form, creating 78–81
   Response form, Hidden property 90
   Response form, illustrated 65
   Response form, making Reply to Folder action
    unavailable 86
   Response form, opening in Design mode 86
   Response form, properties 80
   Response form, publishing 81, 87
   Response form, Read page editing 79
Product Information page
   ComboBox fields, adding and binding 450
   DataBase Record Created field 451
   defined 448

Product Information page *(continued)*
   Document ID fields 451
   Document Summary 449
   illustrated 449
   keywords 449
   Multi-Line option, setting 449
   Resize With Form option, setting 449
   Resize With Form property 449
   SendGeneralCorrespondence button 454
properties
   Action Name, Vacation Request form 202
   Administration, Document Tracking application 472
   Administration, setting 258
   advanced control, setting 143
   Advanced dialog box, Outlook Form Designer 19
   Advanced, setting for controls 125
   AutoArchive, setting for folders 492
   BackStyle 144
   Business Card Request, setting 374
   By Discussion Topic view 423
   CheckBox control, Contacts form 54
   ComboBox control, Contacts form 49
   Contacts form, setting 54
   Control Display, setting 140
   Control objects 311
   control, displaying 125
   Controls collection object 310
   Conversation 247
   Conversation Index 249
   Create Offering action 216
   creating user-defined fields 146
   dialog box, folders 25
   dialog box, Outlook Form Designer 19
   Display, BusinessCardName controls 340
   Display, Document Information page 446
   Entry ID, identifying Assigned Help Task items 418
   Entry ID, MAPIFolder objects 299
   Explorer object 296
   Form (Inspector) object 308
   form, basic characteristics 109
   Form, setting procedure 133
   Forms page, viewing 229
   General, setting 256
   Hidden, Marketing Handoff form 437
   Hidden, setting for the Product Idea Response
    form 209
   Hidden, setting for the Training Management
    Response forms 221
   Importance, Assigned Task item 406

properties *(continued)*
  initial value, clearing for the Product Category
    field 79
  Items collection 302
  MailItem object 305
  MAPIFolder object 298
  message, filtering 252
  Multi-Line property, setting for Product Information
    page 449
  NameSpace objects 295
  object library, defined 286
  object, getting 287
  object, setting example 287
  PostItem object 305
  Product Category, setting 69
  Product Ideas form, setting 76
  Product Ideas Response form, setting 80
  Resize With Form, Document Information page 446
  Resize With Form, Product Information page 449
  setting on the Response item 422
  Store ID, MAPIFolder objects 299
  StoreID, identifying Assigned Help Task items 418
  Task Discussion, viewing properties 420
  TextBox control, Contacts form 52
  using to create conditions 266
  Validation, BusinessCardName fields 340
  Validation, Document Information page 446
  value, OptionButton control 171
PropertyChange event 322, 411
protocols supported for hyperlinks in Message
  controls 166

## R

Read events 322
Read pages
  Art Approval form example 186
  Assigned Help Task form 408
  Assigned Help Task form, illustrated 389
  Business Card Request form, illustrated 334
  Business Card Request, editing 363
  Course Catalog Entry form, illustrated 212
  editing for Product Ideas form 73–76
  Help Request form 387, 388
  Help Request form, determining 400
  Help Request form, Technician names 395
  illustrated 121
  Product Ideas form, illustrated 74
  Product Ideas Response form, editing 79

Read pages *(continued)*
  setting properties for controls 132
  tab order, setting 132
  Vacation Request form 197
  viewing in Run mode 132
Recipients collection object 315
Reply forms
  backup copies, creating 208
  characteristics 203
  custom for non-Microsoft Exchange users 210
  defined 207
  publishing to forms libraries 208
  Show Action On option 204
  Subject Prefix option 205
  This Action Will option 204
  values copied from original forms 205
ReplyAll events 323
Response forms
  copying values to 218
  creating 220
  Hidden property, setting 221
roles 261
rules
  advanced conditions, specifying 265
  applying to items not matching conditions 265
  conditions, specifying 263
  creating 263
  folders, overview 262
  simple conditions, specifying 264
  specifying actions 268
  syntax 264

## S

Save Form Definition With Item option, clearing 478,
  480
Script Editor *See* Outlook Script Editor
script-level variables
  Help Request form 399
  overview 287
security
  Business Card Request folders 336
  controls 132
  Document Tracking folders 434
  folders 258
  Help Desk folders 393
  Product Category controls 78, 79
Send events 324

SendNotification procedure, Document Tracking
   application 439
Separate Read Layout
   defined 121
   specifying for pages 122
Set Status Changed procedure 412
shared fields 116
shortcuts
   folder, inserting 166
   URL, inserting in Message controls 166
Show Action On option
   Course Offering form 219
   Reply forms 204
SpinButton controls 184
StoreID properties, Assigned Help Task items 418
Subject fields
   initial values, overview 163
   initial values, setting for Art Approval form 189
   Task page 444
Subject Prefix option
   Course Offering form 218
   Reply forms 205

**T**

tab order
   Compose page, Product Ideas form 73
   Document Information page 448
   Read page, Product Ideas form 75
   setting for form controls 130
tables, Tracking Information 430
TabStrip controls 182
Task Discussion in Help Desk 390
Task page
   Document Tracking, overview 444
   hiding 444
   Subject field 444
Tasks forms, creating procedure 118
templates, using to create forms in Outlook 119
TextBox controls
   Assigned Help Task form Flag field 409
   Contacts form, adding 51
   defined 169
   labels, Contacts form 53
   multi-line options 170
   properties, setting for Contacts form 52
This Action Will option
   Course Offering form 219
   Reply forms 204

threaded conversations, Discussion folders 11
Ticket IDs
   creating 400
   value, Help Request form 399
TipText, Document Information page 447
To field
   preaddressing for Art Approval form 189
   setting values 161
TOTAL field 152
Tracking Information table
   defined 430
   opening 442
Tracking page, Art Approval form 186
Training Management
   application, overview 211
   folder, illustrated 211
   folders, opening 211
   forms 212
   forms, testing 221
   Response forms, setting the Hidden property 221
tutorial, Library Order application 325

**U**

UserProperties collection object 313

**V**

Vacation Request
   application, overview 196
   folders, opening 196
   forms, Actions page 198
   forms, described 196
   forms, naming 202
   forms, Read page 197
   forms, testing 208
   Message form, Address Form Like A option 203
   Message form, When Responding option 203
validation formulas, creating 158
values
   Approval and Status page, setting 457
   Help Desk item, copying to Assigned Help Task
      item 405
variables
   assigning 288
   lifetime 288
   limitations in Visual Basic Scripting Edition 287
   MyDate 402
   names 287
   procedure-level, overview 287

variables *(continued)*
  scopes 288
  script-level, Document Tracking form 461
  script-level, Help Request form 399
  script-level, overview 287
  setting 288
  setting to store initial information for Item Open
    events 411
  Status Changed 412
  Ticket ID value 399
  Trimmed variables 401
  Visual Basic Scripting Edition 287
Variant data type
  defined 288
  subtypes 288
VBScript
  folders, opening 278
  programming forms with Forms Designer Script
    Editor 22
  variables 287
views
  Beta Participants, creating procedure 40
  By Production Manager, Document Tracking
    form 471
  By Requester Name, creating 379
  ByDocument Status, Document Tracking form 470
  columns, adding 236
  columns, defined 232
  columns, removing 237
  Combination fields 238
  conversation threads 247
  custom, showing for folders 234
  customizing 23
  defined 232
  different item types 423
  Discussion Topic 423
  Document Tracking folder 470
  Filter, defined 233
  folder, design tools 23
  Format, defined 233
  formatting 255
  Groups, defined 233
  initial, folders 259
  Microsoft Exchange, automatically generating 257
  new, creating 234

views *(continued)*
  Outlook 232
  Potential Beta Participants, creating 36
  Potential Beta Participants, Product Category
    view 90
  Potential Beta Participants, saving 39
  Product Category overview 63
  Product Category, creating 87–90
  Request Status, creating in Business Card Requests
    folder 376
  settings, saving 255
  Sort, defined 233
  testing 257
Virus Check\Posted page, Document Tracking
  form 460
Visual Basic
  Expression Service, Outlook Form Designer 20
  Outlook, caution about using Help 279
  Outlook, Help overview 278
  Outlook, using Help 279
  Scripting Edition 111
  Scripting Edition variables 287
  using with Automation to control Outlook
    sessions 23
Voting buttons
  actions, automatically setting 192
  described 185
  options, setting 190
  responding to Art Approval items 193

# W

Web sites
  Help and Web Sites folder, contents listed 16
  Help and Web Sites folder, opening 16
  Microsoft Outlook 278
  Microsoft Outlook, overview 15
  Microsoft Visual Basic Scripting Edition 277
  shortcuts 17
When Responding option
  Course Offering form 217
  Message forms 203
While You Were Out forms 154
Write events 324

# Register Today!

## Return this
### *Building Applications with Microsoft® Outlook™ 97*
### registration card for
### a Microsoft Press® catalog

U.S. and Canada addresses only. Fill in information below and mail postage-free.  Please mail only the bottom half of this page.

---

**1-57231-536-9A**          ***BUILDING APPLICATIONS WITH***          *Owner Registration Card*
                            ***MICROSOFT® OUTLOOK™ 97***

NAME

INSTITUTION OR COMPANY NAME

ADDRESS

CITY                                                        STATE            ZIP

# *Microsoft*®*Press*
## *Quality Computer Books*

**For a free catalog of
Microsoft Press® products, call
1-800-MSPRESS**